# Promises to Keep

# Promises to Keep

## A Political Biography of Allan Blakeney

Dennis Gruending

Western Producer Prairie Books
Saskatoon, Saskatchewan

Copyright © 1990 by Dennis Gruending
Western Producer Prairie Books
Saskatoon, Saskatchewan

Cover photograph by Bob Howard
Cover design by Bob Young/BOOKENDS DESIGNWORKS
Printed and bound in Canada by John Deyell Company
95  94  93  92  91  90      6  5  4  3  2  1

The publisher acknowledges the support received for this publication from the Canada Council.

Western Producer Prairie Books is a unique publishing venture located in the middle of western Canada and owned by a group of prairie farmers who are members of the Saskatchewan Wheat Pool. From the first book in 1954, a reprint of a serial originally carried in the weekly newspaper, *The Western Producer,* to the book before you now, the tradition of providing enjoyable and informative reading for all Canadians is continued.

**Canadian Cataloguing in Publication Data**

Gruending, Dennis, 1948–

    Promises to keep

    Includes bibliographical references.
    ISBN 0–88833–324–2

1. Blakeney, Allan.  2. Saskatchewan - Politics and government.  3. Prime ministers - Saskatchewan - Biography.  I. Title.

FC3527.1.B43G78  1990    971.24'03'092    C90–097116–9
F1072.B43G78  1990

# Contents

Acknowledgements      vii

Prologue: The New Deal      1

1    Jeddore      5

2    Dalhousie and Oxford      12

3    The Civil Service      20

4    Politics      31

5    Medicare      38

6    Opposition      46

7    The Waffle      56

8    Leadership      69

9    New Deal '71      77

10    Premier Administrator      84

11    Premier Politician      96

12    The Farm      104

13    The North      114

14    New Deal '75                           126

15    Potash                                 136

16    Uranium                                151

17    The New Politics                       169

18    Economic and Social Policy             178

19    Constitution                           189

20    Defeat                                 213

21    Life after Politics                    231

Notes                                        244

Index                                        262

# Acknowledgements

The labour which went into this book belies any stereotype of a writer working in isolation. Thanks to my friend George Melnyk, who repeatedly urged me to write it. Heather Wood spent months in the archives, speedily reading a mass of historical records and distilling them on computer discs. She also transcribed dozens of interviews. Charlene Dobmeier, who has worked with me previously, again provided prompt and competent research from Saskatoon, and helped with transcribing. Eric Simpson did research and interviews in Nova Scotia, and Larry Powell helped with interviews in Saskatchewan. Elaine Wood transcribed throughout the winter. Rick Engel generously lent me extensive files on potash. Every writer needs a computer guru, and mine was Keith Fortowsky.

My thanks as well to Dr. James McCrorie at the Canadian Plains Research Center at the University of Regina for arranging a Research Fellowship, which provided me borrower's privileges at the university library. A grant from T. H. McLeod and the Douglas-Coldwell Foundation arrived just as the research bills were mounting. The staff at the Government of Saskatchewan's Legislative Library, and at the Saskatchewan Archives Board were especially helpful. Jane McHughen and Elizabeth Munroe were good sports at Western Producer Prairie Books, and Donald Ward, a fine editor.

Allan Blakeney endured 15 lengthy taped sessions. Our agreement was that he would provide interviews and access to his papers, but that he would not see the manuscript prior to publication. The Blakeney papers at the Saskatchewan Archives Board are an invaluable resource. Mr. Blakeney, in the interest of truth and scholarship, has been generous in granting permission to researchers to use them, a commendable practice. Anne Blakeney was also generous with her time, and helped locate dozens of photos.

My final and fondest thanks go to my family. My wife, Martha Wiebe, helped with research, transcribed interviews, and read the entire manuscript. Her comments were perceptive, and her support, as always, was unflagging. My daughters Anna and Maria paid many visits to my small office in the garage, and provided a continuing supply of art for my bare white walls—sketches of flowers, trees, smiling yellow suns and happy-faced children. Their enthusiasm was catching.

## A Reading Note

I have written this book as a narrative uninterrupted by textual notes, but it has been thoroughly researched. If you are interested in just the story, read straight through. If you want sources, I have provided them in the Notes section immediately following the text.

Most quotes in the text are taken from interviews which I conducted with the people quoted. The sources for other quotes are provided in the Notes. In a very few cases, I have used unattributed quotes because of an agreement with interviewees who provided certain comments on the understanding that they not be attributed. Those few cases are indicated in the text.

# The New Deal

When Allan Blakeney swept to power in June 1971 he had promises to keep—about 140 of them. They had been printed months before in a slim blue-on-white booklet called *New Deal for People*. Someone in a Prince Albert constituency office had wanted a promotional matchbook with the letters "NDP" on the cover. It seemed clever. Provincial office picked it up, and it became the campaign slogan.

When he was elected leader the previous July, Blakeney had appeared to represent an old deal rather than a new one. If delegates had gone with the new wave, they would have chosen Roy Romanow, the youthful challenger. Blakeney represented continuity. He had been a civil servant in the Douglas governments of the 1950s before moving into politics, and he had a traditional Douglas-style social democratic agenda to fulfill. He also had an agenda of his own.

Ross Thatcher had staked his political success on attracting capital to a "New Saskatchewan." His attempt did not survive the first recession. Blakeney was convinced that he could not rely on private corporations to provide much needed diversification. He wanted government not only to control both the pace and the terms of development, but to be a major player in it. He thrust the state into the economy to an extent Douglas had never attempted. He brought to the task a mixture of intellect, stamina, and experience unusual in Canadian politics. A gold medalist in the law school at Dalhousie, his theoretical knowledge of politics and economics had been enhanced at Oxford University, where he studied on a Rhodes Scholarship. He spent five years as legal secretary to the Government Finance Office, a central organization which provided advice to Crown Corporations. He headed the Saskatchewan Securities Commission for several years before launching into politics and the cabinet. That was followed by a seven-year stint in opposition, the leadership race, and finally the election.

As premier, he was immediately in his preferred element—building, fine

tuning, and running a government, dealing brilliantly with a broad spectrum
of issues and a constantly shifting mass of detail. He performed those tasks
with a range and discipline which was quite remarkable, but which, in
the best Saskatchewan tradition, he was careful not to flaunt. Asked by
a reporter how he would like to be remembered, he said, "People can
say about us, 'They run a pretty good shop'." He was the ultimate civil
servant.

The people side of politics did not come easily to Blakeney. He had
to work at it. He showed great determination in applying himself to the
task. Early on he attempted to downplay the inevitable comparisons
between himself and Tommy Douglas. He liked to tell reporters that,
although he was premier, he was really only a "retreaded" civil servant.
In that description he was being honest, if typically understated.

Early in his career he worked diligently to improve his platform
performance. He has a slight lisp, a lingering hiss on his s's. Jack Kinzel,
his speech-writer of many years, tried to compensate for it by avoiding
strings of sibilant words. Blakeney practiced his speeches in front of a
mirror at home, and repeated them in cars or buses as he was driven to
events. He still has a trace of Maritime accent, with an emphasis on hard
sounds and consonants, hard on the "c," hard on the "r."

Despite his brilliance, journalists never considered him good material
for the 30-second clip. At his weekly news conferences in the basement
of the Legislative Building in Regina, he drank tea and fielded questions
like a professor, providing deliberate answers, often in maddening detail.
He would frequently take time out in front of the cameras to run his finger
down a column of numbers to be sure he had exactly the right statistics
for potash or grain exports. He loved precision, but he also had an innate
caution, a belief that a politician's every word was on the record forever.
He was unusually truthful to journalists, although he was frequently and
privately piqued that they knew so little. He admits a preference for the
days when reporters were mainly from newspapers, and reported facts rather
than impressions. He was aware of his limitations as a politician. He was
also comfortable in his strengths, and firm in his belief that politics was
an honourable profession. He was a decent man in public life.

Blakeney defies caricature. Cartoonists left him alone. He is five foot seven,
a bit pudgy, with the soft and unremarkable body shape of someone who
has spent his life behind a desk. His short hair, now grey, is straight, with
a perfect part on the left. One of his mannerisms is to run a smoothing
hand from the part down to the top of his ear. His face is pleasant, fleshy
and round, almost bland. In his years as premier he developed a generous
jowl. The eyes are the most changeable aspect of his face. They are a light
liquid blue, and when he is concentrating on someone in conversation
their roundness gives him the appearance of an excited schoolboy—the

kind of appearance, says his wife Anne, which made certain women feel maternal toward him. When he laughs, he has friendly crinkles around his eyes. It's a hearty laugh which friends remember as a distinguishing characteristic since childhood.

It is an open, friendly face when he's relaxed; it is the stiff, inexpressive face of a poker player when he's not. In fact, poker is one of his pleasures. In the 1960s he began to play with the press gallery crew, a practice which grew into monthly at-home sessions with the same players for more than 20 years. He's reputed to have been the sharpest player in the group, mainly because none of the others could match his powers of recall. The image of the gambler is intriguing because of the high-risk political games at which Blakeney excelled—the nationalization of the potash industry, the constitutional negotiations—but it is undermined by the fact that he would never join a poker game that was more than penny-ante.

Thrift and a modest lifestyle are lifelong habits. He treated the government as he treated his own household. Shortly after the election of 1971 he had Ross Thatcher's license plate—[1]—removed from the black Chrysler New Yorker which was reserved for the premier. Thatcher's cabinet ministers had had similar plates, numbered in order of descending rank. Blakeney had those removed, too. He loved the egalitarian streak in Saskatchewan people, their expectation that even the premier should not outgrow his hat size. He drove the Chrysler for seven years.

His private life was exactly that. He drove himself each evening to a house he and his wife had built in his working class constituency of Regina Elphinstone. He always took work home: reports to read, his correspondence (he refused to send a letter he hadn't read, and frequently his assistants got their work back with red marks and suggestions for changes). His idea of a good time on the two Sundays he took off each month was to sleep in, to watch football or baseball on television, and maybe to read a mystery novel. His telephone number was always listed, but Anne took the calls and protected his privacy.

The longer he spent as a cabinet minister, then premier, the more isolated he became socially. He accepted it as an inevitable part of the job. He did not want to appear to play favourites in caucus, and he believed that most people outside politics acted differently in the presence of a premier. His old and trusted friends, however, describe his warmth and wit in a way which would surprise people who did not know him well. He will join heartily in a sing-song, and particularly likes old hymns, which he remembers to the last word. He loves to talk about ideas. In private, he has a quick sense of humour, which he rarely demonstrated in his political life.

Blakeney gained a national reputation as a pan-Canadian statesman who cared about the integrity of the federation and the aspirations of Quebec, and at the same time demanding a new deal for the West and the Maritimes. During the constitutional negotiations, he remained the point of contact between anti-Trudeau hardliners like Lougheed and Lyon, and the pro-federal forces led by Bill Davis. He was supple, always ready to negotiate, to make a deal. Trudeau was wary of him; he thought Blakeney was indecisive at best, disingenuous at worst. There was respect between them, but also bad blood. Their contact brought out the pride and competitiveness in each.

In the early 1980s, as interest rates soared and recession loomed, the immediate benefits of Blakeney's state capitalism were not always apparent. He and his senior ministers were looking over their shoulders at the emerging Conservatives, aware that society was changing but not knowing quite what to do about it. In 1982 the Tory deluge came. Blakeney was not only defeated, but routed, by Grant Devine, whose government spent the following years pursuing their New Right agenda—a shredding of government services and the wholesale sell-off of Crown Corporations.

Devine has confidently predicted that social democracy has met its Waterloo in Saskatchewan. The Conservatives, with their agenda of privatization, believe they will so discredit the Blakeney legacy that it will be smashed forever. These conflicting visions of society are being debated with particular ferocity now. Once again, as in the Medicare dispute a quarter of a century ago, a small, poor province far from the centres of power finds its citizens locked in a fierce partisan struggle which could have an impact far beyond its borders.

Blakeney observes the fracas from a distance. He stepped down as leader in 1987. He has made a gracious transition from public figure to private citizen. He appears comfortable, and at peace with himself. But his life is by no means over, and, as this book will indicate, he has missed no detail in recent political debates.

# Chapter One

# Jeddore

Allan Blakeney's ancestors are Welsh on his mother's side, English on his father's. He has more information about the English line of the family, but identifies ethnically with the Welsh. Even when he was Premier of Saskatchewan, he usually ventured out on March 1st to celebrate the feast of Saint David, the patron of Wales.

His mother, Bertha May Davies, was born in Rhondda, a spot about 25 kilometres north of Cardiff where two mountain valleys meet. Her people were miners. Bertha trained as a nurse, then moved to London. It was there that she met John Cline Blakeney, a young Canadian soldier who had been wounded in action during the First World War. He had shrapnel in his arm, and he'd frozen his feet in the trenches. They were married in 1919 in the valley. Bertha's family gave her a Bible and wished her good luck in Canada.

The heartland of Allan Blakeney's ancestors in Nova Scotia is Jeddore, a protected harbour up from Halifax along the east shore. The coast there is dotted with rocky inlets and bays ringed with pine and spruce. The soil is poor, and the area is sparsely populated. The main industries are logging and fishing. Two settlements, West and East Jeddore, face each other across the narrow inlet. The tiny village of West Jeddore is a combination of wharfs, stacks of wooden fish boxes, and small houses in need of paint. A larger wooden building is the Jeddore Seafood plant, where the local fishermen bring their catch.

As the inlet bends, and the road with it, a white frame church comes into view. It is boarded up, with no sign to name it, although it is painted and in good repair. It is the West Jeddore United Baptist Church. Beside it, on a steep hillside, is the cemetery, rimmed with green pines; it overlooks the harbour mouth which opens onto the Atlantic horizon. The Blakeney family plot is about halfway up the hillside. It contains the white rounded headstones of John and Elizabeth Blakeney, Allan's grandparents. In the same cemetery there are similar headstones for Luke and Sarah, his great grandparents, and their children, Luke and Silas.

Jeddore is about as far from the seats of power and privilege as any Saskatchewan hamlet. Allan Blakeney never lived there, but that is where he anchors himself. His family has roots in the village and its Baptist church which go back more than 150 years. The route which his ancestors took to get there was by no means direct.

Blakeney's knowledge of antecedents on his father's side goes back to 1066. "Legend has it," he says, "that the Blakeney family were in England soon after the Norman Conquest." Legend later places his branch of the family in Norfolk, bordering on the North Sea. There's a village there called Blakeney, which may have been named for someone in the family. In the 1600s some or all of the Blakeneys travelled to northern Ireland where they were granted land by the British monarch. They stayed for approximately 100 years; the existence of Mount Blakeney and Castle Blakeney implies that the family left its mark.

A Blakeney family left Ireland in the 1760s aboard the "Earl of Donegal" bound for South Carolina, where they took up a land grant inland from Charleston. The American Revolution soon posed a dilemma. They chose the Loyalist side. When they lost, the families were forced off their land. At least two of the brothers—Chambers and David—moved once again, this time to Nova Scotia. They travelled in 1782, a year or so ahead of the greater wave of Loyalists, and arrived in Halifax aboard the troopship "Argo." Halifax was then a muddy garrison town, cold, squalid, and unhealthy.

Walter Stewart describes the Loyalists as having left a legacy of "loyalty, conservatism and hard work." All these terms describe Allan Blakeney, a man who, on those few occasions when he is moved to talk about it, reveals a certain pride in his Loyalist background. He is too cautious to describe himself as anti-American, but he does admit to being "quite a nationalist." He has a fondness for British traditions and institutions, including the monarchy.

He believes he is descended from the Chambers Blakeney family which, after a short time in Halifax, found its way along the coast to Ship Harbour. The land was not good for farming, and there was hardship. The family moved back to Halifax, then down the shore again in the early 1800s to become fishermen and later merchants at Jeddore.

Blakeney's father, John Cline Blakeney, only completed grade six. His father before him had been a relatively prosperous merchant at Jeddore, but died when John was young. The family business fell on hard times. There was no money, and no time for education, something John frequently regretted later in life. He loved reading and discussion, according to Allan, and would have been a good university student.

Neither John nor Bertha ever provided much detail about their hospital romance. They appeared genuinely fond of one another but, one suspects, not given to spontaneous displays of affection. Nor did John talk about his time at the front, but one thing was clear to Allan: "It was a terrible experience for him, and he was not at all interested in anyone talking about the glories of war." Perhaps that is why Allan showed little interest in joining the army when he came of age in the waning days of World War II.

In their first years back in Canada, John and Bertha scrambled to make a living. They spent some time in Windsor, Nova Scotia, then in Halifax, where John spent a few months at the Maritime Business College. He also sold for Fuller Brush, and worked briefly as a carpenter, although he wasn't particularly handy. He even went west on a harvesting excursion. In 1923, after several years of uncertainty, the family found its niche in Bridgewater, Nova Scotia, where John set up a wholesaling business, supplying fresh fruit by truck to small stores in the area.

Their oldest child, Beryle, had been born in 1920. Allan Emrys Blakeney was born in Bridgewater on September 7, 1925. The youngest child, John Davies Blakeney, arrived in 1930.

Bridgewater was then a town of about 3,000, west along the coast from Halifax and inland on the La Have River. It was a retail service and railroad centre, never a fishing or seafaring town, although wooden ships had been built there. In the 1920s and 30s boats came up the La Have to load lumber harvested from the forests farther inland. Nor was it noted as an industrial centre; it did have a few factories, but there were no wealthy local industrialists, in the manner of nearby Lunenburg. There were people like the Blakeneys, of British extraction, and a good number of Germans, who had also arrived as United Empire Loyalists. The largest church was Lutheran, but there were others too: Baptist, United, Anglican, and the Salvation Army. There was a hospital, a newspaper, and a good school.

John Blakeney's business took off quickly in the 1920s, but barely survived the 30s. At the tender age of 14, Allan was pressed into service as the family bookkeeper. On school days, while his father was on the road, Allan hurried home to do the ledgers, to run daily deposits to the bank, and to check in his father's drivers at night. Even so, the books would not have balanced without help from John's brother, a more prosperous fruit merchant in Halifax. "It was tough times," Blakeney recalls. "My father fell behind and probably would not have been carried had they not been brothers."

The family's fortunes began to improve late in the 1930s, but the Depression had left its mark on Blakeney: "I always grew up thinking that money didn't come easily, and we shouldn't spend it unless there was a reason." Blakeney's personal life has always been characterized by thrift and a lack of ostentation; as premier he insisted that those habits be accepted in government. His later aversion to government deficits probably owes much to his youthful experiences with shaky family ledgers.

Still, the Blakeneys were more prosperous than most. Their home was comfortable, with two storeys and four bedrooms. It was on a large lot on Dufferin Street, shaded by maple trees. It was a good neighbourhood. They always drove a car, albeit a second hand one until 1947 when they bought a new Pontiac. Allan's parents went to Boston or New York once a year. They took him to the New York World's Fair in 1939. Both he and his sister Beryle attended university, she during the Depression. John Blakeney spent time as a member of the town council, and acted occasionally as an election scrutineer for the Conservatives.

It is this vision of respectability and happiness which Blakeney prefers to remember. He has described his family's existence as "a modestly comfortable life," and his boyhood as being "serene" and "steeped in security." There is a good deal of evidence to support that description, although it deals rather quickly with what appear to have been some significant family difficulties.

In 1926, when Allan was only six months old, his mother went back to Wales to nurse her own mother through her last illness. Blakeney was left for six months with a woman named Ma Gilnacht, a family friend who also ran the 1940s equivalent of a day-care out of her home in nearby Mahone Bay. Another family crisis occurred when it appeared that Blakeney's brother John might die from a lung infection. "He was in the hospital," Allan recalls, "and my mother brought him home where she was able to give him 'the proper treatment,' as she said." Bertha and a local doctor operated on John in the Blakeney house, cutting out a piece of his rib and draining the lung.

Bertha was a "trooper," Blakeney says: "a very practical, the-world-is-out-there type of person." She became ill in 1940 with a bone disease which kept her in bed for almost a year, and probably explains the frequent presence of a maid in the home. Blakeney's father also had health problems, the legacy of his war wounds. He had a series of operations on the foot which had been frostbitten in the trenches, and to remove shrapnel which remained embedded in his arm. Despite these problems, and a shortage of money during the Depression, it was to all appearances a solid household. It was a family and a life which had convention stamped all over it.

Blakeney appears to have been intellectually closer to his father. One gets the sense of his mother as a pragmatic person who instilled, somewhat sternly, the Protestant work ethic. His father was more of a dreamer, someone who liked to read and discuss. Allan was never close to either of his siblings, attributing this to the fact that his sister was five years older, and his brother five years younger. John agrees that they were not a particularly close family. No doubt it was a household where affection existed, but its expression was muted and somewhat formal.

The Blakeneys attended the Bridgewater Baptist Church, a white clapboard building overlooking the La Have River on the edge of town. They were faithful in their religious adherence, but retained an independence of thought. As Baptists, it was theologically sound for them to do so. The Bible is accepted as God's revelation to humanity, and every believer has liberty to interpret the scriptures.

"My dad," Blakeney says, "had a certain measure of scepticism. My mother equally. Dad, for example, would have laughed if anyone had said the Baptists are going to be saved but those Presbyterians are not. This scepticism would have been part of my upbringing."

Indeed, it was this scepticism which resulted in the family's making pragmatic choices which sometimes collided with their religious loyalties. Blakeney's sister Beryle attended Mount Saint Vincent, a Catholic university, even though her parents were not fans of the Roman church, with its sacraments and clericalism.

Blakeney recalls fondly his years of weekly attendance at Sunday School. He says his Baptist formation had a lasting impact upon him; but there is an ambivalence here. He has never made a public confession of faith, nor has he ever been baptized—both common and expected Baptist rituals. He says, rather lamely, that he never got around to it. A more likely explanation is that he is an extremely private person, and would have felt self-conscious in the ceremonies, particularly the church's practice of having the adult fully immersed in water during baptism.

Blakeney came, intellectually, to his own religious conclusions, particularly through the study of moral philosophy at Oxford. He says he believes in a "spirituality, a third dimension after body and mind." He does not believe in much of the Christian creed—the divinity of Christ, the virgin birth, an afterlife for individuals. He admits to a "measure of agnosticism." Despite his formation, his rationalism has prevented the conventional commitment of a true believer. What he does cherish is the Baptist concept of the "priesthood of all believers," where people are called to use their gifts as they see fit in the service of God and society. It's an egalitarian theology which places great emphasis on the intelligence and discipline of the individual. It is a concept which stresses works over rituals. Blakeney says that theology has guided him in political life. "It is something that one thinks about—the connection between politics and ethics, about the right thing to do."

Part of the Baptist code was a spurning of liquor, although Blakeney says his parents were not purists about it. The family entertained frequently, but almost always without liquor. Nor was it much a part of Blakeney's life, either at university or later in politics. One of his tricks at social functions, as premier, came to be described by his staff as the "Blakeney Scotch." He would have one drink of scotch or rye with coke, and spend the rest of the evening with glass in hand, but refilled only with coke.

He abhorred drunkenness in public life. A fondness for liquor was no way to get promoted either in Blakeney's Cabinet or on his staff.

Allan started school early, in September of 1930, and was out of the first grade while still only five. He admits to being "kind of a bright kid," an opinion which is shared by his childhood friends. He was also curious, nervously energetic, and socially awkward. Jo Eisenhauer of Lunenburg, who has known him since the fifth grade, says, "You knew the standing in the class, and you got prizes for being the top in English or the top in math, and Allan would always carry off most of them. He entered into everything that was going on."

Almost everyone from Blakeney's school days remembers his high level of enthusiasm for almost any task. He wasn't very athletic, but he was irrepressibly energetic. Frank Gow, one in a household of boys who lived next door, remembers Blakeney as "reserved but also hyper. He couldn't stay still. He shook all over when he laughed." The big laugh is also a trademark. Jo Eisenhauer says he's always had it. "When I watched him on T.V. [as a politician] and he would laugh and giggle after he had made some comment, it was so typical of what he was like as a kid."

As a child he was plump, apple-cheeked, and small for his age. The early start at school, and his diminutive size, caused some problems. He felt he was not well developed socially. "I could never dance as well as the people in my grade, and frequently couldn't play games as well because they were bigger and older. I always had that problem as I went through school. It's no big deal."

In addition to the bouncy and energetic boy, Blakeney had a far more reserved and intellectual side. Another of the Gow boys, Donald, recalls: "Sometimes when the parents were talking politics in our sitting room, he listened when the other kids didn't. He was inclined to intellectual affairs. He would rather listen to parents than play Parcheezie." Ralph Simmons, another neighbourhood boy, adds: "Allan was the studious type, not too out-going or forward."

In high school Blakeney spent much of his time with a schoolmate named Barbara McAuley. He often went to her house, on Saint Phillip's Street in a poor area of town. They would sit on the back porch and talk for hours. Although she counted him a loyal friend—and still does more than fifty years later—she recalls that he always visited her house. She never went to his. "In fact, I don't know if I imagined this or if it's true, but I got the impression somewhere that his mother was not pleased that he used to walk up to Saint Phillip's Street so much." Another schoolmate, Margie Haughn, says: "He would never allow his parents to drive him to school. He didn't want people to know his was the type of family to have a car."

Blakeney graduated from Bridgewater High School with top marks in

1942. He was 16 years old. In the photo of that year's badminton club, Allan stands in a white team sweater, a racquet over his right shoulder, pudgy and chubby-cheeked, a half head shorter than the boy beside him. Badminton was the only sport he played with skill, but what he lacked athletically, he made up for elsewhere. He was on the Student Council, the current events club, and the social committee. In the Best and Most categories, the editors of the yearbook had him sharing honours as the Most Studious, Most Ambitious, and Most Talkative student.

In its biographies of Grade 12 students, the yearbook points Blakeney toward public life: "Allan wishes to be a lawyer and a politician." Blakeney says he was already thinking about it. His father was a Tory, and he included his son in the circle. "I remember the election of 1935," Blakeney says, "and listening to some of the arguments. I would have been only 10 then, and I still can remember some of these speeches over the radio and my dad commenting on them." Despite John Blakeney's interest in politics, he believed it was a risky business, and he had mixed feelings about his son's considering it.

There was no doubt, however, about Allan's going to university. Both parents encouraged their children. Blakeney's sister Beryle began university in 1937–38 and later graduated with a Bachelor of Science degree. His brother John wasn't interested; like his father, he went into the fruit wholesaling business.

John Blakeney wanted Allan to be a lawyer. He felt strongly enough about it to insist upon his son's attending Dalhousie University in Halifax because of its law school. The minister at the Baptist church had argued that Allan should go to Acadia University in Wolfville, a Baptist school. Barbara McAuley says: "I think he had a family that expected things of him. He could always talk to his father about these things, even when he was a young boy." Blakeney agrees that it was his father to whom he talked; his mother, although she approved, was not much involved in the discussions. He packed his diploma and left Bridgewater for Halifax.

# Chapter Two

# Dalhousie
# and Oxford

The law school at Dalhousie had a Dickensian feel about it. The old brown benches had names carved in them—from antiquity, it seemed. Law students took their classes in the Forrest Building on the edge of the campus. They shared the building with students from the sciences, dentistry, and medicine. The budding lawyers became accustomed to the pungent odour of formaldehyde from the medical labs. Law classes were small, with fewer than 20 students, all male. The entire campus had only about 1,200 students.

Allan Blakeney arrived in Halifax with a regional scholarship. At 17 he was still his father's lad, and found the city intimidating. He boarded in a house where no other students lived, and found it difficult to meet people that first year. "I was essentially a fairly gregarious person," he says. "I liked discussing and arguing with people, and I found it kind of lonely living alone."

In his second year he moved into residence at Pine Hill Divinity Hall, an old building near Mount Pleasant Park. Pine Hill housed both United Church and Anglican theology students, but other young men lived there as well—arts, medical, and dental students, engineers, about 130 in all. As he had in high school, Blakeney joined every organization in sight. He was a member of the Pine Hill Students' Society; he was the circulation manager, then the advertising manager of the university yearbook; he was a member of the debating society, vice-president of the law society and, in his final year, vice-president of the Student Council. He had the best marks in his law class each year—his best subjects were Property, Sales, and Corporations—and won the university gold medal in law.

"We used to meet in the basement of the law building for coffee and sandwiches, and to discuss cases," Blakeney's classmate Kendall Kenney recalls. "Blakeney wasn't a colourful character, but he was a quiet leader and universally regarded as a good student and a reliable person."

The traits which had begun to show in high school also characterized Blakeney at Dalhousie. He was enthusiastic about almost everything, a compact bundle of energy, but he could also be private and remote. He has been described by an old law school acquaintance as "one of the boys who was never one of the boys." It's a trait which Blakeney has long recognized in himself, and which he still finds puzzling. "I'm not one of the boys with anybody," he says, "and I don't know why I'm not."

The war was on when Blakeney began university. The port city of Halifax was very much aware of it, and so were the students. Halifax was a naval centre, full of men and short of housing. A prefabricated building was erected for naval training right on campus. The Student Council got involved in "war work" through blood donor drives, dances to raise money for the Red Cross, even investing council reserves in victory loans. Enrollment was down because young men were away in the services. The rhetoric of patriotism was everywhere.

Blakeney wasn't eligible for enlistment until 1943. He spent some time in the Canadian Officers Training Corps, where he says he "developed a poor opinion of the Canadian army." He then enlisted in the University Air Training Corps, and in 1944, at age 18, he attempted to join the air force. He was told that they weren't taking any more recruits. He does not appear to have been crushed by the news.

The war did have one lasting effect on Allan Blakeney: it turned him into a CCFer. The later years of World War II were a time of intellectual ferment; soldiers and civilians both were determined that a new society should emerge from the ashes of Europe. "There were discussions of rebuilding the social structures of England with Sir William Beveridge's plans. And there were proposals for rebuilding the social safety net in Canada. All these things were in the air. It was a time of idealism," Blakeney remembers.

They were heady days for the CCF. Everyone feared mass unemployment and a return to the Depression when thousands of soldiers became civilians again. The social democrats captured the popular imagination with their demand to have the country do in peacetime what had been done in war—put all Canadians to work. That could only be done through centralized planning and a socialized state. They also called upon government to cushion the shock of the expected post-war slump through a series of social programs, including unemployment insurance and medicare. The CCF slogan of the day was "Left Turn Canada," and voters appeared to be paying attention. The CCF became the official opposition in Ontario in 1943, and the following year formed a government in Saskatchewan. In 1945, the national party won 16 per cent of the vote and elected 28 MPs.

Blakeney had been attracted to the CCF during his first year at Dalhousie. He and another student organized a campus club called The Round Table. They invited speakers to the campus to talk about political ideas. Among those speakers were two men organizing for the CCF, attempting to plant fragile seed in the barren Loyalist ground of Nova Scotia. One of them was Fred Young, later an elected member for the provincial NDP in Ontario. The other was Lloyd Shaw, whose father, like Blakeney's, was a Conservative, a businessman who owned a brick plant. The elder Shaw, however, had become angry with the provincial government's corruption and turned to the CCF. The young Lloyd grew up in the party, and organized for it in Nova Scotia and Ontario. He worked closely with David Lewis. Later he went into the family brick business and became an oddity—a millionaire CCF businessman in Nova Scotia.

Shaw was in his late 20s when he got to know young Allan Blakeney: "He was a good student, a good worker, and he had lots of energy." It was in Shaw's rented suite in the Cornwallis Manor that Blakeney got his first CCF membership. Shaw's small daughter Alexa was playing in the next room. Alexa McDonough later succeeded in doing what her father had not: she won election as an NDP candidate in Nova Scotia. Like her father, she came to lead the provincial party.

Blakeney's political choice at university was an unusual one in Nova Scotia, and it changed his life: "I became more and more attracted to the ideas of the CCF, and became convinced that this was the way I wanted to go." Kendall Kenney says, "Allan was a product of the 30s—the effect of the Depression and the pre-war period—where there was no effective way for the disadvantaged to live more than a bare existence. And I think the response of thinking people was to want to change that. There was a resolve that if we can raise this sort of money for a war, then we can do it to give support to the economically disadvantaged."

In Blakeney's university world of ideas, the triumphalism of the CCF was tempered by the influence of at least one professor who had a lasting influence on him. George Wilson, an historian and a dour Scot of the George Grant variety, was cynical about politicians, and sceptical of all establishments. He reserved a particular venom for pomp and circumstance. "This type of scepticism will undoubtedly have made a mark on me," Blakeney says, "because I was very impressed with George Wilson. He would have made me very suspicious of the governments who were going to solve all the problems. That goes for governments of the left as well as of the right."

John Blakeney, who had been Allan's political mentor before he went off to university, was disappointed with his son's choice. He believed the party's ideas weren't sound, and that they had no future, a prediction which has proven largely true in Nova Scotia. Blakeney's mother, less doctrinaire in her politics, was unconcerned, but the decision of John Blakeney's boy to get involved with the CCF caused a mild scandal in Bridgewater.

The party had little impact on campus, and some of Blakeney's fellow law students were contemptuous. Clint Havey, a retired lawyer who graduated with Blakeney in 1947, remembers the day Fred Young came to speak to law students about the CCF: "Somebody spoke up and asked him how long he thought it would take before there was a CCF government in Nova Scotia. He said maybe a hundred years. This was a peculiarity to which people were entitled but it wasn't taken seriously." Blakeney took it seriously. When he graduated in 1945 his university yearbook predicted a future in "law and Canadian politics." It was apparent that the politics would be CCF.

Molly Schwartz was a tall, blonde young woman studying zoology. In 1946 she was one of only two women on the student council. The yearbook described her rather patronizingly as "adding grace and charm" to the group. Allan Blakeney was on the council, too. Choosing his words carefully, he says, "She was a very distinctive looking blonde girl. A good looking girl. Fresh complexion and that sort of thing. I would have seen her."

Molly's mother had been a nurse; her father was a doctor who practised out of the family's large home near the public gardens in Halifax, a desirable location at the time. She lived at home while attending university, a twenty-minute walk away. She had been born with a congenital heart defect. The family considered her frail and probably protected her excessively, perhaps as the result of the childhood death of an elder brother. By the time she began school her health appeared better. She continued to avoid vigorous activity, but otherwise appeared to have a normal, if protected, childhood.

During Blakeney's final year at Dalhousie in 1947 he and Molly were going steady. Campus social life was highly organized. The university calendar was filled with dances where students jitterbugged under the watchful eyes of chaperones. Blakeney had a second-hand tuxedo and wore it frequently. They also went to movies, and on Sundays for walks in the park. He went to her house for Sunday supper, and afterward they would sit in the family living room. "Depending on the seriousness of a courtship," he says, "the parents would absent themselves, or they wouldn't."

Molly's dearest friend was Budge Wilson, whom she had met in grade three. Wilson doesn't remember how Molly met Allan Blakeney, "but I do remember that she admired him greatly before he ever took her out. Molly was a little bit shy and she would have admired the kind of presence he had then and has now."

The remarkable thing about Blakeney then, Wilson says, is how amazingly he was like Allan Blakeney now: "It's extraordinary how little he has changed. It's extraordinary how mature he was then, and though he has done so much he still has that boyish, enthusiastic quality that he had then. When I dig out pictures I notice how much he looked the way he looks now."

Blakeney still pays occasional visits to Wilson and her husband in Nova

Scotia. She says another thing which has not changed over the years is Blakeney's curiosity, and the breadth of his knowledge. "He was interesting to talk to. He was never someone to talk small talk. He always had something to say. He always had a good laugh and used it. He found things funny and admired other people's sense of humour, and he was amusing himself. All these things are still true of him."

Throughout his years at Dalhousie, Blakeney continued his friendship with Barbara McAuley from Bridgewater. In 1945 she was diagnosed as having tuberculosis, and spent a couple of years in a provincial sanatorium. "I want to tell you something about his loyalty," she says. "There were times when I was at the San at Kentville, many times, when he would hitchhike 60 miles from Dal in Halifax weekends just to cheer me up." She survived her bout with tuberculosis and still lives in Nova Scotia. Blakeney also visits her on his annual trips home.

Blakeney's professors suggested that he attempt a scholarship in law at an American university, perhaps Harvard. His preference was Britain. He had planned all along to apply for the Rhodes Scholarship to Oxford. He didn't get it in 1946, but he was chosen as Nova Scotia's Rhodes Scholar for 1947. In his application, Blakeney described his principal university interests as "debating, discussion groups and student government." He said he intended to practice law and get into politics in Nova Scotia.

In the summer of 1947, he boarded ship for England. He and Molly Schwartz were "quasi-engaged"; they had an understanding, but no formal arrangement.

The Rhodes Scholarship to Oxford is a mark of distinction for any Canadian student, but in post-war England the lustre was somewhat tarnished. Britain in 1947 was cold, dark, and deprived. Scholars that year received from the university a sombre note informing them that many goods and foods were unavailable and others were strictly rationed. Fish was available, but sauces and fats in which to cook it were not. One might look forward to between one and three eggs a month in winter. Fruit juice, canned tomatoes, rice, peanut butter, and biscuits were not available. Blakeney decided to live in residence at Queen's College. The food was drab and rationed, down to bread and potatoes. "Those potatoes," Blakeney recalls, "were sprinkled with meat dust and called meat pies, or sprinkled with meat dust of a different colour and called shepherd's pie. There were powdered eggs and milk, there was ice cream which seemed to have been made without dairy products or sugar. It tasted like cold chalk."

The residences were stately old buildings of Georgian limestone, set in a quadrangle which contained a chapel and library, and overlooking a grass square with a fountain. But they were drafty and uncomfortable as well. Blakeney had his own bed and sitting room with a fireplace, supplied with poor quality, sooty coal—also rationed. Large windows overlooked the courtyard, and "there was never any significant difference in temperature between the outdoors and the inside except within four feet of the fireplace." The rules of Queen's College were strict, even by the staid standards of the 1940s. Residents were not allowed out after eleven. Nor were they, without permission, allowed to venture more than three miles beyond the centre of Oxford.

Blakeney registered in a two-year course called "Modern Greats" which emphasized economics and modern history, with some attention to philosophy. In contrast to the house rules at Queen's College, the courses of study were loosely organized and left almost everything to the student's initiative and discipline. Blakeney recalls being assigned tutors, meeting with them individually and discussing a plan of work, which included the professor suggesting lectures which the student was free to attend or ignore. The same professor would suggest books to read, send the student away, and expect an essay the following week. After two years he wrote a comprehensive exam. Blakeney liked the system, although he found that he had to read more and rely less on his memory than he had in his law classes at Dalhousie.

His mandatory reading list during his two years at Oxford included Bishop Barclay and David Hume, Descartes, John Stuart Mill, and Bertrand Russell. He was especially interested in moral philosophy and ethics, and still likes to quote what sound like his class notes of long ago. In economics he was interested in the work of one of the Oxford dons, Sir William Beveridge. He had heard about Beveridge, and read his work, before he left Canada, and his reading list at Oxford included Beveridge's *Full Employment in a Free Society.* "That was the great blueprint for democratic socialism," Blakeney says. "It's a book that I studied with some care."

There were vigorous debates about economic policy among professors who alternated between teaching at Oxford and planning the country's economy at Whitehall. "G. D. H. Cole was giving a series of lectures on why the British steel industry should be nationalized, while another professor of economics was heaping scorn on the very idea," Blakeney recalls. "It was interesting to be in an institution where two leading professors were dealing in the most vigorous terms about the nonsense of the other." This tradition of informed debate—critical, analytical, but never personal— impressed Blakeney. It later became his trademark as a politician.

He was determined to use the Oxford experience to expand his horizons, "to make myself a little bit more than a Nova Scotia boy who was quick in making notes." He had made several decisions. "I was not going to take an advanced degree in law. I was going to take philosophy, politics, and economics. It gave me confidence that I understood something in economics. There's an awful lot of nonsense written and talked about in economics. The political and moral philosophy assisted me in dealing with the problems which I encountered in my work and my life. It gave me a level of confidence. I don't know whether that came from studying at Oxford or from having won the Rhodes Scholarship. It came a little bit from both."

He had earned his law degree and gold medal at Dalhousie, but in England there was less pressure to compete. He decided to take a relaxed approach toward marks and exams. "I wanted to travel a bit, play a bit of hockey and badminton, get a feel of U.K. politics. I wasn't going to be able to do all that and get a first." He thought he could get a second without too much work, and he did.

He played on the university badminton and hockey teams, a less impressive athletic achievement than it sounds. His playing hockey for Oxford was a triumph of choice over natural ability. Almost anyone who could skate would do, but being on the team meant several touring trips to the continent. Clint Havey, a friend from Dalhousie, says that "Al's skills as a hockey player had escaped detection at Dal." The team travelled within Britain, and to Holland, Germany, France, Switzerland, and Austria. It was composed largely of Canadians who liked to drink beer and sing on the bus. The badminton group was more serene.

Blakeney did little dating because of his informal engagement with Molly Schwartz. He wrote to her weekly, and maintained correspondence with other Bridgewater and Dalhousie friends. He spent some vacations with the families of British friends from school, others with his mother's relatives in the Rhondda Valley. His parents came to visit during the summer of 1948.

When he left Canada in 1947, Blakeney's membership in the CCF had already come to the attention of the party. He soon had a letter from David Lewis, the national secretary, who also had been a Rhodes Scholar. Lewis encouraged Blakeney to take a close look into the British Labour movement, and offered to arrange a meeting with Morgan Phillips, the Labour Party secretary. Blakeney followed Lewis's advice, and came to several conclusions which were vital to his political development.

"These were highly skilled people," he remembers, "yet they had all manner of problems transforming Britain. That told me that government and political ideology were something that did not consist of a checklist, but of a direction and an approach. I became very sceptical of people who said Marx didn't say it, or that's not in accordance with Marx. None of that makes sense to me. As I look back on life, it never did. That makes me a much more pragmatic socialist than some I've run into, and it also makes me exceedingly sceptical of campaigns for privatization, and that type of thing. I'm not just sceptical of the nostrums of the right. I'm sceptical of the nostrums of the left as well."

Lloyd Shaw's letters kept Blakeney posted on CCF events in Canada. Ever the optimist, Shaw referred glowingly to the CCF's chances in Nova Scotia. He assumed Blakeney would return to the province, and told him his chances of winning election would be "excellent indeed." While at

Oxford, Blakeney subscribed to *The Commonwealth*, the Saskatchewan CCF newspaper. It was a gesture of social democratic loyalty, but he says, "Saskatchewan was a tremendously remote place to me at that time."

His pragmatism, his political formation in Nova Scotia and at Oxford, were entirely academic, the product of classrooms, debates, and reading lists. He had never knocked on a door or organized a poll. He had never been on strike or walked a picket line. He graduated from Oxford in 1949 with a Bachelor of Arts degree and a more sophisticated world view, but with no experience in practical politics.

With his Oxford classes and exams completed, Blakeney and four friends packed themselves into a 1931 Austin and headed for Budapest to attend a Communist Youth Festival. Blakeney had little ideological interest in the festival, but says it was an excuse to escape the drabness of post-war Britain. There may have been more vitality on the continent, but Europe in 1949 was still digging out from the waste and rubble of war. It was an astonishing and disturbing sight for a 19-year-old from Bridgewater, Nova Scotia. They drove through Germany, still devastated, and spent a short time in Prague. In Budapest, they stayed in student residences for 10 days. Travelling back to England, the five students travelled through Yugoslavia, Trieste, and Venice, across Italy, into France to Paris, and back to Britain.

Blakeney decided to return to Nova Scotia to complete his articles but, much to his father's disappointment, he decided he wanted to live elsewhere in Canada. It was a case of youthful wanderlust. He expected to return in a few years to practise law, and to get elected as a CCF politician. He did his articles in Lunenburg with a lawyer named W. P. Potter. He was close enough to Bridgewater to live at home and commute.

Allan Blakeney and Molly Schwartz became formally engaged late in 1949. The arrangement was sealed with a $140 diamond ring from Birks. In September 1950, he was admitted to the Nova Scotia bar, and they were married in the Schwartz home. A few close friends were invited. Barbara McAuley, Blakeney's former schoolmate in Bridgewater, was one of them. Molly's friend Budge Wilson had moved to Ontario, and was unable to attend. Both the bride and her mother wept during the ceremony.

Photographs of the couple and their parents were taken against an artificial backdrop set up on the lawn. Blakeney is short-haired, clean shaven, and appears slimmer than in his high school days. He is wearing a dark suit with a boutonniere in his lapel. Molly, a shade taller, looking fresh-faced and healthy despite her medical history, wears a flowered hairpiece and a long dress, buttoned down the front. Blakeney bears a strong resemblance to his father—a small man with the same round, intense eyes, seemingly standing at attention. After the photos, tea (but not liquor) was served. Both families believed that wedding celebrations should remain modest.

# Chapter Three

# The Civil Service

The myth has it that Allan Blakeney became a convert to socialism and went looking for a laboratory; the CCF government in Saskatchewan was the obvious place for him to put his ideas to work. That's tidy, but a bit too simple. While it is true that he became a CCFer at Dalhousie and remained one at Oxford, his main interest when he graduated in 1949 was to find a job after seven years at university.

During his final year at Oxford he had been fishing for jobs with the federal government, and at several law schools. Nobody had anything immediate to offer. He sought advice from Jim Milner, his former professor at Dalhousie. Milner referred him to George Tamaki, a Dalhousie graduate working as legal secretary to the Government Finance Office (GFO) in Saskatchewan. Blakeney in turn wrote to Tamaki, saying that he was "interested in the experiment being carried on by the present government of Saskatchewan." Tamaki's reply indicated that there might be something for Blakeney after he had completed his articles.

Blakeney continued his search, concentrating on law firms in the growing cities of Vancouver and Edmonton. By February 1950 he had landed a job with the Edmonton firm of Newell, Lindsay, Emery, Ford, and Jamieson. He travelled west alone (he and Molly had not yet married) and found a room in a boarding house for $20 a month. He was close enough to walk to work. Molly's older sister Mardi had moved to Edmonton earlier; she remembers seeing him frequently and darning his socks. The law scene was busy and promising, but he didn't stay. In late April 1950 he was offered an interview with the Saskatchewan government, and he flew to Regina. Tamaki had decided to leave the Government Finance Office. Blakeney was offered the position, and accepted for June 1.

In September he returned to Nova Scotia to be accepted to the bar and to get married. For a honeymoon the newly-weds followed the scenic Cabot Trail around Cape Breton Island. They were driving a friend's car. On their way out to Regina, they ran off the road near Simcoe, Ontario.

Molly, who was driving, wasn't injured, but Blakeney smashed his head into the windshield and was in the hospital for several days. He still bears a small lump and a scar above his right eye.

When they drove into Regina, Blakeney remembers, it "wasn't Paris." They were bruised, disillusioned, and homesick, and had no intention of staying long. "I never had given any thought of spending my career in Saskatchewan," he says, "because it just wasn't on anyone's list." They rented a small apartment with two rooms and a bath. Blakeney went to his new job with the Saskatchewan government and Molly, a lab technician by training, settled for work at the public library.

Blakeney walked into the best civil service in Canada, in the most unlikely of provinces. A mere six years earlier Saskatchewan had had the highest per capita debt in the country; it was nearly bankrupt, and its credit rating was poor. The province was just emerging from the battering it had taken during the Depression, then the war.

The war, and a return of the rains, produced a moderate prosperity, but Saskatchewan was a poor province in 1950. The majority of people lived in the countryside. The lights winking in the windows of farm houses at dusk and throughout the night were of coal oil and kerosene lamps. Many farmers were just replacing their horses with rough-riding gas tractors. Thousands of children attended one-room schools where the teacher had to arrive early to light a fire in the wood stove. Gravel and dirt roads became impassable during rainy weather, and in winter people left their cars and trucks out at the main road to avoid being snowed in when the fierce storms arrived.

In 1950, Regina still didn't seem to believe that it had a future. The two most momentous events of the 1930s had been the Regina Riot in 1935, and the spectacle of hundreds of unemployed men digging a lake— Wascana—by hand. During the war there was work but few consumer goods. People were forced to sacrifice again. The Depression mentality survived into the 1950s. Most of the city had been built in, or before, the 1920s. There were plenty of unpaved streets and wooden sidewalks, and one traffic light. The city fathers refused to pave new streets or to build new subdivisions. There was an acute housing shortage. Many houses still had wooden privies in the back yard. If a house had a basement, it was likely rented as a suite. Rooming houses were filled.

Blakeney's job was as understudy to George Tamaki, the secretary and legal advisor to the Government Finance Office. The GFO acted as a holding company and provided services to the crown corporations. Tommy Douglas had a fervent belief, common among Depression era socialists, in the possibilities of the centrally-planned state. The CCF had come to power with an ambitious set of policies, and proceeded to put many of them into place. They included a health planning commission, progressive trade union legislation, co-operatives, and expanded rural and social services.

In the early years of government there was great enthusiasm for public ownership; this was consistent with the almost Biblical denunciations of capitalism made in the Regina Manifesto. The government's concern was both for the delivery of essential services and for the diversification of Saskatchewan's fragile economy. Crown corporations were the favoured method of organizing public involvement. It wasn't an idea original to the Douglas government, but one to which the Premier added new levels of sophistication. Public companies were created for timber, fur, fish, and the mining of sodium sulfate. A few projects—a box factory and a shoe factory—didn't work out, but most of them did. Telephones, automobile insurance, bus transportation, a northern airline, and an air ambulance service were all brought under public control.

These projects, all occurring at the same time, strained the budget and the administration of a poor province. Late in 1945 Douglas had set up the Economic Advisory and Planning Board, which was to spawn a series of innovations. George Cadbury, scion of the Cadbury chocolate family in Britain and a lifelong member of the Labour Party, visited Saskatchewan in 1945. He was interested enough in the experiment to agree, when invited, to make an unlikely move to the Canadian hinterland. The tall, shaggy-browed Cadbury became Saskatchewan's most important bureaucrat: chairman of the new Advisory and Planning Board, and the province's Chief Industrial Executive. The board consisted of both hired planners and several cabinet ministers, including the Premier and Clarence Fines, the Provincial Treasurer. It was a think tank for the cabinet, and all new major planning began there. Cadbury's minister was Douglas himself, and the Planning Board answered to cabinet through him.

Cadbury's role as Chief Industrial Officer was to bring some central planning and organization to the crown corporations. In 1947 the Planning Board split, with half of it becoming the Government Finance Office. The GFO was also responsible to a committee of cabinet, with Clarence Fines as chair. By the time Blakeney arrived in 1950, much of the impressive administrative machinery was in place. Blakeney's role was to help consolidate that machinery as it applied to crown corporations. He was too young to have been preceded by a reputation, but Cadbury says Blakeney had obvious credentials: "He was the winner of the Rhodes Scholarship. That was obviously a public achievement. But in Saskatchewan he was totally unknown at the time."

In addition to being a holding company for the growing number of crowns (about 18 by then), the Government Finance Office was a central service agency for them, offering accounting, financial, legal, and industrial relations services. Each crown had a manager, but it also had a minister-in-charge. Blakeney acted as secretary at every meeting, the person directing the flow of information. He also provided legal advice to the Industrial Development Fund (later SEDCO). Cadbury was pleased with his performance, and there was no question when Tamaki left in the fall of 1950 that Blakeney would succeed him. "I had no hesitation," Cadbury says. "We were very fortunate to have gotten the right person. He was popular with the corporations. He had to chase them for information. It was a difficult job."

Blakeney is anything but sentimental, but he talks of that period in the 1950s with special enthusiasm. Everything was new. He was working hard and learning all the time. He remembers attending a budget meeting on the afternoon of Christmas day. He was able to apply his academic knowledge in law and economics, and his early experience in his father's wholesale business was valuable when it came to running public corporations. He honed his skills as both a negotiator and a legal draftsman. He wrote and negotiated the contracts for both the IPSCO steel mill and a cement plant in Regina. In both cases business people raised part of the capital, and the government guaranteed bonds for the remainder. It was an early example of the joint venture, which is common today, but wasn't then.

The government placed its public sector emphasis on utility and service corporations, where it had a monopoly—power, telephones, a northern airline, and auto insurance. Blakeney became convinced that public ownership could work as efficiently as private enterprise, and often with desirable social goals attached: "In 1955 SaskPower took natural gas quickly and cheaply to all sorts of people, to small places in Saskatchewan which were not getting gas at that time. It made me believe that a great deal was possible and that there was no mystique in private management."

The Saskatchewan civil service was a small one by today's standards, but it contained a cadre of bright young people who had been attracted by the challenge of what was advertised as "the socialist experiment." Tommy Shoyama, Al Johnson, Don Tansley, and Meyer Brownstone (the civil service at its higher levels was exclusively male) were Blakeney's colleagues. They and their wives formed an educated, urbane social circle. Regina didn't offer many cultural events, so the favoured entertainment was house parties with beer, conversation, and the occasional sing-song—a socially tame, but intellectually stimulating, prescription.

Tommy McLeod, a former Deputy Provincial Treasurer, was a member of the group. Blakeney was shy, he says, someone who had intellectual tastes: "Obviously he would sooner read than indulge in idle chatter." Nonetheless, he says, "Al was part of the group from the beginning. His wife, Molly, was an extremely charming person. She didn't set out to be a model hostess but she was a delightful person. We were in and out of each other's homes all the time. Al was one of the gang."

Meyer Brownstone remembers the day he and Blakeney rented a boat and borrowed some gear to go fishing near Fort Qu'Appelle, east of Regina. They had found a spot and dropped their lines when a boat came speeding across the lake toward them. It contained an RCMP officer. They were both charged with fishing without a licence, and the equipment was seized. When their day came in court, Brownstone pleaded guilty. Blakeney chose to fight the charge, and served as his own lawyer. The officer who charged them was in the courtroom, and Blakeney subjected him to an hour's cross-examination. The questions placed in doubt whether the officer could hear what Blakeney had told him above the noise of the motors out on the lake. "It went on and on," Brownstone recalls. "The judge was in hysterics, and finally dismissed the case. I said 'Dammit Al, what about me?' He said, 'Well, you pleaded guilty'."

The Blakeneys lived for three years in their modest suite in Lakeview, an older neighbourhood near the Legislative Building, known for its tree-lined streets and stuccoed houses. They couldn't afford to buy, and there were few houses available in any case. Blakeney took a rambling old streetcar along Albert Street to his office downtown, and frequently returned home for lunch. They didn't own a car for seven years after their marriage because "Molly didn't believe that we should spend money frivolously." In 1957 they bought a second-hand Desoto.

Co-operative development was one of the pet phrases of the Douglas government, and groups of left-leaning civil servants in Regina became involved in the credit union and retail co-operatives. They also set up housing co-ops. In 1952 the Blakeneys and a group of six other families formed the Lakeview Co-operative Building Association. They bought land near Hill Avenue and Montague Street (then at the southwestern edge of the city, now several miles inside the city limit). They built six houses, providing much of the labour themselves. There are black and white photos in the family album which show Blakeney with a partly-framed house behind him. He is wearing a fur hat, and he's bundled in several layers of clothing: a rotund carpenter, complete with an apron full of nails.

There is a story about his deadly prowess with a hammer. "It's a famous incident," says Tommy McLeod, who was one of the partners in the co-operative. "Allan and Stan Watson from Saskatchewan Government Telephones were straightening out a piece of tin pipe. Stan was holding it over some support underneath, and Al wanted to know where to hit it. Stan put his thumb down and said, 'Hit it right there.' Al did. Fortunately, he did not have to make his living as a carpenter." The Blakeneys moved into their house on Montague Street in 1953. It was an indication that Saskatchewan had begun to exert a hold on them. He became involved with the neighbourhood cubs and scouts, and as a founding member of the Argyle Road Baptist Church.

Despite her heart condition, Molly lived a normal life. She gave birth to two children: Barbara May in 1953, and Hugh Emrys in 1955. After Barbara's birth, Molly no longer worked outside the home. She was not an enthusiastic housekeeper, but she also refused Blakeney's suggestion that they hire help. Her friend Budge Wilson says that Molly appeared happier and healthier than she had ever been.

Most of the child-care fell to her. Blakeney was as involved with his children as most other fathers in his neighbourhood in the 1950s, which meant not much at all. Despite the progressive activity of the Douglas government, Saskatchewan remained a socially conservative, agrarian society. Expectations regarding women were entirely traditional.

Those limitations may not have been felt keenly by Molly Blakeney, the product of a conservative family and society in Loyalist Nova Scotia. But others, including George Cadbury's wife Barbara, chafed at the restrictions. A well-educated woman who had been active in the Labour Party in Britain, she found that something quite different was expected of her in Saskatchewan. "Women didn't feel they could participate," she says. "The atmosphere was very male. The rights of today were unthinkable then." Despite the objections of men who said it was no job for a woman, she decided to run for the Co-op Refinery's board of directors. She later became the first woman representative to the Co-operative Union of Canada.

Blakeney's job, and his friendships with the bureaucratic élite, placed him in a privileged position to see the government at work. His work also brought him into contact with the CCF cabinet ministers. "I got to know the cabinet well because they were all chairmen of crown corporation boards. I'm sitting there as secretary, spending my life at meetings chaired by cabinet ministers, five or six half-day meetings a week: Fines, Lloyd, Jim Darling, Charlie Williams, and J. H. Brockelbank" [the father of John Brockelbank, later an NDP MLA].

The Premier was "Mr. Douglas," and that formal relationship remained until Blakeney went into politics himself. Blakeney, however, found it easy to work for the Baptist minister who had become a politician. Douglas was as comfortable in a pulpit as on a campaign platform. His politics were an extension of his social gospel theology. The leadership of Protestant ministers like Woodsworth, Knowles, and Douglas left an indelible imprint on the CCF. People like George Cadbury, the British Quaker, and Allan Blakeney, the young Baptist from Bridgewater, felt at home in Saskatchewan, helping to build the new Jerusalem.

If Blakeney had a political mentor, though, it wasn't the irrepressible Douglas, but the sharp-pencilled Clarence Fines. It was from Fines that Blakeney learned his most significant lessons about government. A Regina school teacher, Fines had become involved in the Saskatchewan CCF in its earliest days. He is generally credited with putting the province back on its feet when he became provincial Treasurer. He was a dapper man known for the bow tie he frequently wore, and for his shrewd personal investments (even while he was Treasurer). After the election of 1944, Fines began to produce a string of balanced budgets. He was cautious, and a member of the party's right wing.

As Treasurer, Fines was responsible for the Government Finance Office, and Blakeney saw him every week. The experience left a lasting impression. "I've rarely met a person," Blakeney says, "who had a more orderly mind, who understood the principles of public administration as well as Clarence. He spent a lot of time getting quality people. He insisted on performance. He attempted to define the job he wanted you to do. Then he told you to go and do it, not to come back and ask him about it."

There existed a strong camaraderie among the politicians and senior bureaucrats, including Blakeney. They were sympathetic to the aims of the government, and everyone knew it. Many of them, according to Meyer Brownstone, a former Deputy Minister of Municipal Affairs, had been attracted to Saskatchewan to help build the "co-operative commonwealth." They found their services valued and appreciated by a government which believed in planning and professionalism in the civil service. They stayed, even when they could have made more money elsewhere.

That close and informal connection between civil servant and politician had a lot to recommend it. But it was also fertile ground for patronage, and the Douglas government was certainly not free of it. Civil servants were expected to believe in the program, but they were not expected to get involved in the party. Most of them didn't. Blakeney, however, was active in the CCF, and his appointment was through Order-in-Council rather than the usual civil service hiring process. He argues that patronage exists only when the people hired are not the most qualified for the jobs. If Douglas was guilty of excessive patronage, the fact escaped his party. Provincial conventions continued to pass resolutions demanding that the government hire socialists. Colleagues of the day find it difficult to recall where Blakeney fit into the party ideologically. As a civil servant he didn't speak out publicly on political issues, but he was sympathetic to the party's right, represented by people like Fines and Brockelbank, the Minister of Natural Resources.

By the mid-1950s, the national CCF was embarrassed by the stridency of the 1932 Manifesto, and wanted to replace it with something more moderate. Blakeney was a member of the Regina Lakeview CCF Club, and participated at the local level in preparing drafts toward a new statement. Two nights a week for a year, he served on a committee led by party stalwart J. Fortesque McKay. Blakeney was not a Regina Manifesto socialist. The urgency and the almost prophetic sense of grievance were both alien to him. He did not arrive in politics from a dusty farm or a bread line. He came from a Tory Loyalist tradition, the child of a middle class family, an intellectual who had studied at Oxford.

In his view, many of the things called for in 1933 were unnecessary, and others had been won. He wasn't interested in the eradication of capitalism. He believed the financial tyranny of the 1930s had been modified by the 1950s. There was a Bank of Canada, something which had not existed during the Depression, and private banks had come under some public regulation. He thought the old CCF (and Social Credit) had placed undue emphasis on the benefits which would flow from public control of the financial system. He believed, as the Saskatchewan CCF had come to believe, that farm land should not be socialized, but privately owned, and that the CCF needed a more modern definition of both capitalism and socialism. Blakeney's was a line which would disappoint the Old Left in the Saskatchewan party, but his profile then was not such that he attracted their attention.

The review process, which was occurring across the country, resulted in the Winnipeg Declaration of 1956, a sanitized rewriting of the Regina Manifesto. The new declaration avoided a clarion call to socialism and the nationalization of industry. It talked instead about a positive role for private industry in society. Much of that re-thinking flowed from the experience of Canada's only CCF government. Faced by a lack of money and public tolerance, Douglas had softened the party line. Blakeney was there when it happened, and he approved.

Blakeney left the Government Finance Office in 1955 to become the chief officer for the Saskatchewan Securities Commission. New oil and uranium discoveries were attracting unscrupulous promoters, and the commission wasn't equipped to police the marketing of securities. Blakeney was brought in to put some muscle into the operation. He also retained his position as legal advisor to the Industrial Development Fund. The securities work was highly technical, and he found it unexciting, but it did give him an insider's view on how companies are financed, and the confidence that he knew how business works.

He took the job because he was asked, but he was also determined to get into politics. The Securities Commission could not be used as a base for that. Given the non-partisan role which he believed he had to play as securities officer, Blakeney withdrew from his activity in the CCF and even stopped going to party conventions. By 1957 he had arrived at two conclusions: he would take the political plunge in the next election, and he would do it from the base of a private law practice. He began to search for likely law partners. By year's end he was ready to make his move.

During the night of December 27, 1957, Molly Blakeney awakened her husband to tell him she was ill. He took her pulse and immediately called a doctor. Before the doctor arrived Molly had died from a Stokes-Adams attack, a type of heart disease characterized by extreme slowness of pulse.

What happened then and in the following days remains a blur in Blakeney's usually commanding memory. He rarely talks about it. He does remember calling his neighbours, Marj and Bill Haney, at five in the morning. He told them his wife had just died, and asked what he should do. They were there in minutes. Blakeney remembers with gratitude and admiration how they organized around his tragedy: "Marj is from Wilcox and her husband is from Cabri. They just moved in like a group of people would in rural Saskatchewan and they took over."

Molly's death came as a shock to her friends and family, but it became less so after they had thought about it. Budge Wilson had begun to believe that the Schwartz family's earlier fears had been misplaced. Mardi Gordon, on the other hand, believes her sister Molly was fortunate to have lived as normal a life as she had. Regina friends like the Haneys knew that Molly often did not feel well, but the Blakeneys had learned to live with her condition.

The months of that winter were bleak ones for Allan Blakeney. Molly's death is an event which he has submerged as deeply as possible in his memory. He says there was no time to be depressed or introspective that winter. But Molly's friend, Budge Wilson, remembers a letter from him: "I remember exactly the term he used. It was 'my bitter blow'."

He had no family in Saskatchewan, so he depended on friends and people from his congregation at the church. He had the Family Service Bureau send in housekeepers immediately following Molly's death. Later he hired a housekeeper, who moved into the basement suite with her young son. She looked after the children six days a week, and Blakeney was with them on Sundays.

He had been poised to move into private law practice early in 1958. He delayed, but only briefly. In April 1958, he became a partner in the firm of Davidson, Davidson, and Blakeney. He practiced mainly corporate law on behalf of small companies.

Anne Gorham was learning to ski at Mount Baker in Oregon during the Christmas holidays in 1957. When she returned home to Victoria, there was a telegram pinned to her door. Her friend Molly Blakeney had died. Days later, Anne received Molly's letters, one inviting her to spend Christmas in Regina, and another thanking her for the gifts she had sent. They had known one another from childhood in Halifax, had both been born in 1927, had attended the same United Church Sunday School. They had also been classmates in science at Dalhousie. Their families, both well off, had cottages near one another at Green Bay in Lunenburg County.

Anne, a slim, freckled, reddish-haired woman, had met Blakeney when he was dating Molly, although she did not get to know him well before he went away to Oxford. Anne's father was a food wholesaler, and Nova

Scotia was small enough that he knew Blakeney's father, John. She was in Montreal working on her Master's degree in botany when Molly was married in 1950, so she missed the wedding, but she had been at the bridal shower earlier in the summer. When she moved to Edmonton in 1952, Anne got off the train in Regina and spent a weekend with the Blakeneys in their two-room apartment. They showed her the foundation which had been poured for their new house. They visited one Christmas in Edmonton, and another year Anne spent Christmas in Regina. Anne later moved to Victoria, where she taught botany at Victoria College. She also began to work toward her PhD through Washington State University.

In April 1958, about four months after Molly's death, Blakeney wrote to Anne saying that he would be visiting Victoria and would like to see her. "He was still in a state of bereaved shock when he came in the spring," Anne recalls. He didn't say it in so many words, but he was there to begin courting her. She took the hint, however subtle, and not long afterward she stopped to see him in Regina on her way to visit her family in Halifax. She visited Molly's parents, too. They had heard from Blakeney about his trip to Victoria. The codes, though unspoken, must have been clear. "They made me feel very welcome," she says. "They didn't come right out and say they thought we would marry—so many things were guessed at."

There began a communication—a courtship—which was both leisurely and formal. It consisted mainly of letters, which almost took the form of pre-nuptial contract negotiations. "A lot of writing back and forth," says Anne, "and deciding whether we were suited to one another, or interested in one another." His two children were an attraction to her rather than a liability. He told her he was considering politics. She was not a CCFer, but she was prepared to become one. Her letters were more easily personal than his. Her questions about his personality were likely to draw responses "about low cost housing, the life of a politician, and recommending books by Eugene Debs," a labour and political leader in turn-of-the-century America.

She had been a career woman, interested in science and the outdoors, but by 1958, at age 31, she wanted to marry and have a family. "I'd had my fill of concert going," she says. The prospect of pursuing a PhD was not of much interest to her. "When I was 21 I wasn't ready for marriage. I was a slow starter, but this was fine."

Blakeney describes their relationship with typical understatement. "I renewed acquaintances with Anne in the spring of 1958. It was casual at the outset. She came down to Regina at Christmas 1958 and we decided to get married." They announced their engagement at a year-end party at Al Johnson's house. Blakeney wrote to the Schwartzes to inform them and received a warm letter of congratulations. They were married in Victoria on May 23, 1959, in the back yard of the family Anne had lived with while she taught there. Much like Blakeney's first wedding, the ceremony was small. Nineteen guests signed the register. Anne wore an olive green, handwoven silk dress, and a beige straw hat.

Their honeymoon consisted of a driving trip on Vancouver Island, then back to Saskatchewan via the Columbia River and Grand Coulee dams. Blakeney admits a fascination with dams and waterfalls, but Anne confesses that she saw more of dams on that trip than she needed. They settled into his home on Montague Street. Anne persuaded the housekeeper to stay for a while, and began to learn from wives of Blakeney's friends how to be domestic, particularly how to care for children. If it began as a rather formal and cautious liaison, it has been a happy one. Anne gave up a career and inherited a family, and appears never to have regretted either decision. She says she's "of an older generation."

Blakeney was poised for the political career he had always wanted, but which would probably have been impossible had he remained a single parent with two small children. He wanted to contest a nomination in the four-member Regina constituency for the election which was expected in 1960. His problem was that he was unknown outside the public service. He became vice-president of the Regina constituency in 1958. He began to be seen at the obligatory CCF whist tournaments and teas, and to develop a cross-indexed list of CCF members in Regina. He ran for the school board in the fall of 1959 under the banner of the progressive Civic Reform Association. He didn't win, but he placed respectably.

He had been preparing himself for politics since high school—the law degree, Oxford studies in economics, his decision to go first into the public service, then into the security of a law practice. His plan might have been made impossible by his wife's death, but by 1959 he had succeeded, quickly, in putting his personal life back together. One can presume a single-mindedness throughout. He plays that down. He had always intended to get into politics, and he helped the opportunities present themselves. The 1950s were a decade of preparation. Now he had to get himself nominated and elected.

# Chapter Four

# Politics

The Trianon Ballroom, a landmark in downtown Regina, was known for more than its dances. An elegant old building with hardwood floors, balustrades, and balconies, it was used also for less delicate pursuits. On the evening of April 19, 1960, it was packed with more than 1,500 people in what guest speaker Tommy Douglas described as the biggest CCF nominating convention he had ever attended.

The city of Regina was one big provincial constituency served by three members, all of them CCF. Redistribution was adding a fourth, and all would be chosen in this crowded, smoky hall. There was little doubt that two of the four nominations would go to the incumbents—Marjorie Cooper, the only woman sitting on the CCF benches, and Charlie Williams, the personable but barely competent Minister of Labour. The added seat, and the resignation of Clarence Fines after 16 years as MLA and Provincial Treasurer, had opened things up. Fines was unquestionably competent, but he had created a controversy by leaving his wife, and there was constant gossip about the wealth he had accumulated from shrewd personal investments while he was Treasurer. He'd had enough of politics and clicking tongues, and wanted to leave the province. There were four contestants for what were considered the two vacant positions—Ed Whelan, a civil servant and president of the Regina CCF; Henry Baker, the mayor; a trade union nominee named Ernie Smith; and Blakeney. The betting was that Baker, with his high profile as mayor, would win one nomination. The other was up for grabs.

Blakeney was well known in the senior civil service, but not in the city. His speech was mediocre, but that was more than offset by the virtual laying on of hands by Clarence Fines. He made an unusual gesture by nominating Blakeney. "The CCF must look for younger men," Fines said, "and Mr. Blakeney could do a much better job than I have done." The CCF had always prided itself in constituency democracy, in allowing local people to choose their own candidates. The signal being sent by Fines was apparent to everyone in the hall.

In the ethos created by the CCF, the values of the farm and small town were held as almost sacred. In that definition Blakeney was a newcomer, even though he had been in the province for 10 years. He had no mud on his boots or callouses on his hands, and had never attended the one-room schoolhouse, credentials which Saskatchewan people appreciated in their politicians. Fines's nomination helped Blakeney overcome the handicap of being considered an outsider to the province.

Blakeney had caught the eye of the Premier. They had a rather formal relationship, but he knew Douglas well enough to sound him out about the nomination. Douglas encouraged him, and told an interviewer years later that he had persuaded Blakeney to run. Some of the cabinet ministers had been involved in Blakeney's campaign, as had a group of his CCF friends in the senior civil service. He was the Establishment candidate.

While the ballots were being counted that evening Douglas outlined the CCF platform for the election expected in June. He was interrupted by the news that Cooper and Williams had been nominated. He continued, making the best of a chaotic situation by saying blithely that his speech was like baloney: "You can slice it as thick or as thin as you wish." Blakeney was nominated on the second ballot, and the third was inconclusive. Douglas continued with his speech, saying that medicare would be the most important issue in the campaign to come.

Whelan emerged as Regina's fourth CCF candidate on the final ballot. The "younger men" Fines referred to ended up being a civil servant and someone who had been a civil servant until just two years previously. This indicated the close liaison between the government and some of its employees, and it was a sign that the government had been around for long enough for that kind of relationship to exist. The loss was a blow to Baker, one which he never forgot.

Within a few days of being nominated Blakeney was in the midst of his first provincial election campaign. The CCF theme was "Tested and Trusted"—hardly a call to arms. The party intended to run on its record and on the charisma of T. C. Douglas. But the 1960 campaign became a bitter, single-issue contest, with doctors pursuing an aggressive campaign against medicare.

The College of Physicians and Surgeons, which combined the role of trade union with licensing body, raised $60,000 in a levy on its members, and the Canadian Medical Association provided an extra $35,000. That was more money than the CCF spent on its entire campaign. A public relations man, hired from one of the big breweries in eastern Canada, came to Saskatchewan to produce a publication called *The Weekly Mirror.* It was antagonistic to the government and sympathetic to the Liberals. Every household in the province received a folder with a reprint of an article from the *Toronto Star* in which a doctor was quoted as saying that Saskatchewan physicians wouldn't practice under the plan. Citizens would, instead, be stuck with imported practitioners whom he described as the "garbage of Europe." It was a fierce political baptism for Allan Blakeney. He began the campaign in a reasoned fashion, attempting to discuss housing, welfare rates, and economic diversification as well as medicare. He was forced to respond to the single-issue campaign being waged by the doctors. He carried the offensive pamphlets to meetings in the immigrant neighbourhoods of east Regina, known locally as Garlic Flats. "The kit was saying, 'You will be left with nothing but the garbage of Europe.' So I would go down to the Hungarian hall and read this thing, just read it carefully. And it was just as if you were hitting them with a wet towel. They were saying 'Who the hell are those people'?"

Although this was to be only the first round of a bigger battle, the doctors' campaign was a bust. It allowed the CCF to fight the election on health issues—home turf for them. The government was re-elected with an increased majority, although the popular vote fell by five points. Ross Thatcher, the new leader of the Liberals, squeaked out a victory over the CCF in the Morse riding and took his place in the legislature as well. A former CCF Member of Parliament, Thatcher had bolted the party in 1955 to become one of its most trenchant critics. He became provincial Liberal leader in 1959, and was pathological in his determination to wipe out socialism in Saskatchewan.

As a neophyte politician Blakeney expected to remain a backbencher for at least the first four years. Douglas surprised him. When he made a minor cabinet shuffle within two months of the 1960 election, Allan Blakeney, who had never sat in the red-carpeted Legislative Assembly as a member, was sworn in as the Minister of Education. He was not yet 35 years old, the youngest minister in the fifth consecutive Douglas government.

Douglas wanted him for Treasurer, a move which Blakeney resisted. He thought the post should go to Woodrow Lloyd, which it did. While Douglas's invitation indicated confidence in Blakeney's ability, it spoke also to the void left by the retirement of Clarence Fines. Fines had been, since the CCF victory in 1944, the government's financial arbiter, Douglas's backup man, the pragmatic administrator who said what the government could or could not afford. Fines had done his own talent scouting before leaving, and he had given the nod to Blakeney as his successor.

Blakeney was immediately appointed to the powerful Treasury Board committee of cabinet, and later as Minister-in-Charge of the Saskatchewan Government Insurance Office, both hard-side, economic jobs. He was a quiet man around the cabinet table, inclined to listen, and pick his spots to intervene. But he knew the issues and he knew the civil service. Bureaucrats with whom he had worked now faced the unnerving experience, during Treasury Board sessions, of having to answer his questions about their programs.

As Education Minister, one of Blakeney's immediate tasks was to complete the organization of the province into larger school units. Woodrow Lloyd had introduced the changes earlier, insisting that bigger units and schools could provide better education than the local one-room school-house. The argument made sense on the grounds of efficiency, but the loss of local schools was seen as another example of the changes undermining the rural community. Many people resented it, and it gave ammunition to the opposition's Big Brother charges against the CCF. By 1960, most of the province had been reorganized. It was left to Blakeney to complete the task.

He also inherited the task of setting up a new university campus in Regina. It was largely through his efforts that the city received not only a campus, but a 900-hectare park. He was negotiating for university lands with the federal government, which had an agricultural research station at the city's edge. He and Al Johnson decided that the new campus should be integrated with the Legislative buildings along Wascana Creek. There were parks and gardens surrounding the Legislature on the south side of Wascana Lake, and on the north shore as well. Blakeney and Johnson thought the area of the existing parks could be extended along the shoreline all the way out to the new campus.

A decision on assembling land had to be made quickly. Johnson wrote the Wascana Park proposal over one weekend. Blakeney presented it to cabinet the following Tuesday and won agreement. "I think I can say that I was the key political figure in getting it going," Blakeney says. Initially, he ran the planning for the proposal out of his offices at Education, but when the project grew too large he found a ministerial assistant to handle it. Wascana Park—an oasis of trees, lawns, waterways, picnic sites, and bicycle trails—has become the physical highlight of the semi-arid city built on the low shores of Pile-o'-Bones Creek. It has been extended—always along the shores of the creek as it runs diagonally through the city—from the university in the southeast, to well beyond the RCMP training barracks in the northwest.

Blakeney's appointment to the cabinet also meant personal changes. After a mere two years of practising law, he withdrew from his partnership. He and his family continued to live on Montague Street in Lakeview. The woman he had hired as housekeeper after Molly died continued to live in the basement. That freed Anne to accompany her husband to the round of school openings and graduation ceremonies to which the Minister of Education was invariably invited. She often drove while Blakeney sat in the passenger seat rehearsing his speech aloud.

Anne was not someone with a life interest in politics, and after Blakeney's appointment to the cabinet there was a period of adjustment. She had expected to become a housewife, cooking, cleaning, caring for two children and a garden. There was little debate about the traditional division of labour in the household. The more difficult question revolved around her role as a political wife.

Journalists have frequently described her as someone who avoided politics. That's misleading. She is a self-contained individual. She kept her distance in some important ways, but she was always involved. She worked in her husband's shoe-string nomination campaign in 1960, updating telephone lists, and she helped campaign in the provincial election that followed. Later, when he ran for the leadership, she was again a valuable campaigner. She has a reserve about her, a properness, but she likes people and has a direct and easy manner with them. Party workers say she was more effective on the doorsteps of the constituency than her husband was. She soon understood that Saskatchewan was a traditional place: after CCF suppers the men pushed back their chairs and talked farming and politics, while the women bustled about clearing and washing the dishes. A botanist with a Master's degree, she rolled up her sleeves and worked with the local women. It was not a progressive tradition by any means, but it was a real one. She was a hit. Constituents still describe her as "down to earth," which in Saskatchewan is always a compliment.

Blakeney established himself quickly as a capable and valuable minister. He did not create enemies, and he was not easily identifiable with any party faction, either of the left or of the right. If anything, he was closer to senior civil servants like Johnson and Shoyama, who by his admission had come to wield an ever greater influence in the last Douglas governments.

By 1960 there was mounting pressure on Tommy Douglas to run for the leadership of the new national party which would amalgamate the CCF with organized labour. The move was born of electoral desperation and a belief that a British-style Labour Party could work in Canada. The reaction in Saskatchewan was largely negative on both counts—losing Douglas, and linking with labour. The party's reluctance to part with the man who had led it to five consecutive victories is easy to understand, but there was also resistance to seeing the party change from a Saskatchewan-style CCF, dominated by farmers and the legacy of the Social Gospel, to a largely urban-based labour party. There existed a kind of Saskatchewan snobbery —the legend of overcoming dust and hardship through organized political action—which was difficult to give up. The major figures within the provincial CCF were ambivalent. Douglas, the recently-retired Clarence Fines, and Woodrow Lloyd, were at best uncomfortable with the idea, though for the most part they maintained a confident public face.

Blakeney believed that labour was too limited in its outlook, that it cared too much for the pocketbook and too little for the co-operative commonwealth. But he also recognized that a party based on the Social

Gospel and a waning rural populism was going nowhere. Nationally, the CCF had suffered a shocking defeat in the 1958 election, electing only eight MPs and winning a mere 10 per cent of the popular vote. Blakeney had observed the Labour government of Clement Attlee in action when he studied at Oxford, and he had been impressed. In a 1961 letter written to a friend in Britain, Blakeney described the emerging NDP as an amalgamation of the CCF with trade unions "to form what is essentially a right wing socialist party." He was comfortable with the label.

Douglas left to lead the federal NDP in the summer of 1961. There was consternation at losing him, but a clear feeling, at least in caucus, that he would be replaced by Deputy Premier Woodrow S. Lloyd. Before his election in 1944, Lloyd had been a school teacher from rural Saskatchewan and president of the Saskatchewan Teachers' Federation. He became the Minister of Education and retained the job until 1960, when Douglas appointed him Provincial Treasurer. In the leadership convention that followed Douglas's departure, Lloyd easily defeated the only challenger, Ollie Turnbull. He moved quickly to juggle his cabinet, and named Blakeney as his Treasurer. That didn't surprise anyone; what did was Lloyd's decision to breach protocol and swear in Blakeney third in order of precedence, after Lloyd himself and Deputy Premier John H. Brockelbank. The practice had always been to name ministers in order of their length of service in cabinet, and Blakeney should have been considerably further down the list. Lloyd was sending a clear signal that Blakeney was a young man with a future, but the move created some resentment among the longer-serving ministers.

Blakeney delivered his first budget in March 1962. He added a bit of dash to the event by revising a tradition borrowed from Clarence Fines. For years on budget day Fines would don a necktie adorned with a cornucopia—the curved lamb's horn of plenty—overflowing with fruit and ears of grain. It was an odd symbol for Saskatchewan, subject to periodic drought and economic hardship. It was a signal from Fines that he was balancing the budget. On March 9, 1962, Blakeney arrived in the House wearing a tie made from cloth of the Saskatchewan tartan. Anne had made the tie, but the design came from Lillian Bastedo, wife of the Lieutenant-Governor. The horn of plenty would have been inappropriate in 1962. The economy had been poor. Saskatchewan had suffered one of its worst years of drought since the 1930s, and farm incomes tumbled. Nationally, unemployment had risen to a post-war record of 11 per cent. Blakeney's choice in 1962 was either to run a deficit or to reduce services harshly. He did make some modest cutbacks, but he came in with a deficit of $2.4 million on expenditures of $174 million.

Blakeney delivered more than the numbers in his budget speech. He provided a philosophy of governing which was to change little over the succeeding years: there are two types of politicians—those who see the government's role as minimal, keeping law and order and protecting the role of the private sector, and those who see in the state an instrument for providing important public services, creating growth while pursuing greater equity for its citizens.

Twenty months after being appointed to the cabinet, twelve years after his first days in Regina, Allan Blakeney was a man to watch. He entered a government which was honed and organized, a tuned machine. Yet he remained untried by crisis. Medicare changed all that.

# Chapter Five

# Medicare

At Christmas in 1961 the Blakeneys began a genteel annual tradition: Anne wrote a simple letter which was duplicated and sent to family and friends. That first year it was on white paper, and appears to have been written on a portable typewriter. It was less than a page long and painted a picture of contentment. In July of that year, mother, father, and two kids had piled into a government issue red station wagon and headed east on the new Trans-Canada Highway. He went to the NDP founding convention in Ottawa, while she continued on with the children to visit family in Halifax. Later, they drove home along Highway 2 through the northern states, to an autumn of Brownies, new shoes, and piano lessons.

A year later, the family letter had a sharper, almost an angry tone. Most of it was devoted to the bitter medical care dispute—the tension of endless rounds of negotiations for Blakeney as the doctors' strike loomed in June; the task for Anne of fending off threatening calls at all hours; and finally the hot potato of the Health Ministry being tossed to Blakeney to get the medicare plan up and running. It was the kind of year a family doesn't forget.

Tommy Douglas had made his promise for a universal, tax-financed, publicly-administered medicare plan in 1959. He knew the doctors weren't happy about it, but he was confident that a combination of government persuasion and public pressure would bring them around. He promised that any plan would have to be acceptable to the doctors, but he underestimated their antagonism.

By June 1961 Douglas had announced his intention to seek the leadership of the federal New Democratic Party. Some of the doctors took comfort from that. Others were alarmed by their lack of success in negotiating with the Minister of Health, Walter Erb, and feared for what would happen after Douglas left. The Premier had appointed an 11-member committee to make recommendations on health care. It was led by Dr. Walter Thompson, the former President of the University of Saskatchewan, and contained representation from the medical profession, labour, and the public. The committee was putting the final touches on its report during the summer. Walter Smishek, a member appointed by labour, was approached informally by a small group of doctors. They were meeting with the committee on a Sunday at Regina's posh Assiniboia Club. The doctors privately asked Smishek to carry a message to Douglas. They wanted a new Health Minister; their choice was Allan Blakeney. Smishek passed the request on, but Douglas did not want to make a change so near his departure.

The Saskatchewan Medical Care Insurance Act was introduced on October 13, 1961. The College of Physicians and Surgeons had asked, and Douglas had promised, that the doctors would be given a chance to review the legislation before it was introduced. Douglas broke his promise, but he had reason for haste; he wanted at least to introduce the legislation before he left. It was a missed opportunity, and it helped to poison the atmosphere. The act was passed on November 17th, and it fell to Woodrow Lloyd to be medicare's founding father in Saskatchewan. The plan was based on the Thompson Committee recommendations for a fee-for-service plan, supported by taxes and administered by a public commission. While the legislation outlined the plan, it did not say exactly how the doctors would be paid. That crucial point was left to future negotiation.

When Lloyd shuffled his cabinet after Douglas's departure, it was clear that medicare would be the government's priority in the months ahead. Health went to Bill Davies, a former union leader and an MLA from Moose Jaw. Davies told Lloyd that Blakeney would be a better choice, but the Premier said he needed Blakeney as Treasurer. Blakeney wasn't involved in drafting the original legislation. Lloyd quickly named a special inner cabinet committee to deal with the issue, and Blakeney was on it. Its role was to negotiate a plan with the doctors, to draft legislation, to establish the machinery to run the plan, and to make contingency plans as a doctors' strike loomed.

The doctors refused to appoint members to a commission which would administer medicare. At a meeting early in 1962 they passed a motion warning individual doctors against accepting appointments. The commission was finally established without their participation in January 1962. It contained three doctors, but only one, Dr. Orville Hjertaas, was a practising physician.

The government wanted a doctor to lead the Saskatchewan Medical Care Insurance Commission, but the only Saskatchewan physicians available were CCFers who would have been unacceptable to the profession. A few doctors were sympathetic, but they were not prepared to break ranks with an organization which granted their licences to practice. Eventually Davies turned to the civil service. Deputy Treasurer Al Johnson refused the task. Don Tansley, a young economist who had been director of the Budget

Bureau and Deputy Provincial Treasurer, took the job, but not before asking if the position included danger pay.

Tansley and Blakeney had begun working in the civil service on almost the same day in 1950. They were friends as well as colleagues. Shortly after Tansley's appointment to the commission in 1962, the two talked about what had to be done to avert a crisis. Tansley couldn't get the doctors to participate on the commission, and Bill Davies couldn't get them to the negotiating table. It was obvious they were witnessing a delaying operation, and they began to plan "what if" scenarios. Both Tansley and Blakeney possessed a sense of gamesmanship; they tried to put themselves in the doctors' shoes, to anticipate every means—publicity blitzes, petitions, demonstrations—whereby the profession might sabotage medicare. They concluded that the doctors would delay for as long as possible, then refuse to practice under the act. They would bill their patients directly and encourage them to go to the government to be reimbursed—in effect, setting the fee-for-service themselves rather than negotiating it with the Medical Care Insurance Commission.

Blakeney made plans to defend against the tactic, and he convinced cabinet that he should prepare legislation in case the talks got nowhere. As the winter session of the Legislature moved toward spring in 1962, there were still no negotiations, and the April 1st date for the introduction of the plan was fast approaching. Early in March, Davies moved the commencement date back to July 1st. In a letter to the profession, he said doctors could suggest amendments to the legislation, but only until March 28th. The College then agreed to meetings late in March, but they went nowhere. On April 13th, Blakeney's legislation was introduced. The government tried to slip it past the opposition by calling it "housekeeping," and much of it was, but one section contained a bombshell: it anticipated action the doctors would take, and moved to prevent it. Blakeney's legislation stipulated that the government (as insurer) would act as agent for the patient (as customer) in dealing with the doctor. Doctors would therefore have to send patients' bills directly to the commission, which in turn would pay the doctors. Effectively, physicians would not be able to practice outside the plan, and they would have to negotiate with the commission for their fees. It allowed the government some control over costs, and it also allowed the commission to take legal action on behalf of patients if doctors refused to use the plan. The patient, on the other hand, was free to ignore the plan and pay the doctor directly, but would then receive no money for the doctor's fee from the commission.

Blakeney and Tansley decided that, if the doctors were going to harass the commission, the commission would challenge the medical bills they submitted, and thus force them into negotiations for fees. He was thinking ahead to July 1st. But July 1st was a long way off, and the April legislation was heavy-handed enough to antagonize the doctors even further. The

College responded by calling a special general meeting in Regina for early May in the Trianon Ballroom. At that meeting the doctors served notice that they would not co-operate with the plan, and they gave a hostile response to Premier Lloyd when he came to address them. Just before he walked into the packed hall, he learned that Walter Erb, the Health Minister he had demoted the previous November, had bolted to sit as an independent. He later moved to the Liberals.

The tension at the medical convention was palpable. The situation was made more volatile by the federal election campaign which was in progress. Tommy Douglas was running in Regina. There were virtually no medicare negotiations occurring; each side began to prepare for the battle to come. The physicians and their supporters began to organize the Keep Our Doctors committees which, in turn, organized meetings, petitions, and cavalcades in an attempt to defeat the government. A group of pro-government supporters organized committees called Citizens in Defence of Medicare. They wanted to create counter-demonstrations and disrupt opposition events, but Lloyd, fearing violence, urged them to stay home.

Blakeney was constantly at Lloyd's side during an incessant round of meetings. Tim Lee, Lloyd's Executive Assistant, says, "Staff Barootes was the hatchet man for the doctors. He was a brilliant negotiator, but he met his match in Blakeney. They squared off. Lloyd was the strength of the team, but when he needed a negotiator he allowed Allan to go to work." Later, after face-to-face negotiations broke down, Blakeney held a series of secret talks in an attempt to build some bridges to the doctors. He spoke with Donald K. McPherson, a well-known Regina Tory lawyer who had served on the Thompson Committee and had close links with leaders of the College. He was also in contact with Fred Hill, a rich Regina businessman with close Liberal connections.

Tommy Douglas almost lost his deposit in the federal election of June 18th. That gave a psychological boost to the doctors, and probably contributed to their intransigence. A bunker mentality was developing among provincial cabinet ministers, and there was some talk of capitulating to the doctors' demand that the government withdraw the act. Blakeney, in the privacy of cabinet, threatened to resign if they did not go ahead; it was probably a tactical move to stiffen the backbone of wavering colleagues. He also informed cabinet that he had Order-in-Council legislation ready in the event that the doctors attempted to go to the courts to have the act declared unconstitutional.

As July 1st approached, the Saskatoon Board of Trade warned tourists to stay away or risk their lives. Provincial media coverage was shamelessly slanted against the government. The Saskatoon *Star-Phoenix* carried a "countdown" to the strike day. The editorial page compared Douglas's Saskatchewan to Franco's Spain, and asked rhetorically, "Can't It Happen Here?" A weekly newspaper, *The Indian Head News,* carried a full page advertisement in June which read, in part: "You are going to lose your doctors. . . . It will be too late when the pain comes in the middle of the night. When the baby suddenly starts choking, when the good farm worker is mangled in the power takeoff, when the car plunges off the road and scatters dusty bodies in the ditch, when the heart attack comes . . . if this sounds emotional or even hysterical—good."

The strike occurred on July 1st. People were gripped by a fear which was heightened by news that the Canadian Medical Association was helping doctors who wanted to leave Saskatchewan, and by warnings from doctors co-ordinating emergency medical services that surgery might soon be unavailable. The political temperature was running as hot as the weather. The Keep Our Doctors Committee was active. Its organization and events involved many doctors and Liberal party activists. Their line was that medicare was totalitarian, a step on the road to a communistic loss of freedom. There were emotional KOD rallies; the rhetoric was volatile. The government and its supporters bitterly accused the province's press, with the exception of the CBC, of sensationalist coverage, with an uncritical focus on the activities of the KOD committees.

The fever reached its height when Father Athol Murray—a diminutive, tobacco-stained, rugged individualist who had founded Notre Dame College at Wilcox—addressed a KOD rally Friday, July 6th in Saint Paul's High School auditorium in Saskatoon. The speech was carried live over a network of private provincial radio stations. Murray said that a "wave of hatred" was sweeping the province: "There have been deaths, there will be violence, and there could be bloodshed." He ripped off his clerical collar and said he could "smell" three reds in the audience. "Tell those bloody commies to go to hell when it comes to Canada," he shouted. "I loathe the welfare state, and I love free swinging freedom." At another KOD rally in Prince Albert, Murray was quoted as saying, "This thing may break out in violence and bloodshed any day now, and God help us if it doesn't."

Someone spray-painted "commie" on the stucco wall of Premier Lloyd's house. Bill Davies tried to convince his wife to take their children to stay with relatives on a farm. When she refused, he borrowed a 10-gauge shotgun and kept it standing in a wastebasket beside his bed. Blakeney's home telephone rang at all hours. People who would not identify themselves shouted that he was driving the doctors away. The police became concerned enough that they began to guard the homes of ministers.

There were news conferences daily. Blakeney attended many of them at Lloyd's side. The Premier, a thoughtful man who detested emotionalism in politics, was so harassed that on July 4th he quietly slipped out of the province for six days. His Executive Assistant, Tim Lee, bought the airline ticket in his own name, and booked Lloyd into the Waverley, a nondescript hotel in Montreal. "Lloyd was under enormous pressure," Lee recalls.

"There were doubts among some of his colleagues about whether to proceed." Lloyd wanted to meet with Frank Scott, the poet, constitutional scholar, and a doyen of the CCF. Scott urged him to stay the course.

While Lloyd was secluded in the hotel with Scott, Blakeney and others in Saskatchewan covered for him. "We ran a scam while he was away," says Blakeney. "We parked his car in front of the building, and moved it, and put his office lights on and off." Lee says, "I lived a block away from the Lloyds. I picked up his car in the morning, drove it to the Legislature, and parked it. I ordered up his lunch from the cafeteria, and I ate it. When anyone called I said the Premier was busy." The media caught on after Lloyd's third day away, but they never did find out where he went.

On July 9th, Lloyd came home and made an announcement which had arisen out of his meetings with Scott and others in Montreal: Lord Stephen Taylor had been invited to Saskatchewan to advise the government on the medical crisis. Taylor, a British peer and a member of the Labour Party, had been one of the architects of the British National Health Service.

The momentum, which had worked against the government in the first days of July, then began to shift. The bitter fight in Saskatchewan attracted media attention from around the world. With the arrival of the international press, the story began to be told more objectively.

A giant Keep Our Doctors rally was being planned for Wednesday, July 11th at the Legislative building in Regina. Organizers were predicting a crowd of 40,000. It was a warm, sunny day. Two young women in shorts, halters, and sunglasses carried effigies of Woodrow Lloyd and Tommy Douglas, saying "Down With Dictators." The organizers presented a petition to a grim cabinet, demanding that the government abandon its legislation. Lloyd refused. Ross Thatcher, who had scheduled a Liberal caucus meeting to coincide with the demonstration, made a theatrical run at the Legislative Chamber's closed doors, and was widely photographed kicking them. Although there was no session in progress, Thatcher told reporters the government's locking the opposition out of the Legislature was "just another indication that freedom is being extinguished in Saskatchewan."

The crowd which gathered at the steps of the Legislature numbered four thousand people, not forty thousand. They were loud, but they were peaceful. Athol Murray's rantings were the closest anyone had come to calling for violence. For his efforts, Murray was ordered by his archbishop to take an extended vacation out of the province. Blakeney believes that Murray's speech actually broke the momentum of the anti-medicare forces, because for the first time people actually believed that violence might erupt.

An airlift of doctors from Britain and other parts of Canada had by this time produced 100 physicians. Many Saskatchewan doctors were quietly going back to work. On July 10th the College offered to resume talks, and dropped its earlier demand—suspension of the medicare legislation.

The government, in turn, offered to convene a special session of the Legislature to pass amended medical care legislation.

The tall, bushy-browed Lord Taylor arrived in Saskatoon in a flurry on July 16th. He had been invited as a government advisor, but he soon became a mediator, shuttling back and forth along the riverbank between the College's offices in the Medical Arts Building and the cabinet's headquarters in the fortress-like Bessborough Hotel. According to his own accounts, Taylor listened, cajoled, threatened, and finally helped to bring about an agreement. But by the time he arrived the College's negotiators were already meeting with Lloyd, Blakeney, and other cabinet ministers. In an interview after the strike Blakeney described Taylor as someone whose "dramatic gifts were considerable, if slightly of the ham variety." The doctors' strike ended with the signing of the Saskatoon Agreement on July 23, 1962.

Within six weeks of settling the strike, Lloyd shifted Blakeney to the sensitive Health portfolio. He had plenty to do. For months the medicare negotiations, then the strike, had claimed the attention of politicians and people in the department. Morale was low. The immediate task was to get the Medical Care Insurance Commission working according to the terms negotiated by the Saskatoon Agreement.

One of Blakeney's more delicate tasks was carried out entirely behind the scenes. Lieutenant-Governor Frank Bastedo refused to pay his medical care premium on the grounds that he was a federal government employee and shouldn't have to pay the provincial tax. Blakeney considered laying charges. The Attorney-General, Robert Walker, called the federal minister, Davey Fulton, and informed him of the plans against the Queen's representative. Bastedo paid.

The Saskatoon Agreement created a problem of both politics and conscience for Blakeney and his colleagues. The strike had spawned a grassroots network of community clinics. By late June, 1962, groups of medicare supporters decided to take matters into their own hands. Early in July a clinic opened in Prince Albert, and another in Saskatoon. They were conceived as co-operatives in which doctors would work for lay associations. A province-wide Community Health Services Association had been organized by mid-July, with the intention of establishing such clinics everywhere. There were 25 local co-operative health associations by the time the strike ended, although not all of them had doctors.

For the clinics to work effectively, they had to have an income which would allow them to allocate resources where they were most needed. The clinics wanted block payments from the government, from which they would pay their doctors a salary. The College of Physicians and Surgeons was hostile to the point of paranoia about the clinics, and the government caved in to their demands. The Saskatoon Agreement clearly indicated that, while doctors might work for clinics, it must be on a fee-for-service basis. That meant doctors earned the money directly, and made it difficult to organize any consumer led organization of medical practice.

The activists behind the clinic movement ranked among the most stalwart supporters of the CCF, before and during the doctors' strike. Two members of the Saskatchewan Medical Care Insurance Commission, Dr. Sam Wolfe and Saskatoon lawyer George Taylor, both old-time CCFers and active in the community clinic movement, felt they had been sabotaged by their own government. The clinics' difficulties were compounded by the difficulties their doctors had in obtaining privileges to practice in Saskatchewan hospitals. While hospital boards are publicly financed, committees controlled by doctors made recommendations about who should receive privileges. Clinic doctors were often shut out. If they had no hospital privileges, they were effectively prevented from practising. Blakeney appointed a Commission of Inquiry in 1962, but the judge became ill and his replacement didn't complete the report until December 1963. As a result, an appeal procedure was established, but the delay had wounded the clinics.

The dispute over hospital privileges reached right into Blakeney's household. In 1964, when Anne was expecting her first child, her clinic doctor was still waiting to be granted privileges. She had the choice of changing doctors or having a home birth. The legislative session had opened on February 6th; at 6:30 the following morning she gave birth—at home. She had the care of two doctors (they made house calls then) with portable oxygen tanks and anaesthetic should it be needed. David Allan Lloyd Blakeney (the Lloyd in honour of Woodrow) was a child of medicare, and a symbol of just what a difficult time even the Minister of Health had with the strike and its aftermath.

# Chapter Six

# Opposition

The medicare dispute focused the energies of the Lloyd government, but it also created a sense of fatigue at its centre. It was the last great hurrah of the CCF government elected in 1944. The feverish and radical activity of the 1940s was long gone. Throughout the 1950s Douglas was the epitome of folksy moderation, charming and reassuring toward an electorate which was moving farther each year from the memories of the Depression. Within the party, the adroitness and commanding personality of Douglas restrained the antagonism between those who believed passionately in the Regina Manifesto, and others who had become more pragmatic and conservative through the experience of power.

Woodrow Lloyd called an election for April 22, 1964, and lost. Allan Blakeney is convinced they were defeated because of medicare. If so, the government met defeat with integrity, defending a worthy policy. Ross Thatcher had described medicare as "civil conscription," and the Lloyd government as totalitarian. By 1964 he was promising to extend benefits under the plan, although he continued to accuse the government of heavy-handedness in introducing it. Thatcher won by uniting, under the Liberals, the previously fragmented right-wing opposition to medicare in 1962. A so-called non-partisan organization was established by businessmen in Saskatoon with the object of defeating the government. The Saskatoon *Star-Phoenix* and the Regina *Leader-Post* both supported moves to unite the opposition behind Thatcher. He caused further disillusionment in the government by luring both Walter Erb and Hazen Argue from the CCF to the Liberal ranks.

The CCF popular vote in 1964 declined by less than one per cent from 1960, yet the party lost 12 seats. The Liberals gained eight percentage points, mainly from people who had previously voted Social Credit. The Socreds, who in 1960 had gained 13 per cent of the vote, ran only three candidates, and their support collapsed. The Conservatives did not run a full slate of candidates. Thatcher did well in the countryside, a fact which probably had something to do with the CCF amalgamation with labour in 1961. Sparsely populated seats, then as now, were over-represented in the Legislature. Thatcher won 41 per cent of the vote, the CCF 40 per cent, but the Liberal success in rural Saskatchewan allowed them to defeat the CCF by 33 seats to 25.

The movement which had propelled the CCF to power in 1944 had grown weary. It was replaced by the more captivating rhetoric of Thatcher, and his promises for a prosperous new Saskatchewan driven by competitive rather than co-operative principles. For the CCF, and Allan Blakeney, seven lean years had begun.

Blakeney won easy personal victory in Regina in 1964, but the immediate result of the government's defeat meant that he had to go job hunting. An opposition member's salary did not support a family. The transition was not an easy one. The brokers and contractors who had told him he was a genius when he was a minister in Finance and Health were not nearly as friendly later on. His old law firm did not want him back because he was an NDPer, and the firm wanted work from the Thatcher government. He approached several other firms, but they also saw him as a liability.

Eventually he occupied an empty office in a Regina firm being created by Jim Griffin, who had been a lawyer with the Saskatchewan Government Insurance Office. Blakeney hired a secretary and went to work on his own. Griffin was waiting for another partner, John Beke, to arrive. When he did, Blakeney entered into a partnership with them, one which stipulated that he would neither participate in nor profit from any government work they did. His practice was mainly small commercial work, real estate, wills, small business, and estates. He did some court work, but has never appeared at a major criminal or jury trial.

Despite the loss of government, Blakeney gave no thought to getting out of politics. If he felt hurt or unappreciated, he didn't tell anyone. He frequently reminded himself that almost every politician loses some time. It was another example of a rationalist approach which attempted to drain the passion from the defeats (and the victories) of politics. He was in for the long term.

Home life became less hectic. As related in Anne's Christmas letter of 1964, they purchased a cottage on Last Mountain Lake north of Regina, and the family began a tradition of spending at least part of the summer there. They continued to live unostentatiously in their Lakeview bungalow. They continued to rent out the basement suite, often with the understanding that tenants would do some child care when Anne accompanied her husband to political events. Blakeney no longer drove the government car which had accompanied the office when he was a cabinet minister. Their family car was a grey Volkswagen Beetle until 1966. That year they followed an old Saskatchewan tradition: the family travelled by train to Ontario and picked up a new car, a red station wagon, at the factory. They drove it home, saving the freight cost of having the car shipped west.

There was time for trips away—a family drive to Florida to spend a Christmas with Blakeney's mother, who wintered there. For Allan, there was a trip to Wales and Europe one summer with his mother, sister, and brother. He spent five days at Expo in 1967. Anne spent time in Ontario, where her mother now lived. Almost every year they got back to Nova Scotia for quiet visits with friends. His pleasure trips were often tacked onto business, especially after he was elected to the NDP federal executive in 1968.

But if Blakeney's life was less hectic, it was only marginally so. He was rebuilding a law practice. Lloyd had appointed him Finance critic, so there were heavy duties during those months when the Legislature was sitting. The months following 1964 were taken up with getting the party over its shock, and trying to rebuild toward the next election.

The older Blakeney children, Hugh and Barbara, entered their teens while their father was in opposition. They remember him as being busy at the office, and preoccupied at home. Gone almost entirely were the days when he would stop for a brick of ice cream on the way home from church on Sunday mornings, then take them to King's Park in the afternoon. Barbara Blakeney thought it was normal to have a father who was usually home only briefly for supper before leaving again. She often went to visit school friends who lived on a farm. "After supper," she says, "I was prepared to shut up, and when their father goes away to start goofing around again. But the guy didn't leave. He just hung around. In my house he had to go to a meeting, of course, and I thought that's what everyone did."

Anne was the homemaker, and the communicator with the children, and, when necessary, the disciplinarian. If the children wanted to ask him something, they asked it through her, a pattern which continues even today. His major domestic contribution came on his rare Saturdays off. According to his children, he would assemble them and deliver, in his best Boy Scout troop demeanour, a series of staccato orders: "Switch off any 10 lights and report back to me." "Close any 10 cupboard doors and report back to me." "Mow the lawn and report back to me." These bursts of home energy were sporadic and short-lived. He was more relaxed during the Christmas and summer holidays. He particularly liked long trips in the car, and time at the cottage.

Anne had confined her political work to the constituency when her husband was a minister. Although women had been involved in the early CCF, she admits that by the later years in government most cabinet and caucus wives saw their role simply as supporting their husbands. No one in the CCF was encouraging them to do more. The loss in 1964 came as a rude shock to the political wives: "There was a real upsurge of women's participation from '64, and I was part of that." Anne became vice-president of an NDP provincial women's committee. She also became involved in organizing child-care classes through the Board of Education. Most of that work came to an end in 1967 when she became pregnant again. Margaret, the Blakeney's youngest child, was born, in hospital, in October 1968. Anne continued to do volunteer work in a day care once or twice a week.

Gruff and bull-voiced, Ross Thatcher thought he had received a special mission from Providence to declare Holy War upon socialism and wipe it out in its Canadian birthplace. His single-mindedness verged on political nihilism. The results of the 1964 election confirmed in his mind the sanctity of his mission. He believed that what he called socialism, CCF style, led to economic stagnation and big government. He had frequently used the traditional tactic in Saskatchewan politics of smearing the CCF as communists.

His vision of the New Saskatchewan was of a province which was friendly to private and foreign investment. He once said the only thing wrong with foreign investment was that there wasn't enough of it in Saskatchewan. His formula for making the province attractive to capital was simplistic, and by now only too familiar: reduce corporate royalties and taxation, slash the size and influence of government (especially by attacking social spending), sell off government-owned enterprises to the private sector, and bring the labour movement to heel. He couldn't wait to get at the job. The results of the 1964 election in many ridings were so close that Lloyd managed to hold tenuously to power for almost a month, although the outcome could have been in little real doubt. Nevertheless, Thatcher began immediately to act as though he were Premier. His first directive was to order a freeze on all hiring in the civil service. He trusted no one but himself. As he appointed his cabinet, he had each minister sign a letter of resignation, which the Premier kept in his files. The condition of remaining a minister was to cut departmental spending by 10 per cent. Most ministers complied simply by ordering a straight cut in every line of their budget. Those cutbacks were supposed to result in the tax reductions which Thatcher had promised during the campaign.

He sent a message to the civil service by the highly public firing of David Cass-Beggs, General Manager of the Saskatchewan Power Corporation. There began a minor bloodbath which involved some of the key civil servants of the previous CCF governments. As Blakeney says, "The purge was not comprehensive, except at the top. He got rid of some good people and he did not replace them with people of the same calibre." The firings had an immediate effect on Allan and Anne Blakeney; within months, most of their closest Regina friends had left town. The autumn of 1964 was a time of farewell parties. Though suspect in Regina, people like

Johnson and Shoyama moved quickly and easily to Ottawa where they occupied senior civil service positions in the Pearson government. Others, like Don Tansley, David Cass-Beggs, and Meyer Brownstone, landed on their feet in other provinces.

Thatcher's major initial move was to declare a royalty holiday for oil companies, which had been large donors to his campaigns. In the 1965–66 budget he fulfilled his promise to reduce sales and purple gas taxes while bringing in a modest surplus. He was his own Treasurer, and he drafted the budget without much help from anyone. The elaborate CCF machinery fell into disuse as Thatcher undertook the task of trying to run the entire government by himself. In private life he was a rancher, and he owned a small string of hardware stores. His prescription for business success was simple—run your own show, and when in trouble cut costs. He brought the same hardware store approach to governing.

His industrial strategy was simply his advertisement that Saskatchewan was open for enterprise, and it appeared to produce results. The New York-based Parsons and Whittimore announced in 1965 that it would build a $65 million pulp mill at Prince Albert. Despite Thatcher's aversion to public ownership, he had to offer a joint venture to get them. The deal was condemned by the NDP as a sell-out: the government guaranteed or provided 80 per cent of the capital in return for 30 per cent of the equity.

Thatcher's reign also coincided with the potash boom. In the 1950s, Douglas had decided to leave development of the potash industry to private capital. The American mines in New Mexico were becoming old and expensive. Douglas gave the capitalists a long-term promise of low royalties. By 1962 there were two mines, and U.S. Borax planned to build a mine at Allan, east of Saskatoon. The Allan announcement, made after Thatcher was Premier, was followed by others, until the tall head frames of ten mines towered above the flat wheat fields. Saskatoon became the self-proclaimed "Potash Capital of the World." The mines were the most apparent symbol of the New Saskatchewan Thatcher had promised. He frequently mentioned them as an example of what government working with enterprise could do.

Thatcher made his moves on the labour movement in 1966. The Liberals revised the Trade Union Act to make it more difficult for unions to organize plants or to win strike votes. In September 1966 a strike by members of the Oil, Chemical, and Atomic Workers at SaskPower gave Thatcher the opportunity he had been awaiting. He responded to the strike with Bill 2, which allowed the cabinet to end any public sector strike which it believed was contrary to the public interest. The legislation also established a compulsory three-member binding arbitration board.

Thatcher called a snap election in October 1967. He had stacked the electoral deck by a gerrymander which had been produced by an electoral boundaries commission comprised of four Liberals. He campaigned on his theme of the New Saskatchewan, promising prosperity under free enterprise. The campaign became nasty, with the NDP's newspaper, *The Commonwealth*, calling Thatcher a tyrant. He took the bait, waving the newspaper at rallies and shouting, neck veins bulging, that the socialists were running a campaign of malice, hatred, and fear. There was also an NDP whisper campaign on the doorsteps which accused Thatcher, a diabetic who periodically had to be hospitalized, of being an alcoholic. Thatcher added three seats to his majority and improved slightly on his share of the popular vote.

Campaigns between Liberal and NDP supporters were rowdy and rough, and debates in the House were thunderous; but there was an element of respect. Despite their antagonism toward him, NDP members knew Thatcher ran an honest government, with no more than the usual amount of patronage. "He was a good politician," Blakeney says. "He was a hard-nosed guy. He had a direct, sometimes even abrupt way about him. So that was his stock and trade. No nonsense Ross. Mind the store. He ran his government with an iron hand, participated in most decisions, and by my standards delegated far too little of the decision making." While Blakeney respected Thatcher's honesty, they held fundamentally differing views. Blakeney was not profligate by any means, but he expected a great deal from a government and its civil service. Thatcher wanted lean government, and less of it. "I think the calibre of his public servants seriously declined," Blakeney says. "He didn't need as good a public service because he wasn't initiating any new programs. I think Ross didn't keep the team about him that could provide the analysis for a large organization. But he was a good operator. Within the lights of a small organization, he would run a good hardware store."

Despite their differences, Blakeney says he actually liked Thatcher: "When he met with me he was always very cordial. I used to watch him in public, and it always struck me that people responded warmly to him. He had a nice smile, a nice method of shaking hands. When Ross wasn't under pressure, when he wasn't snapping because he was too busy, then he was a very personable fellow."

The only one of his ministers that Thatcher trusted at all was Davey Steuart, now a Liberal Senator. Steuart was known for his fiery speeches and his quick sense of humour. He admits he prided himself in never allowing the facts to interfere with a good speech. The NDP called him "Landslide Davey" because of his habit of winning his Prince Albert seat by the slimmest of margins. Steuart says the Liberals made a mistake in under-estimating Blakeney, based on his early performance in the House: "He never was that comfortable performing and pounding the table. But he got better at it. I think he realized that if he wanted to win he had to develop that side, and he did." Steuart didn't expect Blakeney to succeed Lloyd as leader; but Ross Thatcher believed he would.

Gordon Barnhart, the Legislative Clerk after 1969, says there was no doubt that Blakeney was Lloyd's most trusted lieutenant. "The contrast between Lloyd and Blakeney was quite marked," he says. "Lloyd was quiet, a true gentleman who had a very logical approach, but not flamboyant. Blakeney was rational and factual, but could turn on the fire too." Barnhart recalls Blakeney's habit of laughing nervously just as he was about to make serious points in debate, a potentially debilitating habit which he overcame. Another habit, which he retained, was a practice of rubbing his hands together vigorously, in great glee, when he scored a point in a debate. He loved debates; he had since his university days.

Thatcher's 1967 campaign had concentrated on the brave new world open to Saskatchewan under his free enterprise leadership. He reversed himself immediately after the election. Promises of prosperity had filled the smoky halls during the campaign, but Thatcher walked into the first caucus meeting after the election and stunned his colleagues with his announcement that he intended to embark on a harsh austerity program.

There was a glut of grain on the world market, which meant bulging bins and lower prices for Saskatchewan farmers. The growing international inventory of grain meant that less fertilizer was used, and that hit the potash industry, which had been chaotically overbuilt. Thatcher feared a recession and a reduction in government revenues. His instinctive reaction was to cut spending. He slapped on a six per cent salary ceiling, not only for civil servants, but for the employees of companies with government contracts. The government took over line-by-line control of educational spending by school boards and the University of Saskatchewan. There was an effective ceiling on teachers salaries, too, backed by the big stick of Bill 2—the Essential Services Act—with which he threatened to legislate teachers back to work if they went on strike.

The budget of March 1968 was prepared by Thatcher, but it was read by Dave Steuart, who had been appointed Treasurer. Steuart had the unpleasant duty of announcing not only a series of cutbacks, but also a new array of taxes. Old taxes were reinvented, and new ones added, including a "utilization fee" for everyone using the hospitalization and medical care plans. Steuart later joked that he may have been the first Treasurer ever to read his speech from under his desk.

As Finance critic, Blakeney led the attack. He called it the Black Friday budget. Liberal times, Blakeney never tired of saying, were hard times. The NDP described Thatcher's utilization fees as "deterrent fees," and won the battle of semantics when the term stuck. The NDP called them an unconscionable tax on the sick.

These attacks in the Legislature coincided with several important trends, which breathed new life and militancy into progressive elements both within and outside the NDP. The most important was Ottawa's response to the farm crisis. Trudeau's powerful Saskatchewan lieutenant, Otto Lang, came

up with a program called Lower Inventories for Tomorrow (LIFT), under
which farmers were forced, if they wanted federal subsidies, to take land
out of production. It was antithetical to their most basic values, and they
were enraged. The federal government followed that with a Task Force
on Agriculture which recommended moving large numbers of inefficient
farmers out of the industry.

Westerners did not like Pierre Trudeau, who had succeeded Lester
Pearson in 1968. Some of their reasons were the wrong ones—Trudeau
was from Quebec, and he was an intellectual rather than a populist. He
was also arrogant, and seemed not to understand or care about what was
happening on the farm. Thatcher thought Trudeau was a socialist, and
fought him. He fought almost everybody. The two of them had alienated
a lot of people in the province by the late 1960s. Medicare had given the
anti-CCF forces something to rally around in 1962. The recession of the
late 1960s gave progressive forces an issue, and the arrogant, cigar-
chomping Thatcher provided them with a caricature to denounce.

The 1964 defeat had been terribly dispiriting for the CCF. Many believed
they would not have lost if Tommy Douglas had stayed. Woodrow Lloyd
was much admired; he had earned his spurs on the CCF long march. But
he was a plodding man without Douglas's spark. He lived in mute contrast
to Ross Thatcher's take-charge manner and brash eloquence. Lloyd
recognized his own lack of charisma, and considered stepping down. He
talked to friends and advisors in the party following the loss, and they
apparently advised him to stay on. His decision to do so was reinforced
by the many well-wishers who sent him letters while he was laid up with
a bad back early in 1965.

Lloyd told his troops that they had allowed themselves to become so
preoccupied with good administration that they had overlooked "essential
revolutions" which were occurring around them. Lloyd's interests were
in ideas and policy, but during Thatcher's first mandate he had to refocus
the caucus into an instrument of opposition. He spent a great deal of
time and energy trying to attract new candidates, but he was hampered
in his efforts by the CCF's war-horses, many of whom chose to run again
in 1967 and were in a favoured position to win their nominations. Despite
that, several new people elected in 1967 became party leaders in the next
decade—Roy Romanow, Jack Messer, Gordon Snyder, Ted Bowerman. Lloyd
doled out shadow portfolios for his caucus members. He instituted a buddy
system, whereby a sitting MLA would be responsible to a constituency not
represented by the CCF. Blakeney's responsibility was for Milestone, held
by Liberal cabinet minister Cy MacDonald.

The CCF waged a much better campaign in 1967 than they had in 1964.
Their platform was thoughtful and comprehensive, and aimed at young
people; but it wasn't enough. Lloyd's indecision about the leadership

surfaced again before the 1967 election, but the people he polled asked him to stay. His daughter, Dianne Lloyd, says he was a victim of both his sense of responsibility and his vanity.

There was muted talk of running someone against him at the 1968 convention, but it came to nothing. Blakeney had been approached by dissident MLAs to run against Lloyd at an earlier convention, but he curtly refused. Lloyd told some of his confidants that he would not lead the party into another election; he also told his Biggar constituents in April 1969 that if they chose him as their candidate he would remain as leader. His vacillations made it difficult to know his real intentions.

Lloyd lacked Thatcher's charisma. He was at his best as a political philosopher, and after 1967 he proceeded to instill some new ideas into a party whose intellectual force had peaked 15 years earlier. He appealed to constituencies to take on once again the role of serious policy debate. The once vibrant constituency organizations, the backbone of the CCF, had atrophied. Their role in policy formation, once the focus of frequent and heated debate, had dried up as well. Lloyd encouraged the formation of small, constituency-based study groups to talk about issues. There were task forces on agriculture, housing, and education, which reported to the provincial conventions. In a series of policy seminars, people began to talk about radical solutions to the problems in agriculture and the natural resource industries. As early as 1965, Lloyd questioned the NDP's earlier decisions to allow private capital to develop Saskatchewan resources. He began to analyze the effects of foreign ownership, and he mused aloud about increased royalties, joint ventures, and publicly-owned oil and potash developments. On another level, he organized special seminars for his caucus on issues in education, agriculture, and the environment. At these conferences, experts and other non-party people were invited to present ideas and engage the caucus. He set up a committee which worked on a long-term program for the next NDP government. While he was not successful electorally, Woodrow Lloyd did succeed in rebuilding the party in both policy and organization.

Blakeney was Lloyd's political confidant and trusted lieutenant. As Finance critic, he shared much of the burden in the Legislature. His skills at analysis and problem solving were valued. He always made himself available to speak at nominations or constituency events. Yet he is not remembered as having played a major role in revitalizing the party in the 1960s. He believes he carried his load during those years, but his was a supportive role. "I'm not as good a communicator, guide, educator, and mentor as Woodrow Lloyd," he says. Lloyd is best known for ideas in opposition; Blakeney for programs in government.

Early in 1969, Allan and Anne Blakeney moved their family from Lakeview into a poor neighbourhood in the Regina Centre constituency which he represented. "If I was going to represent that area," Blakeney says, "we were going to live there, and my children were going to go to school there." In a small bay, ringed by austere wartime houses, they had built for themselves a modern two-storey home. With its grey-stained vertical wood siding, its enclosed second-floor deck, and small windows, it appeared an architectural compromise between the competing impulses of privacy and duty. It was a house designed with politics in mind. The Blakeneys wanted a large living room so they could have constituency meetings there. The basement had a large room for even bigger meetings. The kitchen was long and narrow so that several people could work at food preparation and washing dishes. "They had bake sales in the basement," David Blakeney says, "garage sales in the garage, and constituency meetings once a month in the living room. It was also an outside scrutineer's office every election."

If the house stood out in the area, so did the family. Barbara recalls that when she was a teenager, and sensitive about her peers, politics in the house could be an embarrassment. "So you bring some friend home, you're fifteen, and there's all these people in your living room singing 'Oh Canada' or 'God Save the Queen'."

The Blakeneys' presence at King Street in north central Regina was another indication that they were in politics permanently. Blakeney had toyed with the idea of switching to federal politics for the 1968 election, but Lloyd talked him out of it. Blakeney had his own provincial leadership ambitions, but he was also loyal. He approached Lloyd, hoping to receive some clue about his plans. But the leader gave no clear signal. He merely told Blakeney that he was a valued member of the team. He would be sorry, Lloyd said, to see him leave. Blakeney stayed.

# Chapter Seven

# The Waffle

Late in October 1969 the Waffle Manifesto was debated by the NDP federal convention in the cavernous Winnipeg Auditorium. The building was filled to bursting. The Waffle was a radical leftist group within the NDP which got its unlikely name when one of the participants at an early meeting said, "If we're going to waffle, I'd rather waffle to the left than waffle to the right." The convention rules allowed seven speakers on each side before opening it up to the floor. The party Establishment called on its heavies: Dennis McDermott of the auto workers; Tommy Douglas, the aging but revered leader; Ed Broadbent, a young MP who had flirted with the Waffle in its early stages, then withdrew; and Allan Blakeney, the federal vice-president. The main speakers on the other side were Mel Watkins, Laurier LaPierre, Cy Gonick, Gerry Caplan and, from Saskatchewan, Walter Smishek, an MLA, and Carol Gudmundson, a vice-president of the provincial party.

The resolution was in the form of a seven-page document bearing the title, "For An Independent Socialist Canada." It began by saying, "Our aim as democratic socialists is to build an independent socialist Canada. Our aim as supporters of the New Democratic Party is to make it a truly socialist party." The document went on to talk about Canadian subservience to "the American empire"—a militarist and racist power conducting a "barbarous" war in Viet Nam. It called for an explicitly socialist program in Canada: "Capitalism must be replaced by socialism, by national planning of investment and by the public ownership of the means of production." For 70 minutes the convention was consumed in passionate debate, with competing choruses of shouts, boos, catcalls, and applause. Douglas, who had been attempting to avoid any painful splits, eventually spoke against the manifesto, calling it "ambiguous and ambivalent." Among the Saskatchewan delegation, Woodrow Lloyd remained stubbornly silent, despite entreaties by the Waffle camp for his support. When a standing vote was called, however, Lloyd pushed himself heavily to his feet in support of the Waffle motion. It lost by a vote of 499 to 284.

The federal party executive, which included Allan Blakeney, responded to the manifesto with a long counter resolution which had been drafted by the NDP National Council. It was called, "For A United and Independent Canada." It pledged NDP action to achieve Canadian economic independence, and for a program of "selective nationalization" to curb foreign investment. It was passed by the convention the following day. (Woodrow Lloyd voted for that one, too). The Waffle Manifesto had failed on the floor, but it had succeeded in moving the party's policy agenda to the left for years to come.

On the convention's last day, Blakeney was elected party President. He was studiously low key at the news conference which followed. He described himself to reporters as a "slightly left of centre moderate" (his colleagues in Saskatchewan would have described him as a right-of-centre moderate). He favoured some of the manifesto's principles, but not its stridency. He attempted to alleviate the situation by saying that the party owed "a real debt" to the manifesto's authors.

On the convention floor, Blakeney opposed the Waffle Manifesto, and so opposed Lloyd. "This was just a 60–40 judgement call," he says. "Woodrow thought it was more important to encourage openness to new ideas, that there was nothing wrong with their slogan of an independent socialist Canada. I was saying I saw nothing particularly wrong with the slogan, and I didn't have any quarrel with our considering new ideas. But no socialist party is going to get anywhere unless we organize elections, and that involves organizational loyalty. I think there was a feeling that the people who were pressing for the Waffle cause were people who were unwilling to go out there and do the slugging. All they wanted to do was talk." The debate raged throughout the summer and fall of 1969, and it was still far from finished. As national party President, and Deputy Leader in Saskatchewan, Blakeney might have been expected to play a major role in that continuing debate. Yet he didn't. He was Lloyd's most competent member of caucus, but he was a loner by temperament and a pragmatist by inclination. No faction in the party claimed or damned him. He was more interested in political organization and wielding power than in long debates and extra-parliamentary activity.

He regarded himself as a Canadian nationalist, but he disliked what he considered the imported, extremist rhetoric of the New Left. He thought it unsuitable to political debate in Canada, where the system still provided an opportunity for democratic change. In purely personal terms, the brash and loose-living 60s culture left him cold. Frank Coburn, a Saskatoon psychiatrist with a long history in the CCF, illustrates with an anecdote: "At an NDP National Council meeting in Toronto in 1969 we got through the business late on a Saturday afternoon. Al, Jack Shapiro, and I decided to go and see the musical *Hair*. We were able to get tickets, but not sit together. We met outside the theatre after it was over. Jack and I were on cloud nine. Al said he didn't think it had much of a story line."

There was a gap between the Wafflers and much of the older rank and file—differences in appearance, style, and decorum, and the choice of words and language. Those who disliked or disagreed with the Waffle held two other abiding fears: that it was at best a loud and dissident caucus within the NDP, and at worst a Marxist Trojan horse attempting to work its way into the established party. They feared that the Waffle's intemperance would hurt the NDP in elections.

The allegation of infiltration was made in Ontario, particularly by David Lewis. It wasn't a concern for Blakeney in Saskatchewan, where there was a long tradition of a farm and labour left within the party. Many of the young radicals—so-called "red diaper babies"—bore the names of families known for their decades of activism in the CCF: names like Coburn, Taylor, Kuziak, Kowalenko. But the idea of a dissident caucus did pique Blakeney. "There's no place for sniping at the structures, in the guise of advancing new ideas," he says. "If you want to change the structures, change them. But don't tell us that the current ones are bad. Tell us what ones will be better." Still, the view from the Blakeney household after the 1969 convention appeared rather sanguine about what was considered a youth movement. In her Christmas letter that year, Anne Blakeney described the convention as "lively, vital, and encouraging in coming to terms with the much talked about generation gap." There were others in the provincial party, however, who felt more threatened about what had happened at Winnipeg.

Woodrow Lloyd was a large, fleshy man, overweight but not obese. He was balding, but retained thick grey eyebrows and a moustache. He wore bifocals with thick black rims. He could easily have been mistaken for a conservative middle-aged school principal in town for a Rotary convention. The description would not have done him justice.

By 1969 the NDP had swung to the left under Lloyd's leadership. Convulsions within the Saskatchewan party—the losses to Thatcher, the painful process of evaluation—were occurring at a time of political ferment. There was a resurgence of militancy among farmers and organized labour, and it coincided with a wave of New Leftism sweeping through student populations in the Western world.

The National Farmers' Union was formed in 1969 to represent farmers throughout English Canada, but the union was always strongest in Saskatchewan. It was farm union members who dumped rotting wheat in front of the Bessborough Hotel when Pierre Trudeau came to Saskatoon in 1968. It was their tractors which frequently blocked the highways in demonstrations. Union president Roy Atkinson, a barrel-chested (and stomached) wheat farmer from Landis, was a commanding presence. Atkinson was an old time CCFer, and he just happened to live in Woodrow

Lloyd's riding of Biggar. Farmers were angry at Trudeau and Otto Lang and, despite his protestations, they saw Thatcher as an enemy too. Teachers and trade unionists were also infuriated by Thatcher's anti-union legislation and his wage controls. The Saskatchewan Federation of Labour had a tradition of supporting the CCF, although it also had had its disputes with the party. SFL leadership during the Thatcher years fell to Bill Gilbey, an uncompromising tough talker, a Communist Party adherent in his younger days, and one of the organizers of the famous On-to-Ottawa trek in 1935. For a few years in the 1960s the CCF's Old Left, always a minority within the Saskatchewan farm and labour movements, was joined in a loose coalition with a younger group of students and academics—the New Left.

A series of complex, but related world and Canadian events created the phenomenon now known as "The 60s." The most important event in the development of that political culture was the Viet Nam War and the people's movement against it in the United States. The American New Leftists condemned the U.S. as an imperialist power, but the U.S. remained their obsession nonetheless. They knew little about Canada, and cared less. In Canada, people like James Laxer and Melville Watkins, both Toronto political economists, began to say that, while Canada might be a partner to American imperialism, it was also one of its colonies, albeit better treated than most. They attempted to move the New Left critique onto a Canadian nationalist level.

The Waffle arose from the close contact of a group of intellectuals at Ontario universities between 1967 and 1969. Laxer and Watkins were part of that group, as were Saskatchewanians Lorne and Caroline Brown. Lorne Brown was from an old CCF family, and had been president of the provincial CCF Youth in the early 1960s. The Wafflers hoped to move the NDP to a left-nationalist stance. They believed that only socialism would provide indigenous control of the Canadian economy and culture (some Marxists would argue that the Waffle was much more nationalist than socialist). The Waffle emphasis on widespread public ownership as a means of taking that control was reminiscent of the Regina Manifesto's call for a "planned and socialized economy." It was a similarity which touched a responsive chord with some of the Old Leftists in the NDP.

There were differences, however, between the Old Left and the New. The Waffle brought to the left a preoccupation with local participation in decision-making, and women's liberation (the latter was most certainly not a priority in the old CCF). The old CCFers were strongly parliamentarian; their emphasis was on political organization. They believed if they could win control of the national government, they and their planners could deliver the New Jerusalem. The Waffle added the New Left interests in extra-parliamentary activity—street politics, mass actions, and community development.

Woodrow Lloyd believed both the Saskatchewan and the federal NDP were in need of new ideas, but most of his caucus were oblivious to the ferment of the 1960s. Lloyd was much more in tune with developments. He spoke against the Viet Nam War, and against the U.S. stationing of nuclear warheads in the Dakotas, just south of Saskatchewan. In 1969 he tried to attend the Democratic Convention in Chicago, but was turned away at the door because somebody wasn't satisfied with his credentials. For the next several days he walked the streets of Chicago, watching as Mayor Daly's police billy-clubbed and water-hosed students protesting against the war. Those experiences, his reading, and the opinions of his own children, all had a profound effect on his thinking.

By 1969 the policy debate Lloyd had encouraged in the party was in full swing. The provincial convention that spring debated and passed resolutions which had begun in earlier policy seminars devoted to agriculture. They called for curbs on corporate farms, a prohibition on foreign ownership, and a crown corporation which would buy farmland on the market, then lease or sell it back to farmers who were trying to get established. The resolutions passed at a time when only a few members of the Saskatchewan party were aware of the Waffle or its impending manifesto. At the June 1969 provincial convention, the party elected a left-leaning executive. Bev Currie, a young farm union militant from near Swift Current, won election as Party President over Pemrose Whelan, a long-time party volunteer and the wife of Regina MLA Ed Whelan. It was a development which left the Whelans and some of their supporters embittered.

Debate, even division, between left and right in the party was not new. But the experience in opposition was. Lloyd had lost two elections. There was a concern that he was no match for Thatcher on the hustings, a belief the Liberals shared. Lloyd recognized it, too, but gave mixed signals about his plans. The caucus was getting restive, at times even petty. There was a minor uproar when Lloyd returned from a summer vacation sporting a beard. Some caucus members thought that was an electoral liability in Saskatchewan. The caucus included a group of disgruntled older MLAs, and a restive group of young Turks, including Jack Messer, Ted Bowerman, Roy Romanow, John Kowalchuk, Myro Kwasnica, and Adolph Matsalla. They thought it was time for a change of style, away from the old CCF mold. Romanow admits they were restless: "When you're first time around you're young, you're going to create the revolution. What needed to take place as we saw it was a set of new policies and feisty political actions by the new breed of political people. We saw ourselves as that little crowd."

Romanow and the others perceived Blakeney as a member of the old guard. He had been in government, in cabinet, and in the civil service. "We acknowledged his brilliance and his policy analysis," Romanow says, "but we felt that he was perhaps a little too bureaucratically oriented." Blakeney, in turn, was aware of the growing disenchantment with Lloyd's leadership in the caucus, but he remained a supporter. "The people who opposed Woodrow," he says, "somehow felt that he just couldn't win the next election. But I didn't share their conclusion."

The aftermath of the Winnipeg convention debate spilled like molten lava into Saskatchewan. The national party Establishment said that the Waffle did not have widespread support. In Saskatchewan, however, the Provincial Council had debated, and endorsed, the manifesto shortly before the 1969 convention. Approximately half the Saskatchewan delegates in Winnipeg had supported the manifesto. Lloyd had supported it because he thought the party needed such debates. Most of his caucus were less concerned about opening up the party than they were about the election they might face within the year. They were angry that the Waffle, and Lloyd, had given Ross Thatcher ammunition for another red-scare campaign.

Blakeney was among those who believed that Lloyd had made a political mistake at Winnipeg. Lloyd thought the federal party had become too dominated by labour, and was becoming too conservative. Lloyd did not apply that same description to the Saskatchewan party, because it was undergoing a rejuvenation under his own leadership. His mistake, Blakeney says, was to believe that everyone would separate the arguments as rationally as he did.

The Waffle in Saskatchewan continued to meet and to organize after the Winnipeg convention. They were accused of wanting to establish a "party-within-a-party," but insisted their intent was to move the NDP back to a socialism worthy of the Regina Manifesto. The party continued with its flurry of educational and policy seminars throughout the countryside in the winter of 1969–70. Those seminars became hothouses of debate, particularly about agricultural and resource policies. The Wafflers were on hand, vociferously, to put their positions forward.

The struggles went beyond policy. In 1969 the party had hired Gordon MacMurchy, a tow-headed, lantern-jawed farmer from Semans, as a party organizer. MacMurchy had been a school trustee, and active in co-operative organizations and in CCF politics. He had run in the 1967 provincial election, but lost. His skill was in organization, and his turf was rural Saskatchewan. MacMurchy suggested to a young United Church minister named Don Faris that he apply for the vacant job as Party Secretary. Faris had worked briefly for the Douglas government, and later went to work in Africa, but had to return when his wife became ill. He was living in Davidson when he met MacMurchy, and followed his advice.

Clare Powell was then the party's Publicity Director, and worked in the same office as Faris and MacMurchy. "They were travelling around the province a lot," he says, "and bringing back stories about how much discontentment there was with Woodrow Lloyd's leadership. It seemed to me it was cause and effect. You wondered how much of it was actually happening, and how much they were encouraging people to think about it. That disturbed me." Fred Gudmundson, an organizer for the National Farmers' Union in Saskatchewan and a Waffler, received reports from NFU members that NDP meetings in the countryside were being used to undermine Lloyd: "MacMurchy had an undue amount of influence in calling on constituency organizations to say we have to have a meeting to discuss the organization of the party and raise memberships and so on. Under the guise of these meetings, questions about the leadership were always brought up." Faris and MacMurchy both deny that they did anything to undermine Lloyd. "That's totally false." Faris says. "That's just politics."

When the winter Legislative Session began, Lloyd antagonized some of his older caucus members by shuffling critic responsibilities to give more prominence to younger MLAs. The shuffle included a physical move from the front to the back benches for some members, including Bill Berezowsky and Leonard Larson. They were angry, and much to Lloyd's annoyance they went public with their unhappiness. The Liberals gleefully fanned the NDP divisions by shouting over to the demoted MLAs, asking them to speak more loudly from their back benches. Dave Steuart told them they were so far away that he couldn't hear them.

Tension within the party increased when the Waffle decided to contest selected provincial nominations. One of them was Moose Jaw South, where the incumbent, Bill Davies, was retiring. The member for Moose Jaw North, Gordon Snyder, decided to run in the South constituency because it was a safer seat. John Conway, a sociologist at the University of Regina, also contested the nomination. Conway was originally from Moose Jaw. The Wafflers were organized, and convinced the constituency executive to set a nominating convention for January, 1970.

Davies was furious; he believed the Wafflers had set the early date for their own benefit. He and Don Faris intervened to have the convention delayed, much to the annoyance of Conway's camp. Faris claims he acted at the request of Woodrow Lloyd, who disagreed with the Waffle's tactics. Davies campaigned for Snyder. When a snowstorm snarled traffic on convention day, Davies, an old railroader, hitched a ride to Moose Jaw on a CPR caboose. He nominated Snyder, a move which helped to ensure Conway's defeat. Publicly, the NDP could not but support contested nominations as a sign of life within the party; but sitting members did not appreciate it. To them, a nomination challenge from the Waffle was simply another indication that the left was trying to take over the party.

The struggle also spread into the New Democratic Youth organization. At an NDY convention in Regina in March, debate erupted over a resolution proposing a strong "extra-parliamentary role" for youth. The Waffle supported such activity, which included assistance at strikes, on picket lines, and general community activism. A counter resolution, which carried narrowly, stated that the youth group's main role was to further the goals of the senior party. There was also discord at the Provincial Council and the Executive, because some members believed a paid youth organizer was actually working on behalf of the Waffle. There were attempts to have grants to the NDY frozen.

Lloyd, who was sympathetic to greater openness in the party, had begun to run out of patience with the revolutionary leftists in the youth movement. In a pointed letter to Bev Currie in December 1969, he wrote, "I think it is some time since the youth movement has added anything to the party. I do not think they speak for young people. I do not think they communicate to any group of young people except a very small group. I do not think they enlist the support of any new people to take part in achieving the objectives of our party as I understand them. On the contrary, I think they have discouraged and even driven some young people away. You will gather that I have completely run out of confidence so far as the Saskatchewan Young New Democrats is concerned."

It was a Waffle meeting planned for Saskatoon at the end of March, however, which sparked open revolt in the caucus. Advertisements inviting party members to "help found a Waffle group in the NDP" appeared in *The Commonwealth* earlier in the month. Lloyd had become concerned about the Waffle's plan to have its own caucus within the party. He was not happy about the meeting. Bev Currie had been openly associated with the Waffle and the plans for the Saskatoon meeting. His was one of the names on a discussion document which had been circulated prior to the meeting.

Lloyd had known the Currie family for years, and was fond of Bev, but he had become critical of Waffle activity. He had voiced those criticisms at an executive meeting earlier, and on March 23rd he wrote to Currie, warning him about the Saskatoon meeting. He didn't question Currie's intentions, but he did challenge his judgement: "The intention of the Waffle group may not be to establish 'a party within a party.' In my opinion, however, it is inevitable that it will be so considered. Undoubtedly if a 'permanent' group is established the news media will be soliciting comments from me. As I see the situation at the moment I have no option other than to be critical. This can well put a number of us on a collision course. That which is a hell of a way to run a railway is a disastrous way to run a political party." Lloyd sent copies of the letter to Blakeney, Douglas, and several others. To the caucus, already restive, the Saskatoon meeting was evidence that the Waffle was attempting to become a party-within-a-party.

The document to which Currie had attached his name included a section on agriculture. It called for Land Bank legislation which would allow the government the "initial option to purchase retiring land at assessed value." The assessed value of land is a very low figure, used for purposes of establishing municipal taxation. It is invariably a figure well below market value. Some NDP caucus and executive members chose to interpret the document as promoting the compulsory nationalization of farmland at fire-sale prices. They saw red.

The winter Legislative Session went into its last week before a recess for Easter, which in 1970 came early. On the afternoon of Tuesday, March 24th, the NDP caucus held an emergency session which passed a terse resolution moved by Gordon Snyder and seconded by Ted Bowerman: "That the caucus meet tonight at 10 pm to discuss the question of the Waffle caucus and our position thereto."

Caucus did meet at ten o'clock, after the night sitting of the Legislature, and following an angry discussion it issued another motion: "That this caucus convey to the Provincial Executive caucus' extreme concern with the actions of the provincial President in acting as a sponsor of the Waffle group activities, and that we request a meeting with the Provincial Executive before Friday" [March 27]. There were no detailed minutes kept during those two extraordinary caucus meetings, but the motions from each told their own story. Blakeney would certainly have attended them, but he says they do not stand out in his memory. He thought that Currie had acted foolishly and should have his hands slapped.

Some of the executive members summoned by the caucus members were indignant. According to the party constitution and custom, the caucus did not have authority to summon the executive. Some members, like Saskatoon lawyer George Taylor, refused to attend. Currie was reluctant, too, but Lloyd urged him. "Woodrow phoned me at home on the farm," Currie recalls. "I remember Woodrow saying, 'We have to have a meeting or all hell will break loose'." Currie acceded to Lloyd's request, and called what he considered an "unofficial" executive meeting.

As the MLAs and executive members shuffled uneasily into the conference room, with its thick carpets and high ceiling, they found Lloyd seated on one side of the long table, quiet and austere, smoking a pipe which he lit and slowly drew on from time to time. Beside him was his friend and past party President, Frank Coburn. Currie was on Lloyd's other side in what, it appeared, would be the hot seat that night. The others were ranged around a U of long tables: Carol Gudmundson, a young teacher and a party vice-president, was the only woman among them. She was a member of the leftist slate elected at the 1969 convention. Fred Gudmundson, her husband, had tried to convince her to stay home, but she drove in, finally, because she wanted to support Currie if he was attacked.

Allan Blakeney was sitting beside her, quiet and seemingly oblivious to the tension in the room. Walter Smishek was there, perhaps Lloyd's closest personal friend among the caucus members. Seated across the table were members of the new corps of MLAs: Ted Bowerman, big, red-faced, and sandy-haired, a man who spilled out of his suits and gave every impression that he would be more comfortable fighting forest fires than sitting behind a desk; Jack Messer, confident and cocky, independently wealthy, a gentleman farmer from Tisdale; and Roy Romanow, a smooth, dark-haired young lawyer from Saskatoon. A skilled orator, Romanow had performed well against the Liberals in the Legislature. Among the members of the executive present were John H. Brockelbank, a dean of the party who had not run for re-election in 1967, and Robert Walker, a bony-faced, towering man at six and a half feet. A Saskatoon lawyer and a former Attorney General, he had lost his Hanley seat in 1967. Walker could be blunt and caustic, and was known as a loose cannon. Jack Shapiro, a Regina businessman and good friend of Lloyd's, was there to represent the Provincial Council to the caucus. He was a Waffle sympathizer.

The emergency meeting was called to order by Fred Dewhurst, the caucus chairman, and a former Speaker of the Legislative Assembly. What happened next has never been fully documented. No minutes were kept, and people disagree considerably in how they repeat the story. It remains a dark and unsavoury family secret which most of those at the meeting have not discussed publicly for 20 years.

Currie was to begin by defending his actions. After that each member present could speak once. "I remember saying at the start that the party is always developing new ideas," Currie says, "and that I didn't necessarily endorse everything the Waffle was saying, but I endorsed the document as being worthy of being sent around. I think my opening statement was fairly low-key." He recalls that caucus members Gordon Snyder and Eiling Kramer criticized him for allowing his signature to be attached to a Waffle document. Brockelbank made the same criticism, scolding Currie for his lack of "sagacity."

Then the meeting took a new direction: "Bob Walker stood up, and it was almost as if he had forgotten what the meeting was called for." Walker shifted the focus from Currie to Lloyd. Most remember Walker speaking harshly. Currie recalls him beginning in an almost friendly way, telling Lloyd he had always been a supporter—with Lloyd puffing his pipe and nodding. Walker said there was dissatisfaction and unrest among party members about Lloyd's leadership. He had lost two elections. Maybe he had been around for too long. Perhaps it was time for a new face.

At this point a major discrepancy occurs in people's recollection of the events. Some remember that the restive young MLAs, including Ted Bowerman, Jack Messer, and Roy Romanow, joined in attacking Lloyd's leadership. Romanow insists that he remained quiet: "There were a series of people who either defended or attacked. I didn't take part in the debate at all. I don't think Al Blakeney did either, by the way. That I can recall." Others, like Currie and Carol Gudmundson, believe they do remember Romanow participating. Jack Messer does not deny speaking: "I spoke to the issue that evening and I think it would be correct to say that if you were speaking to the issue, you were obviously speaking to leadership as well."

As to the tone of the meeting, Messer says, "Not surprisingly, it wouldn't be friendly. It was a very serious discussion with some vigorous debate, and some very strong emotions. I don't recall that there were any significant personal accusations, but one can't debate that subject matter without making reference to individuals." Lloyd's loyalists were slow to react to the attack upon his leadership. Frank Coburn, Walter Smishek, Bill Davies, and Jack Shapiro all say they spoke on Lloyd's behalf. They used most of their time to argue that the meeting had been called to talk about the President and the Waffle, not the leadership. They did not, however, come vigorously to Lloyd's defence. All now say that they were caught off guard by Walker's attack. Lloyd later admitted privately to being devastated by what he considered a lack of support from his friends.

According to the rules of the evening, Currie was to speak last. He asked why the caucus was worried about the left, when it was traditionally the right wingers in the party who defected and did it harm; he mentioned Ross Thatcher, Hazen Argue, and Walter Erb. He asked why a leader recognized well beyond the borders of the province as great and wise did not have the respect of his own caucus. Lloyd had sat silent throughout. He stood after Currie's concluding remarks and, as Currie recalls it, "He said, in a fairly low key way, certainly not pounding tables or anything, 'My resignation is on the table, and you can pick it up when you decide.' Then Dewhurst adjourned the meeting as if he hadn't heard anything, saying it was sure nice to have these get-togethers, and something good can come out of this. He thanked us all for coming."

Lloyd walked out, and the recriminations began immediately. Carol Gudmundson accused Lloyd's supporters of abandoning him. One of them, Frank Meakes, began to weep. He was a loyalist and an ardent admirer of Lloyd, and had even lived with the Lloyd family after his wife died. He had spoken during the meeting, but did not appear to recognize what was happening. Jack Shapiro made an ironic comment about the significance of a leader being betrayed on Holy Thursday. The executive gathered to consider what had happened. Walker requested that some of the MLAs be invited to sit in as well, but other executive members told them to get lost. They decided to ask Lloyd to reconsider his resignation. Then everyone scattered into the night.

Was this meeting, which resulted in Lloyd's resignation, an event where emotions spontaneously got out of hand? Or were events planned with deliberation by some members of Lloyd's caucus and executive? There is a conspiracy theory. It was discovered that some MLAs, the majority of them, had met informally to talk over their troubles. Several, including Matsalla, Kowalchuk, and Kwasnica, were renting a Regina house from former MLA Marjorie Cooper, who was away for the winter. Were the gatherings just beer-and-vittles gripe sessions? Or were they more formally plotting to undermine the leader? Some MLAs, including Smishek, Blakeney, Davies, and Frank Meakes, had not been at the house. Was that just a matter of social patterns, or of design?

Jack Messer, a frequent guest there, says the meetings were "informal," and it would be unfair to describe them as more than that. "Obviously," he says, "when you have these kinds of circumstances, people have been meeting and talking. Whether you want to interpret that as caucusing, I think is somewhat improper. Everyone has their circle of acquaintances and that applies in caucus as well." Romanow says the house was a "way station for socializing and gossiping." He admits that the activities of the Waffle and Lloyd's leadership would have arisen: "At some point or other, I'm sure they were talked about. But to say that it was a meeting place where people planned with deliberateness strategic moves to achieve results is totally wrong."

There is the question of Walker's conduct. Did he act alone and spontaneously? Or, was there a plan that he would lead an attack on Lloyd and his leadership? The meeting had been demanded by the caucus, not by the leader. It had been called to talk about Bev Currie and the Waffle, but the focus had shifted to Lloyd. Currie is convinced that there was no set up, that Walker, who could be unpredictable, was thinking out loud and acting alone. The fact that he was Roy Romanow's law partner, however, led to suspicion among Lloyd's family and his loyalists. "The truth," says Romanow, "is that I did not know of Walker's intervention. I was not even sure if he was coming down to the meeting. I had not spoken to him for days before that time on this issue at all."

Walker's version of the meeting came in a letter which he later wrote to *The Commonwealth*. He admitted that in the meeting he called for a leadership convention. "I reminded my listeners," Walker wrote, "that two election defeats inevitably lead to pessimism and grumbling by party workers, and this tendency was increasing. I urged Woodrow to announce that he was putting his leadership on the line." Walker denied that his actions were an attack. Lloyd had already decided to step down, he said, and had told him so. Walter Smishek believes Lloyd would have announced his resignation within weeks of the session's ending. Before he could walk through that door, he was pushed. He didn't have to resign. He could have fought for his leadership. His decision to leave was the result of a sense of fatigue and disgust, and the fear that his struggle to remain would tear the party apart.

Allan Blakeney was Lloyd's friend of 20 years, his Deputy Premier and trusted lieutenant, and someone who was considered loyal to the leader. What did he do when Lloyd was being attacked? The crucial difference in recollections here is whether Blakeney entered the debate at all that night. Carol Gudmundson, who was sitting beside him, says that she tried to convince him early on that the meeting had been called to dump Lloyd. "He did not say anything during the meeting," she says, and when Lloyd resigned, "Blakeney turned to me and said, 'I did not have anything to do with this, Carol. I did not know this was happening." She believed him.

Gudmundson's recollection of Blakeney's role is supported by Jack Shapiro, Currie, and Roy Romanow. Bill Davies and Walter Smishek, on the other hand, say that Blakeney did speak on Lloyd's behalf. Blakeney's recollection of the evening is "imprecise." He believed the meeting was called to talk about the Waffle, and he was surprised by the attack on Lloyd. He believes he spoke once during the meeting, relatively early, in an attempt "to keep the temperature down." He agrees that he did not defend Lloyd, and in retrospect says he regrets that, but neither he nor other Lloyd loyalists knew until it was too late that the "surrogate issue of Woodrow's leadership" would come up. He believes that Lloyd's critics were, if not organized, at least prepared. Blakeney attempted to have people commit themselves to secrecy at the meeting's end.

The night of Lloyd's resignation occurred more than 20 years ago. The recall of participants in any event that far in the past is bound to differ. In this case, memories may be even more selective, because no one in the NDP wants to be remembered as a person who helped to banish the esteemed Woodrow Lloyd. And yet, despite the respect Lloyd commanded, he had probably stayed too long. Friends like Bev Currie admit there were "rumblings" about his leadership, and they didn't come only from the caucus.

Blakeney was in an awkward position. He was Lloyd's friend, and had been his most trusted minister. He was also the most likely successor. He would have been aware of the criticisms of Lloyd's leadership. He did not participate in those criticisms; nor did he mount a defence. Most likely he saw the sequence of events as something he could not control. He saw the guns being trained, and he ducked into the trench.

# Chapter Eight

# Leadership

Allan Blakeney had always planned to run for the NDP leadership after Woodrow Lloyd left, but now he wasn't sure. The manner of Lloyd's departure was unsettling; it left him with deep doubts. Jack Shapiro, the party's delegate to caucus, says he confronted Blakeney on his lack of support toward Lloyd during the emergency meeting. He says Blakeney felt terrible, and wondered whether he was worthy of succeeding Lloyd. "He explained that he had always had a personal failing in not being able to relate to people on the level of feelings," Shapiro says. "At an emotional level he recognized that he was frequently not able to rise to the occasion. He acknowledged that he was not able to come to Woodrow's defence because it was at a level of feelings that he was just not able to deal with. In his childhood, his family, and his lifetime, feelings were not the strong point." Walter Smishek also recalls approaching Blakeney and urging him to run for the leadership in the days following the Holy Thursday meeting. Blakeney, dispirited, said he was reluctant.

Lloyd held no personal huddles with Blakeney following his resignation. Blakeney doesn't recall Lloyd talking to him about his pain. "He might have talked to Walter [Smishek], who he knew a little better. I think he regarded me as a bit of a cold fish. Walter is a much more sympathetic person in many ways." Lloyd did, in fact, meet with Smishek, even wept in his presence; but it was Blakeney he encouraged to run for the leadership.

The party began to plan a July convention. Initial media speculation had a handful of people interested—Blakeney, Regina Mayor Henry Baker, Jack Messer, Roy Romanow, and also Smishek. Blakeney was the first to announce his candidacy, in mid-April. At his Regina news conference, he mentioned Lloyd's encouragement. He did not provide details on policy, or on who might support him. His priorities were to unify the party, and to attract voters who had previously supported the Liberals; his obvious hope was to break the anti-NDP coalition. He had little to say about agriculture, Saskatchewan's perennial issue: only that he understood farm problems and could discuss them with rural people. He said he wanted the ideas of the Waffle, but they should be funnelled through regular constituency channels. He thought the party should avoid the word "socialism" because it no longer had a clear meaning. He did not anticipate any great shifts in NDP policy under his leadership. For a month he was the only declared candidate. Then on May 15th, Roy Romanow declared his candidacy at an early morning news conference in Regina. He was described in the *Leader-Post* that day as being 32 years old. The *Star-Phoenix* said he was 34. He was actually only 31, but thought a few added years might improve his chances of winning. Blakeney wasn't surprised that Romanow ran, but he didn't perceive him as a real threat: "He was a personable young man, and I thought he wanted to establish his name and his place in the party." They met secretly, early in the campaign. Blakeney offered to build bridges as soon as he won. Romanow made a counter-offer: "It was rather arrogant, now that I look back on it, a suggestion that somehow Al Blakeney could help a Roy Romanow government. He didn't quite agree with that. He was too much of a party loyalist to say no, but too much of a proud person to say yes." At that meeting, Romanow and Blakeney agreed to refrain from public attacks on one another during the campaign. That was in character for Blakeney, who never liked personal confrontation in politics.

Although he had been around for much longer, Blakeney came forward without backers. Romanow, on the other hand, appeared at his Regina news conference with caucus supporters Ed Whelan and Ted Bowerman. Whelan's presence was surprising, since he and Blakeney had first been nominated at the same meeting 10 years earlier. They had shared many stages and campaigns. The leadership campaign began in earnest with Blakeney emphasizing continuity and competence, Romanow concentrating on style and an ability to communicate. His campaign was modelled on the new era of television politics in the United States. He was photogenic, and had an easy way with people. There was a glitz and excitement to his campaign that Blakeney couldn't match.

As caucus members began to line up, they mirrored the divisions which had occurred during the later years of Lloyd's leadership. Romanow drew his support from the centre-right of the party, with an emphasis on the younger MLAs: his close friend Jack Messer, Kim Thorson, an Estevan lawyer, and John Brockelbank, an MLA from Saskatoon-Mayfair who became campaign manager. Kwasnica, Kowalchuk, and Matsalla, renters of the house where the informal caucus meetings occurred, all declared for Romanow, as did Bill Berezowsky. For the latter group, ethnic loyalty was an added factor. Blakeney's support came from old-time activists, and from sitting and ex-MLAs who had ties reaching back into the Douglas governments. They included Toby Nollet, the former Minister of Agriculture, Fred Dewhurst, Everett Wood, Neil Byers, Auburn Pepper, Bill Davies,

Frank Meakes, Eiling Kramer, Wes Robbins, Orville Hjertaas, Cliff Thurston, and Cliff Whiting. Federal MPs Les Benjamin, Lorne Nystrom, and John Burton all declared for him. Benjamin's support was important because, as the previous Provincial Secretary, he had a network of contacts. Blakeney, although well known to party insiders, did not have Romanow's high profile, and appeared weak in rural Saskatchewan.

On May 25th a Waffler entered the race. Don Mitchell was a 26-year-old political economist and farm union organizer. Publicly, Mitchell denied being an official Waffle candidate, but he was prominent in the group, and made his decision to run at a Waffle steering committee meeting in Watrous. Another Waffler, political scientist John Warnock, was his campaign manager. Mitchell's support came mainly from the NDP youth movement and some members of the National Farmers' Union. Mitchell opened with an attack on Romanow and Blakeney, accusing them of "the bankruptcy of image politics, soft-sell policies, and dead-end reform."

Romanow and Blakeney had taken a cautious approach to the Waffle. The left had been strong at the 1969 provincial convention, and had shown well in Winnipeg. They appeared to be on the move, but neither of the favoured candidates was comfortable with that. Mitchell's criticisms brought an immediate response from Romanow, who was acclaimed in Saskatoon-Riversdale the next night. His speech had a sharp, new ring. He welcomed debate and dissent, but he was a "non-adherent to the Waffle movement." He warned that the Waffle must abide by the party rules. "Where Waffle conflicts with this position, I totally reject it."

Blakeney's nominating convention was held in Regina the same evening. The Waffle question came up there, too, when a youthful member of the audience proposed that members have the right to organize within the party. Blakeney's response was carefully diplomatic. He voted in favour of the resolution (which failed), but he said that debate concerning the Waffle was causing confusion within the party. He blamed that as much on those who were reacting to the group as he did on the Waffle itself. He warned against creating a separate caucus in the party. He also paid tribute to Woodrow Lloyd, and the meeting passed a motion of appreciation to him.

Early in June, Saskatoon alderman George Taylor announced that he, too, was in the running. Taylor, a silver-maned labour lawyer who had the distracting courtroom habit of continually removing and cleaning his glasses with a white handkerchief, was a veteran of the McKenzie-Papineau Brigade in the Spanish Civil War, and of various other socialist causes. He had been an NDP candidate on other occasions. He usually declared late, then campaigned only part-time, because his busy law practice did not allow him a greater commitment. It was that kind of campaign which cost him victory in his 1968 federal campaign against Otto Lang in Saskatoon. This late in the provincial leadership race, Taylor was unlikely to win and knew it. His ties were with the labour movement and the party's Old Left. His support came from people like Frank Coburn, who thought Blakeney was too conservative and Romanow was "superficial and ambitious."

Mitchell and the Wafflers were disappointed by Taylor's entry, because it dashed their hopes of a coalition between the Old Left and the New. By the spring of 1970 the Waffle had alienated much of the traditional left in the party by its refusal to abide by consensus politics. They also committed an unforgivable sin in the eyes of the old-timers by using the capitalist press to attack the party. People like Taylor and Coburn, a self-confessed "Regina Manifesto man," sent out strong signals that they wanted young people with radical ideas involved in the party, but ultimately they didn't take the Waffle leadership bid seriously. "It's one thing to be the gadfly and the stimulators," Coburn says, "and another thing to lead the party."

Taylor's candidacy was meant to show the old guard's anger over what had happened to Woodrow Lloyd. "We wanted to send a signal that someone who had been close to Woodrow and had agreed with his policies was going to run for the leadership," Taylor says. Blakeney was in an odd position: he was seen as a Lloyd man by the Romanow forces, but he was unacceptable to the Old Left. Taylor says it may have been unfair to Blakeney, but "there was a sense about him that he was not a native Saskatchewanian, and could not really wear the mantle of leadership here. He was seen as something of an outsider." The old guard compared Blakeney to Douglas and Lloyd, and found him wanting. Douglas was almost universally popular. Lloyd was less so, but he had his own following. As for Blakeney, Frank Coburn says, "Al was not a populist. Al talked a city idiom. He talked like a Rhodes Scholar."

Lloyd had quietly warned his staff not to take sides in the leadership race. Clare Powell, the party's Publicity Director, says that Bill Allen, Don Faris, and Gordon MacMurchy were "working openly for Roy Romanow. I felt if they were doing it, I could do it as well." He called Blakeney to tell him what was happening, and offered to work for him in the campaign. Blakeney quietly put Powell to work writing campaign literature and leaflets. Don Faris, who was Party Secretary, denies that the staff took sides in the leadership race.

Don Mitchell's candidacy had the immediate effect of sharpening the policy debate, particularly around agriculture. The 1969 party convention had called for curbs on corporate and foreign ownership of farm land, and for a Land Bank. That theme was picked up once again at a policy seminar in Yorkton in February 1970. The Land Bank idea was an echo of the "use-lease" program in the CCF's 1934 election platform. The farm crisis had returned in a modern form in the late 1960s, and that ignited some of the old sparks in Saskatchewan. The Wafflers were the most enthusiastic proponents of the Land Bank.

Mitchell was a major architect of the controversial Waffle agricultural policy, the paper which had precipitated the caucus revolt and Lloyd's departure. Mitchell called for a Land Bank at the news conference announcing his candidacy. He wanted the government to buy land and lease it back to farmers. He said nothing about their option, eventually, to purchase the leased land. Romanow responded sharply; he "emphatically disagreed" with any policy suggesting the "nationalization of farmlands." Mitchell denied that his idea would involve nationalization. It would allow for voluntary sale by farmers to the state. The same farmer, or others, could then lease it. The Waffle policy, however, did not include an option-to-purchase. It was intended gradually to build up a permanent quantity of publicly-owned farm land.

Wafflers, including Bev Currie and John Conway, said the policy had been deliberately misinterpreted by their opponents. That may have been so, but the Wafflers were sending out confusing messages. The paper they prepared for the Saskatoon founding convention in March would have reserved for the government the first right to purchase all farmland coming onto the market. The land would be purchased at "assessed value." A later article by Conway in *The Commonwealth* indicated that the Wafflers had really meant the land would be purchased at the higher "productive value." He repeated, though, the intention to allow the government first option on all land purchases, and recommended expropriating farm land owned by foreigners and corporations.

Romanow's 18-point agricultural program talked about loans and grants to young farmers, and about controlling foreign ownership. It said nothing about any land banking program, voluntary or otherwise. Blakeney remained vague about his proposals for agriculture. His policy announcements dealt mainly with completing the earlier CCF social welfare agenda—a pre-paid drug program, a children's dentistry program, and the rebuilding of health education and welfare programs which he said had deteriorated under Thatcher. Blakeney's speeches also focused on having the province pick up much of the property tax burden for education.

The centrepiece of the leadership campaign was a series of town hall meetings at which the candidates shared a platform. There were speeches from each of them, followed by a question and answer period. The meetings were chaired by paid party organizer Gordon MacMurchy. He later ran for Party President at the July convention, and the left said he had used the public meetings to raise his profile. Blakeney talked about experience, Romanow about style. Neither dealt as extensively with policy issues as did Mitchell. As the last of the meetings occurred before 500 people in Saskatoon's Centennial Auditorium, it was clear that Mitchell did not expect to win. He had been in the race to put forward a socialist program. George Taylor had a message to deliver about democracy in the party. The resignation of Woodrow Lloyd was never broached directly in a speech or question period during the campaign, but no one could miss Taylor's inference when he said, "I reject the concept that we are an appendage of our elected representatives." It was a slap at those who had forced out Lloyd.

While the leadership race was grabbing the headlines, the trench battle between left and right was being waged with bitterness and ferocity. It was in this atmosphere that the leadership convention began in Regina. On Thursday, July 2nd, effusive tribute was paid to Lloyd. Tommy Douglas came home to describe him as the "conscience of the party." Currie announced that a portrait of Lloyd would be hung in the Legislative Gallery. The tributes, and Lloyd's reply, made no mention of the manner of his leaving. The following day the façade began to fall away. At a Waffle caucus meeting, a scuffle occurred when two reporters had their tape recorders grabbed and their tables pulled out from under their elbows before being escorted from the room. The convention later barred reporters from all panel policy discussions. Members attending the agriculture panel faced a package of resolutions which had been changed considerably by a convention amendments committee; it had shelved proposals for limiting farm size, and for the nationalization of the farm machinery industry. It did, however, keep a carefully-worded proposal for a Land Bank. By this time Romanow and Blakeney were publicly supporting the idea as well.

The struggle between left and right continued on the convention floor. John Brockelbank was stepping down as party Treasurer. In his report, he repeated the accusation that Currie had misused party funds to hire a youth organizer who worked for the Waffle. A month earlier Currie had explained that the entire executive had approved the hiring. Brockelbank's repetition of the allegation at the convention left the Currie camp seething. During the speeches preceding the presidential elections, MacMurchy made a further reference to the charge, which made the left even angrier.

The leadership race was between Blakeney and Romanow. The crucial question was where Taylor's old guard and Mitchell's Waffle support would travel after the first and second ballots. The betting was that it would go to Blakeney as the candidate who was less objectionable to both camps, but that expectation blew up during the presidential elections. Blakeney had noticed "Currie for President" posters taped to the bottom of his "Blakeney for Premier" posters in the convention hallways. He had his campaign manager read a statement saying that the Currie posters had not been attached by Blakeney workers, and that Blakeney was not endorsing Currie. That was interpreted in Currie's camp as a signal to the convention that Blakeney was supporting MacMurchy. Immediately the rumour began that Blakeney and Romanow had agreed to support MacMurchy as president. MacMurchy won by a vote of 469 to 306. Blakeney says he stayed out of the race for president, but voted for MacMurchy because he was the better organizer.

Currie and Mitchell supporters spent Friday night threatening to withhold support from Blakeney. The action shifted on Saturday from the Hotel Saskatchewan to the more spacious Regina Armoury—an apt location, given the militant tenor of the convention. It was a drenching hot July day. There was a crowd of 1,600, about half of them voting delegates.

Blakeney expected to lead on every ballot, and was shocked when Romanow collected 320 votes to his 286 on the first. Mitchell received 187 votes, about 22 per cent. Taylor finished last and was dropped from the ballot. Romanow won the second ballot, too, but gained only 20 votes. Much of Taylor's vote went to Mitchell. Early in the campaign, Romanow had come out harder against the Waffle than had Blakeney. Later, he tried to build bridges to Mitchell, but Mitchell was having none of it. Now, Mitchell and his New Democratic Youth supporters held a brief caucus, and decided to abstain on the third ballot. Romanow gained only slightly, but Blakeney gained almost 100 votes, and that gave him the victory. Significantly, 96 people sat on their hands.

An analysis of the numbers indicates that the left, represented in different forms by Mitchell and Taylor, comprised about one third of the vote. When their candidates were defeated, they moved decisively to Blakeney. However, a group almost as large abstained on the final ballot. They were young Mitchell supporters who became the core of an identifiable Waffle formation. In the end it was a combination of the NDP old guard and the New Left that saw Blakeney as preferable. Romanow, guilty or not, was punished for what had happened to Lloyd. It was a victory less crystalline than Blakeney would have hoped for, but it was a victory nonetheless. Romanow had shown surprising strength, and had run a more vigorous and appealing campaign. "There was a feeling," says Blakeney, "that Romanow was younger and more charismatic, not as bureaucratic."

Blakeney had been around for years, had proved his mettle in cabinet and caucus, but he had not gathered a large popular following. His leadership effort had been organized, efficient, and unexciting. He had not yet arrived as an effective campaigner. In his victory speech he promised party unity. The NDP would not be a "one-man show," he said, but a team effort. The people he collected would make up for whatever shortcomings he might have as leader. He built the promised bridge to Romanow, saying that there was likely a cabinet position for him and for Jack Messer should the NDP win the next election. He proffered an olive branch, but made no promises, to Don Mitchell. Mitchell's strong showing meant that his ideas must be heard, and Blakeney encouraged him to seek a nomination.

Blakeney had bided his time. He had travelled deliberately, but in a linear way, never making a move which took him away from what was doubtless his goal—the leadership of the Saskatchewan NDP. He had not appeared too eager for the prize. That would not have been appreciated by NDPers in Saskatchewan, where the culture dictates that you may (modestly) accept the passing of a torch, but you will never be forgiven for lusting after it. He brought great intelligence and a profound background in government to the task of leader. Now it remained to be seen whether he could muster the political mettle to deal with Ross Thatcher.

# Chapter Nine

# New Deal '71

Ross Thatcher was expected to call an election in the spring of 1971. Reporters dogged his every step, but Thatcher was playing coy. At a Liberal coffee party in Saskatoon on May 18th the podium bristled with microphones, and television lights bathed the room. If he was going to call an election before summer, he had to do it that day. To the disappointment of journalists, and probably of his supporters, he finished his speech and sat down. The lights and cameras were switched off. Then Thatcher bounced back up and called for attention. He had something to add: there would be an election on June 23rd.

Blakeney spent his first ten months as leader getting himself and the NDP into fighting trim. There had been a smooth transition. Lloyd was congratulatory, and pleased that it was Blakeney who had succeeded him. The retiring leader sensitively left the country almost immediately for an extended holiday in Scandinavia and Britain. The Liberals were secretly delighted that the NDP had chosen Blakeney as leader. It was Romanow they had feared. Romanow was a better and a more exciting speaker; they thought he would be a more formidable opponent. Thatcher spoke contemptuously of "little Allan" and "little Allan in wonderland."

In the NDP inner offices there was a frank assessment of the leader's image, his strengths and his weaknesses. He was perceived as competent, straight, and "rather square." Thatcher was fiery, but he had a leather-lunged platform style, honed in the days of radio and town hall debate. He was a bombastic, one-man band. "I think someone made the judgement that you could never make me into a competitor with Ross Thatcher," Blakeney says. "Nor was I ever going to be a tribune of the people like Tommy Douglas, who could encapsulate their hopes and fears in a phrase. I was always going to be the quasi-scholar or the re-tread public servant who would analyze the problems and say, this is what we ought to do."

Blakeney's television style was also wooden, and he readily agreed to intensive sessions to sharpen his performance. But these attempts to project image were rudimentary. Blakeney was not very malleable; what you saw was what you got. He was sincere, intelligent, and reserved. No amount of coaching or invention would make him talk like a farmer or look like a truck driver. The NDP decided to play a team game. They put forward program alternatives, and made the messages simpler than they had traditionally done. Their strength was in policy. Lloyd had had a program committee as early as December of 1969. The decision at the 1969 convention to have wide-ranging policy seminars throughout the province provided dozens of resolutions for the 1970 leadership convention. Now the job was to distill them into a platform.

Within a few days of the convention, Blakeney had named an election policy committee, choosing Walter Smishek to lead it. The committee met frequently during the fall and early winter. Blakeney had many tasks to attend to, but he also played a role in policy formulation. There was heated debate on some issues, particularly the Land Bank proposal. Eventually Blakeney prevailed in his insistence that an option-to-purchase must be part of the program. The Land Bank would not attempt to change the dominant system of land tenure: farms owned by families, with some rented land to complement it. Blakeney also continued Lloyd's practice of conferring with groups who were upset with Thatcher—teachers, trade unionists, native leaders—to learn what they wanted from the next government.

The result was an exceptionally detailed program. Early in 1971 the policies were reworked into a concise and popular prose package called *New Deal for People*. The party didn't wait for an election call, but published tens of thousands of slim, blue-on-white booklets and released them in February, just as the Liberals were tabling their Speech from the Throne. The NDP removed some specific promises and numbers so they would have announcements to make during a campaign, but most of the program was published in the New Deal booklet. It was delivered to every household in the province. "We wanted to have it contrasted with the Liberal program in the Throne Speech," Blakeney says. "We wanted them to ridicule our program in the Legislature, which was successful. When you get the government talking about the opposition's program, you're moving right along."

The NDP called it a "blueprint for the 70s." It was 21 pages long and divided into sections—Agriculture, Values of Rural Life, Labour, Taxation, Resource and Economic Development, Pollution, and so on. Each section offered a brief statement on an issue or problem, invariably blaming the Liberals for waste, mismanagement, and sell-outs. Then it proceeded with a numbered list of NDP policies to remedy the situation. It contained well over 100 promises.

Thatcher decided to run on his record—responsible, tight-fisted government. He also attempted to cast this as another round in the mortal battle of free enterprise against socialism, a theme the Liberals had pursued in every provincial election since the 1930s. His major promise, one which followed his sweeping back-to-work legislation, was a vaguely-defined proposal to introduce Labour Courts to replace strikes. He also promised a second pulp mill and an iron ore mine, both to be financed by foreign capital. He ran a personalist campaign, with rallies starring the leader. At each stop the banner read "Saskatchewan is Proud of Ross Thatcher." He travelled in a Government of Saskatchewan Navajo airplane, insisting that he had Premier's duties to attend to during the campaign. Before the election he had suffered a slight stroke; his diabetes was acting up, and he became harsh and irritable.

Blakeney, in deliberate contrast, was low key. He travelled the province in a bus rented from the Saskatchewan Transportation Company. He said he wanted to be on the ground "where the voters are," an obvious reference to Thatcher's high-flying campaign. The STC bus was chosen because it was a friendly symbol: carrying passengers and light freight, the buses were reassuring sights in hundreds of towns. They had the advantage of allowing Blakeney to send out a positive message about crown corporations. In a news conference the day after the election call, he said the issue was agriculture. He shrugged off Thatcher's attempt to make this another free enterprise versus socialism campaign by asking the Premier to define socialism. He offered to debate Thatcher about it. He asked why the government needed Labour Courts when they already had back-to-work legislation in Bill 2.

The NDP machine had been idling. Now it was thrust into high gear. The orange day-glo signs went up literally overnight. The pamphlets and literature were all ready at the printer, awaiting only the election date. By the morning following Thatcher's announcement, they were printed and on their way to the constituencies. The Blakeney Bus was ready to roll. Blakeney's daily routine was to start at 8:00 A.M., hitting as many main streets and nursing homes in as many towns as possible before an evening rally which might not end until midnight. He spent much of the day walking along main streets. Blakeney has flat feet, an affliction for a politician. He took along a bag of shoes, and another of socks, and changed both frequently. His mobile campaign team included a clergyman named Gerry Miller, who was his executive assistant; his press aide Bruce Lawson, a rangy, bearded Australian with an icy demeanour; and the suave communicator, Jack Kinzel. A former radio announcer in the United States, Kinzel had been hounded by McCarthyism, and came to work for the Saskatchewan CCF in the 1950s. He was a gifted speech writer, and a political and communications analyst. It was Kinzel who had taken the NDP policy and rewritten it as the *New Deal for People* booklet.

Before the campaign began, Kinzel prepared speeches in shorter and longer versions for every conceivable issue and topic. Once the writ was dropped, he stayed a day ahead of Blakeney, talking with local NDP activists about local issues. Then he rewrote the set speeches, inserting local flavour and colour, and sometimes including election promises specific to the location. When the Blakeney bus rolled in for the evening rally, Kinzel was there to meet it. "We'd review the material and get everything set for the event, and then probably even before it happened I'd move on to the next location," Kinzel says. He tried to steer Blakeney away from polysyllabic words, and his penchant for qualifiers—the result of his precise legal mind and fondness for detail. Blakeney was aware of his oratorical weaknesses. He wanted everything scripted, and he seldom departed from the prepared text.

At each evening rally he attacked the Liberals, but he also outlined NDP promises—abolishing deterrent fees, abolishing Bill 2, a two-price system for wheat, plans to pave main streets in small towns. He returned again and again to that perennial Saskatchewan election issue, the loss of population. He charged that there were 17,000 fewer people in the province in 1971 than there had been in 1964. These messages were complemented by a door-to-door canvass and literature drop. They had tested those techniques in a by-election in Kelvington in 1969, and had them ready for 1971. "We took the intensive urban organizing style of eastern Canada," says Don Faris, NDP Provincial Secretary, "and applied it as best we could to Saskatchewan, with intensive sign campaigns, two or three canvasses of every home, and good election-day organization." The NDP did no professional opinion polling, but relied on forms completed by its canvassers, dividing people into "supporter," "undecided," and "hostile."

The NDP had decided by early 1971 that every attempt should be made to link Thatcher to unpopular federal Liberal policies, especially in agriculture. He was attacked on broken promises regarding reduced taxation, and for the poor performance of the economy. Finally, taking a page from the nationalist debate popularized by the left, Blakeney hit Thatcher on the "sell-out" of Saskatchewan resources to the multi-nationals.

The television and radio ads, the speeches, the door-to-door canvass and the *New Deal for People* booklet all reinforced the themes that Thatcher was in collusion with Ottawa, and that both were callous, remote, and uncaring. Blakeney constantly repeated the refrain, "A Liberal is a Liberal is a Liberal." The NDP pounced on the federal Liberals' Task Force on Agriculture, which had advocated a corporate model for agriculture with the exodus of thousands of "inefficient" farmers. The NDP created one very effective television commercial. It showed a hand descending on a toy farm yard and wiping the buildings and fences off the table. A voice then said that the Liberals would do away with two of three farms.

The NDP railed at corporate agriculture and at the "capitalist economic doctrine" of Trudeau, Lang, and Thatcher. They countered with a promise to promote the maximum number of family farms. They proposed to restrict corporate and foreign ownership, and set up a Land Bank. They would provide low-interest loans to young farmers; they would support marketing boards, and guaranteed prices for farm products. They hinted at legislation which would declare a moratorium on farm debt. They promised to keep local hospitals and schools open, to develop a public housing corporation, to build more rinks and halls and ball diamonds, to decentralize government services, and to help small business.

The promises aimed at small towns and small business were important. The NDP was strong in the working class areas of the cities, and in the parkland farm belt, following a line roughly from Yorkton to North Battleford. "The places where we had the most difficulty," Blakeney says, "were the places that were small-townish, where the community leaders were main street merchants, who were not NDPers."

The NDP loudly opposed Thatcher's potash pro-rationing deal with the Americans, which set a floor price but also meant production quotas and layoffs in Saskatchewan mines. Blakeney vowed to extract higher royalties from the multinationals, and hinted at public ownership and crown corporations in the resource industries. Blakeney said a second pulp mill and an iron ore mine which Thatcher had promised were going to be re-examined. He would read the fine print on the deals, and analyze their effects on the environment. He promised to control pollution, and to set up an Environment department. For the citizens of the north, Blakeney promised a separate department which would provide economic development and greater autonomy.

When he had run for the leadership a year earlier, Blakeney had emphasized traditional NDP health and social programs. Now he promised a publicly-financed prescription drug program, a dental program for children, support for community clinics, more day care centres, and a higher minimum wage. There was to be a human rights code and a commission to enforce it, and an Ombudsman. Those projects had been high on Woodrow Lloyd's list. Blakeney also wanted a toll-free telephone line to provide citizens with government information. In response to two blatant gerrymanders by the Liberals in the 1960s, he promised an independent electoral boundaries commission.

The campaign began with a bang, but it soon started to flag. Kinzel says that many organizational problems occurred because Don Faris divided his focus; he was Party Secretary, responsible for provincial organization, but he had also won the nomination in Arm River, a rural constituency north of Regina. He had to spend time campaigning. Gordon MacMurchy, the Party President, was also a candidate. The early NDP crowds were small and subdued. Blakeney thought it was "a minor disaster." This was the first Saskatchewan campaign to receive much television coverage. There were blinding lights and whirring cameras in Elrose, but the people refused to applaud his speech. Nobody had coached them. They didn't want to appear impolite on television.

After the rally, Blakeney spent an uncomfortable night in the local hotel. He is a cold sleeper, who piles on extra blankets and wears heavy pyjamas and even socks to bed. He was very discouraged the next morning. Kinzel, who had gone on ahead, recalls that Blakeney blew up when they talked on the telephone. "He hadn't slept, he felt awful, the food was terrible. He'd come down and he couldn't get lemon for his tea. He always has lemon with his tea. Elrose was the low point of the whole affair." Kinzel got on the telephone to ensure there would be better organization in Shaunovan, the next stop. When the Blakeney bus hit the outskirts of town, it was met by a horn-honking car parade which escorted him to his motel. The rally that night was a roaring success, and the campaign went into orbit. The NDP crowds grew in size and enthusiasm. Two days before the election Blakeney spoke to 5,000 people in the Regina Armoury, where a year earlier he had won the leadership. His platform style had improved markedly. He knew by then that the election was his, just as Thatcher and Dave Steuart knew that they were gone.

On June 23rd, the NDP won 45 of 60 seats, and grabbed 55 per cent of the popular vote, the highest ever in the province. The size of the victory surprised Blakeney as much as it stunned Ross Thatcher. The Liberals had obviously under-estimated Blakeney, who had performed superbly in the campaign, displaying an uncanny logical ability to puncture the rhetoric of his opponents. That didn't surprise the Liberals; what did was Blakeney's ability to express a vision for the people in his depressed province.

Subdued and dignified on election night, Thatcher walked into the crowded, sweltering NDP headquarters, an abandoned supermarket in north Regina. When he was spotted, there was an initial chorus of boos, but Blakeney grabbed the microphone and called for silence. Thatcher congratulated him on a "magnificent election," and promised to have the government offices cleaned out in a few days. Woodrow Lloyd was there, too, wearing a beard and looking relaxed. The reins of government, he said, would now be back in the hands of the people. Blakeney made plans to take over as Premier on June 30th. He had prepared himself for the job in a way that few Canadian politicians could match—brilliant academic qualifications and long experience in the senior civil service, the cabinet, and in opposition; and he came to office with the detailed *New Deal for People*.

The celebration later that night was at his house. A steady stream of NDP activists and well-wishers came and went. Blakeney stood at the door, alternately grinning widely and delivering his loud belly laugh. He had prepared earlier in the week for a victory party by having friends go to the liquor store and buy a case of whiskey. When Anne Blakeney discovered the purchase, she cursed the extravagance and had the liquor taken back.

When Blakeney heard about that, he wrote a new cheque and sent his friends back to the store. He had the last word. Given the expectant crowds that night, it was fortunate that he did.

# Chapter Ten

# Premier Administrator

Allan Blakeney was sworn in as Saskatchewan's tenth Premier by Lieutenant-Governor Stephen Worobetz on June 30, 1971. He took the oath of office just after 10 A.M. in the red-carpeted, oak-paneled Legislative Chamber. The galleries were filled with invited guests, including Woodrow Lloyd and Robert Walker. Anne Blakeney received a surprise when she arrived in the gallery above the house with the three oldest Blakeney children. The commissionaire didn't know who she was, and refused them entry until she produced their invitations. Immediately after Blakeney took his oaths, eight other cabinet ministers were sworn in. The entire ceremony took 45 minutes.

Blakeney opted for a small cabinet, keeping the Treasury and Industry portfolios for himself. Roy Romanow was sworn in first among the ministers and named Deputy Premier. Jack Messer, the new Minister of Agriculture, was next. Blakeney's friend and long-time colleague Walter Smishek was third, with Everett Wood, Gordon Snyder, Ted Bowerman, Neil Byers, and Gordon MacMurchy following in that order. Wood was the only member who had previous cabinet experience, and MacMurchy the only minister who had never sat in the Legislature. Their average age was forty-two. Six of the eight would remain in cabinet throughout the Blakeney years.

Blakeney had three big jobs to tackle immediately, and a trust to maintain. He had defined agriculture as the major issue in the campaign, and the NDP had made a page of promises, featuring the Land Bank. Messer, a wealthy farmer, was given the job of setting it up, a task he pursued aggressively. The NDP had also promised a new deal to northern native people through a separate department for northern Saskatchewan. The northern seat had gone, narrowly, to the Liberals. Ted Bowerman was a Shellbrook farmer who had been a smoke jumper, a game warden, and a conservation officer. When the Department of Northern Saskatchewan was created, he became the minister. Finally, the bargaining restrictions Thatcher had slapped on trustees and teachers (an important NDP support group) had become a major irritant. Thatcher had introduced area bargaining; negotiations occurred in each school unit, but he dictated the salaries from Regina. It was a recipe for frustration. Gordon MacMurchy had been a school trustee, and he was a crisp negotiator. Blakeney told him to get the teachers and trustees to agree on an acceptable method of bargaining. MacMurchy set up a system whereby salary negotiations occurred provincially, with local bargaining for conditions of work.

In making his choices Blakeney attended to those immediate priorities, and to the usual considerations—skill, background, ethnicity, religion, geography, and the importance of both rural and urban representation in cabinet. There was also a symbolism apparent in his choices. He had made peace with his leadership rival, Romanow. In fact, the Romanow supporters appointed to cabinet outnumbered the Blakeney supporters by four to three. Blakeney did not succumb to the temptation to surround himself with loyalists. Romanow's friend and supporter, Jack Messer, was sworn in ahead of Blakeney's friend Smishek. Romanow and Blakeney never became close friends, but they had a good first-man, second-man relationship.

The closest Blakeney came to representing the New Left in cabinet was in the appointment of Smishek, who was seen as a sympathizer. The left had been virtually shut out in the nominations, and in elected party positions. John Richards, a young political economist and a Waffler, had been elected in the Saskatoon University constituency. Blakeney considered him too inexperienced for cabinet, but hinted at future possibilities. The Premier made a small gesture to the left by appointing Richards as Legislative Secretary to Smishek in Health. In his victory speech at the leadership convention, Blakeney had encouraged Don Mitchell to run for office, but when Mitchell sought the NDP nomination in Moose Jaw North he was defeated; Gordon Snyder, an MLA, worked against him.

Blakeney's caucus and executive in 1971 were right of centre; but party policy was more to the left than it had been at any time since 1944. In his cabinet appointments, Blakeney was sending a message about party unity. He was reaching out to his own supporters, and to Romanow. His appointment of Walter Smishek, who had supported Taylor, was a message to the left.

Within days of the first round of appointments, Eiling Kramer was added as Minister of Natural Resources. A rancher and auctioneer from North Battleford, Kramer had been an MLA since 1952, and had served briefly as a minister in the Lloyd government. When Blakeney overlooked him, Kramer lobbied vigorously for an appointment and Blakeney gave in. Six months later he added two more ministers. Kim Thorson, an Estevan lawyer, and John Brockelbank, the son of party pioneer J. H. Brockelbank, were both appointed early in January 1972. Thorson became Industry Minister, Brockelbank Minister of Public Works. Both had been Romanow supporters. Blakeney added five more ministers during his first administration. Three were young men: Ed Tchorzewski, Don Cody, and Elwood Cowley, who took over Finance from Blakeney in May 1972. The others were veteran MLAs Wes Robbins and John Kowalchuk. Cowley and Tchorzewski were to play continuing, important cabinet roles.

Blakeney sent another signal by keeping the Finance and Industry ministries for himself. His would be a government interested in economic development and diversification. "We wanted to put an economic underpinning under what we hoped would be a broad social service safety net," he says, "and you can't do that in Saskatchewan unless you have a more diversified economy."

By the time the cabinet was sworn in, Blakeney was already ensconced in his office, with its silver and blue tapestried walls, and fireplace with oak-trimmed mantle. He had photographs of Woodsworth, Coldwell, Douglas, Lloyd, and David Lewis placed on the wall behind his desk. The suite of offices, including the gilded cabinet room with its burnished oval table, lies behind the Legislative Building's second floor façade: six sandy brown marble columns which stand on the roof of the first floor entrance. Behind those columns a row of tall arched windows looks into the cabinet room. To one side of the room are the offices of the Cabinet Secretary and the Premier's Deputy Minister; to the other those of the Premier and his receptionist. The predominant view from the windows is of the manicured flower gardens sloping toward Wascana Lake. Across the lake is a treed park, then the office buildings of downtown Regina. Blakeney's secretary, Florence Wilke, made the move with him to the Premier's office. She had a history in government service going back to 1944, and had worked for Lloyd, then Blakeney, in the opposition office. She was in charge of his schedule, and met with him regularly. She lived in Blakeney's Regina constituency, where she served on the executive. Given her history in the party and her sensitive jobs in the legislative offices, she was a good source of intelligence for Blakeney. Clare Powell came from the party office to become the Cabinet Press Secretary. Gerry Wilson continued as Blakeney's Executive Assistant, but they didn't get along. Wilson soon left.

Jack Kinzel also moved to the inner sanctum. He was initially Clerk of the Executive Council, and ran the Premier's office. His role included organizing Blakeney's schedule, deciding which delegations he would see, and which speaking engagements he would accept. He organized a small staff to see to the mail which began immediately to pour in and never really stopped. Blakeney also wanted Kinzel as his major speech writer, and an advisor on communications and potential trouble spots. In the early days, Kinzel also organized Blakeney's contacts with the party. Blakeney soon saw that Kinzel had too many jobs. By the end of 1971, the Premier had decided that his role as writer and advisor was paramount, and should be separated from any cabinet support role. No matter what his changes of title over the years, Kinzel always remained on Blakeney's bus during election campaigns.

Beyond the Premier's office there was the imposing task of rebuilding the machinery of government, which Blakeney believed Ross Thatcher had allowed to rust. Blakeney needed civil servants who could do the more ambitious work he had in mind, but first he had decisions to make about the people in place. He turned to an old-time friend and civil servant Grant Mitchell. A sandy-haired man with a sad face, Mitchell had worked for the Douglas and Lloyd governments in water management and the environment. He survived the Thatcher years, although he hadn't been kept very busy. Mitchell's wife June was the daughter of Marjorie Cooper, a former Regina MLA. All were trusted friends of Blakeney. Mitchell, a professional civil servant, knew almost everyone in government. He was "a shrewd observer of people," Blakeney says. His immediate task was to compile a list of all the Deputy Ministers and senior civil servants. They made a chart, then Mitchell and Blakeney pored over the names. They were divided into several categories: those who would stay where they were, those who would be promoted, and those who would be moved. Blakeney didn't want a purge, and he knew Mitchell wouldn't recommend one. To help with the task, Mitchell called in Mel Derrick, a veteran civil servant he thought was being under-utilized in a middle-level administrative job.

A few people were fired, but not many. Almost everyone else retained a job, although many people were shuffled. Thatcher had run a shoestring operation; Blakeney wanted more planning and more programs. There was room to move people, often with salary increases; Blakeney thought Thatcher's civil service had been poorly paid. A year after Blakeney took over, the staff in his office had grown from eight to fifteen. The total spent on salaries had more than tripled, from $50 thousand to $170 thousand. Davey Steuart says Blakeney handled civil servants sensitively. "If they were getting up towards retirement he just moved them aside. I used to call them the ghosts wandering around the Legislative Building."

Blakeney's lack of partisan fervour was a continuing source of frustration within the NDP. Some members probably wanted patronage appointments; others believed on principle that Blakeney should hire socialists if he wanted a socialist program. In 1972, the Regina Wascana constituency passed a resolution expressing concern over the number of key civil service personnel "who hold neither our philosophy nor believe in our policies." Similar complaints had dogged Tommy Douglas over the years, and Blakeney was probably less partisan in his hiring than Douglas.

Mitchell's second major task was to recruit new people, and he quickly completed a short list for the senior jobs. He looked immediately to the administration faculty at the University of Saskatchewan's Regina campus. The dean there was Wes Bolstad, a slender man with a warm, unhurried drawl. Bolstad had worked in the Budget Bureau in the 1950s, and in Woodrow Lloyd's office after 1962. He had left for the university after the loss in 1964. In the summer of 1971 he was camping in the Cypress Hills when a call came from Blakeney. He drove back to Regina, where Blakeney offered him the post of Cabinet Secretary. Bolstad did not begin full time work until about a year later, but he immediately began to help in setting up the machinery of government. Keith Saddlmyer, who had worked for the federal government, was recruited as the interim Cabinet Secretary. Roy Lloyd, a provincial civil servant, was also hired into the nascent central planning office.

Blakeney set up a small task force in August 1971 to come up with recommendations for re-establishing a central planning unit attached to the Executive Council (essentially those offices around the Premier). By early 1972 he had hired Hubert Prefontaine as the Chief Planning Officer. That summer Blakeney appointed a Planning Committee of cabinet consisting of himself, Romanow, Messer, Smishek, and Alex Taylor, then Minister of Social Services.

Soon after the election, Mitchell, Lloyd, Bolstad, and Saddlmyer were dispatched to set up a cabinet retreat for November. It was to deal with the nuts and bolts of government organization: the role of ministers in planning, and how to set priorities for programs. A second cabinet retreat followed the NDP annual fall convention, this one devoted to policy. The annual retreats were Blakeney's way of staying on top of where the government was going, and ensuring that his ministers did, too. They were a throwback to the Douglas days, when similar retreats had been organized by George Cadbury. Blakeney's retreats were usually held at locations like Kenosee Lake. Wes Bolstad planned them and Blakeney chaired them. Bolstad recalls the parade of government experts with their technical reports: "They were bright professionals, so Blakeney would have them there and pick their brains. It was an incredible performance each year. I don't know how anybody could be as bright and know as much as Blakeney did."

Early in his tenure Blakeney sat down with his ministers and talked about deputies. He hired some of them himself, but did not insist, as Thatcher had, upon hiring all of them. When Doug McArthur, a young Rhodes Scholar originally from Watrous, was being considered for Deputy Minister of Agriculture, he spent most of his day in Regina with Jack Messer. He met Blakeney for about 15 minutes, long enough to receive the signal that Blakeney was on top of the decision.

Blakeney placed his own call to Garry Beatty, a gruff, non-partisan civil servant who had worked in the Douglas, Lloyd, and Thatcher governments. In 1966 he had joined the Administration faculty at the university campus in Regina. Blakeney invited him to lunch and asked him to become the Deputy Minister of Finance. He came on a leave from the university, but he stayed. "Blakeney was galvanizing by the power of his intellect," says Beatty. "He had the ability to attract people."

Blakeney placed great emphasis on Finance, and its Budget Bureau. He wanted budgets which were well prepared, then scrutinized regularly as the year progressed. He also wanted to take the best advantage of shared-cost programs being offered by Ottawa, a burgeoning source of income in the 1970s. Many of the brightest people were recruited to Finance, which became a training ground for those who later became Deputy Ministers and top-ranking civil servants. Blakeney himself was most comfortable in the "hard side" of government; and it was with the high-fliers in Finance that he appeared, socially, to be most at ease. The Finance people were often drawn from public or business administration programs, and they were frequently resented for showing little obvious empathy for social democratic ideals.

Allan Blakeney carried with him in 1971 a detailed model of the governing structures he intended to put into place. Many of them harkened back to his experience as a civil servant, and later a cabinet minister. Cabinet was central. Blakeney did not, in his own words, "want to be the minister of everything," as he thought Ross Thatcher had been. He was a delegator, and placed great emphasis on process.

The ministers regularly met on Tuesdays in the large cabinet room off Blakeney's offices. They gathered at about 9:30 A.M., with Romanow always seated to Blakeney's right at the oval table. The meetings continued through a sandwich lunch into at least mid-afternoon. Wes Bolstad, the Cabinet Secretary, sat in a corner away from the table and took notes. "Blakeney really expected ministers to be there," says Bolstad. He wanted cabinet to deal with policy, not administrative detail, with recommendations and not with problems. Blakeney, recalling his experience as Legal Secretary, insisted on a streamlined paper flow. The procedures became increasingly refined: "The cabinet agenda had to be on paper. I wanted an outline of the problems, but with some recommendations. If it wasn't worth someone's time to figure out what the answer was, or at least recommend an answer, then why was it worth ours? Back to the Fines kind of approach."

Roy Romanow says Blakeney was a stickler for process, rules, procedures, and thoroughness. "Bring in the Kentucky Fried Chicken, and we would sit there until one or two in the morning, with ministers half asleep, and Al stuck on the stray animals act amendments. But there were occasions when this held us in good stead."

The Premier gave short shrift to any civil servant who came with problems rather than recommendations. Stories are legion about the devastating Blakeney cross-examinations. His staccato questions, delivered in an icy and impersonal manner, would bring an unstructured presentation tumbling down on its unfortunate presenter—again, much in the manner of his mentor, Clarence Fines. If the Premier was at times curt with his staff, he was gentler, although no less effective, with his ministers. If a minister was carrying a proposal prepared by a deputy, but was not knowledgeable about it, a few penetrating questions by Blakeney could prove embarrassing. "He could cut your idea up quickly," Elwood Cowley says. "Three sentences. He quit, and so did you."

The meetings, although serious, had their lighter moments. Cowley, particularly, was known for his cynical sense of humour, and his quick rejoinders. He was also the minister who lived the hardest. A colleague says: "He would come into cabinet, unshaven, after a hard night of poker playing and beer drinking, and you'd think that he was dead or asleep, or both. Then he would contribute most creatively to the agenda item before them. Blakeney appreciated him because he was more ingenious and creative than Blakeney himself in some areas." Blakeney had no appetite for the high stakes, all night poker games, but he did like Cowley's mind. He would sometimes repeat Cowley's witticisms at home to Anne.

Blakeney insisted that ministers leave their departmental hats at the door. They were the Executive Council, and expected to consider the needs of the whole government. If departments were having turf wars, he wanted them worked out in advance, often by having Bolstad sit down with the Deputy Ministers. He wanted everyone to participate in cabinet discussion. He did not want ministers "lying in the reeds." He chaired the meetings and led the discussions. Several of his ministers describe him as school masterish, always wanting to be sure that everyone understood the issues. He worked on the basis of consensus. "If there was something he was uneasy about or that cabinet was divided about," says Cowley, "he'd worry the damn thing to death."

In the House, Blakeney obviously relied on certain ministers, particularly Romanow, Messer, and Cowley. He showed no similar need around the cabinet table. He had his own categories for ministers and tended to look to them for help in those areas. He relied on Kramer and MacMurchy to tell him what people were thinking in the country. Cowley provided political advice, Romanow tactical advice. Ed Tchorzewski gave guidance on how the party might react to certain issues. Once in cabinet, the political categories of left and right became less important. Blakeney looked to ministers for the specific skills they brought to the table to advance the government's program.

Blakeney did not have an obvious lieutenant, as Tommy Douglas had in the tough-minded administrator Clarence Fines. Romanow says Blakeney would have liked a Douglas-Fines model: "I would be the bean counter, on top of the nuts and bolts of cabinet, the financial side, the civil service side." Blakeney may have been disappointed when it became obvious that those weren't Romanow's interests. "As it turns out," Romanow says, "we might have changed roles a little bit. I think Al channeled me into the area of being the politician. I became one of the chief political operators of the government."

Blakeney also had a clear idea of the administrative relationship his ministers should maintain with senior civil servants. His description was formalized in a lecture he gave around the oval table shortly after the election, one he repeated every time a new minister was added. It came complete with a chart. "It would have cabinet and ministers on top," says Wes Bolstad, "then there'd be a very hard line drawn, with Deputy Ministers below that line. He was telling ministers they were not to get involved in the administration of their departments. And he would tell the deputies, 'Don't delegate problems up to ministers. Your responsibility as public servants is to look at policy options, weigh them, make a recommendation as to what you think best'. His favourite expression was, 'Well, what do you recommend?' "

That was the Blakeney Lesson in Public Administration. When, in later years, he pulled out the chart, veteran ministers like Jack Messer would moan, "The Speech," and reach for a newspaper. "The Speech" passed into literature when Blakeney gave it as an address to a national conference of the Institute of Public Administration of Canada. It is central to his view of how to govern. The emphasis is on public servants to create policy options. The role of the cabinet minister is to add a political component, testing those ideas out on the public, and also informing the planners how supportive people will be of a policy, whether it's medicare or a new park. The politician also explains policy to the public in a way that will build support. In Blakeney's view, any policy which falls outside the "range of public acceptability" cannot be pursued, no matter how good it might be from a technocratic point of view.

The contradiction in this approach was that it placed great emphasis on planners to provide ideas, but did less to encourage people, in the NDP or the public at large, to engage in the same exhilarating process. This emphasis on central planning, rather than on a broader community, caused the dynamic agrarianism of the earlier CCF to wane during Blakeney's years. Some argue that the trend would have occurred in any event.

Tommy Douglas was always in a hurry during his 17 years as Premier, driven by what his biographers call a "manic energy." He was known to explode in frustration at motorists blocking his way on narrow gravel roads when he was late for a meeting. Blakeney was more controlled, but he also believed there was never a moment to spare. He organized himself, and the affairs of government, with a cold relentlessness. He was thoroughly disciplined, and demanded the same of those who worked with him.

He kept regular office hours, driving himself to work and usually arriving about 8:30 A.M. As often as they could, he and Anne would swim in the mornings at the Lawson Aquatic Centre, a public Olympic-sized pool complex near Taylor Field. He wanted no appointments before nine. He used his first minutes in the office to read his mail. He expected the staff to provide him with letters and memos which he had to see immediately, selecting out others which they could answer and he could sign. There was a set turn-around period for correspondence. He also met briefly with staff members to give instructions or to receive information about specific things to watch for during the day. He did not like surprises. He had a vast filing system, and he stayed on top of those files the same way he had in his law practice.

He usually worked until 6:00 or 6:30 in the evening, but went home slightly earlier when he had evening events. He occasionally returned to the office after supper, but more often took work home with him. He kept a stack of reports at the office marked "Read Only," and selected several each evening on his way out. He browsed through them after supper, making notes, at times dictating into a pocket-sized machine he carried with him. He was a stickler about correspondence (his staff often thought he was a fussbox), and refused to sign any letter he hadn't read. He demanded precision in both written and verbal communication. One correspondence secretary remembers her fear and trembling at being summoned into the Premier's office; she received a friendly, but firm, lecture on the nature of split infinitives. Blakeney did not want his writers to use the word "hopefully," and he instructed staff about the proper use of the word "presently." He would not tolerate jargon. Wes Bolstad sent a memo to staff in 1978 instructing them that: "[The premier] avoids the use of words with Latin roots."

Cabinet met on Tuesdays. On Wednesday mornings there was a regular news conference in a small studio in the basement of the Legislative Building. Blakeney sipped tea brewed in a small stainless steel pot. He might have an announcement, or he might simply respond to questions. He provided answers in detail that sometimes left reporters with glazed eyes. He usually whizzed through these encounters without anyone laying a glove on him. It was his Press Secretary's job to brief him about what to expect. Clare Powell, the first Cabinet Press Officer, says he was shifted into another position because Blakeney didn't feel he was anticipating journalists' questions accurately enough. Powell was informed of his impending move not by Blakeney, but by Kinzel.

Flo Wilke, Blakeney's secretary, says the Premier was not above dressing down a staff member whose performance he found wanting. But he would have them moved, not fired; and he would always have someone else break the news. "I think he found it impossible to tell them that directly," she says.

Following the Wednesday news conference, Blakeney met for half an hour with his speech writers. Together they reviewed the engagements. Blakeney wanted to know about the audience: was the message meant for the people in the hall? Were they sending a message to an interest group? Was the speech aimed at the entire electorate? While the writers made notes, he would pace the floor, throwing out themes he wanted to communicate, providing a framework and a background. Garry Aldridge, who wrote for Blakeney late in his administration, says that the outline "off the top of his head would have more detail than most people get by sitting down to write a first draft." The writers would then go away to gather detailed research and put the speech together.

Ted Bowen, a late arrival on the Premier's speech writing staff, says, "He understood rhetoric and literature and history. I would throw Northrop Frye into his speeches from time to time." Blakeney has a caustic sense of humour, but was cautious about using it. He did not like media scrums, and would privately refer to them as a time to "throw the Gainesburgers" to reporters. But he would never make such a comment in a public statement. He did like zingy one-liners which he could use, then move on. A certain understatement came naturally to him. He rarely departed from his prepared texts. He did not want to say anything that would come back to haunt him. He kept in mind the image of a tape recorder running endlessly. He believed everything he said was public material, and he treated it carefully.

He was rigid about keeping to his schedule in the office. Staff members who wanted to see him on short notice were greeted icily. Says Flo Wilke, "He demanded that his staff provide what he needed to manage his time. He did not tolerate interruptions." Cabinet and caucus members got the message that the careful access applied to them, too. Ed Whelan says it was annoying: "It took three weeks to get an appointment. With Tommy Douglas it took 30 seconds."

Blakeney's control over his agenda included building in time to stop and think, free of interference. Ted Bowen's most lasting image of Blakeney is of the Premier sitting quietly in the half light in his office, staring silently out the window while clipping his nails with a large pair of scissors. Blakeney wanted everything around him organized. He wanted the staff to do most of their communicating with him in writing. He did not want to read about problems without reading about recommended solutions, preferably several. He wanted material well in advance of deadlines, and his way of showing unhappiness with shoddy or late work was to delay responding to it. He wanted verbal communication to be considered and concise. In his mind it was all quite simple. He had a mental model of how things should be run, and he had to bend his staff to it in ways which would create time and space around himself. "I always tried to get people to think about who should do what, because that's what you've got to think about when you're in government. Not only what 'we' are going to do, but who are 'we'?"

When he was to travel out of town, he wanted to know who was in charge of planning the trip and who would be accompanying him. He wanted a complete briefing before leaving. He was careful never to make trips accompanied only by a female aide. He expected events to move according to schedule. If someone wanted to prolong a conversation, his aides would move in to rescue him. The assistant in charge of the trip was expected to write thank-you letters and to pick up on matters of concern which had been raised. Aides who accompanied Blakeney on the road were advised through senior officials like Bolstad or Kinzel that they should not make small talk with the Premier. If he wanted company, he would initiate the conversation.

There was a good deal of staff turn-over in his office—partly because it was used as a training ground, but also because it was not a happy place to work. Blakeney had high expectations and a seeming inability to compliment good work. Even Bolstad, who "liked Blakeney a lot," says, "I can only remember one time in six years that he explicitly commented on or gave me any praise for anything I did, and that was something I'd written. He put an annotation in the margin: 'Good job, Wes.' And I kept that. It would have helped if he'd complimented people a bit more, but that was just the guy." Murray Wallace, the Premier's Deputy Minister for a brief time, says he once suggested, gingerly, that Blakeney toss out a few compliments among the MLAs and staff. Blakeney noted curtly that he couldn't remember when anyone last told him he was doing a good job as Premier.

Excellence in public administration was a legacy of the Douglas and Lloyd governments, and Blakeney expected it, too. He believed that social democrats offer "high service" governments, and to do so they need a sterling civil service. Doug McArthur says, "We felt as civil servants that we worked for a Premier who wanted us to be the best. He had very high standards, but he recognized and appreciated the civil service. If you functioned professionally and competently, you would be recognized in his government." Recognition took the form of added responsibility.

The work was constant and demanding. Weekdays it was the office, night events, and frequent travel. On weekends there were often party meetings. He wanted at least one Sunday free every two weeks. He would nap and watch sports on television, and perhaps go to church. On the Friday afternoons preceding such weekends he might be found in the stacks of the Legislative Library, searching for a mystery novel. His idea of relaxing was to be cocooned at home. The Blakeneys rarely went to movies, the theatre, or the symphony, because he knew he would have to respond to people, which he did not consider relaxation. For the same reason, his idea of a vacation was to be out of the province. The annual summer Premiers' conference was usually an opportunity for a long driving trip. Beginning in 1975 Blakeney and Anne took an annual winter holiday in Hawaii. For two or three weeks they would book into a light housekeeping suite on the west island of Kauai, where they would relax in the sun.

He admits that during his years as Premier, Anne was virtually a "single parent." He was less available to his younger children, David and Margaret, than he had been for Hugh and Barbara. When Margaret, the youngest, was in grade school, she wrote a brief portrait of her father for a class composition, describing him as short, with a scar on his forehead and always sleeping. Barbara recalls visits with him when she was a university student in Saskatoon. "I'd be booked in—you know, 'fifteen minutes to see your daughter'—usually at his hotel room. I'd sit there and talk to him while he shaved. There was absolutely no way to see him if you weren't part of the itinerary."

Close social contacts for the Blakeneys waned in direct proportion to his succession through the political ranks. Many of their closest friends in the bureaucracy had left after Thatcher's victory in 1964. The Blakeneys maintained an easy and open contact with them, but did not see them often. The Lloyds left in 1971 when Woodrow went to work for the United Nations in Korea. He died there, suddenly, in 1972. The Smisheks, Walter and Ruth, remained friends throughout, and had a cottage near the Blakeneys on Last Mountain Lake. The list of close cabinet and caucus friendships ended there, although there were Christmas parties and the odd sing-song. The latter would include the families of politicians such as Gordon Snyder, and civil servants like Grant Mitchell or John Burton. Occasionally, Blakeney would invite an out-of-town MLA home for supper during the Legislative Session.

Blakeney believed that for a Premier isolation is part of the job: "The more senior your political office, the fewer friends you have." He was aware of the dangers of being on better social terms with some members of cabinet and caucus than others, and the potential accusation that he played favourites. Like Tommy Douglas before him, he chose to isolate himself. At the Premier's level, friendship cannot always survive politics.

# Chapter Eleven

# Premier Politician

When Bill Parker was Allan Blakeney's Executive Assistant, he had special responsibility for Regina Elphinstone constituency. Together they would plan door-knocking forays, and Blakeney would dutifully have them written into his schedule. One sunny afternoon, Parker knocked lightly on the Premier's door, and poked his head into the office. He asked his boss if he was ready to go.

"Go where?"

"Selling memberships in the constituency."

"What if I don't want to?" Blakeney snapped.

Eventually he did go, but he wasn't happy about it.

What Blakeney really liked was administration—taking ideas and putting them into an organizational form. That was fun. It was politics that was the hard work. Ed Whelan, a practised tea party politician from north Regina, says that "In a crowd Blakeney wasn't worth a damn. He would stand in a corner and talk to two people about the GATT agreements." Allan Blakeney is basically a shy man. He had to force himself to maintain personal links to the party, and to press the flesh on Main Street. His favoured meet-the-people exercise was his annual bus tour. Each summer for a week or two the Blakeney bus would be rolling into the false-fronted main streets of Saskatchewan towns, stopping so he and Anne could visit with men at the Pool elevator office, or have tea with blue-haired citizens at the nursing home. He appeared happiest when he was on the bus as it rolled past the black and gold fields. He would stand in the step at the front, treating reporters and aides to a running commentary about the ethnic mix in the town ahead, or long-term crop yields in the municipality just past.

These summer visits were highly organized. Aides were sent ahead to plan the social stops. Others accompanied him when he stepped off the

96

bus. He got much better at these visits, but he never found them easy. He was uncomfortable with prolonged casual conversations. When he lost interest, his eyes began to wander, leaving the person to whom he was talking feeling slighted.

Blakeney's self analysis is revealing: "I've never found it easy to go out and glad-hand. I always think I should have a purpose. I have a certain fondness for precision, and that is really a disability, because an awful lot of human discourse depends on the exuding of warmth or sympathy. I'm a literalist. Frequently I'm listening to what people are saying rather than what they are conveying. But that's always been true, and I'm not sure you can change that."

There were other personal quirks for which aides had to compensate. Blakeney could remember discussions in great detail, but often not faces or names. Frequently he didn't appear to recognize people he should have known. John Burton, a former Member of Parliament, became one of Blakeney's senior planners. They met socially. Burton's son James tells of a party at his parents' house attended by the Blakeneys: "He happened to come and talk to me. His first question was how I knew the Burtons. When I said who I was, he immediately knew more about my life history than I did."

Bill Knight, who had worked on Blakeney's leadership campaign, went to work for the provincial party as secretary after he lost his seat as an MP. Knight says Blakeney frequently walked past cabinet colleagues without acknowledging them: "He was famous for this. He would get so cranked up, he'd concentrate so damn hard on what was going to come into play, that he wouldn't really be seeing them."

Blakeney had another potentially damaging quirk. Many aides and acquaintances have stories of the Premier walking down a city street or sitting in a campaign bus, talking to himself. Again, Knight says, that arose from his habit of abstracting himself from the events around him. Knight's favourite story comes from his days as Blakeney's Principal Secretary: "One of the receptionists said to me, 'You'd better go down to the cafeteria. I think the Premier is talking to himself and it's kind of unnerving everybody.' He was sitting at a table all by himself—this was a pre-budget period. He was practising how he was going to deal with the debate. I just grabbed a coffee and sat down in front of him and said, 'Hi.' He gave a twitch, and then he said, 'Hi, I was just thinking.' So we started talking, and then he was fine. Anybody could have snapped him out of his trance." Blakeney was aware of this and other image problems, but he was sanguine about them. He doesn't think they affected his performance as Premier.

Blakeney was always attentive to his Regina Elphinstone constituency. He did the obligatory door knocking, and took his turn, along with other MLAs, at an NDP urban office on weekday evenings, meeting the public.

Constituency executive meetings were often held in his living room, bake sales in his garage. "If there was a fowl supper in Elphinstone," says Flo Wilke, "that had better be on his calendar, because he was not going to miss it. He knew enough to be visible. He liked those people." While he may have liked them, Blakeney also felt some impatience with them, and he was capable of being caustically humourous at their expense. One aide recalls the Premier saying that the "good folks" in Elphinstone did not like native people or people on welfare, spied on city work crews, which they suspected of loafing—and they all voted NDP. He was more at home with farmers than with the urban poor. He had a hearty respect for the ability of rural people to quickly organize themselves around any issue.

Anne Blakeney was much involved in the constituency and the neighbourhood. She had neighbour women in for coffee. She volunteered at the school, attended nearby Saint John's United Church, sang in the choir, and became involved in latch-key programs for school children. It was Anne who knew the names of party and community people they met at church, or at the shopping centre. She hosted constituency teas and bake sales. She was admired for her willingness to roll up her sleeves and plunge her hands into the dish water. Never a stylish dresser, she is recalled fondly by one constituent as "Ms Polyester and Sensible Shoes."

The Blakeneys had an agreement about her political involvement. She did not want a high profile as the Premier's wife. She chose the events she wanted to attend. She worked in election campaigns and accompanied him on his summer bus tours, but she did not speak about issues. No one had elected her to make public pronouncements. When she was invited to attend celebrity events, she replied that she was not a celebrity. When invited to be an honourary patron of organizations or events, she would most often demur, with the observation that she suspected she was being asked because she was the Premier's wife.

Blakeney attended Provincial Council meetings regularly. He didn't leave the meetings after his reports, but stayed, listening and taking notes. The council generally met four times a year and, like the fowl suppers, they had to be on his calendar. He maintained a proper relationship with the party, but it was stiff and formal, and unsatisfying to many of the NDP faithful. He never had the kind of easy rapport with party presidents that T. C. Douglas had had with Carlyle King, or Woodrow Lloyd with Coburn or Currie. That lack of rapport carried over to the party rank and file. One worker, who was involved in almost every Blakeney campaign, says, "There were two groups of troops—the party and the government, and he wasn't all that grateful to the party, the people who put him in the Premier's chair."

Blakeney has a self-confessed difficulty being soothing or reassuring. He treated conversations as if they were briefs to be dissected. He is intellectual and he is competitive. When members of Provincial Council had criticisms, they could expect tightly reasoned and sometimes sharp retorts. At a meeting following the 1971 election, councillor Don Kerr asked Blakeney why he had made a statement in support of wage and price controls when it wasn't party policy. Blakeney replied that the NDP believed in a planned economy; controls were the only way to reduce unemployment without severe inflation; therefore, his position fit party policy. Kerr's notes from the meeting indicate that Blakeney's answer was followed by a healthy round of applause. People may not have felt entirely comfortable around him, but they had great respect for him, even awe. Increasingly, they were prepared to follow wherever he led.

There was some discomfort in the party following the NDP convention in 1971, the first after the election. The Premier responded to directives from the convention by saying that the party, while important, offered just one of the "many inputs" to be considered in arriving at policy. As Premier, he had to govern for everyone. It was a debate that reached back into the early years of the CCF—the demand that constituents have the power of recall over elected members, and that the Premier and cabinet be bound by the policies which had been approved at conventions. Tommy Douglas had signed a recall letter before being elected federally in 1935, but once in power provincially, he decided it would be impractical. Few party members in 1971 expected the power of recall over anyone. But there was some suspicion that Blakeney had his own category for the party, and kept it in that mental drawer. The party was important for winning elections, and it was useful as a sounding board for policies created by the planners. But Blakeney knew that only a minority of Saskatchewan people were committed NDPers. He had to appeal to a broader group of people to stay in power.

He tended to delegate party and political tasks to ministers who would play that role for him—MacMurchy, Cowley, Tchorzewski. Bill Knight, as Party Secretary and later as Blakeney's closest advisor, also played a major political role. "I'm not as skilled at party organization as I am in party policy or governmental organization," Blakeney admits. "I never was a really skilled politician in terms of being able to figure out how to win X riding by candidate selection, or by organizing so and so's campaign." He also appointed a cabinet political committee, usually containing the same triumvirate. They had special responsibilities relating to party organization and election planning. "Blakeney was happy to leave political strategy to somebody else," Wes Bolstad concurs. "He would sit in on meetings of the election planning committee, but he wasn't really an initiator. He would certainly have his input, but he was quite happy to have someone else looking after the politics of it."

His reticence to mix it up politically had its dangers for an NDP government. There were complaints that after 1971 party conventions became less open; that too much of the agenda had been set in advance;

that cabinet ministers and their executive assistants manipulated conventions to ensure that panels and plenary sessions came up with the results they wanted. Those complaints grew into a chorus over the divisive issue of uranium development.

Walter Smishek says that cabinet made a mistake in giving so much power to the political committee. "They, for all intents and purposes, ran the political party organization. The party became reliant on the government. At our conventions we did everything possible to defuse conflicts, and damn, within the political structure conflicts are healthy. We were afraid that somehow the party was taking on the government. And why not? The party should have its antennae out politically and it should be advising government. Instead, we almost reversed the roles." Blakeney admits that the party after 1971 was not as strong on philosophy and education as it might have been. In his defence he says that governing was a consuming task, and he and his ministers had less opportunity for reflection than they had had in opposition.

A problem for Blakeney in his first years as Premier was the NDP's deteriorating relationship with the Waffle. Waffle candidates had been shut out of party positions at the 1970 convention, and those who ran for provincial nominations all lost. The Wafflers suspected the party was organizing against them from head office. President Gordon MacMurchy admits there was some skirmishing, but there was no deliberate shut-out. "They were organizing. Others were organizing. That was going on, but if a shut-out was taking place, it was by the delegates who came to the convention."

As the NDP was preparing for the 1971 provincial election, there was also intense activity on the federal scene. Tommy Douglas had stepped down as leader, and the national convention was set for Ottawa in late April. Throughout the spring, the Saskatchewan Waffle organized vigorously on behalf of Jim Laxer, the Waffle leadership candidate. Laxer finished a surprising second, behind David Lewis but ahead of Ed Broadbent. Carol Gudmundson, the former Saskatchewan NDP vice-president, ran for national president and lost. Behind the scenes the convention was a bitter one, and it deepened the divisions within the Saskatchewan party.

After the convention Woodrow Lloyd wrote a personal letter to Lewis. He said he had noticed "potentially ugly symptoms" at the convention, and urged Lewis not to marginalize the Waffle. Lloyd went on to tell Lewis that he saw similar signs of intolerance at home. "I am undoubtedly influenced by my reading of the signs and symptoms within Saskatchewan's 'Party officialdom' (Let me immediately and gratefully say that I exclude Allan Blakeney from responsibility for these signs and symptoms. I include the hope that he won't be a partial victim of them)." Lloyd, who was impatiently awaiting his United Nations posting, proceeded to tell Lewis that "there are those (like our provincial Party President and Secretary) who are obviously uncomfortable because of my policy position on many items and even my physical presence." MacMurchy was Party President, and Faris was Secretary.

The party's internal squabbling subsided during the 1971 election campaign. Many Wafflers worked against the Liberals; others quietly withdrew. Soon after the election, however, the Waffle picked up on its earlier criticism of the NDP. There was another battle at the provincial convention in December 1971 for control of the party executive and council. MacMurchy, now an MLA, nominated Alvin Hewitt for Party President, and Hewitt defeated the left candidate, Dr. Frank Coburn. None of the left's 12 candidates for Provincial or Federal Council was elected. Then in May 1972 the Lewises, Stephen and David, forced the expulsion of the Waffle from the Ontario party. They said it had become a party within a party. There's a common misconception that the Waffle was expelled in Saskatchewan, too. In fact, they left on their own. By 1973, the remaining Wafflers had come to a number of conclusions. They believed they had been successful in moving the party to the left on policy, but had lost the battle for positions of influence. They despaired of the NDP under Allan Blakeney ever delivering socialism as they defined it. In the Moose Jaw Union Centre on Thanksgiving weekend, 1973, the Waffle decided to go its own way toward building a new Marxist party. They believed there was a base of people who wanted a new socialist alternative. They were full of optimism, and even had membership cards printed.

A few days before the Moose Jaw meeting, a Waffle delegation met with Blakeney for an hour at the Legislative Building. They wanted to inform him of their impending decision. Sheila Roberts (then Sheila Kuziak) was one of the Wafflers at the meeting. "It was a very polite conversation," she remembers. They asked why the left had been shut out of positions and nominations. Blakeney saw it not as exclusion, but as their lack of a sufficient power base within the party. They disagreed with him about how closely the cabinet should adhere to party policy as decided at the convention. Blakeney gave his speech about being Premier for everyone. "The tenor of Blakeney's conversation," says Roberts, "was that if we were going to split, he didn't want to see any rancour in public. He didn't want us denouncing the party. He wasn't trying to persuade us to stay, but he wasn't trying to tell us to get out. He never tried to force anybody out."

Blakeney had never treated the Waffle with overt hostility. He had spoken and voted against them during the Waffle Manifesto debate at the Winnipeg convention, but not in inflammatory terms. While the caucus battle swirled around Lloyd and his tolerance for the Waffle, Blakeney remained aloof, and refrained from red-baiting. But if he was not unfriendly toward the left after becoming leader, nor did he build any bridges to them. John Richards, the lone MLA openly associated with the Waffle, says now that many caucus members considered the Wafflers to be flakes and electoral liabilities. On the other hand, he says, the Wafflers *were* intemperate, immature, highly emotional, and arrogant. They gave their critics some good ammunition. "Marxist-influenced people engaged in awful *ad hominems* on the other side. There was not an appreciation of the complexity of life. They basically disliked sloppy social democratic parties. And because it was the only game on the left in town, they would tolerate being part of the NDP under the guise of the Waffle. But they really didn't like it."

Richards says it was a tragedy for the Saskatchewan NDP that the ideological and generation gaps could not be bridged. As leader, Blakeney should have insisted those bridges be built, but he didn't. "Had he been prepared to say to us, 'Look, you guys, you are a minority sentiment within the party; you aren't going to run this show. But, on the other hand, I do think you are a valuable component and should have some share of the prizes. . . .' Had that kind of back room dealing taken place, I think a good deal of the polarization could have been avoided."

Left to itself, the Waffle began almost immediately to implode. The original 1960s leftist movement within the Saskatchewan NDP was an eclectic mix of those who wanted a revival of the old-time CCF, and a few Marxists, but the latter were in the minority. As the battles with the party became more bitter, some of the social democrats melted back into the mainstream of the NDP. Many of the remaining Wafflers were Marxist academics. They began a series of bitter quarrels over what path to follow. It all ended with factions (of sometimes fewer than a dozen people) denouncing each other variously as Stalinists, Maoists, or Trotskyists. Richards resigned from the caucus in the summer of 1973 and voted with the Waffle to leave the NDP. When he ran as an independent socialist in the 1975 provincial election, few Wafflers did anything to help. Some denounced him as a careerist social democrat. He finished last among the four candidates. He had, he says, learned a bitter lesson about sectarianism.

The Waffle's departure reduced tensions within the NDP. The 1973 convention was the quietest in years. Blakeney was able to stand unobtrusively in the food line waiting for a box lunch. Later in the day he sat alone in a corner of the hall during the convention plenary, scribbling occasional notes, but mostly just listening. It was frequently Wafflers who had pushed many of the progressive policies in the New Deal for People program. They were the passionate people, the people with ideas in a party which was generally much more interested in organization and winning elections. The NDP in the later 1970s became a much less interesting place to be.

The classic line is that Blakeney was a crack administrator, but he was not a good politician. That analysis grew partly out of nostalgia for the days of the early CCF. He was underrated because he was constantly being compared to Douglas. Don Faris points out that Blakeney's victory in 1971 was by a larger margin than anything Douglas had ever achieved, so he must have had some appeal. Bill Knight adds that a politician has to be judged not only on the ability to make rousing speeches and remember everyone's name, but on the ability to get elected, to govern, and to get re-elected. "He had brains and discipline. He combined them with an incredible knowledge of a whole range of issues. . . . So he could fight a battle with the federal government on health care like nobody else. He could handle the constitution. He could switch back to economic fights over the ownership of industries and the like. He had the agility to move philosophically within the party to handle its changing moods and positions."

Blakeney was not a populist, but rather a team player, a party politician. He had stamina and energy. Roy Romanow, using a hockey metaphor, says Blakeney was also a competitive politician who used his elbows in the corner whenever necessary. He was a good judge of people. He used his ministers and civil servants to their best advantage. He was a process man who surrounded himself with competent people, not sycophants. His personal stock rose greatly after his victory in 1971. His way of dealing with his lack of popular appeal was to accept that it was more important to be respected than to be liked. He was exceptionally competent, and voters recognized that. Within his own party, the combination of his victory and his careful handling of the caucus divisions which had arisen under Woodrow Lloyd placed him firmly in control.

# Chapter Twelve

# The Farm

Allan Blakeney liked to tell reporters how Saskatchewan farmers traditionally saw government as "the hired help," how when the Grain Growers held their annual meetings early in the century, they expected the whole cabinet to attend and to answer for itself.

Blakeney won in 1971 not because he looked at home on a tractor, but because of an effective slash and burn attack on the federal Liberals' 1969 Task Force on Agriculture. By 1971, Saskatchewan was in the third year of a recession triggered by a crisis on the farm. A bushel of the finest red spring wheat sold at the country elevator for $1.32, the worst price since the Depression. When Senator David Kroll visited the Prince Albert area in 1970 gathering impressions for his poverty report, he was shocked by the dilapidated housing, rickety vehicles, and despair he saw on some of the farms. Some farmers bartered wheat for tractors, or for meat and groceries. Others ran their machines on used oil begged from local garages.

The main thrust of the task force was that the market should be allowed to take its toll. The report predicted that by 1990 two-thirds of Canadian farmers would be out of business. In rural Saskatchewan the reality was as harsh as the prediction. In the ten years ending in 1971, 17,000 farm families had been lost. In a province so dependent on farming, this was devastating. The provincial population shrank by 44,000 between 1968 and 1972.

Blakeney and the NDP campaigned on a promise to maintain the "maximum number of family farms." Rejecting the "capitalist economic doctrine" in agriculture, they vowed to revitalize rural Saskatchewan. If there was any inconsistency in railing against capitalism while vowing to retain a capitalist organization of agriculture based on family farms, it did not raise eyebrows in Saskatchewan. Everyone knew that the slogans meant protecting the farmer—a little capitalist—against the pin-striped Bay Street banker, or the Montreal railroad president—the big capitalists. That's how the CCF movement originated.

The NDP rural recovery plan included grants and loans to farmers to diversify into livestock production and new crops, and a whole package of tax relief programs and grants to brighten up the face of small-town Saskatchewan. But its centrepiece was the proposed Land Bank. The party was more enthusiastic about it than Blakeney was. It wasn't a policy he had emphasized in his campaign for the leadership. To party insiders he quoted former Agriculture Minister Toby Nollet, who had said that problems in agriculture could "not be solved by tinkering with tenure."

The debate over land tenure was not new. In 1931 the Saskatchewan section of the United Farmers of Canada had called flatly for the nationalization of all farm land, which would then be leased back to farmers. The CCF backed away from that, but did propose a use-lease program in 1934. In the context of Depression foreclosures, the proposal was concerned more with guaranteeing permanent tenure than with an ideological commitment to public ownership. It became a political liability, however, and it was dropped before 1944.

Land tenure received little government attention again until 1957, when the massive report of the Royal Commission on Agriculture and Rural Life devoted a full 200 pages to it. The problems were clear: thousands of small farmers were being weeded out, land was being concentrated in fewer hands, and the rural community was suffering. Reflecting the views it had heard in extensive public hearings, the commission continued to prefer private ownership, but expressed a bias against large, corporate, and absentee farmers. Although many briefs had called for it, the commission's report did not recommend limits on farm size. There was, however, a muted recommendation for something very like a Land Bank, with the government purchasing "large holdings of productive land offered for sale," and allocating it to "neighbouring uneconomic farm units." The report implied that such land would be rented, not sold, to the smaller farmers.

The Douglas and Lloyd governments made no attempt to introduce land banking, or to limit farm size. Thatcher's policy was to promote farm credit for land purchases and diversification; in fact, he forced many farmers leasing government land to buy it or lose it. The tenure issue surfaced again during the farm crisis of the late 1960s. The NDP's search for new answers led them back to the old ones. The left, particularly, pushed the issue, and the provincial leadership convention in 1970 accepted the principle.

After the convention, internal party debate swirled around the option to purchase. The left wanted a Land Bank as an alternative to private ownership, providing long-term leases on publicly-owned land. The debate was especially heated in Provincial Council during the winter of 1970, as the party was drafting the *New Deal for People* booklet. There was no doubt where Blakeney stood: "I took an active part in some of these battles, saying we really have to have the right to re-purchase. We always intended that, but I said it had to be stated. It was not our purpose to have a vast store of land owned by the Government of Saskatchewan." Blakeney perceived the Land Bank as a method of transfer from one generation to another, not as a fundamental change in the system of tenure. The CCF had long since abandoned the idea of public ownership of farm land as politically unacceptable in rural Saskatchewan. In Blakeney's mind, there would be no dusting off the earlier CCF use-lease proposal.

Doug McArthur, a young, reddish-haired, nervously energetic Rhodes Scholar from Watrous, was working as a consulting economist in Toronto when the call came from an assistant in Blakeney's office. It was a few days after the election in 1971. They wanted him to interview for a job in the Department of Agriculture. He flew to Regina to meet with Jack Messer and, briefly, with Blakeney. They were setting up a planning and research unit and wanted McArthur to lead it. They were also trolling for a new Deputy Minister of Agriculture. McArthur was promoted in the summer of 1972.

His most important initial planning task was to set up a series of country meetings in 1972. They played to packed halls. There was plenty of interest, but also some uneasiness about what form the Land Bank might take. In a rural community nothing strikes so close to the bone as land and the arrangements for its use. Some of the controversy within the party spilled over into the public hearings. There were recommendations from the Waffle, for example, that farm land be publicly owned and leased back to farm families. Others wanted nothing to do with any government ownership.

Blakeney appointed Jack Messer as Agriculture Minister. Messer came at farming from an unusual angle. His parents had lived in Saskatchewan, but moved to Vancouver where they did well in real estate. Messer returned to the University of Saskatchewan, and later got into farming almost as a sideline. Land was cheap in the 1960s, and once he had some he could borrow against it for his other business interests, mainly in seismographic exploration. He thought it a good idea for young farmers to rent government land and put their own money into diversification, or into off-farm investments. That would provide some security for the times when farming was in a down-cycle.

Messer presented his vision of the Land Bank to cabinet in December 1971. For someone who had been accused by the left of being cool to the idea, he made an aggressive push for it. The program would promote having as many family farms in Saskatchewan as possible. Its intention was nothing less than the creation of a complementary system of land tenure based on crown ownership. For people to choose a continuing lease option, the rents should be pegged at a level below the government's cost of borrowing money to buy the land. Messer and McArthur both agreed to an option to purchase, but they wanted to make renting land more attractive than buying it. Other ministers argued that rents should be set at the province's cost of borrowing, which would mean about seven per cent of the land's market value. Throughout the summer and fall of 1972, Messer argued before cabinet that the Land Bank was a "powerful adjustment tool for Saskatchewan agriculture," and that rents to farmers should be kept low. He won the day; rates for the program's first year, 1973, were pegged at five per cent.

The Land Bank needed a commission to run it. Messer proposed Gib Wesson and Ross Moxley as people who might act as Land Bank commissioners. Wesson was a non-political bureaucrat, an old hand from the Department of Agriculture's Lands Branch. He had also worked for Co-op Trust and the Saskatchewan Wheat Pool. Moxley was a young Rosetown lawyer. Neither was a farmer, but there was also a concern in cabinet that they lacked the requisite "philosophical outlook." Messer was annoyed, but added the name of David Miner as a third commissioner. Miner was a farmer from Speers and a former provincial vice-president of the NDP. Wesson, who was named chairman of the commission, initially viewed Miner's appointment with suspicion. He thought it might insert an element of patronage into the allocation of land, but he says now that Miner "kept his shirt-tails pretty clean" and became an effective commissioner.

Cabinet approved the Land Bank regulations in August 1972. After leasing for five years, farmers would be eligible to buy the land at prevailing market prices. Doug McArthur drafted much of the legislation, and had the program objectives clearly in mind. People would be free to buy, but they would not be assisted to do so. "We were concerned that the option to purchase not undermine the main tenure option that the Land Bank was attempting to introduce. There would be no credit. If people purchased, they would have to pay cash, and at market prices. We made it fairly unattractive, not with a particular meanness of spirit, but simply because the Farm Credit Corporation was there to handle purchases. We were trying to set up a very different kind of option."

The program immediately attracted a great deal of interest. Letters began to flow into Blakeney's office. One man, originally from Saskatchewan and about to retire from the Canadian Forces, wrote from New Brunswick to inquire about the land he thought was being distributed, and asked if the Premier might save some for him. Closer to home, the program created a buzz in the countryside. In the first year, applications poured in from 2,100 farmers who wanted to sell. The commission made offers on 600 parcels of land. Fifteen hundred farmers applied for leases. The applicants were judged on the basis of a point system, with preference given to younger farmers who looked promising but whose holdings weren't too big. In cases where a retiring farmer wanted to lease to a younger family member, the transaction was made without reference to the point system.

By 1975, the end of the NDP's first mandate, the commission had bought about 600,000 acres of land, and it had 1,300 lessees. The Land Bank was enjoying some success. For 1975, the average lessee was 32 years old, so the program was allowing younger people either to get into farming or to add to their operations. One lessee in six was a direct descendant of the person who had sold to the Land Bank, so it was allowing the transfer of land within families. One lessee in four was someone who had owned no other land, an indication that new people were coming into farming—in most cases farm kids who had left and wanted to return. The program received press attention, most of it favourable, all over North America. George McGovern visited Saskatchewan in 1975 and later introduced similar legislation, without success, in the United States Congress.

Despite its obvious successes, the program was fraught with difficulties. Doug McArthur calls it an "administrative nightmare." There were more farmers wanting to sell than the Land Bank could accommodate. Where offers were made, there were inevitably criticisms from sellers that they hadn't been offered enough. In 1974 a man from Chamberlain, north of Regina, wrote to the Premier to complain that he had been offered only $64 an acre for land he wished to sell to the Land Bank: "My neighbour across the street sold three quarters last spring for $80 per acre. The next closest neighbour bought a quarter for $82 per acre. Please consider again and at least offer a fair price." On the other hand, farmers buying land on the market claimed that the Land Bank's presence as a potential buyer drove prices up. Virtually all farmers wanted more land, so there was intense competition for it.

But it was the process of selecting lessees that became most controversial. The application for land through the commission was a public process. For every farmer who received land, there might be as many as 20 who didn't. That made for a lot of unhappy farmers. "It wasn't only the non-recipient," Jack Messer says. "It was the family of the non-recipient and the neighbours. It created a lot of problems for us."

In small communities people all know their neighbours' politics. The suspicion of patronage frequently accompanied the distribution of land. Elwood Cowley, who represented the rural riding of Biggar, says, "There was no political patronage, but that turned out to be a problem, too. No one was impressed when the local Tory got land. New Democrats were mad, and the Tories wouldn't vote for us, anyway." Messer agrees that the claims about political patronage were simply never true: "I can say with the highest level of comfort that land was not awarded on a political basis, and we paid a significant penalty for it. This whole process of allowing people to make application and going through the process of selecting the most competent, politics excluded, just got us into more trouble."

Ironically, the Land Bank was also undermined by the return of agricultural prosperity. In the early 1970s large grain sales were made to the Soviet Union and China. Wheat which had been selling at $1.30 a bushel was selling at $5.00 two years later. The good times began to roll once again. Battered old trucks disappeared from the wide main streets of prairie towns, to be replaced by gleaming new half tons. In winter the truck boxes often sported new ski-doos; in summer they were outfitted with campers. Bright new bungalows began to sprout in farm yards, replacing the gaunt, two-storey farm houses with their lightning rods and peeling paint. Some farmers began to go to Hawaii in winter, to Phoenix, or on Caribbean cruises. People who had been fearful that every strange car coming down the lane was the sheriff or the banker were now making sales of $100,000 a year and feeling like wheeler-dealers.

Good times altered the depressed land market. Between 1973 and 1978 the Land Bank's average purchase price almost tripled, from $54 to $143 per acre. And those figures underestimate the real situation, because the commission in 1976 stopped making offers in regions where prices were most buoyant. In some areas, land which had fetched $100 an acre in 1970 sold for three to eight times as much by the end of the decade. That didn't seem to deter farmers. Wild inflation and land speculation had arrived.

The people at the Land Bank were concerned. Soaring prices were driving up rents for lessees. The Land Bank was charging a percentage of the market value of the land, so rents were carried up with prices. Messer had fought for rental rates of five per cent in 1972, and won. With interest rates rising the next year, he announced a "10-year rate" of 5.75 per cent. But in November, rents were raised again, to 6.5 per cent. Serious inflation was underway in Canada, and the cost of government borrowing to finance the program kept going up. The rates were raised again in 1975. The lessees were not amused, and the government began to search for a new formula.

As 1978 approached, the first farmers renting land in 1973 became eligible to purchase. By that time the land was worth, on average, three times what the government had paid for it. It was a potentially explosive political situation. The government stood to realize a big capital gain. People who thought it was all right for farmers to make money that way didn't think the government should be doing it. On the other hand, if the government sold land at 1973 prices, the lessees would have a windfall capital gain. That would incite increased envy and anger among neighbours who had applied for land and been refused.

A Land Bank with an option to purchase was not a socialist program, but that didn't prevent Davey Steuart, the new Liberal leader, from making a high noon stand as early as 1972. The Liberals charged that the Land Bank was not a transfer system, but the first step by the NDP in setting up a "landlord system of farming under which farmers are merely tenants of the government."

After Steuart launched his attacks, hundreds of letters began to arrive at Blakeney's office. He was forced onto the defensive, and attempted to recover by criticizing the logic of the Liberal attack. At the government's rate of acquisition, he said, it would take 300 years to buy up Saskatchewan's available farm land. But Steuart's attack had little to do with logic, and everything to do with emotion. He touched a raw nerve among Saskatchewan's rural population, many thousands of whom were descended from Ukrainian, Polish, Hungarian, and Rumanian immigrants, in countries living under communism. Elwood Cowley, the principal political minister in the cabinet, saw that the attack was leaving its mark. "[The Liberals] would say that your parents and grandparents left the Ukraine, or wherever, to get away from government owning all the land and look at what these damn socialists are doing to you. You might as well have stayed in the Ukraine."

In the 1975 election, the Liberals went after the Land Bank as a plot by Big Brother to turn farmers into serfs. The NDP tumbled by 15 per cent in the popular vote, and they took a beating in many rural seats. The lesson they chose to take from their losses was that the Land Bank was unpopular. Many members of the caucus made a hasty retreat. Blakeney also draws a rueful conclusion from the experience: "I think it was Harry Truman who used to say in quite another context, that when wheat is $2.00 a bushel farmers are all Republicans. When it's $1.00 a bushel they're all Democrats. Some of that was true in Saskatchewan. When farmers are prosperous they don't want government intervention. When they're not prosperous, they do."

The Land Bank's glossy annual reports took on a more contrite tone. The confident, smiling visage of Jack Messer was replaced with the more quiet, sombre face of Edgar Kaeding, who succeeded him as Agriculture Minister. In its statement of objectives the Land Bank no longer talked about "a new system of land tenure." The report in 1976 contained a newly-drafted statement on objectives which mentioned the word "lease" only once, and emphasized that participation in the program was by the "free will" of those wishing to sell to or rent from the Land Bank.

Gib Wesson, the Land Bank's Chief Commissioner, remains perplexed and somewhat bitter about what he perceived as a lack of political support: "My personal feeling is that a lot of the MLAs at the time felt that it was not in their public interest, and they were trying to shoot it down just as much as the Liberals were." Wesson says that the government's uneasiness translated into a lack of financial support, and that was the "turning point" in the Land Bank's fortunes; it went from a successful to a stale program. It never owned as much as two per cent of the province's farm land, it was not big enough to affect tenure in any significant way, but it was big enough to excite opposition.

Doug McArthur, who had left the Department of Agriculture by 1974, says it was an easy program to attack because of its classic political overtones, and because of the large number of people who did not win in the competitions for land. He says he could understand the opposition from Liberals and Tories, but there was opposition from the left, too: "The opponents of the Land Bank in the party felt they had been betrayed somehow because of the inclusion of the option to purchase. They didn't understand how much that criticism hurt, how much the Land Bank needed support." It was a program, he says, which had to be sold, and no one seemed prepared to do it. The left dismissed it as nothing more than a real estate agency, and people on the NDP right, much like their Liberal neighbours, didn't agree with any public ownership of land.

The 1975 election indicated that there were political problems with the Land Bank, but a full two years later nothing about the program had changed. In 1977 Blakeney took control. He told Kaeding that he wanted a frank "political assessment" of the program. Kaeding's officials prepared a long brief which concluded that the problem was one of poor public relations. Blakeney and cabinet already knew that. They asked for another document, one which contained recommendations. Kaeding agreed, but asked for a committee of cabinet to help him out. He got no takers. Dunsky's, the government's favoured advertising agency, was already at work on a public relations program. Blakeney was concerned enough that, before he left for his August vacation, he instructed that no publicity go out until he had reviewed it. Kaeding's people skittered around nervously, searching for options.

Blakeney had also asked the cabinet's chief planning officer, Roy Lloyd, to get involved. Lloyd thought he had a solution, and went to the Maritimes to present it to Blakeney. The work was done by Ken Rosaasen, then an economist with the Department of Agriculture, now a professor at the University of Saskatchewan. He had been unimpressed with earlier talk of a "new tenure system." The leases were a marketplace distortion. They were subsidies to lessees which were not available to other farmers. As an alternative to the Land Bank, Rosaasen proposed a rental-purchase program which would resemble a rent-to-purchase agreement on a house, with emphasis on the purchase. The proposal reversed what McArthur and Messer had tried to do, which was to encourage long-term leasing. "If public ownership of land was an implicit objective," Rosaasen wrote, "it would not be met by [my] program."

Blakeney read the report and thought that, at the least, it offered some solutions. He told Kaeding to take a close look at it. A civil servant named Byron Hindle polled some of the ministers on the proposal and reported to Cabinet Secretary Wes Bolstad. Kaeding hadn't originated this research, even though he was the minister in charge. He recognized the change for what it was: "a departure from the concept of providing [an] alternate land tenure system." Gordon MacMurchy said it was too much like the

Farm Credit Corporation. Elwood Cowley said any proposals which got the NDP completely out of the Land Bank would suit him. Cowley had decided that the only people who liked the program were the successful lessees, and left-wingers in the NDP. After the 1975 election he wanted out of it.

Cabinet did not go for Rosaasen's idea, and Blakeney accepted their wisdom. Rather, they chose Kaeding's option: the government would provide a subsidy for a lessee purchasing the first quarter-section; those who wanted to buy more paid market prices and raised their own money. Cabinet also approved a complex rental formula, one which meant lower, rather than higher rents. Faced with changing the program fundamentally, cabinet opted only to tinker with it. Despite its political problems, the Land Bank was carried into the later Blakeney administrations.

Farm income improved dramatically in the mid-1970s, but Blakeney remained determined to diversify the economy. Within agriculture, he shifted the policy emphasis from land tenure to rural services and transportation. Communities had been hit hard by the farm depression and the continuing loss of population. Farmers might move into towns and build fine houses as prosperity returned, but streets and sidewalks were in a state of disrepair. The shambling public buildings and businesses along the main streets of Saskatchewan towns were a throwback to another era. The government created a new Community Capital Fund for streets, roads, rinks, and swimming pools. These programs had a distinct political advantage over the Land Bank. Politicians would much rather cut ribbons and smile for the weekly newspaper photographers than answer angry mail from frustrated applicants for leases.

There was also a flurry of planning activity around service and industrial development. There were hopes and plans in 1971 for the decentralization of industry into small towns, but they were only modestly realized. All the signs pointed to a continued deterioration in rural Saskatchewan. A study by Peter Woroby, a University of Regina economist, concluded that not all small towns could be saved. The government should stream some of its own services—like libraries and nursing homes—into the healthier centres. The report was never made public, nor, says Blakeney, was it ever adopted: "We operated on the principle that not all small towns could be saved—nor should be saved—but we weren't going to select among them. We did try to bunch a few government services in towns which we felt would grow, but we didn't do a lot of selecting."

There was another study in 1976, led by historian John Archer. He concluded that Saskatchewan, with its hundreds of small rural municipalities, had an inefficient form of local government. The logical decision that many small municipalities should be merged into fewer, larger ones had been considered by the Douglas government, but scrapped because of local opposition. Blakeney sidestepped it again. He didn't want to offend rural leaders—Reeves, Councillors, and, perhaps most important, the rural Municipal Secretaries, who were influential people in the countryside.

Archer also concluded that it would be better to have all farmsteads along major all-weather roads, and proposed government incentives to have farmers move their houses and buildings. It would have saved money on providing services like school buses and snow ploughs. Blakeney the technocrat was drawn to the idea, but it set off political warning bells: "We looked a little wistfully at some of the things that, ideally, could be done. But we weren't at all sure that the folk in rural Saskatchewan felt they made a lot of sense."

The CCF began as a farmers' movement, and in 1944 it became a farmers' government. The forces of change bearing down on the rural community, however, were inexorable. Blakeney's best plans were stymied in some respects by the indomitable facts of geography and international economy. The government spent millions of dollars lending farmers money to feed hogs rather than grow wheat for export. When international wheat prices rebounded, many of the hog barns sat empty as farmers went back into wheat. The Land Bank was an attempt to slow down the concentration of land ownership and its attendant depopulation of the countryside. It was a good program, but it faltered. Saskatchewan farmers appeared to oppose even that modest amount of intervention. There were occasional calls, harking back to the days of the Royal Commission on Agriculture and Rural Life, for a limit on farm size. Blakeney rejected them. "There was clearly a lot of resistance to that idea among Saskatchewan farmers," he says, "certainly among those Saskatchewan farmers who were members of the New Democratic Party. They weren't interested in the arguments. Their gut feeling was that it wouldn't fly." The CCF had begun as a party of small farmers, but that was no longer true of the NDP. Blakeney had within his own caucus some large landowners, including Dwayne Lingenfelter, Reg Gross, and Allan Engel. Blakeney came armed with programs, but ultimately wasn't able to deliver on his promise to revitalize the rural community. For a few good years in the 1970s he was able to stem the flow of people leaving the countryside, but ultimately the NDP foundered—partly through their own inconsistencies, but mostly through events they couldn't control.

# Chapter Thirteen

# The North

The sun blazed down on La Ronge throughout the clear June afternoon. By evening the light had softened, but an oppressive heat remained trapped inside the thin walls of the Kitsaki Indian Band Hall. The nondescript frame building sits on a rocky rise just off the south end of Main Street, which winds its way through the reserve and then 150 miles south through forest to Prince Albert. By meeting time the room was packed to overflowing. La Ronge, an old fur trading and fishing centre, had become a northern civil service town. Some government workers were there to meet Premier Blakeney, dressed tonight in a conservative blue suit. But the bulk of the crowd were native northerners, braided, booted, and mocassined, recruited by the Métis Society for a showdown with the southern politicians. It was one of many which had been occuring throughout the north and in Regina.

The meeting began badly. Blakeney told them their frustrations arose from the hurried pace of change. Southerners had been transferred to La Ronge to make things happen quickly. Someone in the crowd shouted a question. Was the Premier, then, saying that northerners were retarded? A chorus of boos and catcalls, the first of many, greeted Blakeney and his small panel of ministers sitting at the front of the hall. The doors had been left open to allow the heat to escape. At one point a large man from the audience strolled to a side door and urinated from the top step, in view of much of the crowd. It was a fitting symbol of what some in the hall thought of Blakeney's ideas, and perhaps what he thought that night of their criticisms.

Fully half of Saskatchewan is a natural wonderland of forests and lakes. The majority of the people living there are native—Chipewyan and Dene in the far north, Woodland Cree and the Métis farther south. When Tommy Douglas was elected in 1944 most northern native people lived in a traditional manner in their villages or on their trap lines. They were largely self-sufficient, although white clerics, employees of the Hudson's Bay Company, and the police wielded great authority. The CCF government extended health services, and organized some commercial activity. The government created crown corporations to market timber, fur, and fish. Douglas and his ministers had good intentions, and expressed concern for the poverty, poor housing, and lack of health services. But they were also interested in using northern resources—timber, metals, and uranium—to diversify the provincial economy.

In the 1950s and 60s the life expectancy of northern people had increased, and with it the population. That placed a strain on the traditional hunting and gathering economy. Native people also had to compete with ever more tourist sportsmen, lumberjacks, and miners for access to the forests and lakes. They found their way of life changing, and there wasn't much they could do about it. In one generation many people moved from an often meagre self-sufficiency to an equally meagre, but much less dignified, dependence on government welfare payments. During the 1971 election campaign, Blakeney and the NDP had ridiculed Ross Thatcher for the paternalism they said he showed toward native people. Thatcher had established an Indian and Métis Department, and set a minimum hiring quota for natives, both in the public sector and with firms wanting to do business with the government. The NDP said the department had failed because its policies were rooted in the perceptions of the white middle class. Actually, Thatcher's approach to native people shared a basic similarity with that of his predecessors, Douglas and Lloyd: they all believed that the solution to native problems lay in integration. Lloyd and Douglas thought that integrated services and schools, and an integrated labour force, was the way to extend the benefits of provincial society to native people. Lloyd had advocated that federal Indian Affairs responsibilities should be transferred to the province.

By 1970 those ideas were out of date. Indian bands in Saskatchewan had joined others across the country, responding with shock and anger when Jean Chretien's 1969 white paper on Indian policy suggested such a transfer. There was growing talk by 1970 of Indian self-government, and a militant Métis nationalism was emerging.

The *New Deal for People* promised to abolish Thatcher's Indian and Métis Department, to provide more money to native political organizations, and to consult with them in creating new programs. The NDP talked about having the government provide resources for community development, so that native organizations could organize around their own agendas.

Blakeney's response to demands for a better deal in northern Saskatch-ewan was to promise a special government department for the region. He made the promise in June 1971 as he boarded his bus for the second leg of the campaign. He was vague, talking about a department to "plan, develop, and protect the potential of northern Saskatchewan." In the frenetic pace of the campaign he was never called on to elaborate. It wasn't a rash promise. The NDP had been talking about it since at least 1960.

Some people saw the northerners as oppressed and colonized, and wanted nothing less than true liberation. There was a lot of that talk around in 1971, much of it within the NDP. The words "colonized" and "oppressed" did not flow easily from Blakeney's lips. He saw the initiative in more pragmatic terms. A single department in the north would do what many smaller departments did in the south. The object was to improve services. There would also be a measure of community development to prepare local people to take over their own local government: school and library boards, fire departments, town councils, and so on. Once new local governments had been nurtured, the special department would wither and dissolve. It was really a southern municipal model that Blakeney had in mind; he had no intention of turning over traditional provincial powers of government to anyone in the north.

That view clashed with what many native people were demanding. This difference in opinion is central to understanding the ensuing conflict. Blakeney offered programs, but only a measure of power. The Department of Northern Saskatchewan became the biggest political headache in his first term of government. He was excited about the project and committed to it, but it quickly came under fire. The difficulties with the Land Bank paled by comparison.

Blakeney's first obstacle was not in the north, but right in Regina. The Department of Natural Resources had been the pervasive government presence in the north for years. Northern officers of the DNR dressed in police-style uniforms and drove high-powered cars. They delivered welfare payments, offered counselling, and collected taxes, although they were trained mainly as game wardens.

Blakeney lost little time in pursuing the DNS idea. By October 1971 he had a four-member cabinet committee on the job, and he was one of its members. The Department of Natural Resources did not want to lose any turf, and there was immediate opposition from civil servants, which went right to the top. When the minister, Eiling Kramer, began to understand that power in the north would move away from his department, he resisted.

Blakeney became irked at all the foot dragging, and a memo from one of his aides described him as "being mad as hell." Blakeney won't comment on Kramer's role, but admits department officials were being obstructionist: "DNR just wouldn't let go. They didn't want to hammer their troops into line. They thought we were crazy with DNS. I had to make a ministerial change." He appointed Ted Bowerman, who was the Minister of Northern Saskatchewan, to become DNR Minister as well. Kramer went to Highways. Blakeney made the shuffle in May 1972, shortly after the enabling legislation for DNS was passed in the Legislature. He stayed on top of the northern project, insisting that much of the material flowing to and from Bowerman's office also be copied to him. The Premier's close attention was the best indication that this was a project important to him. Throughout the fall and winter of 1972 there was great activity. The old town on the shores of Lac La Ronge became an administrative nerve centre for the north. Dozens of ATCO trailers made the long trip up the highway to serve as government offices, and there was an immediate boom as civil servants arrived in search of housing.

Internal problems came up almost immediately. The planners hired by DNS were generally young academics. Most considered themselves to be left wing, and a number of them participated in the Waffle caucus. Their analysis named the government as one of the agents of northern oppression. In other circumstances the bureaucracy might have resisted hiring them. But the department was new, community development was the catch phrase, and DNS had problems attracting staff to the north. The acrimonious battle between the Waffle and the party Establishment following the 1971 election was played out in the north as well. The Waffle newsmagazine *Next Year Country* regularly carried articles harshly critical of Bowerman, his deputy Wilf Churchman, the church, the Hudson's Bay Company, and the police. The magazine's second issue, in December 1972, ran a story entitled, "The True North: DNS—Re-occupying the Colony."

The planners had departmental allies among the area co-ordinators, whose task was to work as animators in northern communities. They were all impatient with traditional management systems and regulations, in which they saw a bureaucratic attempt to control and delay progress. The DNS bureaucrats were conservative career civil servants under pressure to get programs into place. That group included Churchman, an old hand from DNR. Some of the administrators had little confidence in native people. They also thought the new recruits were irresponsible, and in some cases dangerous proponents of class struggle. The two groups held each other in mutual and growing contempt. Their differences exploded in May 1974, when the planners issued a statement alleging all sorts of improprieties. They called for the resignation of Bowerman and Churchman, and for the disbanding of the entire department. They were fired, and their branch was shut down.

Blakeney had been keeping tabs on the department. By the spring of 1974 he knew that something had to be done. Churchman was removed. Blakeney asked Mel Derrick, one of his administrative fixers, to go into La Ronge to restore order. Derrick was also to search for a new Deputy Minister, but nobody wanted the job. Many of the senior staff, including Churchman, had commuted to La Ronge from Regina, a distance of almost 640 kilometres. Even Bowerman, after a series of tough confrontations with the Métis, began to deal with the north from Regina.

Doug McArthur was purring along happily in Agriculture, organizing the Land Bank, the Hog Marketing Commission, and the loans program to farmers. One day he was invited to the cafeteria for coffee. Derrick and two of the Premier's top men, Bolstad and Grant Mitchell, asked him to take on the job of DNS Deputy Minister. Within a couple of days McArthur had decided to do it. What he found when he got there was that the grand experiment had blown up. "Everything was a mess," he says. "Everyone was tearing their hair out. The place was in turmoil. There were all these factions, and there was a tremendous distrust of the department in the communities. Nobody seemed to know where to go with this thing."

The situation looked so hopeless that within months McArthur wanted out. To complicate matters, his relationship with Bowerman was uneasy. Bowerman hadn't hired him; Blakeney had. The minister didn't know what to make of it. He was seen in caucus as a champion of the north. He was shell-shocked by the battering he had taken there from all sides. Although their relationship later improved, McArthur initially found Bowerman cautious and defensive. Blakeney left Bowerman where he was, but established a Regina-based management committee to help McArthur out. It consisted of some of his trusted fire fighters—Bolstad, Garry Beatty, and planners Gerry Gartner and Hubert Prefontaine.

McArthur moved to streamline what had been an administrative octopus, and to build trust. His major accomplishment in the community was to open and maintain dialogues with local town councils and school boards, and with native political leaders. He may not have succeeded in satisfying them, but he treated them well and earned their respect. When he left the job after an intense year McArthur was exhausted. He'd had enough of front-line government administration. Blakeney had remained in frequent and supportive contact. Now he virtually gave McArthur his choice of assignments. McArthur chose several in succession, each with a low profile.

Jim Sinclair is a big, rugged man with a scar that alters the line of his upper lip. He's a commanding presence: you wouldn't want to meet him in an alley after an argument. A non-status Indian, he grew up in poverty in Saskatchewan, living, dispossessed, along a road allowance. In his twenties he was an alcoholic. Later he quit drinking and got into native politics. He was a Métis Society of Saskatchewan organizer in the late 1960s, and he took over when an exhausted Howard Adams resigned in 1970.

Adams had studied at Berkeley, and returned in 1965 to teach at the University of Saskatchewan. He became MSS president in 1969, and brought with him the revolutionary rhetoric of the American New Left. He talked about the ruling classes, revolutionary development, and self-determination. He grafted the militant Berkeley style onto an analysis of the local Métis situation. He gained notoriety in 1967 for warning that existing conditions for native people could lead to violence. That threat became commonplace later, but in 1967 it made national news. Sinclair did not have Adams's academic qualifications or his political sophistication, but he was a tough and instinctive survivor in the rugged world of native politics.

Sinclair's rugged style had nothing in common with Blakeney's cerebral sense of peace, order, and decorum. There were great differences between them, as their first encounters indicated. The Métis were planning to meet in December 1971. Sinclair wrote to Blakeney, saying he expected him and the cabinet to be in Prince Albert to talk about their *New Deal for People* promises. It was on a cabinet day, but Blakeney and several other ministers flew north to attend a rambling question-and-answer session with hundreds of Métis representatives. Sinclair later presented the Premier with a bill for $15,000. The meeting, Sinclair said, had been an expensive one; the government had benefited from talking to the people, so it should pick up most of the costs. Blakeney forwarded the request to Bowerman, who provided $10,000, but told Sinclair not to submit any more surprise invoices. The government would have to devise a more organized method of support for the society.

It was a pattern which was to be repeated, to everyone's frustration. Sinclair, as leader of the Métis, wanted to deal directly with Blakeney, often on short notice. Blakeney was a process man. He did not like impromptu meetings; further, he felt that the Métis should deal with Bowerman, the DNS minister.

The Premier was also piqued when the Métis Society told him a few months later that at the Prince Albert meeting he had promised provincial money for an arena at Ile à la Crosse. Blakeney's aides had taken detailed notes at the meeting so he could respond to requests. The notes backed his contention that he had made no such promise. A sure way for anyone to gain Blakeney's enmity was to call him a liar. After that first meeting, he had note-takers or a tape recorder displayed conspicuously at any meetings he had with Sinclair.

Beyond the question of style, the two men had a continuing philosophical disagreement. The *New Deal for People* had promised northern self-government and full consultation with native people. To Sinclair, that meant a northern government controlled by natives. The northern treaty Indians had their reserve governments, but Sinclair believed that elsewhere the Métis should be in control. He told Blakeney early on that the Métis wanted "to be planners, decision makers, and part of the total operations of their own development." Early in 1972 he asked for $74,000 to hold consultations with northern Métis about the style of government they wanted. Bowerman reluctantly provided $50,000. Sinclair later presented Blakeney with the results of those consultations. Northern government must ensure that the majority, Indians and Métis people, also had the majority of representatives. Local governments should hold the main power, with a northern council to co-ordinate any programs throughout the region. Ted Bowerman rejected the idea, saying that it would divide people in the north along racial lines. Blakeney had never intended to provide more than limited government responsibility to northerners. "Many people," he says, "felt that the running of the department should be turned over to a northern board which would report to the Northern Municipal Council. The public service really shouldn't be interfering with the organization in the north. That couldn't work. Where was the money going to come from? Who was going to account for it? And furthermore, what were the objectives?"

The Métis were a people in search of redress. They were at the stage of angry articulation of their grievances. In many ways, they were worse off than the Indians, who at least had rights enshrined in treaties. In the south, the Métis lived in city slums or in shacks on the edges of white towns. In the north, they believed they still had a chance to win something. "Look what happened to people in Fort Qu'Appelle and Lebret," Sinclair says. "They were pushed off their lands and they're living on welfare. We felt that in the north we still had room for the kind of growth that we needed." The Métis believed they, too, had aboriginal rights, but they could never convince Allan Blakeney. He readily recognized they had problems, but he said they had no claim to aboriginal rights. Sinclair thought that Blakeney could have provided self-government and land for the Métis, and was bitter when it didn't happen. Nor did Blakeney accept native political organizations—the MSS or the Federation of Saskatchewan Indians—as the only voices of their people. He hoped that, progressively, local governments set up in northern towns and villages would play an important role. His view of the limited role for the Métis Society became another source of tension. By September 1972, Sinclair was angrily telling Blakeney that DNS was "building another empire" in the north. Contrary to Blakeney's promises, he said, the native people and the Métis Society were not being consulted about changes.

The Métis infuriated the NDP when Métis activist Ray Jones ran as an Independent in a September 1972 byelection in the northern Athabasca constituency. The seat had been won narrowly by Liberal Allan Guy in the 1971 election, but the NDP had successfully contested the result. In the byelection, Jones collected 400 votes. Guy defeated the NDP candidate by 30 votes, and the NDP believed it would have won if Jones had not been in the race. The cabinet was even more upset to discover that Jones had done some of his campaign travelling on Métis Society money. Davey Steuart rubbed salt in the wound by telling Blakeney that the Liberals had also contributed to the Jones campaign in an attempt to split the NDP vote.

When, in May of 1973, the government appointed a seven-member Northern Municipal Council, it had essentially the powers of a rural municipality, but it had no power to tax. There was virtually no local tax base. Candidates backed by the Métis Society won four of the five seats. The council was never used by DNS as anything more than an advisory group. Most senior bureaucrats ignored it. The Métis believed that it had been set up for failure.

There were plenty of disagreements between the Métis and the government, but the situation was complicated by the volatile politics of the Métis Society itself. Howard Adams was back on the board by 1973, but he wasn't welcome. There was a power struggle between his supporters and Sinclair's. Cabinet was by then providing the Métis Society and the Federation of Saskatchewan Indians each with about $200,000 a year. Adams alleged that Sinclair was pocketing Métis Society money, and he organized a sit-in at MSS offices in Regina in December 1973 to publicize his case. Sinclair deflected the publicity by holding a sit-in of his own—at the Legislative Building, to emphasize Métis grievances.

Sinclair and his followers succeeded in having Adams dumped as a director early in 1974. Adams charged that Sinclair was living in a house trailer purchased by the MSS, and that he had billed the society for a holiday trip which he and his wife took to Mexico. Adams demanded that the government initiate criminal proceedings. The province and the federal Secretary of State began investigations. The Attorney General, Roy Romanow, appointed a provincial review conducted by prosecutor Serge Kujawa. He concluded that there was no basis for criminal charges. The society's bookkeeping was questionable, but not criminal. Sinclair had indeed taken his wife to Mexico, on a trip of dubious value—he said it was to study revolutionary movements there. Kujawa told Romanow that Sinclair and his directors were using society money "in a manner that appears unjustified," but he stopped short of calling it criminal. Adams angrily insisted that the government refused to crack down on Sinclair because it was trying to buy peace.

The Métis Society had to lay off staff early in 1974. Audits done for cabinet showed that in little more than a year the society had run up a deficit greater than its annual $220,000 grant. Cabinet withheld new money while trying to decide what to do. Rod Bishop, a Métis from Green Lake, walked into Blakeney's office one day in May and warned that if the entire amount wasn't forthcoming the Métis would disrupt Blakeney's northern cabinet tour, planned for June. Cabinet didn't blink, and informed Sinclair on June 5th that it would provide money to the Métis Society on a quarterly basis, rather than annually. The following evening the Métis kept their promise, and confronted Blakeney and other ministers in Kitsaki Hall in La Ronge. Sinclair was there as one of Blakeney's attackers.

There were internal rumblings about dumping Sinclair. He had called the MSS annual meeting for early July in Prince Albert, but then postponed it, saying there was no money to hold it. He blamed the government. A dissident group of Sinclair's executive voted to go ahead with the meeting anyway. There was clearly a move to challenge his leadership. He responded by calling for another demonstration against the government. On Dominion Day weekend, the manicured lawns surrounding the Legislature sprouted tents. Blakeney had had it. The Regina police were called to ensure they took precautions to maintain order. Blakeney also wrote a memo to his own file, which became the basis for later public statements: "I think the public are getting fed up with these sit-ins and tent-ins. I've said before and I say again that these types of tactics do not help negotiations between the government and any organization." And in the same personal memo: "Government has received evidence of a number of large accounts of the Métis Society—unpaid for long periods. We will be insisting on full and complete financial disclosure of the financial state of affairs of the Métis Society before we consider turning over any more money to the society." Métis leaders responded by calling Blakeney a racist.

Sinclair called the annual meeting for September. By that time Blakeney had put the hard-nosed Gordon MacMurchy on the case. He announced that the government would now make payments to the society on a monthly basis. At the Prince Albert meeting Sinclair easily won the leadership, and he launched a slashing attack on the government. He accused Blakeney of trying to smash the movement. He threatened violence, saying that Saskatchewan was a "powder keg," and that the Métis could make previous militant Indian demonstrations at Kenora, Ontario and Cache Creek, British Columbia "look like a picnic."

The hot politics of summer ended in a four-hour blowout between Métis and cabinet delegations in a large meeting room at the Legislature in October. The Métis had prepared a brief with a litany of complaints, but it was all but forgotten. The exchange was bruising and extraordinary. Blakeney opened by saying he would make no commitments at the meeting. Any promises would be put in writing to Sinclair later. Sinclair responded by saying, "The government is to the Métis Society as ITT was to Chile. You are trying to undermine us." He said the government was pushing the Métis to violence. Blakeney, no doubt recalling the Kitsaki Hall meeting, asked why the Métis had chosen to "have a confrontation with the government." The Premier took the precaution of having two aides take notes at the meeting. He did not want anyone saying that he had made promises which he hadn't.

Sinclair's tough and confrontational leadership put him and the Métis on a collision course with Blakeney. The Premier's political style was cool, rational, and highly controlled, based on a rigid, almost British sense of decorum. He did not like people who became aggressive with him. Sinclair refused to play by his rules, and that made for conflict. Sinclair admits that his use of confrontation was tactical. "It was the stuff of Saul Alinsky's books," he says. "We read a little bit about Malcom X. I had some meetings with the Black Panthers in the late 60s and early 70s. I had a meeting with Fred Hampton just before he was shot in Chicago."

Blakeney, too, had read Alinsky (a radical community organizer in Chicago), and he had his own theory about what Sinclair was attempting to do. He believed the Métis needed someone to organize against, and he was it, although he's more sanguine about it today than he was when they were revving their chain saws in the Legislative rotunda.

Blakeney's relationship with the Federation of Saskatchewan Indians was much smoother. The responsibility and most of the expense associated with services for treaty Indians rested with Ottawa. The Indians stood fast on their treaty rights, and the federal government was the focus of their discontent. Blakeney also had a much warmer personal relationship with FSI chief David Ahenakew than he had with Jim Sinclair. Ahenakew, a Cree from near Prince Albert, was older. He had spent many years in the Canadian Forces. His most distinguishing feature was his thick, black brush cut. He liked Blakeney from the first: "I have nothing but praise for that guy. He had a grip on his government, and on the economy of Saskatchewan. He never forgot the ordinary person and that is what I see as his greatest achievement. You gotta be pretty damn smart to be a Rhodes Scholar and you got to have feelings in order to be able to deal with ordinary individuals. His wife is just a beautiful lady."

Ahenakew says Blakeney understood that the Indians wanted to maintain their "treaty-trust relationship" with the crown. They wanted no talk of Saskatchewan taking over services to Indian people. Blakeney and Ahenakew decided that the province could help most by helping to pay for FSI research and communications programs. "We agreed," Ahenakew says, "that we were trying to reach not only Indians, but ordinary citizens and educate them about native issues."

Sinclair was difficult to describe in his partisan politics, and seems to have preferred Ross Thatcher to Allan Blakeney as an individual. Politically, the relationship with Ahenakew was more solid. Ahenakew was sympathetic to the NDP—so much so that they tried to get him to run in 1971. He declined. Ahenakew could talk tough at times, but he never led his troops in occupations or blockades. If Ahenakew and the chiefs occupied anything, it was their chairs at the negotiating table.

Northern Saskatchewan is dotted with Indian reserves, but the Indians felt less concerned about DNS than did the Métis. Ahenakew wanted assurances that DNS would not tamper with the reserves. He and the chiefs wanted DNS people to stay away unless they were invited. After some initial indecision, DNS decided to comply. Ahenakew says DNS was an "expensive white elephant," but it got things done. He thinks the Métis were too critical: "Jim Sinclair is a very direct and vocal person. He took on the world, it didn't matter who it was. He slammed the province, but the province did just as much for the Métis as for the Indians—all the housing, the employment, the infrastructure. Those people all of a sudden realized they mattered. The only thing is, people want the sky."

The outstanding issue for Saskatchewan treaty Indians was land entitlements. Some bands never got all of the land promised to them when they signed treaties. Others had received land only to have it stolen from them by unscrupulous operators, some of them Indian Affairs agents. The Indians had been making that allegation all along. The NDP had promised in 1971 that they would support the researching of land entitlements. Once in power they were as good as their word. The province matched $175,000 in federal money to pay for the research. Once completed, it showed that 15 bands had about a million acres coming to them. Responsibility for settling the claims was divided. It was Ottawa's jurisdiction, but Saskatchewan owned the land.

Blakeney moved quickly to search for a solution. By the summer of 1977 Saskatchewan had agreed to supply Crown land, wherever possible, to provide the bands with their entitlements. Most of those possibilities existed in northern Saskatchewan. In the southern agricultural area, the federal government agreed to pay for the purchase of land wherever it was necessary for entitlements to be settled. The accord was formalized in an agreement called the Saskatchewan Formula. Blakeney appointed Ted Bowerman as minister in charge of entitlements.

The process began in hope, but it soon bogged down. Ahenakew says the federal government dragged its feet because it did not want to pay the costs of dislocation to whites using the land (mostly as community pastures). Provincially, the municipalities and interest groups like the Saskatchewan Wildlife Federation began to organize against the transfers. Ahenakew says NDP ministers, including MacMurchy, Blakeney, and Bowerman, did all they could to help: "The farmers and the municipalities got spooked because they thought they were going to lose their tax base. Bowerman went out there and explained everything. He took on the Wildlife Federation and really helped us. But that cost him politically."

The province had hired a young lawyer, Rob Milen, as land entitlements negotiator. Milen had worked in NDP election campaigns, and briefly for the Premier as an assistant. He says Blakeney was committed on land entitlements: "On this issue, he crossed the line from politician to statesman." Some of the other ministers were not nearly as supportive as Blakeney and Bowerman, and Milen later quit in frustration. He served, eventually, as legal counsel for Sinclair and the Métis. His work with both groups allowed him to compare Blakeney's different approaches toward the Indians and the Métis. He thinks Blakeney was a victim of his own logic. "If there was a document like the treaties," he says, "the NDP was prepared to honour that. However, when it came to rights for the Métis, there was no document. So the notion of any special rights for the Métis cut directly across the grain of socialist-egalitarian philosophy. I think

Premier Blakeney had trouble recognizing any rights to self-government for the Métis or for [non-status] Indians." Blakeney believed in limited self-government for Indians because the concept grew from the logic of the treaties. He believed it illogical to say that the Métis, as offspring of white and Indian parents, had any claim to aboriginal rights. Their problems should be addressed through the usual mix of social and economic programs.

The government's DNS strategy changed the face of northern Saskatchewan in ten years. Those changes were obvious when one drove into any of the towns—Ile à la Crosse, La Loche, Buffalo Narrows, Pinehouse, Cumberland House. There were new halls, community centres, arenas, and especially new housing. There were new water and sewer works. There were new schools with locally-elected boards, and a good number of native teachers, in most cases graduates from the specially-designed Northern Teacher Education Program. There were Local Community Authorities, and every northern town had its mayor.

There were brickbats and resistance from many quarters. Blakeney expected them, but on balance he says, "We didn't do all that badly in pacing it. Occasionally we were a little fast, but that's better than a little slow. The lumps came thick and fast, but in five or six years the worst was over."

What DNS did not do was provide an economic base for people to break out of the poverty cycle. Unemployment, and the alcoholism and violent death which accompany it, continued to be starkly serious problems. The traditional industries—trapping and fishing—were in decline. The forest leases were held mainly by big companies, and the NDP did not change that. The companies hired few native northerners. When uranium development beckoned, Blakeney seized on it as a megaproject which he believed would provide the employment which had eluded the north. But by the mid-1970s the NDP had come to a new realization: the most serious problems for native people were not in the north, but in the cities. Blakeney and the NDP belatedly began to tackle the problems of urban poverty and racism.

# Chapter Fourteen

# New Deal '75

More than a year before he expected to call the 1975 election Blakeney called for a report card on the *New Deal for People*. He had also appointed an election strategy committee by mid-March of 1974. It included several of the people who had created the 1971 program—Walter Smishek, Jack Messer, Frank Coburn, Clare Powell. Smishek was to act as chairman, as he had in 1971. It was an experienced, professional team.

As he surveyed the political landscape in 1974, the Premier might have been excused for a certain lightness in his step. Although he was cautious never to be quoted saying it, the universe—in Saskatchewan at least—was unfolding as it should. Suddenly the province had what everybody in the world wanted, and was prepared to buy: wheat, oil, and potash. After a near crop failure, the Soviets had rushed into the international market. China continued to make large purchases. Prices shot up. Realized net farm income—the money farmers actually had in their pockets—had increased by six times since the depths of the farm crisis in 1969. As international grain shortages replaced the glut of the late 1960s, farmers everywhere began to buy fertilizer again. The mountains of stockpiled potash began to move. Sales more than doubled between 1971 and 1974. In October 1973 the Yom Kippur War had precipitated the Arab oil boycott. Within a few months, oil prices shot from $3 to $10 a barrel; between 1974 and 1975 the government's take increased by 50 per cent.

Next Year Country had finally arrived. In 1975 Saskatchewan became a "have" province for the first time. Farmers began to buy luxury cars. Regina and Saskatoon sprouted new restaurants, lounges, and malls with specialty shops. New subdivisions began to grow, with two-storey houses fronted by the wood-stained doors of double garages.

By mid-March the Chief Planning Officer, Gerry Gartner, had delivered his New Deal report. It was upbeat. Many of the NDP promises from 1971 had been kept, and others were in the works. In the countryside the Land Bank was visible, FarmStart had distributed $20 million in loans, and a

Hog Marketing Commission had been established. People liked the new community colleges, particularly in rural Saskatchewan. The government had instituted the Property Improvement Grant, a rebate on home and land taxes. Cities and towns were getting more money with fewer strings attached, and the Community Capital Fund allowed them to do some badly needed rebuilding.

There were new social and health programs: insured dental service for children, reduced costs for hearing aides and eye glasses, two million dollars a year to subsidize day-care. A tax-financed prescription drug program was on the way. An Ombudsman and a human rights commission had been appointed. An Independent Boundaries Commission was redesigning the electoral map.

The first years of Blakeney government qualify as a reform period by any standards. Yet there was much to be done. Promised new services for the mentally ill had not yet materialized. Nor had the government done much to make prisons into places of real rehabilitation. Ambulance services remained to be improved; regional health councils had not been established; promised housing programs and changes to the Landlord-Tenant Act were behind schedule.

The government had not yet staked out any clear ground on foreign ownership in the crucial resource sector, despite the strong nationalist sentiment apparent in the 1971 campaign. Planners were busily designing options with respect to royalties and taxation, but none had been announced; nor had the intentions of the government regarding public ownership.

Although it appeared strong, the economy had some soft spots. Individual farmers were better off, but that was a condition which could change for the worse as quickly as it had changed for the better. Even in good times people continued to leave the farm. Rising land prices were shutting young people out, and the Land Bank was not a big enough program to alter the situation. Farm prosperity masked the weaknesses of communities, and of the small business sector. Planners said bluntly that the improved farm economy had merely slowed the decline of rural businesses. The establishment of secondary industry was going at a much slower pace than the government had hoped. Still, it appeared to be a good record to take to the people.

Blakeney was lucky in those heady years. He had taken office at a time when international events, more than provincial policies, set Saskatchewan on the road to plenty. Agriculture was his announced economic priority, and it had begun to take care of itself. When grain prices took off, in fact, much of the government's investment in diversification came to naught as farmers rushed back into growing wheat which they could sell for $6 a bushel.

Blakeney had also come to office with high hopes of developing processing and secondary industry beyond the farm gate. Successive Douglas governments had entertained similar hopes, with limited success. Blakeney was determined to create industrial diversification. Early in 1972 he told the *Saskatchewan Business Journal* that he thought the province's future lay not so much in resource development as in the "processing of raw materials," and "the manufacturing of goods through secondary industries for the prairie market." His predictions about the relative importance of industry compared to resource development turned out to be wrong. Saskatchewan was trapped in a continuing role as a supplier of raw materials and a purchaser of manufactured products. People often said, with grim humour, that the province's most precious export was its people, driven to look for jobs and security elsewhere. Blakeney wanted to change that by creating jobs and wealth at home. His strategy was first to diversify agriculture, and then to build food processing plants on that farm base. He also wanted to create secondary manufacturing. Finally, he wanted to add value to non-renewable resources, such as crude oil, by processing them in the province.

The government had some limited success with food processing projects. A malting plant was built with government assistance at Biggar. The Saskatchewan Wheat Pool built a plant in Saskatoon for crushing rapeseed into oil and meal. Moose Jaw got a meat packing plant. The government's instrument in these projects was the Saskatchewan Economic Development Corporation (SEDCO); its method was a combination of grants, loans, and loan guarantees, often in exchange for a percentage of equity ownership. The government purchased a 45 per cent interest in Intercontinental Packers from Fred Mendel in Saskatoon in 1972 when it appeared he was preparing to sell to out-of-province private interests. The meat packing industry in western Canada had been consolidating, and Blakeney did not want to lose another Saskatchewan firm. Within a few years he had sold the plant back to the Mendel family. Other, odd ideas—a noodle factory in the southern town of Mossbank, for example—never happened.

The government also had some success in supporting the manufacture of short-line farm implements—stone pickers, rod weeders, cultivators, sprayers, and truck boxes. Small companies got going in such unlikely places as Vonda, Englefeld, and Frontier. The government's equity involvement in expanding the IPSCO mill in Regina provided the steel needed for manufacturing farm equipment. Blakeney came under fire from labour and the left for using SEDCO to support the most prosperous of the small equipment companies, Morris Rod Weeder of Yorkton, which was the site of some bitter strikes, and strike-breaking.

Plans for heavy manufacturing were generally a bust. An announced Rumanian tractor assembly plant became an embarrassment. When the provincial government began negotiations with a Rumanian state company, there was a fierce argument over whether the plant should go to Moose Jaw or Saskatoon. Negotiations between the Rumanians and Saskatchewan officials went nowhere, and nobody got the plant. After that, plans weren't announced until they were more certain. There were also talks about the government taking an equity position in a tractor plant built by Co-op Implements of Winnipeg. That didn't happen, either. Neither did the Daimler-Benz truck plant, a heavy water plant, or a textiles development project.

Blakeney had entered office suspicious of resource megaprojects. Pulp mills and potash mines in Saskatchewan usually involved the government coughing up cash or guaranteeing loans, and later receiving ridiculously low royalties. It was expensive, and it didn't provide many jobs. Early in his mandate Blakeney had shelved two Thatcher projects—a pulp mill at Dore Lake, and a Choiceland iron mine whose economics looked marginal. Yet it was resource megaprojects, albeit with a new and decidedly NDP twist, which became the centrepiece of Blakeney's economic development strategy.

There was a sentiment in cabinet, expressed most strongly by Gordon MacMurchy, that centres outside Regina and Saskatoon didn't get their share of industry; the government should attempt to funnel development into those communities. That coincided with NDP election promises to improve life in smaller towns. But here, too, the government, although it eventually claimed some limited successes, was not able to revitalize small-town Saskatchewan through industrial development. In some ways rural Saskatchewan was like the north: the government could make life more pleasant by building houses and apartments, hockey arenas, sidewalks, and water and sewer lines, but it could not attract development for a new economic base. The provincial population continued to decline, albeit more slowly than it had in the late 1960s.

The development thrust would have to be in raw resources, with minimal refining. By 1972, the government was struggling with policy. Its overriding principle was a determination to collect more in royalties and taxes. There was also a clear sense that the province had to assert more control over the very conditions of resource development. Cabinet was spurred into action by the shutdown in the early 1970s of most of the private oil refineries in Regina, Saskatoon, and Moose Jaw. A report from the planning and research people raised other questions. What had to be decided, the planners told cabinet, was to what extent the province wanted to control its own development: "Saskatchewan will have to deal differently with economic issues and relationships, and with the dictates of power centres and of technology, than the North American norms." The government would have to take a more active role than was common. In the oil industry, the planners provided cabinet with a range of alternatives, ranging from traditional regulatory measures to outright nationalization.

By late 1973, the Arab oil embargo had lent a greater sense of urgency to government planning. Blakeney devoted a cabinet meeting to a "stock-taking" of what they were committed to doing in oil, gas, timber, potash, steel, and small business. They decided that it was time to up the public ante in the oil industry. The government moved to tax windfall profits away from the companies, a move which resulted in a protracted court battle. Cabinet also opted for equity by creating Sask Oil, an integrated crown corporation. The government saw the company as a window on the industry, but also as an assured source of supply for an enlarged Co-operative Refinery in Regina.

Discussion around specific cases as they arose—in oil, then potash and uranium—led to a provincial resources policy which, in turn, resulted in a broader industrial strategy. Projects would be assessed on the basis of "significant benefit"—how they aided economic stability and diversification, which included the consideration of establishing plants in smaller centres. The government decided to welcome foreign investment in the manufacturing sector, but to limit it in energy and in primary renewable resources, including farming and forestry. Blakeney was interested in joint ventures in non-renewable resources, which might include oil, potash, or uranium. He even went to France and Germany looking for partners for uranium development in northern Saskatchewan.

Blakeney's own ideas about a mixed economy were summed up in a comment to Saskatchewan Wheat Pool President Ted Turner during a cabinet consultation: "The greater the extent to which a project moves away from resource development and toward secondary industry, the less the government wishes to become involved." In the Blakeney governments after 1971 there was little talk, as there had been at the 1969 and 70 party conventions, of nationalizing the food processing or farm machinery industries. When there was stiff competition, and marketing made the difference, Blakeney didn't think the government would do well. In resource industries, where marketing was a less sophisticated operation, he held quite a different view. His opinions were grounded in his experience as a civil servant and minister in the Douglas governments, but they had to be applied to the volatile conditions of the 1970s. He made some bold and determined moves—moves made possible by an improved income, which allowed the government to move into the economy while consolidating social programs.

Armed with his New Deal report card, Blakeney began in the spring of 1974 to plan for the election he wanted to call the following year. His wish list, presented to an evening cabinet discussion in March, included an improved telephone system, particularly in rural areas; new grid roads and bridges; universal sickness and accident insurance; a Saskatchewan

Bertha and John Blakeney at their home in Bridgewater, Nova Scotia in the early 1950s. John, a soldier injured in the First World War, met Bertha, a nurse, in a London hospital ward. They were married in 1919.                                                                    —Blakeney Family Album

Allan graduates with a BA from Dalhousie in 1945. An energetic student involved in debating, the students' council, the yearbook, and the CCF, in 1947 he received Dalhousie's gold medal in law and a Rhodes Scholarship.

—Blakeney Family Album

*Allan met Molly Schwartz at Dalhousie. By 1947 they were going steady, and they were married in Halifax in September 1950. They had two children: Barbara and Hugh.*
—Blakeney Family Album

*Allan helps Barbara skate near their home in Regina's Lakeview neighbourhood in 1959. The Blakeneys joined several other families in a co-operative and built their own home in the early 1950s.*
—Blakeney Family Album

*Anne Gorham, c. 1959. Anne, a school-mate and close friend of Molly's, had remained in contact with her. Molly died suddenly in 1957, and six months later, Allan and Anne began their courtship. They were married in May 1959.*
—Blakeney Family Album

*Blakeney, the Provincial Treasurer at age 36, prepares to deliver his first budget. After his election in 1960, he was immediately appointed to the Douglas cabinet.*
—Saskatchewan NDP Collection

*Woodrow Lloyd, Education Minister from 1944
to 1960, became premier after Douglas left to
lead the federal NDP in 1961. Lloyd appointed
Blakeney Treasurer and, later, deputy leader.*
—SAB, R–A22815, Copyright West's Studio
Collection

*Clarence Fines, Saskatchewan's Treasurer from
1944 to 1960, was a crack administrator and
Blakeney's political mentor. Known for his
balanced budgets and his bowties, Fines believed
Blakeney could succeed him.*
—SAB Photo Art Collection, 55–1J, Copyright
West's Studio Collection

*Ross Thatcher bolted the CCF to lead the Sas-
katchewan Liberals. A blunt-spoken, right-wing
populist, he forged a free-enterprise coalition and
won the 1964 and 1967 elections.*
—SAB, R–A8359, Copyright West's Studio
Collection

*Dave Steuart, Thatcher's deputy leader and Treas-
urer, was known for his fiery political oratory and
quick sense of humour. He admits that he never
allowed facts to get in the way of a good speech.*
—Saskatchewan NDP Collection

*Demonstrators at a Keep Our Doctors rally in 1962 demand that legislation introducing medicare be withdrawn. Throughout the heated controversy, Blakeney was a key government strategist and negotiator and, later, Health Minister.* —SAB, R–A12109 (4)

*A pause during voting at the July 1970 NDP leadership convention. Blakeney, Roy Romanow, George Taylor, and Waffle candidate Don Mitchell all ran. Blakeney won on the third ballot.*
—*Briarpatch* Photo

*Blakeney gives the V for Victory on election night in June 1971. A slashing attack on Liberal agricultural policies and the NDP's alternative* New Deal for People *program gave Blakeney a landslide victory.*
*—Leader Post* Photo, Doug Dicken

*Anne and the children (Hugh and Barbara, the older children; David and Margaret, the younger) leave home for ceremonies to install the cabinet on June 30, 1971. In 1969, Blakeney had moved into his Regina Elphinstone constituency. He said if he was going to represent the area, he was also going to live there.*

—Blakeney Family Album

*Blakeney and his cabinet are sworn in. Blakeney and Anne are centre left. To the right are new ministers Romanow, Messer, Smishek, and Wood. To the left and rear (behind Anne, right to left) are Snyder, Bowerman, Byers, and MacMurchy.* —SAB Photo Art Collection, 71-508-42

*Blakeney held open news conferences each Wednesday morning. He usually sipped tea with lemon and answered reporters' questions with an astonishing amount of detail.* —*Briarpatch* Photo

*Blakeney accompanies her Majesty Queen Elizabeth II on a walkabout during a Royal Visit in 1973. He developed a fondness and respect for British institutions while at Oxford.*
—Blakeney Family Album

*Blakeney had a stormy relationship with the Métis Society and its leader Jim Sinclair. Métis activists erected tents in front of the Legislative Building in 1974 to protest the government cutting off grants to their association.*
—*Briarpatch* Photo

*Dick Collver, an Alberta business consultant, revived the Conservatives for the 1975 election campaign, replacing the Liberals as the free-enterprise alternative to the NDP. He was a brilliant organizer, but an erratic leader.*
—*Briarpatch* Photo

*Blakeney signs the writ for the 1975 election. He is accompanied by ministers Jack Messer (left) and John Kowalchuk (right). In the back row (left to right) are Gordon Snyder, Neil Byers, Walter Smishek, Eiling Kramer, and Gordon MacMurchy.* —SAB, R–B11538(1)

*Trade union demonstrators in the rotunda at the Legislative Building in October 1976 protest against wage and price controls. Blakeney criticized the Trudeau program but imposed a controversial provincial program.* —SAB, R–B11501, Copyright Richard Gustin

*Blakeney and Anne in China to sell Saskatchewan potash in 1976. A bitter tax feud between the potash companies and the provincial government resulted in Blakeney nationalizing half of the Saskatchewan-based production in 1975.* —Blakeney Family Album

*Blakeney and Elwood Cowley. Cowley, a former teacher, became a key minister and, in 1975, was a central figure in the potash takeover. He also plotted political strategy and planned election campaigns.* —SAB, R–B12047

*People in Regina protest the government's uranium policy. Blakeney believed Saskatchewan's rich uranium deposits would pay for social programs and provide needed energy to other countries, but he was accused of being insensitive to environmental and peace concerns.* —Briarpatch Photo

*Blakeney and his ministers in 1978. Front row (left to right): Gordon Snyder, Walter Smishek, Jack Messer, Roy Romanow, Blakeney, Norm Vickars, Don Faris, Ned Shillington. Back row (second from left) Eiling Kramer, Ed Tchorzewski, Neil Byers, Elwood Cowley, Gordon MacMurchy, Adolph Matsalla, Ted Bowerman, Herman Rolfes, Edgar Kaeding, Ed Whelan, Wes Robbins. The men in the right and left rear are unidentified officials.* —SAB, R–A23260(1)

*Blakeney and Douglas at the 1981 opening of Tommy Douglas House in Regina. Douglas had encouraged Blakeney to run for office in 1960. Delaine Scotton, the provincial party president, stands behind them.*
—Blakeney Family Album

*Blakeney, flanked by Roy Romanow, speaks at the constitutional talks in Ottawa in November 1981. Howard Leeson, the Deputy Minister of Inter-Governmental Affairs, sits at centre rear.*
—SAB, R–A22496(4)

*Blakeney, Ontario's Bill Davis, and Trudeau confer at the constitutional talks. A compromise agreement was put together in haste by Romanow, Jean Chretien, and Roy McMurtry and was agreed to by all governments except Quebec.* —SAB, R–A22508(3)

*Within five months of his constitutional heroics, Blakeney was buried by Grant Devine and the Conservatives in the April 1982 provincial election. Devine inherited a balanced budget, but has produced nine consecutive deficits.*
—Leader Post, Pat Pettit

*Blakeney is applauded during the 1983 federal NDP convention in Regina. Beside Blakeney are Tony Penikett, Gerry Caplan, Delaine Scotton, and Ed Broadbent.*
—Blakeney Family Album, Copyright Photo Features Ltd.

*Blakeney announces his intention in August 1987 to quit as leader. The NDP had won more votes, but fewer seats, than the Conservatives in the 1986 election. Roy Romanow succeeded him.*
—Leader Post, Roy Antal

*Blakeney has had more time for his family since leaving politics. Seated in front of his Ottawa home are Hugh (right) with his daughter Victoria, Barbara, and David, with Margaret in the foreground.*
—Blakeney Family Album

*Blakeney pruning trees at the family cottage. While he spends summers in and near Regina, he's been a lecturer in law and public administration at Osgoode Hall in Toronto, and at the University of Saskatchewan.*
—Blakeney Family Album

Pension Plan; a push on urban recreation facilities and housing; and some assurance that the products of crown corporations—forest products, for instance—would be reserved for use in Saskatchewan, a tangible benefit of public ownership. The concerns of some other ministers included programs to provide for the lack of professional services, such as doctors and dentists, in rural areas. Blakeney's notes for that evening include a handwritten instruction to Wes Bolstad: "Cabinet, or a cabinet committee, should also consider in some way the results of the party's policy seminars." That appears to provide limited input for the party into election policy, and supports Walter Smishek's contention that the party had become less important in the political process. Cabinet, not the party, was clearly taking the lead in deciding the NDP's electoral priorities.

By September, the themes were emerging. One was to improve the quality of life in rural Saskatchewan. "We viewed one of the deficient areas in Saskatchewan to be the level of municipal services," Blakeney says. "We wanted better roads, sidewalks, and streets. We wanted to see some new swimming pools and rinks, that sort of thing. The municipalities didn't have that kind of money." A second, important theme centred on what kind of economic growth the province should pursue. That list included greater government participation in resource development; major initiatives in the processing of agricultural, forest, and mineral products; and improved services to small business. It was a move away from the 1971 emphasis on agriculture. "By 1975," Blakeney says, "we felt that we'd given our farm programs time to work. In any case, the stress wasn't there by 1975 and we had some other priorities."

The government had not yet decided how to proceed on resource policy, but it had begun to develop the principles. A number of important decisions were taken at a cabinet planning conference in November 1974. Cabinet wanted to look at acquiring control of the province's uranium resources (the richest finds had not yet occurred). They also decided to open negotiations with Eldorado Nuclear Limited for a uranium refinery which would process yellowcake into uranium hexafluoride. The government wanted eventually to go a step further and produce enriched uranium in Saskatchewan for use in Canadian and foreign nuclear reactors. Cabinet also agreed that day to involve the government more aggressively in plans to bring the potash industry into full public ownership. Finally, they determined to take advantage of any opportunities which might arise in the oil refining industry, a move which led to government participation in the expanded Co-op Refinery and heavy oil upgrader in Regina. It was also the Blakeney government which began negotiations for the heavy oil upgrader in Lloydminster, a project which has often been announced, but never been built.

The 1975 election platform was carefully crafted to include resource policies in a general sense, allowing the government to say later that people had voted for those policies. The province's attempts to tax windfall oil profits, and its emerging commitment to public ventures, put it on a collision course with Ottawa. The federal government wanted a greater share of burgeoning resource revenues, too. Trudeau had also concluded, for reasons ranging from crass politics to statesmanship, that the pendulum had swung too far in the direction of provincial rights. He was going to redress the balance. Tensions were growing before 1975, but they did not come to a head until after the election.

Although the NDP had won handily in 1971, there was a good deal of flux at the party office. The NDP had a problem with losing appointed secretaries to elected office. Don Faris, Party Secretary from 1971, was now in the Legislature. His replacement had stayed in the job for only a short time. Bill Allen, Party Secretary in 1974, was also planning to run for the Legislature in the safe Regina Rosemont seat.

Bill Knight, a casualty of the federal election of July 1974, had a call from Blakeney on the morning following his defeat. The NDP needed someone to co-ordinate the next provincial campaign, then move into the Provincial Secretary's job. Did Knight want it? Blonde, chubby-cheeked, and beaming, Knight's good humour disguises a shrewdness which is both innate and practised. Depending on who you ask, he is either a prince of a man, or not to be trusted. After some days to think it through, he accepted. He served as Party Secretary until 1979 when he, too, left the job to run (unsuccessfully) in the federal Assiniboia seat. After that he moved into Blakeney's office as a senior political advisor. In both roles he developed a reputation as the Premier's political fixer.

When Knight moved into the office in 1974, he did not like what he saw. The party and caucus were complacent. There was a lack of organization. The NDP had not adjusted to changing technology. "We still thought we were running a door-to-door campaign, grassroots based, with little television," Knight says. It wasn't easy to convince campaigners that the town hall meetings and the four-canvass campaign which had worked well in 1971 might need changing. The NDP's polling techniques remained rudimentary, and the party resisted adapting to television.

Blakeney faced an opposition in transition. Ross Thatcher had died within a month of the 1971 election. His personalist style had kept a lid on the aspirations of any young pretenders, and the leadership fell to 55-year-old Davey Steuart. He had been the Premier's loyal deputy, but was, in fact, a year older than Thatcher. The image he tried to project, of a leader with new and dynamic ideas, suffered from his long association with Thatcher. As the Liberals struggled, the Conservatives reappeared in the person of Dick Collver. The Tories had been moribund since their brief, disastrous tryst with power in the 1930s. Collver was a stout, blonde-haired Saskatoon management consultant, and his efforts appeared at first to be another of those earnest but hopeless attempts at political resurrection. The party had fielded only 16 candidates and won a mere two per cent of the vote in 1971. But Collver's skill lay in organization. He surprised everyone in 1975 by putting together a full slate of 61 candidates.

The NDP had a problem on the issues; no single one dominated. There was a spate of new programs, many of them in their early stages. There were emerging resource plans, but they weren't ready to be publicized. The Potash Corporation of Saskatchewan had been established early in 1975. Cabinet intended that PCS would build a new mine at Bredenbury, near Yorkton, but Blakeney did not want to give the Liberals another socialist, Big Government issue, so he refused to make any announcements.

The Liberals, however, had chosen their issues. Steuart homed in on the Land Bank. The NDP, he said, wanted to take over farm land and introduce tenant farming. The Liberals promised to scrap the Land Bank and replace it with guaranteed loans and subsidized interest rates to help farmers buy land. Steuart also took aim at crown-owned Sask Oil, and Bill 42, Blakeney's new tax on the oil industry. The Liberals would develop oil and other resources through co-operation with the private sector, not through government intervention.

Early in May, Queen's Bench Justice D. C. Disberry delivered a court ruling against the government in a potash case. In the 1960s, when an oversupply of potash was driving prices down, Ross Thatcher had set a floor price and established production quotas. He did it under duress from the Americans, whose industry, centred in New Mexico, could not compete with the new mines in Saskatchewan. American politicians were threatening to launch actions against Saskatchewan for "dumping" potash into their market. Thatcher wanted to prevent that, and agreed to impose a floor price and limit Saskatchewan production. Woodrow Lloyd responded witheringly that it was not Saskatchewan's role to make the world safe for American potash. The NDP had called it yet another Liberal sell-out to the Americans, and campaigned vigorously against it in the 1971 election.

The industry had co-operated with Thatcher's plan. In fact, there were allegations that some of the companies wrote the script. The NDP had been contemptuous, but after the election Blakeney did an about-face. He supported the cartel arrangement, which both the industry and governments described as pro-rationing. Central Canada Potash, a joint venture of the Canadian-owned Noranda company and a farmers' co-operative in the mid-western States, took Blakeney to court. The company believed it was being hurt because it was being forced to share its captive United States market with its competitors. Central Canada Potash said the government's pro-rationing was unconstitutional because provinces had no jurisdiction over international trade.

By 1975 the mines were operating at full capacity. Prices had risen and markets were plentiful, so there was no longer any need for the cartel.

The constitutional point, however, remained. The federal government had taken the unusual step of intervening on behalf of the company before the courts. As the resource battles between Ottawa and the western provinces heated up, the potash ruling was seen as important in deciding who had what power to regulate provincial resources. Disberry said that inter-provincial and international trade belonged to Ottawa. Saskatchewan's legislation attempted to interfere in that jurisdiction, and was therefore unconstitutional.

The ruling arrived on May 7th. Six days later Blakeney called the election. The NDP themes were the improvement of life in rural Saskatchewan, and diversification of the economy through resource development. The court ruling allowed Blakeney to put extra emphasis on running against Ottawa. He called for a "mandate to protect our resources," and suggested that a vote for the Liberals would be seen as supporting Ottawa in the resource dispute. He also used the perennial issue of rail line abandonment, saying that only the NDP would fight Ottawa on its plans to get rid of branch lines which farmers needed if their country elevators were to remain open.

The Blakeney Bus rolled along gravel roads and through small hamlets for six days a week, just as it had in 1971. But the campaign did not go well. The initial confidence of NDP candidates turned to fear. The government campaigned on its record and on general issues—quality of life, economic diversification. But Steuart undercut Blakeney in his campaign against Ottawa. The Liberals had introduced pro-rationing, the NDP had continued it, and Steuart promised that, as Premier, he would appeal the Queen's Bench ruling. And both Steuart and Collver said they, too, would oppose rail line abandonment. The Liberals' vigorous campaign against the Land Bank struck a nerve. NDP candidates did not want to talk about it, but they had no choice. The issue was raised everywhere. The Liberals alleged the government was bent on the communistic control of land and the enslavement of farmers. They also charged there was political favouritism in the Land Bank's dispensing of land. Day after day NDP candidates called in to head office for advice on how to respond to the attacks.

The Liberals fought a hard-nosed, fear-mongering campaign. The NDP began to respond in kind. Collver and the Conservatives played a different game. Collver clucked disapprovingly and said that he would take the nastiness and confrontation out of politics. He posited himself as a sane and reasonable alternative. He proposed a Saskatchewan Investment Opportunities Corporation as an alternative to crown corporations for developing natural resources. The assets of all Saskatchewan crown corporations would be transferred to the new company. Citizens would be able to buy shares, and 70 per cent of those shares would, by law, have to be held by Saskatchewan residents. All the shares would be guaranteed by the government, and all board members of the corporation would be Saskatchewan residents.

Dave Steuart knew the future of his party was on the line, and he used every trick—of elbow and knee, of passion and ridicule—he had learned over the years. During his final rally at Regina's Centre of the Arts, he was in full oratorical flight when he was told there was a bomb in the building. "I'm the bomb!" Steuart shouted. "When I explode the NDP will be gone!"

The NDP weren't gone after June 11th, but they were chastened. They lost six seats, three belonging to cabinet ministers, and tumbled 15 percentage points in their popular vote from 1971. The Liberals went down 11 per cent, although they retained the same number of seats. The big winners were the Conservatives, whose vote rose from 2 to 28 per cent. They elected seven members. The Tories took votes from the Liberals, but also from the NDP. Something had changed in Saskatchewan politics. Both the Liberals and the NDP heard the tread of heavy footsteps behind them.

In the mental little black book he keeps for scoring elections, Blakeney marks 1975 as a negative. The NDP vote in 1971 had been unusually high because of Ross Thatcher's unpopularity. Blakeney hadn't expected to hold all of that. He had made some enemies—druggists and dentists, among others—who did not like the new programs in their areas. The NDP had no "over-arching theme." The government was hurt by the campaign against the Land Bank. Its image as landlord wasn't helped by the fact that the land it bought at low prices in 1971 had appreciated, producing a tidy capital gain by 1975.

The Liberals had not been able to reorganize sufficiently, and were hurt by their lack of new candidates. They also suffered because of the growing unpopularity of Pierre Trudeau. Blakeney says the Liberals ran a "very negative campaign" against the NDP, which hurt both parties. "The Conservatives were just around saying, if you don't want to vote NDP and you don't want to vote for Trudeau, here we are. So, they did exceedingly well because they really exploited all of the opposition to us."

Blakeney took two lessons from what was for him a disappointing election. First, he should slow the pace of introducing government programs. Second, given the unpopularity of Pierre Trudeau, he would never refuse an excuse to squabble with him. The growing rifts over resources and the constitution made that an easy decision. It was to become a habit.

# Chapter Fifteen

# Potash

There was an abnormal amount of activity in the basement of the Legislative Building throughout the sun-short days of autumn, 1975. Public Works carpenters had just finished tearing down dividing walls between a number of cubbyholes in Room 43. Without explanation, they were told to put them back up. No nameplates were posted on the doors. The telephones weren't listed in any directory. There was movement in and out of the room at all hours of the day and night, although it was camouflaged carefully. Each of the men working there had his own separate keys to the building so that he could come and go without having to encounter the commissionaire. They chose not to arrive or to leave in groups. They avoided sitting together in the cafeteria.

They appeared to be going about their civil service and planning jobs as usual. But all could not be hidden. Their colleagues recognized the palpable air of excitement, and knew something extraordinary was happening. For that reason an elaborate cover story was created. The government, it was said, believed that Prime Minister Trudeau would soon act unilaterally to impose wage and price controls. A special task force had been drafted from various departments to plot Saskatchewan's response.

Now and then the Finance Minister, Elwood Cowley, would poke his head out of his office across the hall; if the coast was clear, he would shuffle quickly across to Room 43. Allan Blakeney would arrive with studied casualness, then dart through the unmarked door. The mystery team began to call it The Bunker. Inside, they were working on the "Hot Option." The stakes were Saskatchewan's billion-dollar potash industry; the "hot option" was to take over some or all of it. Blakeney was the only one who knew, finally, if that option would be played out. This was one hand he was keeping close to his vest.

The progress of potash policy after 1971 illustrates how Allan Blakeney ran a government. Initially he was cautious, and there wasn't much change.

136

His manner of arriving at policy was complex and bureaucratic, and placed great emphasis on cabinet considering a range of options. He always built in escape routes in case any one choice backfired. He asked for options from the departments, but also from his own group of planners.

The reddish salt known as potash (potassium chloride) was first discovered in Saskatchewan in 1942 during a search for oil. The province was found eventually to have the largest known reserves in the world. The Douglas government gave consideration in the late 1940s to developing the resource publicly, but decided against it. It would have been expensive and risky. The reserves were rich and plentiful, but they were also deep in the earth. Many early, private attempts to mine them had ended in expensive failures.

The Potash Company of America (PCA) went into production near Saskatoon in 1958, although not without flooding problems. At the urging of then Mineral Resources Minister, John H. Brockelbank, cabinet set minimal royalty fees through 1977 in return for the risks PCA was taking. The CCF government was negotiating for new mines, but they didn't arrive until Ross Thatcher's reign. Naturally, he took credit for them. He also extended the low royalty schedule to all companies through 1981. The 10 Saskatchewan mines were owned by a dozen companies, most of them American. They included international heavyweights such as International Minerals and Chemicals, Hudson Bay Mining and Smelting, Pennzoil, Canadian Pacific, Noranda, PPG Industries, and Swift Canadian.

Rash expansion drove the prices down during the farm recession of the late 1960s, and Thatcher chose to co-operate in creating a cartel which set prices and limited production. Blakeney could accept the policy which had been in place since the 1950s, he could dramatically alter it, or he could follow an intermediate policy. He was not lacking for advice. He and his first Minister of Mineral Resources, Ted Bowerman, had a steady stream of potash executives pass through their offices in the summer and fall of 1971. There was no doubt that the companies wanted to maintain the price-fixing arrangement.

On July 21, 1971, W. P. Morris, President of Pennzoil's Duval Corporation of Canada, wrote to Bowerman, and copied the letter to Blakeney. Morris did not want to see an outbreak of competition. "It is the strong conviction of Duval Corporation of Canada," he wrote, "that potash prorationing and floor price control by the government of Saskatchewan should be maintained until such time as the natural economic forces of supply and demand can operate to perform the function of maintaining a viable industry. . . ." The bureaucracy in Mineral Resources could be counted on to take the industry's case to cabinet. Bowerman was soon won over, and he recommended that cabinet retain the plan with no major changes. That meant production quotas, layoffs, idle mines, and a floor price of $34 a ton. Blakeney didn't like it, but he had no alternative policy: in the face of American hostility, Thatcher's plan didn't look so wimpish after all. The difference between the two men was that Thatcher had only one policy: accommodation to the industry. Blakeney began to spin a spider's web of options. As Bowerman was preparing for his first big meeting with the industry, Blakeney wrote him a memo effectively dictating the province's position. They would offer to keep prorationing as the industry wanted. In return, the government would raise the royalties, and charge a fee for administering the prorationing program. It was really a thinly disguised tax. Dutifully, Bowerman made exactly that demand. After the December meeting, he issued a statement saying that the government was not only aware of the benefits of prorationing, but intended to make it work even better. It was a move designed to return more money to the province, but also to buy time while the government developed a new policy.

Bowerman was busy as minister for the new Department of Northern Saskatchewan. Early in 1972, Blakeney relieved him of Mineral Resources, and named as his successor Kim Thorson, a conservative Estevan lawyer. Thorson, too, was soon extolling the benefits of prorationing. But a complication had arisen. The potash producers accused one of their number—IMC—of breaking ranks and selling potash below the imposed floor price. IMC vigorously denied it, but the fracas led to a new demand from the companies: they wanted the government to base the prorationing quotas on the production of the mines rather than on their markets. Production was much easier to measure. Thorson did it, but his regulations worked to the detriment of one mine. The Central Canada Potash Company was owned jointly by Noranda Mines, a Canadian company, and by CF Industries of Chicago. CF was a fertilizer company, owned in turn by 20 regional farm co-operatives in the United States and Ontario. Central Canada Potash had its own assured American market with those farmers. Prorationing was essentially a cartel arrangement which raised prices, forcing them to pay for the industry's over-expansion.

Blakeney was aware of the problem, but he thought the companies would find some informal way to sort it out. He was wrong. Central Canada Potash went to court in July 1972, asking for a quota which would allow it to fulfill its contracts. While the cases and appeals were being heard, the company kept producing in excess of its quota. They lost the first court round. When the province threatened to suspend their licences if they maintained production, they laid off 120 workers. Then in December 1972, Central Canada Potash launched a constitutional court case which argued that Saskatchewan's Potash Conservation Regulations interfered with international trade, which was a federal jurisdiction. Saskatchewan attempted, in an ultimately unconvincing legal argument, to defend the quotas in the name of conserving a resource. Much to Blakeney's annoyance, Ottawa joined in the suit against Saskatchewan. He interpreted that as a declaration of constitutional war: "It signalled that the federal government was going to battle the western provinces for control of our resources, and that we had better sharpen our swords."

Late in 1972 the NDP was still pursuing what it had described as a contemptible Liberal potash policy, and it had provoked a lawsuit. Blakeney was thinking ahead, but he had not moved. In his November convention speech, he talked about some of the policy options open to the government, ranging from relying on private development, through joint ventures, to public control. He was thinking aloud for the party's benefit, and being surprisingly candid. He admitted that the government was working on its development strategy, one which assumed a role for public ownership.

Blakeney had already made the first decisive moves along a road which would lead to public ownership. Earlier he had hired Hubert Prefontaine to lead Executive Council's Planning and Research group. Then, shortly after the federal election in October 1972, he called John Burton, a defeated Saskatchewan MP. Blakeney had known Burton professionally and socially for 20 years, and trusted him. He asked him to join the planning group, and to lead a special potash task force.

Blakeney dispatched Prefontaine to break the news to the minister, Kim Thorson, who was not amused. Prefontaine reported in a memo on December 18th: "I told Thorson that Burton and I could get together with them and study the work done to date, especially by the Nathan people [Washington consultants who had advised against a significant government role]. Mr. Thorson indicated that he was not interested in such a meeting, that he had other pressing matters to attend to, that he was unaware of the Planning Committee's activities or interests regarding potash, and that he had this question independently under consideration. He was quite short."

Blakeney's use of special planners to complement departmental advice was another of his trademarks. Throughout the early months of 1973 his planners were at work, while Thorson ran a group of his own. Both were churning out policy alternatives, and they didn't agree. Thorson wondered why the "central government" was so interested in potash, an interest which he saw as circumventing his department. The differences continued through the summer. The bureaucrats from Mineral Resources wanted private capital, or some joint ventures at most. Burton criticized the department for its timidity, and pushed for greater public ownership. In September, Blakeney intervened. He wanted cabinet to engage in "stock-taking" on a number of big projects, and potash headed the list. He also wanted more than bickering between the planners and Mineral Resources. He instructed them to work together on a document.

By October the new head of Planning and Research, Gerry Gartner, reported that his office was working on a paper which assumed that all further policy "should be based upon the premise that the objective of government policy is public ownership and control of the potash industry." Gartner was also recommending a Machiavellian policy: "If the government is planning to negotiate purchases, it should begin to make potash mines less profitable through royalties and taxes."

Blakeney says now that these were only the options, and he stresses the differences between options and final policies. He always wanted a cafeteria of choices. In 1973, cabinet didn't know where it would go on potash. Blakeney was leaning toward future joint ventures with the industry. "The United States government and business community were not favourably disposed toward publicly-owned corporations. They might find ways to retaliate against us. Much of this could be mitigated by joint ventures. We could still get profits and influence the way the industry developed."

Late in December, Blakeney moved Thorson to Industry and placed Elwood Cowley in Mineral Resources. Cowley was imaginative and tough, and more likely to impose his will on the department. He moved quickly on several fronts. He created a Potash Production, Planning, and Development Division. He wanted more tax money from the industry, and a firm government policy on ownership. By April 1974, he informed the industry there would be another tax—a potash reserves tax. He also indicated officially that the government wanted to become involved as a joint venture partner in any new mines. The government might also build a mine of its own.

The industry was not pleased, but their relationship became even worse after May 1974. John Turner, the federal Finance Minister, included in his budget an income tax amendment which eliminated provincial royalties (including the potash reserve tax) as allowable tax deductions for companies. Turner's move was part of the constitutional power play between the federal government and the provinces over who should benefit from the rapidly rising resource prices. Blakeney considered this the second shot across the bow. The first had been Ottawa's intervention in the Central Canada Potash suit against provincial prorationing.

Turner's budget had an important effect on Blakeney's strategic thinking. They were in court over a tax, and they might lose. If the province owned the mines the tax issue would disappear, because crown corporations did not have to pay federal taxes. Blakeney maintained a keen interest in constitutional matters. He had received a legal opinion in 1972 which had suggested just such a possibility.

Cowley introduced the reserve tax in October 1974, and the industry reacted angrily. Potash executives said that combined federal and provincial taxation would slash their after tax returns to three per cent. Cowley said he might revise the tax if the industry could convince him of the hardship. He wanted to see their books. They refused. Blakeney met with industry leaders early in 1975, but claims he was stonewalled. The companies announced in the spring that they would not only refuse to provide the financial information Blakeney wanted; they would refuse to pay taxes and royalties as well.

Blakeney was annoyed, but not alarmed. "I just put it down to the fact that they were not a very well-organized industry. They had great difficulty mounting an effective lobby, because they hadn't sorted it out among themselves." He found the American potash companies unsophisticated in their dealings with government, in contrast to the oil companies and the European uranium companies.

In early 1975 the government established the Potash Corporation of Saskatchewan, with Cowley as the minister in charge. David Dombowsky, a civil servant who had served as Blakeney's deputy in Finance and Industry, was chosen as President. Blakeney believed the industry was solidly opposed to any joint ventures with the government. After reviewing options from the planners, cabinet decided the government would build its own mine. Dombowsky hired a small staff of experts to secretly develop plans for a $500 million mine at Bredenbury, near Yorkton.

Blakeney and his ministers were busily planning for the election in June. A few days before Blakeney announced it, Mr Justice Disberry delivered his ruling against the province on the Central Canada Potash case. Blakeney denounced the decision as a victory for the federal government, and one which eroded the province's control over resources. Despite the ruling, the potash issue never really caught on in the 1975 campaign. When Dave Steuart charged that the government was planning to waste the taxpayers' money by building a potash mine at Bredenbury, Blakeney responded coyly, saying that Steuart's predictions were usually wrong, but that "he could get accurate once in awhile."

The New Deal '75 literature promised to "speed up direct participation" in the exploration and development of potash and hard rock minerals, and to "achieve a greater measure of public ownership of these resources and industries." That was hardly a stunning policy pronouncement; the government had previously done no exploration or development in potash. The campaign statements were less precise than those of the *New Deal for People* booklet of 1971, and weaker than public statements made by both Cowley and Blakeney.

The industry made its political statement in a campaign of television, radio, and newspaper advertising, and speeches to community groups. The companies announced that they were cancelling $200 million of planned expansion because of the government's reserve tax. Steuart promised that a Liberal government would co-operate with the industry to ensure expansion. The NDP were re-elected with a reduced majority. Blakeney believed that the industry had been waiting for the results, and would then resume negotiations on the new reserves tax. In fact, the government-industry relationship fell apart completely, and that led to dramatic action.

The chain of events which led to The Bunker began almost immediately after the election. The companies' second quarter reserves taxes were due late in June, and they didn't arrive. Blakeney was away. Garry Beatty, the Deputy Minister of Finance, walked upstairs in the Legislative Building to break the news to Romanow. On the same day, 11 potash companies went to court seeking a declaration that the reserves tax was unconstitutional.

Blakeney accepted that as a declaration of "all out war." He wanted the money new taxes would deliver, but he also wanted to see the industry expand. Prices had risen to justify it—from a low of $20 a ton in 1969 to $80 a ton in 1975. The industry was balking, partly because of its dispute with the province, but also because of Turner's budget. The federal Finance Minister's action pushed Blakeney to bolder action: "We were under attack in the courts by the industry, and under attack on the tax front by the federal government. But if the potash mines were owned by the public, both of those attacks could be effectively repulsed." Former MLA John Richards, among others, has said that Blakeney always wanted to leave a publicly-owned potash industry as his legacy. Blakeney says it didn't happen that way: "I read some of these analyses of how we had a great master plan that took five years to unroll, and we put a little pressure here and we produced that result there. I don't know whether those are flattering or not, but they're inaccurate. The actions of the potash industry forced us to make some decisions."

Cowley agrees with Blakeney, although he admits there was a "psychological factor" at play after the 1975 election. "We all felt that we had been a good government. We'd tried the straight and narrow and we'd damn near lost. As potash started to heat up, people who had argued, myself included, for a careful potash policy prior to that, said 'If they want to fight, hell, we'll give them a fight. We'll give the party something to remember, win or lose the next election.'"

Cabinet decided in August to consider nationalization a serious option. The team in The Bunker began to work feverishly. They had to predict what would happen if the government nationalized between half and all of the industry. Ken Lysyk from the Attorney General's department considered legal and constitutional implications. Garry Beatty from Finance assessed the likely reaction of international financiers. John Burton from Planning and Research was to look at marketing. David Dombowsky from PCS had to abandon the earlier plan to build a new mine and think in terms of a corporation which in a few months might have to run several mines and sell potash. Cowley's Deputy Minister, Roy Lloyd, was involved, too, as was the Cabinet Press Officer, Bruce Lawson. Others came and went.

They knew they were pursuing the Hot Option, but they didn't know how likely it was that cabinet would follow it. The air of excitement was cut by an edge of uncertainty. Dombowsky says, "Blakeney has this great, wonderful approach—from his point of view—of keeping all his options open until the very last minute."

As the typewriters clacked and the telephone lines buzzed in The Bunker, cabinet met upstairs far into the night, on many nights. It was easily the biggest gamble Blakeney had taken as Premier, and he was nervous. He soaked up information from his planners, and from his cabinet colleagues. But he didn't stop there. He reached all the way back into the 1950s. He was on the telephone to the "Mafia"—the Ottawa remnant of the 1950s Saskatchewan civil service crowd. Later in August, he paid a visit to them in Ottawa and spent long hours talking over the possibilities. He confided in George Cadbury, his first Saskatchewan boss. Cadbury went off to London to make some discreet inquiries about how a takeover might affect markets.

Blakeney urged his former colleague Don Tansley to come back and get involved in the new potash corporation. Tansley didn't want the job, but thought it would be useful for Blakeney to consult with Maurice Strong, the unorthodox millionaire businessman and Liberal nationalist. Tansley, who was in New York much of that year, arranged a meeting between Blakeney and Strong. Strong liked the nationalization idea, and had some suggestions about where the province might find money for the purchases. He also suggested the name of Douglas Fullerton, a retired Ottawa mandarin, as someone who might make a good board member for the Potash Corporation. Fullerton had advised Quebec on its takeover of Hydro Quebec. Blakeney put Fullerton on the potash board.

In September, Beatty and Dombowsky attended a portion of a special cabinet meeting to discuss the financing of a possible takeover. "David and I came out into the crisp September air," Beatty recalls, "and I thought at that point they wouldn't do it."

In September the crew in The Bunker turned its attention to preparing the way, rather than researching the reaction. Romanow and his deputy, Lysyk, became heavily involved in drafting the specific legislation. They were careful to avoid offending the BNA Act and United States law regarding expropriation and compensation. Some of the work was farmed out to the Toronto law firm of Davis, Ward, and Beck, to prevent rumours from flowing in Saskatchewan. Beatty began looking for money. Dombowsky began to assemble a team which could purchase, then manage, a multi-million dollar potash industry.

Discussions in cabinet carried on interminably through the fall. "We had a lot of people in cabinet who weren't sure where we should be going," Elwood Cowley says. "Blakeney was uncertain, too. He wasn't sure about the will of the cabinet and caucus to carry it through, so the debate went on for three or four months." Blakeney ran interminable cabinet meetings, looking at the options and their consequences from every possible angle. Cabinet's resolve was strengthened by news in October that the entire industry was joining in a lawsuit to challenge the province's earlier prorationing legislation. In the Central Canada Potash case, the courts had ordered Saskatchewan to refund the company's prorationing fees. Now the rest of the industry wanted its money back, too. "That just hit me the wrong way," says Blakeney. The companies who had begged him to keep prorationing were now suing him for doing what they asked. "This was really double-dealing," he says. The companies continued to withhold their reserves tax. The government estimated that they owed $30 million by autumn 1975.

The cabinet process was not without a touch of intrigue. Dombowsky recalls that for one crucial meeting Cowley had a limited number of copies made of the report to cabinet: "He deliberately had us misspell the word 'appropriation' in a different way in each of the documents. If there was a leak, we'd know whose document it came from. But Cowley lost the key, so that if there had been a leak we wouldn't have known anyway."

Blakeney's process of protracted discussion finally resulted in most members of cabinet putting their cards on the table. The big guns—Cowley, Messer, Romanow, and MacMurchy—were all on side. Caucus had been informed of the situation as well. In late October, Blakeney informed the party executive and council. The news never reached the press or the opposition. The Saskatchewan NDP, even in its modern embodiment, has something of a tribal sense of grievance and distrust toward the media, and is capable of quickly circling the wagons. A few days before the Throne Speech, Blakeney's trusted writer, Jack Kinzel, thought something might have stalled. "I proceeded to draft the speech," he says, "on the assumption that the government would move ahead, and nothing happened. Finally I'm within twenty-four hours of my deadline to get the Throne Speech printed. I went in to see Al and explained my problem." The cabinet was ready; the caucus, executive, and council had been informed; but Blakeney talked the issue through one last time in Kinzel's presence. Then he told him to write the Hot Option into the speech. There was no turning back.

The Legislative galleries were packed on November 13th. MLAs, old and new, sat stiffly upright at their desks. Lieutenant-Governor George Porteous read from the speech Kinzel had prepared: "You will therefore be asked at this Session to approve legislation which will enable my government to acquire the assets of some or all of the producing mines in the province."

David Dombowsky sat high in the gallery, facing the opposition side of the house. He had worked for Douglas and Lloyd, for Thatcher and Dave Steuart, and now was playing a key role in Blakeney's potash takeover. "It was high tension," he says. "The shock on the faces of the opposition was incredible. At first they couldn't believe what they were hearing. Then there was a kind of a groan." In fact, some rumours of potash activity had reached Dave Steuart, but he thought they had to do with the Bredenbury mine.

The Lieutenant-Governor continued: "Where the terms for an agreement for sale can be reached between my government and a selected potash company, it will not be necessary to invoke the legislation. Where such an agreement cannot be reached, however, the legislation will enable my government to expropriate the Saskatchewan assets of that company."

Steuart emerged from the assembly in shock. He borrowed a copy of the speech from a reporter, then retreated into his office. Fifteen minutes later he emerged to make a statement. "Totally unnecessary," he said. "This is the greatest risk ever taken by a provincial government, certainly by the province of Saskatchewan."

Blakeney had taken the precaution of placing several strategic telephone calls prior to the Throne Speech. Several were to industry and business leaders. Another was to Alberta's Premier Peter Lougheed. Blakeney respected Lougheed, liked him, and always kept him informed on resource and constitutional issues. The other political call was to Pierre Trudeau. Blakeney was concerned about the American reaction, and how Ottawa would respond when it came. Trudeau was unsurprised, but predicted a negative reaction from the United States. External Affairs later played it straight, giving the Americans the information, but making no attempt to undermine the Saskatchewan position. Otto Lang, however, Trudeau's most powerful western minister, called the move "provincial stupidity," and indicated that the federal government might reconsider its policy of not taxing provincial crown corporations.

The Who's Who of the Saskatchewan Mining Association were on jets that day bound for a technical convention in Winnipeg. When their reaction came a day later, they called the government's action "monstrous," "totally unfair," and "un-Canadian." A hasty survey by Canadian Press of 30 American and Canadian corporations indicated that 29 would be "negatively influenced" regarding further investment in Saskatchewan and (in the case of American companies) Canada. The Saskatoon *Star-Phoenix* editorialized that it was a breach of trust, and a "sad state of affairs." It appeared that there would be a big fight.

Blakeney had some public support of his own, but it was never effectively mobilized. At the NDP convention two days later he asked his supporters to "gird [your] loins" for a fight. The convention's enthusiasm was tempered for a different reason, however: Trudeau had announced a program of mandatory wage and price controls. Blakeney had his criticisms, but he was in favour of some form of controls. The reaction from Saskatchewan's labour unions, and many others within the party, had ranged from unease to rage. The unions were unenthusiastic about rallying behind the government on potash. There was a battle for public opinion, but it was waged by competing advertising agencies, cabinet ministers, and corporate big shots, not by citizens at large. NDP supporters did not take up the cause with the passion they had shown for the medicare crisis in 1962.

It's debatable whether the party would have been up to it in 1975. In any event, they were never really given the chance.

Part of the rationale for buying or expropriating mines was to show some results before the next election, which could be expected in 1978 or '79. Building a new mine would have exposed the government to the danger of delays; shaft flooding and labour strife were only two. The mines had to be purchased quickly to show results as soon as possible. The government had to act on many fronts: legislation, public relations, negotiation for purchase, borrowing money, staffing PCS, and convincing the Canadian and American governments not to retaliate. Blakeney needed a multi-faceted response and he had planned for one.

Through an Order-in-Council a week before the Throne Speech a PCS board of directors had been appointed. Cowley chaired it; other members included Romanow, Messer, Garry Beatty, Roy Lloyd, and John Burton. More board members were added later. Blakeney delegated the major responsibility to Cowley, but wanted to be kept informed. A week after the legislation was introduced, there began another parade of potash company presidents through Blakeney's office. This time he was in charge. He outlined the intent of the legislation, and told them PCS would pay fair market value for any mines it bought—but only after it had inspected them and seen their financial statements. He outlined the arbitration process which would be used if agreements could not be reached. After these initial meetings with him, Blakeney said, the companies could meet a negotiating team led by David Dombowsky.

The reaction was predictably hostile, although some companies, including Noranda, were interested in selling. The Canadian Potash Producers' Association, along with the Saskatchewan Mining Association, set to work immediately on a media blitz which cost them $130 thousand in three months. The Saskatoon Board of Trade mounted its own campaign to attack the government's action. The industry published the results of an opinion poll which indicated that 52 per cent of Saskatchewan respondents were opposed to the prospect of a potash takeover, while only 22 per cent were in favour.

The industry and the opposition won the battle for public opinion in the early months. When the legislation came forward early in 1976, the Liberals mounted a lengthy filibuster. The main task of shepherding the bills through the House fell to Roy Romanow, who led off with a speech of several hours.

The government's own poll in January 1976 showed a result marginally worse than the industry sampling. Fifty-two per cent of the respondents were opposed, and only 19 per cent in favour. Early in February, with the Liberals filibustering, and the industry scoring with the public, Blakeney became agitated. The mood around him was one of near panic. Cabinet Secretary Wes Bolstad wrote notes to his own files about "the Premier's psychological problems related to potash." Bolstad also felt the government's publicity campaign was slow and ineffective. The main strategic thinker on publicity matters, Jack Kinzel, could only agree. He told Bolstad that the government was "in deep shit from a publicity point of view." Blakeney thought things were out of control. He wasn't being briefed. The action on organizing PCS and negotiating for acquisitions was going too slowly. He was even feeling a lack of confidence in Dombowsky and Cowley. Dombowsky, one of a family of 19 from Avonlea, was grateful for the responsibility Blakeney had given him. But he recalls it as a difficult time. "The tensions were so high that everybody was second-guessing everybody else. And I think Blakeney thought that Cowley was a little bit out of control, not reporting as frequently as he might. Blakeney was feeling the corporation is rolling, but he's the CEO and what's his role? His need to know, his need to be on top of things, wasn't being served."

There was a series of meetings between Bolstad and Blakeney, and Bolstad and Kinzel. The bureaucratic response came quickly and on two fronts. The Cabinet Committee on Potash was reformulated, and a Potash Secretariat assembled the civil servants needed to provide support. The cabinet committee consisted of Cowley, who chaired it, Blakeney, Romanow, Messer, and Ed Whelan. Blakeney had made cabinet changes just before the November Throne Speech, moving Cowley to the administratively light job of Provincial Secretary, allowing him to concentrate on potash. Whelan had become Mineral Resources minister.

Cowley was responsible for purchasing the mines and overseeing the organization of PCS. Romanow was in charge of political and external affairs, which included public relations within the province, as well as monitoring and responding to the reactions of the Canadian and foreign governments. The Potash Secretariat answered to Cowley, but was under the daily direction of Garry Beatty. The strategy was to allow PCS to build its company and negotiate the acquisitions, with guidelines provided by cabinet. Most of the remaining load moved to the secretariat. Blakeney's need for paper and detail was met by a 20-page progress report every month. Romanow and other cabinet ministers went on the road to convince people that the government was making the right decision. Caucus members received a regular report, along with a list of questions and answers about potash.

In February and March, the government's chosen advertising agency, Dunsky's, set up an unusual journalistic format featuring the Premier: two half-hour television programs produced for broadcast over a private provincial network. In one of the encounters, Blakeney was questioned by a panel of journalists, including columnist Douglas Fisher, a former NDP MP from Ontario. In the other, he was interviewed by Patrick Watson. The interviewers were given free rein in both cases, and the agreements stipulated that no editing would occur. Blakeney gave forceful performances.

The general public relations campaign, however, did not go well. Blakeney and the cabinet privately conceded defeat on that front, and decided that they would convince people only by good results at PCS. Kinzel's publicity ideas eventually prevailed. The government should go with defensive strategy. It should not initiate debate about potash, but rather wait for the opposition to raise it. The response should be cool and rational, playing to Blakeney's strength, arguing that the takeover was a good business deal rather than trying to justify it on ideological grounds. Kinzel also believed that PCS should not be promoted separately, but as part of the network of crown corporations: "We wanted to put forward the proposition that crown corporations were a legitimate means of government activity and managing a very important and profitable resource."

The wild card, and possibly the most dangerous, was the reaction of the American government and financiers. No one was predicting a replay of the coup in Chile two years earlier, but it was a sobering example of how far the United States government and business élite were prepared to go in retaliating against resource nationalization.

On December 9th the State Department sent a memorandum to the Canadian government complaining about Blakeney's move, and warning that it could do major damage to Canada-U.S. relations. Thomas Enders, the United States Ambassador, made a similar warning, and later visited Saskatchewan. The United States Senate Agriculture Committee passed a resolution which compared the proposed takeover to the behaviour of the OPEC states, but the bill appears to have had only limited interest among the Senators; only six of them voted. The American reaction can only be described as mild.

Part of the reason was Blakeney himself. In early December, even before the American protest was issued, he was in New York talking to the financiers. In September, before cabinet had decided to nationalize potash, Blakeney had received an invitation to speak to the Canadian Club in New York. He informed Garry Beatty of the invitation, and they decided that Blakeney should go into the lion's den to make his case. The speaking engagement was set for several weeks after the announced nationalization. Beatty and Kinzel accompanied Blakeney to New York.

Beatty recalls it as a crucial test. "It was a big crowd of investment bankers at the Plaza Hotel. Normally at these events there is a 45-minute cocktail circuit, then they sit down to dinner and have the speeches later. This night they let them go an hour and a half on the cocktails. Now these were people who were conservative to begin with, and by this time, let's say, they had no inhibitions. When he was introduced, there were a few mutterings and hisses. It was not a friendly crowd.

"He began talking about Saskatchewan. He talked about the history, the culture, how we looked upon things and why. How the province looked upon resources, and potash development. At the end of the speech he got a good hand. In the question period they were direct and pretty damned aggressive. He was brilliant in his answers. It went on for 40 minutes. People were missing their trains home. At the end he got a standing ovation. He was magnificent. It's too bad all the people of Saskatchewan didn't get a chance to see this."

Blakeney made two more trips to New York within the year. He also went to Chicago to talk to CF Industries, the farmer-owned co-operative fertilizer company. He went to a World Fertilizer Conference. The message was always the same: the compensation paid for mines would be fair, and there would be an assured supply of Saskatchewan potash at fair prices. Some companies attempted to maintain an American political lobby against the Saskatchewan move, but they were ineffective.

Saskatchewan had not borrowed abroad on the open market since 1930. But even before the province bought any mines, its credit rating was raised by American bankers from A to AA. That occurred partly because of Blakeney's reception in New York, but more importantly because Saskatchewan was in good financial shape. Resource prices were rising, there was no deficit, and there was $400 million in an Energy and Resource Fund. The province easily raised $125 million in the United States bond market. When Beatty went to Europe to borrow money, he raised $75 million.

In October 1976, PCS purchased the Duval mine near Saskatoon from Pennzoil for $129 million (U.S.) That relieved the pressure to show some results. Critics argued that the government paid too much just to provide those results. Dombowsky anticipated the criticism, and to protect himself against second guessing he prepared a confidential memo ahead of time about the worth of the mine. "We were always within our range of value as pre-determined in the paper. We didn't panic. In fact, I believe in the Duval case that I'd have been authorized to go to $140–$150 million."

Dombowsky's old boss Dave Steuart still thinks Blakeney made a big mistake in getting the government into potash. He also believes that the government did pay too much: "I remember every day the gallery was full of potash people, then one day it was empty." He says the company presidents went missing in their haste to sell when they found what Blakeney had offered to Duval. "I lost my audience right there. I was a very lonely man."

After the Duval purchase, corporate disaffection began to fade. Within the next two years PCS purchased three more mines and a share in a fourth. It cost the government $520 million to buy 40 per cent of the industry. The other companies began to make their peace with the government. Most of the lawsuits were dropped. The American government found that United States corporations were being paid fairly, and that there was no interruption of supply to American farmers.

Blakeney's problems over potash were greater at home than abroad. The court cases over potash and oil were mere preliminary bouts. The main event occurred with the constitutional battles of the early 1980s. The producing provinces, particularly Alberta and Saskatchewan, were determined to use the money derived from provincial control of oil and potash to create a new and enhanced position for themselves in the Canadian federation. In Saskatchewan, the opposition continued to use potash as the most obvious example of the socialist lust for power. After the 1975 election, the Liberals were obviously fading; the Conservatives were the new free enterprise force. By 1978 Dick Collver would have no trouble raising money from the resource companies. The NDP began to look fearfully over their shoulder.

Blakeney denies any ideological or personal motive, but it must have at least occurred to him that he might be remembered for potash, the economic equivalent to medicare, the last great social achievement of the CCF. By the time of the provincial election in 1978 Blakeney's potash gamble had paid off. PCS was turning a profit, even after paying its taxes and royalties. Blakeney's polls told him that 60 per cent of the people approved of public ownership in potash, a complete reverse from the dark days of early 1976.

# Chapter Sixteen

# Uranium

On Easter Sunday 1962 there was a ban-the-bomb parade in Regina. Seven hundred marchers collected downtown, then walked across the Albert Street Bridge to the Legislative Building. They were met by Premier Lloyd and members of the cabinet. Most people in the Saskatchewan peace movement also belonged to the CCF. Nuclear disarmament was their big international issue. It's one of the ironies of history that, while they were marching in southern cities, uranium from the north was being used to build the American nuclear arsenal.

Uranium was first discovered in Saskatchewan in 1935 by prospectors looking for gold. Deposits of blackish-grey pitchblende were found on the shores of Lake Athabasca, near the border with the Northwest Territories. There was little interest in the ore then, but during the Second World War military science identified uranium as essential for the atomic bomb. Suddenly it became strategic material. Canada joined Britain and the United States in the Manhattan Project, which created the bombs that were dropped on Hiroshima and Nagasaki. Those weapons relied on Canadian uranium from Ontario and the Northwest Territories.

Large sales to the United States set off an exploration boom in Saskatchewan. A post-war discovery led to the development of Eldorado's Beaverlodge mine at Uranium City. Throughout the 1950s the major market continued to be the American nuclear weapons program. By the late 1950s, however, the Americans had a sufficient stockpile, and stopped making purchases abroad. Saskatchewan's industry promptly went bust, and hard times hit Uranium City.

The Easter peace marchers could be excused for not knowing what was happening at Uranium City. The activities of Eldorado Nuclear Limited were under a shroud of secrecy imposed by Ottawa. But the Premier and his ministers must have known. In 1960, cabinet commissioned the Center for Community Studies at the University of Saskatchewan to make recommendations about future development in the north. The report mentioned casually that the Uranium City mines had been affected by "declining military demand."

Allan Blakeney was already a cabinet minister on that Easter Sunday in 1962. He knew that Saskatchewan uranium had been used for American weapons. There had been virtually no civilian use for the mineral when production began at Uranium City. Logic led him to believe that others knew as well. Yet, strangely, it never became a topic of debate. Blakeney doesn't find that surprising. People believed that the way to achieve disarmament was to negotiate it internationally. They did not see uranium as the problem, any more than they saw the aluminum which was used to build fighter planes as the problem. The CCF throughout the 1950s and 60s was always in favour of uranium mining. Blakeney's own opinion changed little between his civil servant days and his premiership.

There was a second uranium boom in the 1970s. Canadian companies and others had created a price-fixing cartel, and it was predicted that civil nuclear reactors would create a vast new market. Prospectors once again prowled the scrub forests of the Athabasca Sandstone Basin in northern Saskatchewan. In 1968, Gulf Minerals announced a discovery at Rabbit Lake, a water body adjacent to Wollaston Lake, 350 kilometres north and east of La Ronge. In the same year, the French company Amok discovered three ore bodies at Cluff Lake, on the western side of the same large basin.

The Blakeney government in 1971 began a review of the province's mineral resources policy. But events were moving quickly. Blakeney had no idea that in a few years a business spokesman would describe Saskatchewan as the Saudi Arabia of uranium producers. Yellowcake—the product of uranium mining and primary milling—had been selling for less than $10 a pound. By the mid-70s it was selling for four times that amount. Saskatchewan was estimated to have between 10 and 13 per cent of the reserves in the non-communist world, a figure which was revised upward every year.

In reviewing Saskatchewan's uranium policy, Blakeney played his favoured role as chairman of the board. He wanted a range of options, and he wanted each considered at length. Yet, despite all the planning, Saskatchewan got into uranium joint ventures in an odd way. The Inexco mining company from Alberta wanted to sell part of its interest in a property. It searched for private sector partners and found none. They approached Elwood Cowley, the Minister for Mineral Resources. Inexco's existing exploration partner was the German company Uranerz. Cowley recommended in March 1974 that the government buy in with the Germans. Within a few months, cabinet had set up the Saskatchewan Mining Development Corporation (SMDC) as its vehicle for the purchase.

"If I made one good decision for the government," Cowley says, "that was it." The partnership was rewarded by a major uranium discovery at Key Lake, 270 kilometres north of La Ronge. A policy was born from that transaction. Cowley proposed a new development policy for all northern minerals: the government should use the money that was pouring in from oil to pay for SMDC's joint ventures with private corporations, and any company with an exploring venture worth more than $10,000 (virtually all of them) would have to offer the government a 50 per cent stake in its operation.

Resource policy occupied centre stage in a two-day cabinet planning session at the Legislative Building in October 1974. Cabinet instructed the Department of Mineral Resources to look at buying Gulf's Rabbit Lake mine. The ministers also decided that Saskatchewan needed a uranium refinery to process yellowcake for sale to American and offshore customers. Kim Thorson, the Industry Minister, was instructed to approach Eldorado Nuclear with the idea. He wrote to Eldorado's chairman, Nick Ediger, early in 1975.

Blakeney wanted a uranium mining and milling industry; it was consistent with his other industrial development policies. But by the 1970s other people in the province had come to see uranium as a death-dealing substance. They said it should be left in the ground, and questioned the morality of a government which was promoting its development and sale. Blakeney and most of his ministers couldn't understand the fuss. When he moved to nationalize half the potash industry, he had expected opposition from his opponents and support from his friends. He received both. With uranium it was different. This time his allies were corporate, multi-national, joint venture partners; his opponents were a significant minority of people within Blakeney's own party.

During the green spring days of 1976, strangers arrived at John Wiebe's farm yard near Warman, just north of Saskatoon. Wiebe was an earnest, good-natured Mennonite farmer. He'd had only a few years at school, but through hard work and thrift he and his wife Elizabeth had done well with their dairy. They were approaching retirement. The strangers offered to purchase options on some of Wiebe's land at more than he thought it was worth. He was a curious man, but polite. He asked why they wanted it. They said it was for a planned industrial park. The SEDCO officials neglected to tell him that the park's major tenant would be a uranium refinery.

Rumours began to spread. SEDCO was acting for Eldorado, and Eldorado would build a refinery. It would take the yellowcake that was mined and milled in northern Saskatchewan and, through a series of chemical treatments, transform it into uranium hexaflouride, a middle step on the way to the enriched uranium used in some nuclear reactors.

The Warman area is a predominantly Mennonite community with a long tradition of both food production and pacifism. The people did not know what to think. Many were uneasy. The offer was timely, and Wiebe wanted to sell. Some of his children supported his decision. Others among them said it would be wrong to have their dairy farm become the site of a uranium refinery. He sold.

When Gulf Minerals decided in 1968 to build its uranium mine, there was not a whisper about an independent environmental assessment or public hearings. The Thatcher government didn't even have an Environment Department. In the 1971 election campaign, Blakeney promised a new government department for the environment. After the election there was a surprisingly sharp internal debate about it. The conflicting positions most strongly expressed were those of Grant Mitchell, the influential civil servant, and John Richards, the young MLA from Saskatoon. Blakeney had asked Richards to prepare a report for cabinet. Mitchell wanted an appointed Ecological Advisory Council rather than a department. With a council, he said, "unpopular decisions do not reflect as directly on the government." Richards argued that the government was making a decision which would send a signal to the public about how the NDP viewed environmentalism. If environmental protection was to be taken as seriously as resource development, he said, there should be an Environment Department. Cabinet was divided. Smishek and Romanow supported the idea; MacMurchy, Bowerman, and Byers supported an advisory council. Blakeney favoured Richards's argument, and set up a department in 1972. Major environmental review legislation followed the next year, but it was not until September 1976 that a law on assessments and public hearings arrived.

As late as 1975, the most contentious issue debated at the NDP convention concerned returnable bottles. In 1976 a succession of important events occurred: Amok announced that it wanted to proceed with a mine at Cluff Lake; the provincial government purchased its stake with Uranerz, using SMDC as the vehicle for participation; an unbelievably rich strike was made at Key Lake; then the SEDCO people visited John Wiebe. The government had promised to submit all projects to vigorous scrutiny, and to do it before they were committed. Yet the same government had already created a momentum toward uranium development.

These local events occurred when, internationally, the nuclear power industry was poised for unprecedented expansion. But there was growing disagreement about the wisdom of such development—in Sweden, Britain, France, Germany, the United States, and Canada. Nuclear development became a heated topic of discussion at the United Nations Habitat Conference in Vancouver in May, 1976. A number of Saskatchewan people who attended that conference were later instrumental in the debate at home. One of them, a feisty, fearless grandmother named Maisie Shiell, decided to dedicate herself entirely to anti-nuclear research and activism. Another Habitat participant was Peter Prebble, a Saskatoon university student. He became an anti-nuclear activist, and later an NDP MLA. "In the early winter of 1976," he recalls, "we suspected that Eldorado was looking at the Saskatoon area for the site of a uranium processing plant. In June it became clear they were looking at Warman. We wanted an inquiry at Warman, but also a full scale uranium inquiry. I remember the Environment Department saying we would never get it."

There were two processes under way—one within the party, and the other around Blakeney and the cabinet. Throughout the summer and fall of 1976, the pages of *The Commonwealth* were dominated by articles and letters critical of nuclear power. Prebble and others were making their rounds in the constituencies, and approaching NDP allies such as the National Farmers' Union, to build support for public hearings and a moratorium on uranium development. Another voice raised against development was that of Bill Harding. A former CCF civil servant and a member of the party's left wing, Harding had spent many years working abroad for the United Nations. By 1976 he had retired to Regina, and he immediately became active and respected in the anti-nuclear movement.

Within cabinet there appeared to be little understanding that a significant new issue was emerging—a profoundly altered environmental outlook which connected the issues of peace, health, and the environment. There had never been an environmental assessment of uranium mining in Saskatchewan. Yet upon discovery of the most concentrated ore body ever discovered in Canada, Ed Whelan, the Mineral Resources Minister, was telling his cabinet colleagues there would be hearings only if the public pressed it.

Blakeney appointed Neil Byers as the Environment Minister in May 1972. Byers was a school teacher from Kelvington, and never one of cabinet's leading lights. He was poorly cast for what should have been a major portfolio, an indication that Blakeney probably did not consider it one. Grant Mitchell was appointed Deputy Minister. While he was a capable civil servant, Mitchell, like Byers, had argued against the creation of an Environment Department. Now they were running it. Byers attempted to explain the emerging environmentalism to his cabinet colleagues in September 1976. The government was suddenly getting "bad publicity on development projects." Something had changed. It was no longer "fashionable to be pro-development." Traditional NDP supporters weren't expressing themselves publicly. The vocal ones were environmental activists: "They focus on basic moral and value questions. They tend to believe in confrontation tactics and do not accept compromise easily."

Blakeney saw a potentially divisive battle on the horizon, and set a number of wheels in motion. While he was considering Byers's proposals, Blakeney also heard from his Science Secretariat, led by Dr Leon Katz, a physicist from the University of Saskatchewan. Katz said that the government had a "democratic responsibility" to respond to the moral concerns being expressed. He recommended a Royal Commission. Blakeney appointed a cabinet Uranium Committee in the summer of 1976. It consisted of Messer, Smishek, Byers, and Whelan. He also established an "officials" committee—civil servants who would provide backup and continuity to the cabinet group—chaired by Grant Mitchell. This combination of cabinet committee and secretariat had worked well during the difficult months following the potash takeover.

Blakeney wanted two reports. Amok's Cluff Lake environmental study was imminent, and the government would have to respond. He told the officials' committee that he wanted "at least two points of view" on how a public discussion of uranium development might occur. The message was carried by Wes Bolstad, who also had news for the cabinet Uranium Committee. Blakeney wanted some "solidarity" on uranium development policy. He wanted a proposal prior to the party convention in November. He also had Bolstad send a cautionary note to Whelan. Cabinet was already negotiating with Amok for a road to Cluff Lake. Bolstad warned Whelan not to make any announcement about the Cluff Lake road which could "get the government into trouble"—in other words, not to announce the road before the Cluff Lake hearings.

There had been two major developments within the party over the summer. The Provincial Council wanted a "comprehensive report" on uranium at the November convention. Meanwhile, a joint resolution arrived from 10 constituencies and the Saskatchewan Federation of Labour calling for an "immediate and indefinite" moratorium on all nuclear developments, including mining, milling, and refining; and it called on the federal government to hold comprehensive hearings into the nuclear industry.

The 750 delegates to the NDP convention in Regina's Centre of the Arts engaged in a heated and confusing three-hour debate. The party's uranium committee had not been set up until October 15th, and it didn't meet until early November, barely a week before the convention. There were allegations that the party executive and staff had deliberately impeded the work. Still, the committee did a good job. Indulging in some political theatre, it convened an Oxford-style debate on the main stage. One committee member took a pro-uranium position; a second member opposed; a third acted as moderator. Following that debate, the committee put forward a resolution calling for a provincial inquiry into both the local and global implications of mining, refining, and processing uranium. It called on the government to make no "new" commitments until such a commission made its report. In calling for a halt to "new commitments," the committee stopped short of the multi-constituency resolution for a complete and indefinite moratorium, and there was a sense of outrage that the convention's arrangements committee had not allowed the resolution from the 10 constituencies to come to the floor. It had been set aside in favour of the special committee's less comprehensive resolution.

Cabinet had been unable to reach the solidarity that Blakeney desired.

But they had obviously devised a strategy to head off calls for a moratorium. Blakeney shuffled the cabinet a few days before the convention, demoting Ed Whelan from Mineral Resources to Consumer Affairs. He replaced Whelan with Jack Messer who, along with Cowley, was probably the cabinet's strongest proponent of uranium development. It was Messer who moved into action, telling the convention it was the federal government which should convene comprehensive hearings into nuclear development, since they regulated the sale of uranium and reactors. The province should develop an educational campaign, which would include hearings into the narrower, local aspects of mining, refining, and processing. Messer agreed that no "further commitments" should be made until such hearings had taken place. His amendments won the day. He had headed off the moratorium, and tried to limit any hearings to local issues.

Blakeney sat silently through the debate. During his leader's address earlier, he had said that Amok's environmental impact statement would be released soon. He promised there would be a board of inquiry, and that it would have "wide terms of reference." But uranium mining had been going on for more than 20 years in Saskatchewan without major problems, Blakeney said. He would have to be convinced that it was no longer justifiable. Those concerned about nuclear development didn't get a moratorium, but they came away with Blakeney's promise of an inquiry.

The six weeks between mid-November and Christmas of 1976 were crucial to NDP uranium policy. There was pressure from the industry to proceed, and the government itself was part of that industry. There was countervailing pressure for a moratorium from a significant minority in the party. Blakeney had promised hearings. As he and his ministers drove along the yellowcake road that fall, they appeared to have their feet simultaneously on the accelerator and the brake.

Jack Messer, as Mineral Resources Minister, was bullish on development, but it was the responsibility of Neil Byers, as Environment Minister, to make a proposal for an inquiry. Given their different responsibilities, one might have assumed at least some contention between them. There was none. Less than a week after the convention, Byers came to cabinet with a proposal. Appoint an inquiry, but "based on the premise that the Cluff Lake project will proceed." Amok wanted both a road and permission to begin site preparation at Cluff Lake. Cabinet had been dangling those concessions in exchange for first right of refusal on Cluff Lake shares if they became available. The agreements had been negotiated, but not signed. Byers thought they should all get what they wanted, and proposed that the road and the equity agreements between Amok and the cabinet be announced when he named the inquiry commissioners. If even that amount of delay was likely to cause any problems, he said, road construction could always begin before the announcement. Messer went further. He wanted not only to begin immediately with the road, but to have meetings in the north to talk about mining jobs. "The basic assumption behind this proposal," he wrote to cabinet on November 22nd, "is that the Cluff Lake project is committed."

Bolstad warned Byers that he and Messer were premature in assuming that the project was committed. Their approach could cause political problems—"whether it's credible to hold hearings on a project already committed. Some cabinet members think not." There were objections from ministers like Walter Smishek and Wes Robbins, who were never comfortable with uranium development.

Byers proposed specific options to cabinet early in December. He wanted Messer to set up not an inquiry, but a departmental task force to "improve understanding of the importance of the industry." He also wanted to appoint a Cluff Lake board of inquiry "with hearings restricted to the environmental impact and proposed mitigation measures." This option consciously avoided looking at any implications beyond Saskatchewan's borders in making decisions about uranium mining, milling, and refining. Byers assumed that people were ignorant on the issues, and that low level departmental hearings would convince them to change their minds.

Byers admitted in his submission to cabinet that there was "an increasing concern" around nuclear issues such as India's exploding a bomb (allegedly using Canadian technology), and radiation problems at Port Hope and Uranium City. But he attempted to reassure his colleagues: "The anti-nuclear debate is basically internal to the NDP, [and] one which is being externalized by the CBC. It must be emphasized that the general public is not concerned about uranium mining in Saskatchewan." Byers was obviously out of touch with the depth and dynamics of concern around nuclear development.

Blakeney always insisted that ministers provide cabinet with several options. Byers gave them four. His preferred one was the narrowest and most restrictive, and appeared to contravene Blakeney's convention promise for a board of inquiry with wide terms of reference. The most open-ended option was for broadly-ranging hearings, with all work at Cluff Lake delayed until the board reported. After a spirited debate, cabinet chose the latter option.

Blakeney wrote Byers a blunt and confidential letter a few days later. It amounted to a firm rap on the knuckles: "We're off track somewhere on our New Deal '71 and '75 promises of fully examining environmental factors before approving major new developments. Despite this we have somehow got ourselves into the position with the Cluff Lake mine (and I fear we are doing the same thing with Key Lake) that everyone (Amok, Highways, DNS, the Energy Secretariat) feels we are committed to start implementing various facets of the project the very moment the Environmental Impact Study is completed. To do so would clearly be at odds with our policy." He told Byers to think the process through, and come back to cabinet with something better. It was an ambiguous signal. Blakeney, for good reasons, did not like Byers's habit of simply assuming that all projects should go ahead; but his letter prompted another submission to cabinet, this one jointly from Byers and Messer. They urged the abandonment of the previous week's position on the grounds that it would alienate many people in Saskatoon, which had become the industry's main supply depot. Shutting down work would harm the province's reputation with the uranium companies. Amok should be given conditional approval for site clearing, and the deal for the road should be signed. In return, Amok and the companies exploring for uranium would be asked to agree that if a board of inquiry ruled against mining, they would themselves bear the burden of any losses they had incurred in exploration and development. Cabinet bought it. Blakeney's intervention, through his letter to Byers, had helped to overturn cabinet's decision not to allow development to proceed during the Bayda inquiry.

On December 24, 1976, Byers announced publicly that he would appoint a Cluff Lake Board of Inquiry. It would have the power to say if the project should proceed, not proceed, or proceed with conditions. He said that work would continue at the site. The uranium companies, including SMDC, would continue to look for ore. This was the glinting moment of truth in NDP uranium policy. The ministers had found something they could defend and agree on. They could have development and inquiries at the same time—the accelerator and the brake pedal. Some may have believed they could allow the momentum to build, then turn it off later. It was a naïve position at best, a disingenuous one at worst. It was the sign of a government which had become arrogant.

Cabinet had passed retroactive legislation ordering companies to provide SMDC equity in uranium properties. The industry might have been expected to react almost hysterically to such a sweeping law. On the contrary, they were pleased. Uranium had always been a sensitive mineral, with a high degree of federal involvement and regulation because of its strategic history. In the 1970s, Ottawa once again introduced limits on foreign ownership in uranium holdings. What better Canadian partner than a provincial government? It gave the industry a powerful political hedge against any future federal restrictions or local civilian antagonism. Where the NDP saw a window on the industry, the industry saw reflected an indication that government would ensure conditions which were beneficial to the companies.

This accommodation with the multinationals represented a fundamental shift for the NDP. The CCF movement had been created to provide institutional protection for farmers and wage earners against the ravages of 19th-century capitalism—the banks, the railroads, the grain merchants. The movement had been founded on a sense of grievance and the need for redress. As an outsider with a more privileged background, Blakeney was never propelled by that same sense of grievance. Other powerful ministers, including Messer, Cowley, and Romanow, also represented a break from the old tradition. They were consciously a new breed of entrepreneurial politician, without the old CCF distrust of capital. Opposition to uranium development came from some old CCFers and the young environmentalists, the Bill Hardings and the Peter Prebbles. It was the generation in between—Blakeney and most of his ministers—who were the keenest developers.

The three-member Cluff Lake Board of Inquiry was appointed early in February 1977. It was led by Mr Justice E. D. Bayda, a member of the Saskatchewan Court of Appeal. A political Liberal who had earlier been a partner in a Regina law firm, Bayda was a prominent Catholic and a member of the Knights of Columbus. Dr. Agnes Groome was an education professor at the University of Regina, and a member of the United Church. She had been an unsuccessful NDP candidate in the 1975 provincial election, and had made her pro-nuclear sentiments known. Dr Kenneth McCallum was dean of graduate studies at the University of Saskatchewan, and also a United Church member.

Byers wanted a scientist on the board, and he had approached Dr J. W. T. Spinks, former president of the University of Saskatchewan. As a chemist at the university, Spinks had been involved in nuclear research related to the Manhattan Project in the 1940s. He declined Byers's offer, saying that his views were too well known, and he didn't want to suffer attacks from anti-nuclear groups. He recommended McCallum, another chemist. McCallum told Byers that he had a bias in favour of uranium development, but thought he could look fairly at the issues. It was a panel of relatively distinguished people, but well weighted toward a respect for established opinion and unlikely to propose any dramatic policy change.

Bayda and the others were instructed to hold public hearings and to make recommendations on Amok's proposal at Cluff Lake. They were also asked to investigate the wider question of the "social, economic and other implications of expansion of the uranium industry in Saskatchewan." They chose to interpret that as a mandate to recommend whether the province should proceed with the expansion of the entire industry, not merely the mine at Cluff Lake. They were to report within nine months, a deadline clearly established to allow the company to maintain its schedule to begin mining in the summer of 1978. Bayda argued for an open-ended schedule, but reluctantly agreed to a reporting date of November 1. There was immediate protest from 15 organizations, including the Federation of Saskatchewan Indians, the National Farmers' Union, and church groups. They said it wasn't enough time. They asked for a delay so they could do extra research, and carry out public education. Bayda passed the request on to Byers without recommendation. Cabinet viewed it as a stalling tactic. The request was turned down, and most of the groups boycotted the inquiry.

Blakeney insists today that, while he expected Bayda would recommend development, the government was prepared to back off. "We wouldn't have had a lot of trouble extricating ourselves from it. I was in no sense, nor was the government in any sense, committed to the sponsors of the Cluff project." They may not have been committed officially; but, given their actions, it's almost impossible to believe they would have said no.

Five weeks after the board was named, Jack Messer told the Regina *Leader-Post* that Cluff Lake was a "committed project." Messer says his position was that even if Bayda ruled against development, cabinet would still make its own decision. "After all, Bayda wasn't to dictate to us what we were to do." While Bayda was holding hearings, Messer and a group of officials from the Saskatchewan Mining Development Corporation travelled to the Pacific Rim to talk to potential uranium buyers in Japan and Australia. Messer justifies the trip as necessary business practice: "We had to continue to move ahead with the development that was taking place prior to [Bayda's] decision. We were putting the pieces into place, even though the inquiry was going on." Blakeney says Messer's enthusiasm can be explained partly by the Mineral Resources portfolio. It was, in a sense, the minister's role to promote the industry: "Messer was clearly, in a personal sense, committed. He wanted the project to go ahead. He was certainly not reflecting the view of the cabinet. Cabinets don't have monolithic views." Nevertheless, uranium exploration and SMDC's wheeling and dealing in joint ventures continued unabated while the Bayda inquiry was proceeding. In February 1977, only days after the inquiry was announced, cabinet decided on Messer's advice to increase its equity in Key Lake to 50 per cent. Key was the richest find to date, richer even than Cluff. The irony wasn't lost on Wes Bolstad, who jotted a note to his boss: "In approving the minister's recommendation cabinet was aware of the obvious political problem that it will create, i.e., with one hand setting up a uranium inquiry and with the other investing $70 million (or more) in a proposed uranium mine—this willful action does seem to call into question the government's commitment to public hearings." Cabinet made its final decision to buy 50 per cent of Key Lake in May 1978, just before Bayda delivered his final report.

Bayda gave the green light, with conditions. Amok would proceed at Cluff Lake, and other projects could go ahead, too. Bayda accepted as reasonable the existing standards relating to ionizing radiation and radon gases. That came as a bitter disappointment to environmental groups. They accused him of neglecting the evidence of their expert witnesses. The judge called for continuing studies into the health effects of exposure to low level radiation. The most nagging environmental question was that of disposing of mine and mill tailings which would remain radioactive for tens of thousands of years. Amok proposed to place them in concrete vaults and bury them. Bayda admitted that was only an interim measure, but felt the vaults should be a safe, temporary method of storage. He called for monitoring of the ground water, for surveillance at the site virtually forever, and for continued research into removing radioactive elements during the mining and milling process.

Given the hazards of uranium mining, Bayda had to justify the industry in economic terms. The cabinet's chief planning officer, Roy Lloyd, told the hearings that Saskatchewan stood to reap a bonanza of between $1.5 and $3 billion in taxes and royalties between 1977 and 1990. With those figures ringing in its ears, the board recommended that northerners be guaranteed a generous share of royalties, a percentage stated in written, contractual terms between the province and northern local governing bodies. Bayda, Groome, and McCallum also called for a Northern Development Board, a planning and advisory body separate from the Department of Northern Saskatchewan and answerable to a different minister. The board would be responsible for guaranteeing as many uranium-related jobs as possible to northerners. The suggestions for fixed revenue sharing and a separate Northern Development Board indicated the board's scepticism about DNS's will to ensure a full cut to people in the north.

The environmental groups had attended the hearings on a day-to-day basis. They observed the board's acceptance of existing radiation standards, and of Amok's plans for dealing with tailings. As the hearings progressed, the groups concentrated increasingly on the weapons connection. Their evidence was all circumstantial, but the growing knowledge of the corporate connections between Saskatchewan's uranium players and the weapons industry later became difficult to refute. Amok, for example, was owned in part by the Commissariate de l'Energie Atomique, a French government corporation. The CEA was involved with French weapons testing in the South Pacific. France had refused to sign the international nuclear non-proliferation treaty, and was selling nuclear technology to other non-signatories. Bayda admitted the possibility that uranium from Saskatchewan could find its way into weapons production. He concluded that a decision by Saskatchewan to withhold uranium from the market would be "irrelevant," and merely symbolic, because the mineral could always be obtained elsewhere. That was the position Blakeney had held since the 1950s. Amok proceeded with its mine. Over the summer Doug McArthur, the former Deputy Minister of the DNS, led provincial negotiations with the company for a surface lease. He secured a contract in which Amok promised that half the work at Cluff Lake during its operations phase would be performed by northerners.

Blakeney called an election for October 1978. He predicted that uranium would not be an issue. It wasn't, and he won a major victory. But the uranium issue did not go away.

Throughout the bitterly cold days of January 1980, the town halls in Martensville and Warman were the scene of hearings into Eldorado's proposed uranium refinery. The company took a public relations drubbing. One after another, ruddy-faced Mennonite farmers, sincere Catholic nuns, tweed-jacketed university professors, and school children took their turns at the microphone to plead with the federal environmental review panel not to allow the company to proceed. Leonard Doell, a local farmer and amateur historian, told the panel: "Our forefathers chose this valley because of the potential it had for agriculture. A nuclear refinery does not fit into the dreams that they had or that I have for this area." Sister Gertrude Sopracolle called the proposal "a transgression against life itself." Dr Alan Anderson, a sociologist, asked who Eldorado had employed as their consultants "on the probable social impact of the Warman development?"

The panelists and Eldorado's officials were frustrated. They wanted briefs to be limited to the site-specific environmental and economic effects the refinery might have. They got some of that, but they also received lectures in the history of anabaptism and pacifism. The local community was disturbed by the prospect of having as a neighbour an industry which might pollute the water and air, the cattle and the milk; an industry with the whiff of a weapons connection behind it. The Mennonites had left the Netherlands for Prussia, then migrated to Russia, and finally to Canada. They had made each move because they wanted nothing to do with wars and weapons.

Eldorado was not pleased. The Blakeney government had insisted that the company consider a refinery site in Saskatchewan. Things went smoothly at first. In 1975 a federal-provincial committee began to look for sites. It came up with a list of 11, including the Dundurn military base south of Saskatoon. That list had been narrowed to four by 1976. In June, SECDO began negotiating the purchase of options on the land near Warman, and approached John Wiebe. The company took SECDO's participation there as a signal that the Warman site was acceptable to the province. That's where Eldorado wanted to be. It did not want to invest money in producing environmental impact statements at several locations.

Meanwhile, anti-nuclear sentiment was growing. The 1976 NDP convention debated uranium development. The Cluff Lake inquiry was announced in February, 1977. In April, the Warman and District Concerned Citizens group was organized. Cabinet was beginning to understand that Eldorado had narrowed its choices to the Warman location even before the environmental assessment had begun. For almost two years the province tried to convince Eldorado to consider other sites, and the company refused.

By 1979 there was a new dynamic in the NDP caucus. Peter Prebble contested the NDP nomination in Saskatoon Sutherland in 1978. One of the people working against Prebble's nomination was Dale Schmeichel, who had been an Executive Assistant to Jack Messer before being appointed to a public relations job in SMDC's head office in Saskatoon. Prebble's supporters believed Schmeichel was acting on Messer's orders, and that at least some members of cabinet wanted to see Prebble defeated. Messer denies any involvement. Prebble won the nomination by seven votes, and was elected to the Legislature in 1978. He was the first caucus member to challenge the party's big guns, including Blakeney, Romanow, Cowley, and Messer. He had little help from cabinet, where it really counted, but several caucus members were at least uneasy about uranium development, particularly the Warman project. They included John Skoberg, Bev Dyck, Clint White, and Doug McArthur, the former Deputy Minister in Agriculture and DNS. He had been elected in 1978 and would soon be promoted to the cabinet. McArthur thought uranium mining did not make sense economically, although he says he was "wishy-washy" in his opposition. Caucus held a full-fledged uranium debate in March 1979.

In June of that year the government suffered a major embarrassment, which gave impetus to the anti-nuclear movement. In 1977, while Bayda was holding his hearings, the Key Lake company had approached Neil Byers for permission to drain lakes which lay above the ore body. They wanted to do it in the name of exploration, but it was actually site preparation. The government decided to grant permission not through the Environment Minister, but through Jack Messer in Mineral Resources. He signed the permits in June 1977—ironically, under provincial pollution control regulations. Later, he renewed permission under industrial wastes management regulations. The story didn't break for almost two years, but the revelation cast another cloud on cabinet's intentions and its integrity. The Regina Group for a Non-Nuclear Society (RGNNS) went to court to get an interim injunction against the so-called Key Lake "de-watering." The judge rejected it as meaningless because the work had already been done. RGNSS considered launching a civil suit, but did not have the money. The government's own lawyers informed the department that the action had been "invalid." Ted Bowerman (Blakeney had shifted him to Environment in 1978) admitted that the province had not complied with the "letter of the law." Attorney General Roy Romanow admitted that a "technical error" had been made. It is difficult to imagine a decision more self-serving than the government's allowing the draining of natural water in the name of either pollution control or the management of industrial wastes. It was another indication that development took precedence over environmental protection.

The Regina *Leader-Post* also discovered that the government was pushing ahead with a road to Key Lake even before hearings into that project were held. A cost-sharing arrangement for the $25 million project had been signed quietly with the company in October 1978. Eiling Kramer had been lobbying for a road, and cabinet agreed. In plotting the strategy,

Neil Byers warned of a possible negative reaction: "We may receive unfavourable comments because this road is already decided upon and will be built even though the actual Key Lake mine operation has not been subject to all phases of the environmental assessment procedures." When the story broke, Byers said the province could make good use of the road even if the Key Lake mine did not go ahead. He gave no details of how such a road might be used. When Peter Prebble found out about it, he raised the issue in caucus. His motion to delay until after a Key Lake inquiry had reported was only narrowly defeated.

Cabinet held one of its out-of-town retreats at Saint Peter's Abbey at Muenster in June, 1979. Ministers admitted that they had a problem about the environment. They had an image of being too pro-development, and not giving enough attention to environmental concerns. Their solution was to deal with public relations rather than with the substance of their approach. Bolstad summarized the discussion in a memo to Cowley (with copies to Blakeney and Romanow): "It was suggested that it might be worthwhile to have a high profile fight with SMDC. This would underline that we agree to development only if there are stringent safeguards."

By late 1979, the Key Lake fiasco and the Warman project had mobilized an anti-nuclear coalition in a way the Bayda hearings had not. The refinery would be built not in the north, but near Saskatoon. The hearings were concentrated in one or two locations. That allowed the urban and rural dwellers to make common cause. It would be built in a Mennonite community. The Mennonite connection prodded the churches into solidarity with what they perceived as a threatened religious group. No longer could the industry and government characterize their opponents, as Neil Byers had done earlier, as young, overly idealistic, and given to confrontation—the brown bread and bicycle brigade. Warman was bad news, and the government knew it.

The hearings began in January. Blakeney insisted that someone in government monitor them so the cabinet would be informed of all developments. The co-ordinator at Warman was Jack McPhee, Deputy Secretary to the cabinet committee. McPhee made his final report late in January. He talked about the "well-organized and vocal participation by the anti-nuclear faction," but he admitted the hearings were also "a highly emotional experience" for a large number of local residents. The panel members, he said, "were annoyed by the lack of factual information being provided, and by the repetition of the anti-nuke case." McPhee warned that if the federal panel said no to Warman, Eldorado would probably back away from a Saskatchewan refinery entirely. The company had looked at Saskatchewan to meet the government's objectives, not its own. He concluded with the observation that any further delays would bring the project too close to the next election for the government's comfort.

Messer told cabinet that if the panel said yes, they should push ahead at Warman, despite public objections. If the panel said no, cabinet should convince Eldorado to look elsewhere in the province. In a reference to obvious divisions in caucus, he warned: "If caucus will not support a refinery at any reasonable site in Saskatchewan, then anti-nuke forces in the province will recognize their accomplishment and pursue the attack on mining with increased vigour."

The panel chairman, John Klenavic, had warned citizens that they were mistaken if they thought a show of numbers would influence his advice to the federal Environment Minister. When Klenavic reported in August 1980, it was obvious that, despite his warning, the show of numbers had had its effect. The panel accepted that the uranium refinery was solid on environmental grounds, but said Eldorado's studies on social impact were deficient. The company should come back with more sophisticated research or, alternatively, pursue impact studies at other provincial locations.

Against the solid citizens at Warman, Eldorado and the provincial government came off a poor second best in the eyes of the wider public. Anti-nuclear groups saw it as a complete victory which would lead to an even stronger movement. That didn't happen. The coalition which formed around the Warman refinery did not continue and has not been repeated. Cabinet and a majority of caucus saw it as a lost opportunity. Ted Bowerman, the Environment Minister, invited citizens in his Shellbrook riding to convince the company to locate there. A group of businessmen in Saskatoon approached Roy Romanow to find another location near the city. He politely accepted their petition, but predicted to cabinet that the idea would go nowhere. Eldorado declined all other provincial offers. A Saskatchewan refinery was never built.

The anti-nuclear coalition at Warman included significant numbers of people from Saskatchewan churches. Church leaders were moved by their congregations at least to question the wisdom (and the morality) of the NDP position. It was a challenge which cut deeply, and which created a new political dynamic. With Protestant ministers like Woodsworth, Douglas, and Stanley Knowles in its pantheon, the NDP had a habit of assuming the moral ground as its own. The Saskatchewan party had been accustomed to support from the United Church; there were frequent joking references to the United Church as "the NDP at prayer." Catholics traditionally had been hostile to the CCF, but by the mid-1970s that had changed significantly. The NDP was winning in constituencies with predominantly Catholic populations, and Catholics like Ed Tchorzewski, Murray Koskie, and Herman Rolfes were in the cabinet. The debate over uranium threatened carefully-nurtured relationships with the churches.

Blakeney, particularly, chafed at being challenged on his morals. He countered arguments against the development of nuclear power with his own rhetorical question about how moral it was to deprive the world of energy which was in increasingly short supply. It was an argument which came to be weakened by the increased supplies and declining prices of both oil and uranium. But he believed, and still does, that the world will need nuclear power. Bill Knight, his chief aide during those years, says his boss was tolerant of differences of opinion—to a point—"as long as you didn't try and imply an immorality to him. Then he would just go absolutely snake." A case in point was Blakeney's treatment of a United Church delegation in 1981.

He began to attend the United Church in the mid-1970s, along with his wife Anne, a lifelong member. Blakeney followed her into the congregation of Saint John's United in their Regina neighbourhood, although he attended only sporadically. The Saskatchewan Conference of the United Church had a long tradition of presenting an annual brief to the cabinet. In 1981, Blakeney was waiting when the conference group arrived at a meeting room at the Legislature. The brief that year criticized Blakeney for his uranium policy. He was ready for them. "He just let us have it," says Reverend Joan McMurtry, the minister at Saint John's and also a member that year of the delegation to cabinet. "He was particularly offended with the brief, and the offence was the way it was written, because it accused him of not being ethical and of not having a moral position, of being immoral." Blakeney delivered his sermon, then left the room.

One of the main presenters that day was Reverend David Petrie, a conference official. He recalls the meeting as "intense." In a letter to Blakeney later, Reverend Petrie reviewed their areas of disagreement, among them the weapons connection. Blakeney had challenged them to prove that Saskatchewan uranium went into weapons. Even if small amounts of it did, he said, withholding Saskatchewan uranium would make little difference. "You argued," Petrie wrote, "that if we don't supply the uranium, others will. Surely you know this is the argument used by every prostitute, drug dealer and bootlegger in the world. No, I do not mean to smear you by linking you with these people. I just want to point out that the argument is as invalid here as there."

Blakeney had always thought his politics were driven by a sense of Christian morality, even if he didn't believe specifically in traditional tenets like the virgin birth and the divinity of Christ. "What does the Lord require of thee but to do justly, to love mercy and to walk humbly with thy God?" he asks, quoting the prophet Micah. "Well, what is to do justly? What is to love mercy in that sense of the word from the point of view of what the government of Saskatchewan can do? Those certainly were part of my consciousness, and part of the way that I attempted to carry on my duties." He believed the churches weren't taking account of his moral arguments in favour of uranium development—employment for people in northern Saskatchewan, and the sharing of energy with people in other countries: "I think that there were some very real questions to be debated, and that no one could assume that their side of the argument was necessarily right in moral terms, and the other side was necessarily wrong. Every once in a while I ran into that assumption."

The uranium debate became an annual ritual at NDP conventions. After the Bayda report, Blakeney's position hardened and his patience grew shorter. Doug McArthur says Blakeney saw uranium revenues as the foundation for his social democratic dreams for Saskatchewan: "He's saying, 'We talk about needing to create wealth to have better health care services, day care, and dental care. We talk about wealth creation, and when we find the thing that can do the job for us, we don't have what it takes to go ahead'."

One might argue that the vigorous debate was good for the party, that it prepared the NDP for the later primacy of environmental issues. McArthur says the debate was actually harmful: "The old Establishment, the powerful people in the party, all lined up pro-uranium. They sold it to the membership on the view that most of this environment stuff is soft and mushy, coming from people who can't think straight, who don't understand the nature of the modern economy, who listen to extremists.

"It discredited environmentalists, both at the level of leadership and at the level of the ordinary membership. We would be much closer to a legitimate green party if uranium would have never existed in Saskatchewan, or if we had not proceeded with uranium."

The uranium debate elicited the best and the worst in Blakeney, a mental toughness and determination on the one hand, a petulance and an intense dislike of being challenged on the other. Peter Prebble, who respects Blakeney immensely and calls him a "giant in politics," nevertheless opposed him on uranium. Prebble lined up at the microphones against Blakeney and others during a federal convention debate on nuclear development. The anti-nuclear argument carried the convention, and Prebble says that Blakeney would not speak to him for weeks after. The 1970s debate was so difficult and acrimonious because it was a contest for the heart and soul of a party which has always traded on its morality.

# Chapter Seventeen

# The New Politics

By 1978 Saskatchewan had left the mentality of the dust bowl behind, and was tentatively beginning to believe its new press clippings. After decades of deprivation, it was officially a "have" province, right up there with Ontario, British Columbia, and Alberta. Resource money was rolling in, and farming was fine. The word "wealth" was even breathed now and then, although those saying it immediately looked fearfully over their shoulders.

Blakeney had begun to receive his share of press clippings, too. The national media discovered him after his move on the potash industry in 1975. REGINA'S BLAKENEY: THE ARAB OF POTASH, said the headline on Richard Gwyn's story in the *Toronto Star*. A SHARP TURN TO THE LEFT said Paul Grescoe's article in *Canadian Magazine*. The magazine writers may have visited Regina expecting to find a socialist specimen. You could sense their relief and reassurance when, in Gwyn's words, they found that, with Blakeney, "respectability oozes out of every pore."

As he put the shock of the potash takeover behind him, the headlines soon began to read BLAKENEY'S NEW DEAL, and BLAKENEY'S MISSION. Grescoe quoted a former national president of the Conservative Party as saying Blakeney was the "best premier in the country." Suzanne Zwarun called him "dogged" and "utterly indefatigable." John Dizard, writing in *Weekend Magazine*, said that "only Saskatchewan's Allan Blakeney can match wits with Pierre Trudeau." Blakeney's aides had been courting the national press for years. Now he was finally getting his due.

But there were some long shadows on the horizon, which Blakeney warned could prevent Saskatchewan from taking its rightful place in confederation. At the national level, there was the struggle over the control and price of gas, oil, and potash. Trudeau, acting unilaterally, had kept Canadian oil prices below world prices. Peter Lougheed had retaliated by tightening the taps in Alberta. Blakeney's oft-repeated quote was that Moose Jaw should not be expected to subsidize London, Ontario. Made-in-Canada oil prices, he said, were costing Saskatchewan taxpayers $575 million a year. He supported a national energy policy, but he said Saskatchewan and the producing provinces should not have to pay the entire price of providing cheap oil and gas to Canadian consumers.

Then there were the cases lodged by Saskatchewan oil and potash companies. They had been winding their way through the courts for years. The companies were challenging Saskatchewan resource taxes as unconstitutional, and asking for their money to be returned. In November 1977, the Supreme Court ruled unanimously in favour of Canadian Industrial Oil and Gas in the oil taxation dispute. Chief Justice Bora Laskin ruled that the province had no jurisdiction over the price of resources entering inter-provincial trade. Saskatchewan immediately drafted new legislation. Meanwhile, the province was waiting apprehensively for the other legal shoe to drop in the appeal of the Central Canada Potash case.

The NDP began in 1977 to think seriously about the next election. There was a good deal of nervousness in the ranks. The party had always relied for its political intelligence on coffee row and reports from the MLAs. In 1976 Elwood Cowley, as Provincial Secretary and senior political minister, began to purchase quarterly questions on the Gallup Poll. He was shocked to find that respondents preferred the upstart Tories to the NDP. People didn't like potash; they didn't like the Land Bank; many did not like compulsory seat belt legislation. The Tories were scoring with their criticisms of big government. The Liberals were on their way to collapse.

Dick Collver, an Alberta management consultant, rode in from the west in the early 1970s. He went to work in property and business management for the Baltzans, a family of medical doctors-cum-tycoons, in Saskatoon. He was sandy-haired, full-cheeked, and chubby, with a clean look about him that belied a ruthlessness and unpredictability. Unlike Steuart or Blakeney, he was new to politics. In 1975, Collver took the Tories from 2 to 28 per cent of the popular vote, and won seven seats. Before the Legislature was dissolved for the next election the Tories, through two byelection victories and two Liberal defections, had 11 seats, as many as the Liberals. The Conservatives became the new free enterprise alternative, and by 1977 they were having no trouble raising money from business. The NDP caucus contained some men of little faith; in the dark, post-potash days of early 1977, the unbelievers needed reassurance. Bolstad wrote a memo to Blakeney, reminding him that cabinet wanted him to give caucus a "pep talk on the Tories" to help improve morale.

The NDP had problems in its own house as well. Some people were unhappy with uranium development, and with cabinet's roughshod tactics in promoting its position. Then there was the lingering turmoil over wage and price controls. Prime Minister Trudeau had ridiculed Robert Stanfield for even talking about them during the 1974 federal election campaign, but by October he was on television introducing them himself. The national rate of inflation was running at 11 per cent, and most governments (not Saskatchewan's) were ringing up huge deficits. Interest rates were on the way up; so was unemployment, and unionized labour was striking to catch up.

Blakeney was called to Ottawa for an emergency first ministers' meeting in October, 1974. He had spoken for years of a planned economy along the Swedish lines. Government, business, and labour would sit down and set goals, including the levels of prices, wages, and profits. In return for their share of power, and a negotiated "social wage," workers would moderate their wage demands.

Labour knew about Blakeney's musings, and they were alarmed. They were much more interested in bargaining their next wage increases than they were in any social contract. Larry Brown, the young Executive Secretary of the Saskatchewan Federation of Labour, called on Blakeney privately before the latter went to Ottawa. "I saw us heading for a brick wall," says Brown. "I went over to his office, just he and I, and spent about an hour. He was noncommittal, gave me a good hearing. My desperate attempt was to try and transmit to him how fundamental this would be to the trade union movement. I obviously didn't do it."

Blakeney met with the first ministers. He was deliberately vague after Trudeau's unilateral announcement. He agreed with the principle of wage and price controls, provided the program made some exemptions and adjustments for low income earners. He also warned Ottawa that it would be unconstitutional to impose economic controls on provinces because no "emergency" existed. He did believe that people were concerned about inflation, and that he couldn't afford to duck a program that other governments were embracing.

Saskatchewan eventually opted for an 18-month program called the Public Sector Price and Compensation Board. Labour's response was predictably hostile. The SFL immediately announced a "fightback" campaign. There were major debates at the 1975 and 1976 NDP conventions. In October 1976, a thousand workers jammed into the Legislative rotunda to demand an end to controls. In February 1977, the SFL rallied 4,000 workers to the Legislature for another rally. The campaign in some cases became personal and bitter. Blakeney's Finance Minister, Walter Smishek, had to promote the government line, but he was vilified for it. Smishek had for many years been a representative of the Retail, Wholesale, and Department Store Union. Now his RWDSU card was pulled, and a union scholarship in his name was revoked. It remains a sensitive memory.

Blakeney says his government went easy on controls. The economy was booming and he did not want to lose tradespeople to Alberta: "All manner of settlements were approved in the 12 to 15 per cent range when the federal guidelines were for 10 per cent. The guidelines had little or no effect in Saskatchewan." He denies that his embracing controls had any long term effect on the NDP's relationship with labour: "The Saskatchewan Federation of Labour did not exhibit a high degree of upset at its leadership levels, but individual people in the SFL did."

Larry Brown disagrees: "I'm convinced that what we were reflecting was the reaction of working people. There was a tendency to respond to that by saying that Larry Brown and Gordon Quaale, Len Wallace—people who were saying this was a major political mistake—were not the messengers but the creators, that if we'd have kept our mouth shut everybody else would have accepted it. I think that's crazy." An unattributed quote in the notes from a cabinet retreat in the summer of 1976 has one of the ministers saying, "our relationship with the labour movement is terrible." In February 1977, a full seven months before controls were lifted, Smishek came to Cabinet with plans to remove them.

Blakeney spent the hazy days of August 1978 in Nova Scotia, visiting old friends and the haunts of his childhood. His vacation ended abruptly. Pierre Trudeau read the polls and they were Tory blue. He announced there would be no federal election that fall. That upset Blakeney's own timetable. He had planned a spring 1979 election, but didn't want to risk the confusion of concurrent campaigns. He could wait until the fall of 1979, but then he ran the risk that euphoria from a Tory victory federally could spill over into Saskatchewan. His planners were predicting a softening in the economy. He had already begun tightening up on government programs and civil service hiring. He did, however, have an option. If he moved quickly, he could break with the long New Democrat tradition of spring elections and go this fall.

It wasn't the kind of decision he would make alone. When he got home, he called a quick cabinet meeting. He asked the advice of his political committee—Cowley, Romanow, MacMurchy, and Don Faris. The polls were intriguing, and confusing. They showed a dislike of Trudeau, bordering on rage. The numbers showed Blakeney running ahead of the NDP in popularity. People respected and trusted him more than his party. Meanwhile, Dick Collver was beginning to lag behind his Tories.

The NDP feared Collver. He was appealing to New Democrats as well as Liberal supporters. "We were trying to say if you were an NDP in the past, but really wanted to vote Conservative, we're not very far away from you," he recalls. It might be implausible elsewhere in Canada, but in Saskatchewan there was a traditional affinity between the Conservatives and CCFers. People proudly voted for Tommy Douglas provincially and John Diefenbaker federally. What united voters was their dislike of the Liberals. "The original CCF were elected by the old Tories," says Dave Steuart. "They sent out the word. 'Elect this guy Douglas and the CCF, and get rid of the Grits. Then we can get rid of the CCF any time because they're kind of wild-eyed.' The Tories came to scorn and stayed to pray.

They loved Tommy Douglas because he hit those dirty Grits hip and thigh." The Liberals and the NDP had a relationship which was competitive, but comfortable. Collver was an unpredictable new boy on the block. In his first Legislative speech he lectured members about their decorum, even about chewing gum. He promised to represent something new in provincial politics. But he proved to be an opponent who barred no holds. He once alleged that conditions in Saskatchewan hospitals were "filthy," and accused the Health Department of allowing it. On a later occasion, he charged that there were homosexuals in the cabinet. Eventually, he had to admit a lack of evidence in both cases. Nonetheless, Collver and the Conservatives created a desperate anxiety in the NDP camp.

"After '75 you had the complete collapse of the Liberals," says Bill Knight, then Party Secretary. "It brought out the competitive edge in Blakeney. He found Collver smarmy and threatening and dangerous, and was going to stop him." Blakeney usually refuses comment on the personalities of competing politicians. But he does say, with an edge to his voice, that in 1975 Collver "was a nice, fresh leader who nobody knew." He pauses, then adds: "And with Dick Collver, the less you knew of him, the more effective a leader he was."

While the NDP feared Collver, his clay feet had begun to show. First, there was a nasty lawsuit unfolding between him and his former partners, the Baltzans. They were arguing over property that Collver said had been turned over to him. The Baltzans denied it. Then in the spring of 1978 the Regina *Leader-Post* broke a story about bad debts with the Saskatchewan Government Insurance Office; Collver had signed loan guarantees for a construction company which had gone broke before completing the projects it had undertaken. SGIO wanted its money and couldn't get it.

Collver was suddenly vulnerable, and the NDP was prepared to exploit any weakness. Collver's self-styled image was that of a businessman who would run the province effectively, yet he was unable to run his own affairs. There were rumours about a Swiss bank account. Collver acknowledged there was such an account, but that it was for his daughter, who was studying in Europe. People trusted Blakeney; they didn't trust Collver. A snap fall election began to make more sense. It was unthinkable to have it before the end of the harvest, early in October, but dangerous to hold it much later. Cold weather and freak storms might make it difficult to campaign and bring out the vote. Blakeney called it for October 18th.

Bill Knight had become Party Secretary in the fall of 1974, too late to put a stamp on the 1975 campaign. This time he was ready. He convinced Blakeney that the NDP's approach to elections was outdated. "I flew off to Washington," he remembers, "with two people out of media agencies, Ron Pradnick and Lowell Monkhouse, and we went through a big political seminar on techniques, polling, advertising, research—all the things you do to win. We didn't go east to pick up from the national Liberals or Tories. We headed straight across the border and did a technical raid on the Democrats and Republicans to find something that would fit our operation."

The 1978 campaign was the first in which the NDP used polling. It was also their first electronic campaign; made-for-television events began to replace the traditional town hall meetings and large rallies. "What we found," Knight says, "was that we could turn TV commercials around in 48 to 60 hours. We could respond to issues, poll weekly, and have a multi-faceted radio campaign hitting different audiences. We were a little amateurish the odd time, but we were right on track. We just overwhelmed everybody because it was not expected by our political opponents in '78."

Knight also learned something in the United States about a technique which is now called negative advertising. After the election call, the NDP immediately sucker-punched the Conservatives. Knight led with advertisements saying that if Collver were elected he would "tax the sick" by bringing back Thatcher's hated deterrent fees on health care. "Starting the campaign by blasting the Tories right off the map on health care was basically mine," Knight says. The polls did not show medicare as an issue, but Knight believed he could use it as a symbol. Blakeney and the NDP could be trusted; Collver and the Tories could not.

The Tories hadn't expected a fall election, and they were caught completely off guard by the attack on them. They spent precious time and resources preparing advertisements to prove that the Conservatives had always been in favour of medicare. By the time they were ready, the NDP was into stage two. They began attacking federal resource policies, and saying that only Blakeney could stand up to Trudeau. Blakeney had not forgotten his pledge to himself after the disappointing election in 1975—never to allow the Conservatives to run harder against Trudeau than he did. The party had learned something, too: it could run a campaign that featured Blakeney as leader. The New Deal campaigns of 1971 and 1975 had emphasized the policy and the team. This time it was "Allan Blakeney and the NDP." Party publicists reminded people about the headlines in the *Toronto Star* which had called Blakeney the best premier in Canada.

Early in October, the Supreme Court handed Blakeney the election. It released judgments saying that Saskatchewan's potash reserves tax was unconstitutional, and that the province would have to repay $500 million it had collected under its oil tax, which had been declared unconstitutional the previous year. Blakeney, who was usually respectful toward the judiciary, went on a minor rampage. He said the judgement showed a bias in favour of eastern Canada. He called on Saskatchewan people to support him in seeking constitutional changes to allow the province greater control over its resources.

It was a perfect script. Blakeney was running against Trudeau on resources, and against Collver on trust. The personal campaign against Collver was vicious. One of Blakeney's ministers called Collver the "Richard Nixon of the Prairies." A van carrying an NDP sign in Regina also sported a hand-lettered placard which said "Let us not Conserv(ative) our money in a Swiss bank, but let us share socialistically." Someone discovered that one of the Conservative candidates had once been in jail in the United States. Photocopies of a newspaper article reporting it were placed under windshield wipers. Blakeney knew it was a rough campaign, but says he had nothing to do with the personal attacks. In mid-campaign SGIO named Collver as a defendant in a million-dollar lawsuit. He responded by placing his personal affairs in a blind trust with the respected former Justice Emmett Hall.

The once mighty Liberals were wandering aimlessly under their new leader, Ted Malone. They were caught without a policy or an organization. Malone and a group of Liberal lawyers dreamed up a confusing series of proposals which would see run-off elections until one party had over 50 per cent of the vote. He ran a harsh campaign against labour in an attempt to prevent the Liberal right from going completely to the Tories. Ted Malone was Ted Alone, according to media wags; they weren't far wrong.

Blakeney won 48 per cent of the popular vote and 44 seats. The Liberals were wiped out. The Conservatives added 10 per cent to their vote and 10 seats. But they had expected to win, and they were bitter. Collver was elected in Nipawin. A woman in the subdued high school gymnasium where he had planned his victory party talked acidly about the NDP's "big lie" about medicare, and the "shabby treatment" Collver had received.

The partying was in Regina, where 500 people packed into a small Legion Hall to hear Blakeney's speech. Above the din, one of his supporters told a newspaper reporter, "We did the same things in Pelly. You'd think they would learn." What the NDP had done in the Pelly byelection in 1977 was run Blakeney against Collver, and talk about health care. The Liberals and the NDP had had their pitched battles over the years, but there was always a sense of decorum. Somehow, as the Conservatives went through the process of coming from nowhere to become the opposition, the mood turned ugly. The Tories have never forgotten the 1978 campaign.

A few days after the election, Collver encountered Wes Robbins, an NDP cabinet minister, in the foyer of the Legislative Building. Collver had approached Robbins prior to the election about crossing the floor to sit as a Conservative, and had been rebuffed. As they walked out of the building, Collver offered congratulations and the two shook hands. But then something happened. Robbins, a small and mild-mannered man, says, "Collver made some nasty comments about my mother." By this time the two were on the steps outside, and Robbins delivered a haymaker, sending the Tory leader tumbling down the steps. When reporters heard the story, they began to call Robbins "Sugar Ray." Within a few months of the election,

Collver had resigned as Conservative leader to sit as an independent member of the Legislature advocating Canadian union with the United States. He later moved to Arizona, where he still lives.

After 1978, Blakeney appeared as invincible as anyone can be in politics. The party had been running scared for three years, and Blakeney saved them. "When we defeated Thatcher in '71," Bill Knight says, "a lot of the common talk within the party was, well we were going to beat him anyway; that Blakeney wasn't much of a factor. In '75 the common theory was that the other two parties split, so we won. Again there was no political credit given him—all the credit in the world as Premier, but not as a political leader. In '78, nobody could argue that it wasn't his election."

It was a gleeful group of MLAs that gathered shortly after the 1978 triumph to conduct the campaign post-mortem. Cowley and MacMurchy, the rough and tumble veterans of cabinet's political committee, made their report. "Our polls predicted the final outcome so well," they wrote, "that one wonders if the campaign had any effect." There was also a cynical acceptance of negative campaigning. "The party must be conditioned," they reported, "thoroughly conditioned, to this aspect, so no one cracks under the pressure. If this technique is used, it is essential that the negative move into the positive. It is as important for our workers that they be fighting against something as that they be fighting for something. That should not be too hard to stimulate in 1983 with the Tories as the opposition." There were rowdy times ahead.

The NDP had virtually shut out the Conservatives in the larger cities. Tory strength was in the countryside, what was called the old Liberal "L," down the west side of the province and across the south. Many of those constituencies—Meadow Lake, Kindersley, Swift Current, Estevan—contained large towns or small cities. The 1978 election, more than any other, established the NDP as an urban party, and the Conservatives as the party of the farms and towns. It was a dangerous prescription for the New Democrats in a province where representation is tilted toward the rural seats. Blakeney accepted MacMurchy as the most heeded rural voice in cabinet. In the post-1978 analysis, MacMurchy and Cowley plotted the broad outlines of an NDP rural strategy for the next four years: "Our farm vote is in trouble, but it isn't lost. What we need to do is to give ourselves something to talk about, something that will excite them, and something they can identify with us. Land Bank, FarmStart and the diversification programs are not going to do that. Making wheat and barley and rapeseed as important as oil and potash and uranium to the development of Saskatchewan is essential to restoring pride."

The NDP attempted to turn rail transportation into the issue of pride. Former Justice Emmett Hall had been presiding over a Royal Commission on the prairie rail system. In 1977 he recommended that two-thirds of it be protected, and that the hallowed Crow Rate (which provided federal subsidies for grain transportation) be maintained. The federal Liberals were working to get rid of the Crow. Every farmer was affected by freight rates. MacMurchy thought it the obvious political issue. It had the added benefit of allowing the NDP to bash Trudeau.

MacMurchy and Cowley also saw the constitution as a good issue for a fight: "Ottawa, and the constitution must be an ongoing battle. At the present time, the one thing that our people hate more than the Winnipeg Grain Exchange and the multinational corporations is Ottawa and Central Canada. The person who engineered the Supreme Court decision in the middle of the election campaign deserves a medal." Before the 1978 campaign had ended, Blakeney wrote to Trudeau demanding constitutional changes which would give Saskatchewan control over the sale of oil and potash. The Cowley-MacMurchy political blueprint for the years following 1978 was long on cynicism and short on vision. They accepted negative campaigning and character assassination as a calculated and routine ingredient of Saskatchewan politics. Their approach to national issues was divisive and self-serving. Nowhere was there a hint of statesmanship or the national good. Amid the glee of the 1978 election, the NDP began to look like a party which had become a machine.

# Chapter Eighteen

# Economic and
# Social Policy

Blakeney viewed the outcome of the 1978 election as an endorsement of his economic policies. Resource revenues were approaching $500 million a year, and Saskatchewan had the lowest unemployment rate in the country. The government pushed ahead with expansions at crown-owned potash mines, and maintained a vigorous exploration and development program in uranium. During the campaign, Blakeney had talked about a heavy oil upgrader in the Lloydminster area. The government's employment and investment strategies were concentrated on resource megaprojects. There wasn't as much talk now about secondary industry in small towns. That may have indicated failure on one level, but people like political economist John Richards, a former MLA, say that Blakeney made the right choices in concentrating on resources and their "comparative advantage" rather than repeating earlier, failed CCF attempts at pursuing secondary industry.

Blakeney set up sophisticated machinery to co-ordinate the government's presence in the resource sector. As a young civil servant in the 1950s, he had cut his administrative teeth in the Government Finance Office. In 1978 he created the Crown Investments Corporation, a more complex version of the GFO. The CIC became the holding company for 17 crown corporations: traditional utility companies like Sask Tel and Sask Power, and the newer resource companies, including the Potash Corporation of Saskatchewan, the Saskatchewan Mining Development Corporation, and Saskoil. CIC also managed the equity shareholdings of government in outside companies, such as IPSCO, the steel company. The stakes in the 1970s were exponentially higher than they had been 20 years earlier. By 1979, CIC was the holding company for corporations with revenues of over $1 billion, and assets of $3.5 billion.

The CIC was Blakeney's way of keeping the government on top of what was happening in a growing number of crown corporations. None of those companies made plans to build mines or borrow money without permission from CIC, which also provided advice in areas such as industrial relations, accounting, and legal services. That gave the CIC and its director, Garry Beatty, an immense amount of power.

Beatty was a brusque hard-sider out of the Finance Department. Blakeney had recruited him as his Deputy Minister of Finance back in 1972, and given him major responsibilities on the potash takeover. Beatty insisted that CIC did not want to become "an organization of shadow managers." But that was exactly how some of the crowns perceived it, and they chafed under the control. David Dombowsky, President of PCS and a great admirer of the Premier's administrative ability, says, "I've got some very strong feelings about how we organized to run our crowns and they're not always complimentary. This whole business is to some extent the black side of Blakeney. The paranoia resulted in parallel organizations and shadow management, which I think is overkill and debilitating.

"For example, we'd have on our board a secretary appointed by the minister. We'd have CIC appointments, then we'd have CIC staff that would check our staff. This over-bureaucratization could grind you to a halt. But this suited Blakeney perfectly, because of his need to know. His need to have balances was honed to a keen edge."

Some of the most confident, entrepreneurial ministers, like Messer and Cowley, chafed as well. Had they lived in Alberta they might have led private corporations. In Saskatchewan, with its public sector tradition and its lack of large private companies, they were among the most important corporate people in the province. The CIC, in turn, was Blakeney's elaborate mechanism for independent information about those ministers and their empires.

The crown resource companies were set up as straight commercial corporations. When Jack Messer recommended that the government purchase additional equity in the Key Lake uranium property, he laid out the department's thinking clearly to cabinet: "SMDC should be regarded primarily as a profit-oriented organization, and be expected to operate similar to a private sector company." While he recommended that SMDC be a "model corporate citizen" in its relationships with northern people, Messer warned that "SMDC should not enter into mining ventures providing a rate of return on investment lower than that acceptable by normal industry standards in order to provide employment to northern residents."

Blakeney admits that his government made few attempts to use crown corporations to change the basic relations between management and workers. Government companies made it clear that they were in favour of unions, but they did not see themselves as agents of democratization in the work place. Blakeney's rationale was that, by acting as profit-makers, resource corporations would return millions to the Heritage Fund, which had assets of $900 million in 1980–81. About $400 million of it was returned as a dividend to be used for annual expenditures on roads, parks, and social programs. Another $150 million was invested in crown mines, and in a fleet of cars leased to the railroads to haul potash and grain. The stern international school masters who provide the report cards called credit ratings gave Saskatchewan a glowing AA in 1979.

In May 1977 Roy Romanow told people attending the NDP's Provincial Council meeting in Saskatoon that potash would be to the 1970s what medicare had been to the 1960s. Blakeney, Romanow, and the others placed great importance on good administration and the creation of wealth. Yet the ownership of potash mines didn't grip people in the same way as medicare had. The identity of the CCF-NDP had been as the party of universal health and social programs. The problem was that changes in both demographics and expectations were occurring rapidly in provincial society. The tried and trusted NDP approach of floating universal programs to solve social needs was not suited, for example, to the needs of women, or to the desperate plight of native people. The party was into its second mandate before it began to recognize that a change of approach was needed.

In 1971 Blakeney had turned quickly to health and social programs. One of his first acts was to remove Thatcher's deterrent fees. Chiropractic services were added to the list insured by medicare. Blakeney introduced major new programs in children's dentistry and prescription drugs. There was no staff for a dentistry program in 1971, so it really began with the province setting up classes to train dental nurses. Both programs were well on their way by the 1975 election, and both broke new ground in Canada. There were achievements in social welfare, too, but they were more ambiguous. The most obvious success was virtual full employment during several years. Saskatchewan's rate of unemployment was frequently less than half the national average; in 1975 it dipped as low as 2.9 per cent. The percentage of poor people in the province declined. Saskatchewan maintained the highest minimum wage in the country throughout the decade. The welfare rolls declined between 1971 and 1976. The NDP introduced a Guaranteed Income Supplement to improve the lot of the elderly poor. There were subsidized housing programs for the elderly, and a home care program that worked well. The Family Income Plan topped up the incomes of poor working families with children. Still, the basic social assistance rates remained consistently below the poverty line in Saskatchewan, as they did elsewhere in Canada. Blakeney says he toyed with the "theoretical possibility" of a guaranteed annual income which would include all the poor, but there was a stubborn perception among the public, including NDPers, that somehow the able-bodied poor without work were not deserving.

While there was growing prosperity in Saskatchewan during the 1970s, there was also a wide income gap between the rich and the poor. "It was clear that economic prosperity was redounding to the benefit of those who were economically adept," Blakeney says. "It was the middle class who were able to take advantage of these things." There was a persistent problem with income inequality, and the gap did not narrow under the NDP. In 1981, the richest 5 per cent of Saskatchewan's people earned as much, in total, as the poorest 50 per cent.

Blakeney initially pursued universal programs in the best social democratic belief that everyone would benefit equally. In 1978, after the election, he thought it was time for a new direction. He began to talk about the people who had been missed by the general prosperity, about targeting programs to those who needed them most. At the time he said, "It's going to be a test for Saskatchewan people. They have shown in spades that they can survive adversity. We are now going to find out if they can survive prosperity with the same sense of social cohesiveness and generosity of spirit."

Jim Sinclair frequently said that if conditions did not improve, the violence within native communities would spill over into white neighbourhoods. His predictions went mostly unnoticed; they were seen as attempts to get attention. But Ken Svenson, one of Blakeney's planners in the Executive Council, was no activist. His confidential report in 1976 echoed Sinclair's threat, albeit in the more neutral language of a civil servant. The gap in living standards between whites and natives was increasing, and Svenson, too, warned that the alienation and frustration could boil over. It already had within the native community: one native death in five was the result of accidents or violence. The infant mortality rate was twice that of white children. Fewer than one per cent of native children completed grade 12. Sixty per cent of the native work force was unemployed. Family income levels were one-sixth the provincial average. Sixty-six per cent of admissions to correctional centres were native people. Svenson reported that the native population was approaching 10 per cent of the provincial total, and the birth rate was three times that of whites. Existing government programs weren't working, and things could only get worse.

By 1973, a full 30 per cent of Saskatchewan's native people lived in towns and cities. They arrived in search of work for themselves and better schools for their children, only to be met by an ugly and growing racism. The NDP did little that recognized the new reality during its first two mandates. The Department of Northern Saskatchewan did some good, but the majority of native people lived in the south, and increasingly in the poorest neighbourhoods of the cities.

Blakeney was aware of the problem. In 1974 he wrote in a personal letter to his old colleague Al Johnson: "The major social problem is our inability to devise a strategy for dealing with the social ills of the native population." Blakeney's own home in north central Regina existed in the midst of a neighbourhood where poverty, family breakdown, and failure at school were endemic. He may have been too preoccupied at the office to pay much attention to the local neighbourhood. If so, his wife Anne, who tried to build some personal bridges to native families, surely told him what was happening.

Even before the 1978 election, Blakeney had decided that it was time for the NDP to move. Early in the year cabinet had decided on a thorough review of the government's relationship with native people. Blakeney liked to deal with special secretariats, and would pull a combination of ministers and civil servants together to organize the government's thinking. Once the problem had been analyzed and programs had been put in place, the secretariat would be disbanded. He had used this approach in the oil, potash, and uranium sectors, and he decided to do it with urban native poverty. He named a cabinet committee which included Smishek, Bowerman, and MacMurchy. Don Moroz, a civil servant, was the committee secretary and director of the secretariat. Researchers and planners were pulled in from other departments. Cabinet reviewed two major documents from the secretariat early in 1979. One outlined the dimensions of native poverty in the cities, an update of the work Svenson had done three years earlier. The other talked about what could be done. The report concluded that the problems were lack of education and employment, but added that these were exacerbated by an underlying racial discrimination.

In April 1979, cabinet accepted a four-year affirmative action program proposed by the secretariat. The government could not eradicate decades of prejudice, but it could move in the areas of employment and education. There would be a Native Employment Program in government with the goal of having native people in eight per cent of the civil service jobs by 1984. There would be training money, and subsidies to departments which hired native applicants and trained them. A Native Economic Development Corporation would make investment money available to native entrepreneurs and co-operatives. The thrust in education would be to provide native teachers and teacher's aides, to develop a curriculum more suitable for native students, and to encourage a closer relationship between parents and schools. The programs were to focus on the cities.

Cabinet considered the proposals in April. Some of the documents were leaked to the CBC in September. Walter Smishek, the Urban Affairs Minister, with responsibility for the secretariat, not only allowed himself to be interviewed, but suggested an extended session rather than a few short news clips. He was testing the waters. Some days later, he denied the interviewer's estimate that the program would cost $500 million, and that there might also be quotas set for native hiring in private companies. There had been a quick and negative response from the private sector to any idea of mandatory quotas. The proposal was dropped. Smishek and the cabinet were left trying to make their point through hiring and promotion in government.

Native political organizations weren't impressed, either. Jim Sinclair did not like quotas or affirmative action because he said people in the work place resented the native trainees. The Métis had always proposed that government turn money over to them to create and deliver their own programs. The Federation of Saskatchewan Indians made its usual point about treaty Indians being Ottawa's responsibility, but also asked why there had been so little consultation about the programs. The strength of Blakeney's secretariat approach lay in its ability to marshall government resources quickly; its weakness was that it consulted interests outside government only after the fact. Smishek acknowledges the lack of consultation: "We did not include in the overall planning people of Indian ancestry. They should have been part of the development of the programs which we then started."

In June 1979, Blakeney made a major cabinet shuffle. Among the ministers added were Doug McArthur in Education, and Gerry Hammersmith in the DNS. Blakeney expanded his cabinet group and called it the Committee on People of Indian Ancestry. It included Smishek, who remained in charge of the Social Policy Secretariat and who dealt frequently with the Métis. Bowerman was in charge of Indian land claims, MacMurchy of relations with the FSI. Hammersmith became the DNS minister, and Doug McArthur went to Education. McArthur also played an important role as informal communicator. After his stint as Deputy Minister of DNS in the mid-1970s, he had maintained contact with Sinclair, Ahenakew, and Sol Sanderson, who became Chief of the FSI. The native leaders respected McArthur and trusted him, and his office was often their first point of contact with the government.

The affirmative action hiring programs began with the new fiscal year in April 1980. Blakeney had once criticized Ross Thatcher's quota system for hiring native people; ten years later he was doing it himself. There was precedent for quotas in the surface leases the government had signed with Amok at the Cluff Lake uranium mine, but in that case the quotas were negotiated as the enterprise began. Bringing native employees into existing projects was a slower process. Eight months after the government program began, 50 native people had been hired. Blakeney sent an impatient memo to his ministers. The native hiring program was at a "critical phase," he said. "Already we have raised expectations without achieving significant impact. Native people and program managers are wondering how serious the commitment is. Well, it is serious." Blakeney had been slow to convert to the idea of quotas and affirmative action. He was much more comfortable in the familiar NDP world of universal programs. Once convinced, he was frustrated by the lack of quick results.

There were more promising results in education. McArthur introduced community schools in Saskatoon and Regina, with new curriculum material which was more sensitive to native students. Programs for training native teachers were set up at the universities in Saskatoon and Regina. The Saskatchewan Indian Federated College became affiliated with the University of Regina, but remained under Indian control. The Métis set up the Gabriel Dumont College in Regina.

They were good programs, but the NDP was running out of time. Why had it taken them nine years to get moving? That tardiness is one of Walter Smishek's biggest regrets about his time in government: "I think it was an oversight to a degree, and I don't think we got ourselves organized. We thought that all of the other programs were going to catch the people of Indian ancestry, that they were somehow going to be taken care of. It just didn't happen."

Women had participated in the CCF from its earliest days, drawn by the promise of its egalitarian message. In 1934 the party pledged that, when there was full employment for men in a society governed by the CCF, there would also be full employment for women. They would be partners and equals both in politics and the economy. One of the early activists was Gertrude Telford, a Saskatchewan teacher who had poured her heart and soul into the CCF from its earliest days. She was an organizer, a pamphleteer, a perennial member of council and the executive. When she looked back at it all in 1959, she asked herself why so few women had succeeded as candidates. Her answer: the jealous guarding of "age old prerogatives of dominance by men," and the willingness of women to allow it. She added wistfully that, "there was a time when many of us thought the CCF was to be the answer to women's dream of justice and equality."

It was an unblinking observation after 15 years of the Douglas government. There was always a place for women in the movement, but it was second place. The CCF-NDP fought 13 provincial elections between 1934 and the end of Allan Blakeney's Premiership in 1982. In that time, three women sat as NDP members, none of them during Blakeney's tenure. In the sweep of 1978, there were no female candidates. Throughout much of the decade the NDP seems, strangely, to have been impervious to the demands for women's equality, both in the party and in the larger society.

The government should have been well informed. Throughout the 1970s the push for equal wages, new matrimonial property laws, adequate day care, and affirmative action often came from women who were NDP activists. There were resolutions at the annual conventions calling for greater efforts to elect women candidates, and for more women to be appointed to boards and commissions. Yet the *New Deal for People* booklet, with all its promises, made no mention of women as a group with special needs. That singular lack of attention changed somewhat in the following years, but so slowly that NDP women were perplexed and hurt.

The federal Royal Commission on the Status of Women reported in 1972. The provincial cabinet set up a two-person task force to review the recommendations as they might apply to Saskatchewan. Blakeney appointed Ed Tchorzewski, the Consumer Affairs Minister, to be responsible for the Status of Women. Tchorzewski appointed an advisory committee, just in time for International Women's Year in 1975. The committee continued throughout the NDP period in government. It was appointed by the minister, contained mostly people friendly to the party, had virtually no staff, and its only power was to advise.

Two of the committee's continuing concerns were child care and the appointment of women to boards and commissions. They had some success on the second point. In 1975 there were 1,900 people on such boards. Fewer than 300 (7 per cent) were women. By 1981 that number had increased to 34 per cent. The advisory committee had much less luck with child care. The move by women into the work force was well under way by the time the NDP came to power in 1971. By then half the single women in Saskatchewan and 40 per cent of married women were working outside the home. There was a growing need for child care, in both city and farming communities. In its 1976 report, the advisory committee told the government that existing arrangements did not "meet the need": there was not enough day care, and what did exist was too often in small, dark basements without decent play areas. Reports in the following years had a more urgent ring to them. In 1979 the advisory committee told the minister it "felt strongly" about the government's lack of action. Year after year it called for a universal day care program.

Cabinet resisted the idea. It was prepared to offer subsidies to low income people to help pay for day care spaces, but it was not prepared to build more centres, or to provide operating grants to existing ones. Social Services would support only centres which were run co-operatively by parents, and only if they were non-profit. The big problem was that there simply weren't enough centres, or spaces. Between 1974 and 1979 half the money allocated to parental subsidies wasn't used; there was no place to spend it. A special review committee in 1981 recommended a universal, tax-financed program. The government known for its universal programs would have none of it. "Politically and philosophically as well," Blakeney says, "our cabinet was just not clear whether they wanted a system of institutional day care. We would only put up money for parent-operated day care. We were still very much into empowerment: people should run their own institutions to the greatest extent possible."

The attempt to "empower" women actually made it more difficult for them to find child care. It indicates that cabinet was either out of touch, or stubbornly resistant to knowing what was really happening in families.

Marriage breakups were becoming distressingly common. Eighty per cent of Saskatchewan's single-parent families by 1976 were headed by women. The average wage of women was about half that of men of similar education. There were a lot of poor, single women with children, and their lives were a struggle. Who could expect them to hire a sitter, then head out evenings to a meeting of the parent-run day care board? The cabinet would not accept day care as the foundation for a mobile work force which included large and increasing numbers of women. Nor was it a priority of cabinet ministers, who might have benefited from the insight of women around the table. The phrase "day care" never once found its way into the booklets prepared for the elections between 1971 and 1982.

Blakeney's own traditional rearing and traditional marriages were likely an obstacle to his being more progressive on women's issues. Alexa McDonough, the Nova Scotia NDP leader, has known him since she was a child. Nevertheless, she was one of those to criticize the Saskatchewan NDP government's dismal record in excluding women as candidates. "He came from a totally traditional Nova Scotia Tory background," she says. "He would have come through law school when women were unheard of there. Oxford was entirely male-dominated. And politics was a man's world in those days. He then went into a province where the NDP was the established government party. The women's movement was a much later phenomenon. He just didn't have the exposure."

Feminists were unhappy with Blakeney's position on abortion. He accepted the reality outlined in the Criminal Code. It allowed women to have abortions if the therapeutic abortion committee of an accredited hospital agreed it was necessary. Successive Health Ministers, including Robbins, Tchorzewski, and Rolfes, were opposed to abortion, and many women believed they did nothing to encourage hospitals to establish committees. Blakeney and the ministers were confronted, on the other side of the issue, by an increasingly militant pro-life movement.

In its 1975 campaign, the NDP promised to promote the role of women and to tackle discrimination. It also promised a Career Opportunities Program within the civil service. The Women's Division was created in 1976. It undertook research and public education, and it administered the equal pay, maternity, and paternity leave sections of The Labour Standards Act. It had the power to prosecute employers who violated the act, although it seldom did so. Merran Twigg, who had worked in Social Services, later became Director of the Women's Division. She says cabinet never showed the kind of interest in day care or women's programs that it did in potash, but compared to the other provinces the division stood out: "We were the only division that actually had a program to run where we could take people to court. We didn't have a big enough staff, but we still actually had quite a bit of power. There was a progressiveness in the government that was ahead of the country."

Twigg says she received little response from Blakeney's office, but there was no interference, either: "I had the impression that he was interested, and that he would have liked to be an expert on women's issues, but that it was really pretty foreign to his life." She recalls Blakeney's furtive appearance at an International Women's Day event: "We ran a series of things in the community, showing the film *Not a Love Story,* and then we'd have a discussion. It was mainly women who came, and because I was doing the presentation, I happened to notice this person in the theatre, who was sort of crunched over. It was Allan Blakeney. He wasn't there for any political reasons. He was there to see the film and figure out what was going to be said about pornography. He sat and listened to the speech. He went out in the same way, almost unnoticed."

The government achieved only limited success in a voluntary program to move more women into management positions. Blakeney was frustrated. In May 1978 he wrote to Walter Smishek, who was in charge of the Social Policy Secretariat: "I'd like to see an attempt made to determine, in some systematic way, why females have not been winning competitions for such positions. To have a policy and a plan, and to have this widely publicized among female employees, would at least give them some hope. It would also be a positive step in responding to such groups as the Saskatchewan Action Committee." Blakeney was overcoming his traditional reluctance about hiring quotas. Cabinet began talking about a program to propel women into senior positions, and serious work began that spring on affirmative action programs for women. "It was the first affirmative action with some claws," says Merran Twigg. "We had the promotion and the assignment of women as part of the Deputy Minister's performance appraisal. It actually became a serious program."

Employment programs for women were linked with those for the physically handicapped and for native people. Saskatchewan's human rights code was amended, in effect to allow discriminatory hiring and promotion in favour of those groups. The revised code gave the Human Rights Commission the power to demand that programs be implemented, but that was seldom the approach taken. The government served notice to its departments and crown corporations, but it was much more circumspect with the private sector. Blakeney thought the idea of having every affirmative action program include all three target groups made it too complicated for employers to implement. The private sector, it appears, agreed, because there was no rush to get involved.

The ideals which had given the CCF its vitality and its moral authority were egalitarian. The movement was born of the Depression. It was co-operative and collective—all for one, and one for all. No doubt the Depression experience was later idealized in a sepia-toned sort of way, but it remained a powerful mythology in Saskatchewan into the 1970s. The NDP thought it owned the myth.

When prosperity arrived, it wasn't easy to admit that there were those who did not share in it because of some distinctly non-egalitarian barriers— racism, sexism, and a continuing inequality of opportunity. The targeted programs represented a major, if tardy, shift in thinking and activity. At the height of his power, Blakeney was in an enviable position to come forward with new ideas.

# Chapter Nineteen

# Constitution

The stakes early in 1981 were high. The Canadian constitution was an act of the British Parliament—the musty old British North America Act—and for years Canadian politicians had been squabbling about how to make amendments to it. Prime ministers and premiers had never been able to agree on patriation, the basic question of who in Canada had to concur before constitutional changes could be introduced in the House of Commons. Every time a change was needed, Canada had to ask the British Parliament to do it. It was an embarrassment to everyone, a vestige of colonialism the British had no wish to maintain, and a sign of lingering political immaturity in Canada.

Trudeau and the premiers came within a whisker of achieving an amending formula in Victoria in 1971, but at the last minute, Quebec's Robert Bourassa backed out. He said the proposal gave the federal government too much control over Quebec's social and educational programs. Trudeau began the process again in 1976. He was interrupted by the election of 1979, in which he was voted out of office. After his comeback victory in 1980, he was determined to have done with it. He wanted desperately to enshrine language rights and education—for both French and English minorities—in such a way that they could not be touched by the legislatures or by Parliament. Language guarantees were central to his vision of the country, and had always been his political priority. Constitutional change was also a way of confronting René Lévesque, who had called a referendum for May 1980 to ascertain if Quebecers wanted to leave Canada.

The constitutional dynamic was much more complex than it had been at Victoria. Trudeau's eye may have been on Quebec and the separatists, but other provinces had become insistent about their own issues. The 1970s had seen a constant tug-of-war between Trudeau, who wanted more power for the central government, and the provinces, which wanted a devolution of that power. Trudeau had unilaterally imposed a price for

Saskatchewan and Alberta oil flowing east, and the western provinces were bitter about it. They saw the action as a constitutional affront, and the latest example of Central Canada benefiting at their expense.

Lévesque was defeated by the federalist side in the sovereignty-association referendum of May 20, 1980. Blakeney had been active in the debate, having visited Ontario and Quebec in an April speaking tour. Saskatchewan was not interested in negotiating sovereignty-association with Quebec, he said, because as a small trading province it needed a strong federation. Blakeney was more interested in a new constitutional bargain, one which would benefit Quebec and other provinces. He supported Trudeau's proposal for the entrenched protection of language rights, but demanded constitutional changes regarding resources and equalization payments.

The day after the federalist side won the referendum, Trudeau announced that the constitutional process was on again. In a buoyant and aggressive mood, he said a new constitution would include both a recognition of federal and provincial powers, and a charter of rights and freedoms applying both to individual rights and to collective language rights. But he divided the package. Discussions about the charter should come first, he said, and the division of powers (including resources) should wait until later. He put those proposals to the premiers at a first ministers' conference in September. They were not impressed.

In October, Trudeau announced that he would present Ottawa's amendments to the British Parliament whether or not the premiers agreed. There were among the premiers some who didn't bother to conceal their drawn daggers. Trudeau's and Lévesque's dislike for one another was legendary. Sterling Lyon's feelings for the Prime Minister bordered on hatred. Brian Peckford didn't like him. Bill Bennett and Peter Lougheed weren't exactly fans, either. Blakeney's attitude was ambivalent. Bob Weese, a former director of Saskatchewan's Department of Inter-Governmental Affairs, says, "Blakeney always felt Trudeau did not like him. Al had enormous respect for Trudeau and his intellect, and quite liked him as a person, but their relationship was not positive or easy." And by late 1980 Blakeney didn't trust him.

Blakeney chose not to join with the "gang of six" who vowed to stop Trudeau, but he made it a point to stay on good terms with the other premiers. His best relationships were with Lougheed, whom he liked and respected, and with Bill Davis from Ontario. He also got on well with John Buchanan, a fellow Nova Scotian and graduate of Dalhousie. He could barely tolerate Lyon, and did not respect Bennett's intellect. He was prepared to like Lévesque, and in other circumstances could have co-operated with him; but from the beginning he believed that Quebec was simply out to sabotage the constitutional talks.

Anne Blakeney says that in Hawaii it took a week of sleeping, swimming, and reading novels before her husband would emerge from his political

cocoon and become "human" again. The Blakeneys began slipping away
to the sun in the mid-1970s, a brief escape from the accumulated rigours
of Saskatchewan's politics and its winter. They came to prefer a small,
light-housekeeping suite on the outer island of Kauai. Always efficient,
Anne kept the same shopping list from year to year, so that an hour after
they arrived, they had picked up their groceries and were seated for a
simple meal.

When Blakeney left for Hawaii in January 1981, he had informed
everyone who needed to know that Romanow would be in charge of any
constitutional negotiations. He hadn't yet enjoyed his humanizing week
when Romanow's call came from Toronto. Trudeau, through Marc Lalonde,
had made a final offer to win Saskatchewan's support for constitutional
amendments. Would Saskatchewan sign? It was not unusual that Lalonde
would call Romanow directly, or that the Attorney General and his officials
would enter important negotiations without Blakeney's actually being there,
although nothing ever happened without the Premier's knowledge and
approval. Blakeney and Romanow weren't close; there was a competitive
edge to their relationship. But they were political colleagues who had
developed a way to work well together. Romanow never challenged
Blakeney's leadership, and Blakeney gave Romanow freedom to follow his
instincts.

Romanow gained national attention and prestige throughout the lengthy
constitutional talks. In 1978–79 he had acted as co-chairman of a committee
of federal and provincial ministers who were looking for enough common
ground to begin serious negotiations. He and federal minister Jean Chrétien
starred at widely publicized constitutional hearings in major cities during
the summer of 1980. Romanow had as much freedom as any constitutional
minister, and probably more than most, but it was not always as much
as he would have liked. He found that the rapport he built with Chrétien
and other constitutional ministers was frequently dissipated when their
bosses got together and knocked heads. Despite those inevitable tensions,
Romanow and Blakeney were a good team. There was no more effective
duo in the constitutional talks.

Now, in January 1981, Trudeau was offering Blakeney a deal. Romanow
was calling to say that the feds could be serious; there might be movement.
Blakeney asked him and Howard Leeson, Deputy Minister of Inter-
Governmental Affairs, to fly to Honolulu to meet with him. Blakeney,
Romanow, and Leeson would make a crucial decision concerning the
Canadian constitution in a Honolulu hotel room, thousands of kilometres
from home. Would they hop aboard the Trudeau express, or would they
dig up the rails in its path?

Ross Thatcher used to say that, on a list of 100 priorities for Saskatchewan, constitutional change was number 101. Prairie politicians had always

believed that Trudeau's constitutional approaches were framed with Quebec in mind. That had little appeal in Saskatchewan. Farmers on coffee row weren't talking bilingualism at nine o'clock in the morning, unless it was to complain about the French on cereal boxes. Blakeney had represented Saskatchewan in constitutional negotiations as early as 1962. He knew that Thatcher's observation, though it fell far short of statesmanship, was politically true. So it was with competing feelings of reluctance and public duty that Blakeney approached any constitutional talks.

Trudeau is a liberal individualist. As a scholar and law professor, he had since the 1950s proposed incorporating individual human rights—the freedom of religion, speech, association, and the due process of law—into a Canadian constitution. As Justice Minister in Lester Pearson's government, and later as Prime Minister, Trudeau extended the concept of entrenched rights to linguistic groups as well—the French-speaking minority in English Canada, and the English-speaking minority in Quebec.

Blakeney is a democrat in the British tradition, who describes himself as a "British constitutional lawyer type." He studied law in the Loyalist province of Nova Scotia. Later at Oxford he steeped himself in the study and first-hand observation of British political institutions. He is not in favour of entrenched rights, and that was a fundamental difference between the two men. He had concluded with typical understatement that "the British Parliament has worked not all that badly." Ultimately, rights are protected by Parliament, not by a constitution which is interpreted by the courts.

Blakeney's position, based on his observations of the American legal system, was carefully reasoned: "The charters have been so misused in American history that I just don't believe they add much to the total rights and freedoms of the people. The Bill of Rights was used to strike down laws setting minimum wages, minimum hours of work . . . all these things were seen as being an interference with the citizen's right to contract and sell a service, for any period of time and at any price he wanted. That's not my idea of adding to the rights and freedoms of the people." Counter-arguments did exist; in fact, they constituted a majority position in the federal NDP caucus. The CCF had been calling for a Charter of Rights since the 1940s. Proponents could point to cases, such as the internment of Japanese Canadians during the Second World War, in which people needed protection against the discriminatory practices of an elected majority. And the American courts had made progressive judgements—in the integrating of students, for example.

Trudeau wanted constitutional change. Blakeney still believes that what Trudeau really cared about was language and mobility rights (the ability to reside and look for work in any province): "Everything else was unimportant to him, but he couldn't sell language and mobility because they didn't have any political pizazz. So he wrapped around them all sorts of rights that everyone agreed with and already existed but did have a certain pizazz—a people's package." Blakeney may have underestimated Trudeau's commitment to a charter for individual rights, but he was right in analyzing Trudeau's strategy as one of appealing directly to Canadians. Trudeau knew he was going to have a battle with the premiers over who should have what powers, so he said a "people's package" should be approved first, with arguments over power-sharing negotiated later.

Blakeney wanted constitutional change, too, but not an extensive charter of rights. He wasn't opposed to language protections, but they weren't a big issue at home. Saskatchewan had only a small French-speaking population. For him, resources were the key. When Trudeau talked about a charter of rights as being a "people's package," Blakeney insisted that concerns over who controlled resources was also a concern of the people. The courts had ordered the province to pay back $500 million to the oil companies because its taxes were unconstitutional. That money might have allowed Blakeney to extend the dental program to older children, or to put houses or skating rinks into decaying Saskatchewan towns. The constitution could guarantee Saskatchewan people jurisdiction and income which the courts had refused them. He found Trudeau too centralist on resources, but he believed there was a possibility for negotiation.

There would be great risks in entering Trudeau's wind tunnel of constitutional change. Blakeney knew that by pursuing any deal with Trudeau, he risked neutralizing the potent political weapon of Ottawa-bashing. His political ministers, Cowley and MacMurchy, had told him in the 1978 election post-mortem that Saskatchewan should use the constitution to fight Trudeau, not to deal with him. The battle shaping up for the next provincial election was between the New Democrats and the Conservatives. The Tories were rabidly anti-Trudeau, and stood to gain politically from it. They would have liked nothing better than to be able to link Blakeney with Trudeau. Blakeney was prepared, reluctantly, to forgo the advice of his ministers. "Once Trudeau started on this," he says, "it seemed to me that we had to finish it in a way that was satisfactory to Saskatchewan. This was going to mean some sort of compromise."

Another reason to be involved, surely, sprung from his view of the national good. "One has to remember the mood of the hour," Blakeney says. "As the Parti Quebecois made clear that they were going for separation or sovereignty-association, the possibility of the break-up of Canada as we knew it was a clear and present danger. At the same time there was growing dissatisfaction in Western Canada. Imagine the circumstances under which Alberta would simply cut off the production of oil which was going to be sent to eastern Canada or exported, on the grounds that the federal government was stealing their heritage. I didn't expect that western Canada was going to leave confederation, but if Quebec went, then stranger things might have happened, because there was just that mood about."

Finally, there was the sheer intellectual challenge. Blakeney worked through intricate constitutional problems with the same satisfaction many people find in crossword puzzles. Bob Weese says, "Throughout the piece Al was Saskatchewan's constitutional lawyer, with a little help. It's a job he relished. He probably preferred it to the Premier's job."

The political dangers lurking externally were not nearly as immediate or as painful as the division within the NDP. The constitutional ministers held hearings and met during the summer of 1980, but the September first ministers' conference had flopped. By mid-September, Ed Broadbent had begun some constitution making of his own. He was preparing to contact Trudeau, and he was looking for a package of amendments the premiers could support.

Blakeney's notes indicate that he and Broadbent talked on the telephone on September 16th. They discussed a list of possible amending formulas and charters. Blakeney broke off to consult with his Attorney General. Romanow was alarmed that the leader of a third party in the Commons was attempting what the constitutional and first ministers had been unable to do. "It was Roy Romanow's opinion," Blakeney wrote to his file, "that such a move at this time would be unwise and a possible source of great confusion." Blakeney, clearly uneasy, then concluded the conversation with Broadbent. He could approach Trudeau if he wanted, but the Premier's notes say, "I specifically requested that he not suggest that he was putting forward proposals on my behalf, and I indicated to him that he was not mandated to bargain on Saskatchewan's behalf." Broadbent is an intellectual, but loose and philosophical; Blakeney is no less an intellectual, but he's tight and pragmatic, with a keener sense of detail and a greater experience in negotiation. He wanted to do his own bargaining.

Trudeau announced on October 2nd that he would ask Britain to amend the BNA Act without the consent of Canada's premiers. Trudeau had met with Broadbent for about an hour the previous afternoon, and told him that he intended to act unilaterally. Broadbent wanted a stronger charter of rights and, with Saskatchewan in mind, he pushed for a clear statement that the provinces owned natural resources and had power over them. Trudeau promised to consider that, and Broadbent apparently left the Prime Minister's office a happy man. He called Saskatchewan that same afternoon. Blakeney remembers leaving a caucus meeting to talk to him.

Broadbent outlined the package. "I said I didn't like it," Blakeney says now, "but I said we might well be able to live with it." He returned to repeat to his MLAs what Broadbent had said.

Blakeney watched Trudeau's televised announcement in his office along with Romanow, Leeson, Bill Knight, and Dick Proctor, Saskatchewan's Inter-Governmental Affairs man in Ottawa. Trudeau announced his intention to put the constitutional question to a national referendum. That came as a complete surprise to Blakeney. The first ministers had not discussed a referendum. Blakeney wasn't pleased about the charter of rights, and he noticed that Trudeau made no announcement about resources. Broadbent and Joe Clark followed the Prime Minister with televised statements. Clark attacked Trudeau; Broadbent supported him, but talked about the need for a better deal on resources.

Dick Proctor recalls the scene after the telecast: "Blakeney got up, walked over, turned off the television set, and said 'That's not the package that was described to me over the phone.'" It shook Blakeney's confidence in Broadbent, and he became even more determined that the federal leader not attempt to bargain on Saskatchewan's behalf. Blakeney also took extreme precautions in documenting his telephone conversations with Broadbent, the premiers, and other NDP leaders. One of his assistants, usually Bill Gillies, listened to Blakeney's side of the conversations and took detailed, often verbatim, notes. Beyond any garbled messages, Blakeney differed fundamentally from Broadbent on two points: the acceptability of unilateral action, and the charter of rights. The differences are understandable. The founders of the CCF believed that no real progress would occur until the party won national power. They put great stock in national planning, and the nationalization of industry and the banking system. To accomplish that agenda, they would need a strong central government. They were, by definition, centralists. But the dream of national power eluded them. Success came at the provincial level, particularly in Saskatchewan. Blakeney had been able to exercise power innovatively, introducing new social programs, and paying for them through the profits from public enterprise. But Ottawa had been challenging Saskatchewan's income from resources at every turn. Blakeney's practical experience had caused an evolution in his view of how the country was best governed. He had become more of a provincialist.

"I once believed," he says, "that we could develop in Canada a sufficient consensus to proceed with a fair number of things nationally. I later saw different things happening. Governments have become much larger. People have become unwilling to repose their confidence in governments. People like to deal on many issues with organizations which are a little closer to them. It was easier to do social experiments on a provincial level."

Blakeney's view of Canada as a country with separate but equally important orders of government was offended by Trudeau's unilateral action. "I think it was outrageous for Trudeau to say that he was going to amend the constitution without provincial consent," he says, "and outrageous for the federal NDP to agree. I make no bones about it." Broadbent was less concerned about unilateral action, and makes no apologies for his actions: "I believed deeply at that time that we had to move as a nation to overcome the blockage in constitutional reform, and that ultimately if it had to come to unilateral action, or action that had just the support of a few provinces, it was necessary." Broadbent was branded by some in the NDP as an "Ontario" politician with a centralist's diminished view of the country's extremities. It was a charge that infuriated him. He could point to his immediate insistence that Trudeau add provincial control of resources to the constitutional package before he could expect NDP support. "I want to be fair in my comments about my colleagues in Saskatchewan," he says now. "We got in the negotiating process a number of things that up to that point they had been interested in and hadn't got. I got commitments from Trudeau, in addition to his package of proposed changes, to make further changes toward the decentralized management of resources. As a modern social democrat I deeply believe in that."

Broadbent felt his insistence on behalf of the energy-producing provinces did indicate a thorough and subtle understanding of Canada. In Blakeney's view, the Conservative government of Ontario supported Trudeau mainly out of economic self-interest. Ontario stood to lose by a shift of power toward the provinces because that would mean, among other things, increased prices for western oil. Broadbent believes he took a much more pan-Canadian position than did the Ontario Tories.

Blakeney's and Broadbent's second point of disagreement regarded the charter of rights. Broadbent was articulating the traditional desire of the federal NDP for entrenched rights. Again, Blakeney's opposition had to do with his provincial experience, although it contained personal elements as well. "I'm still aghast that any social democratic party would be in favour of transferring power from legislatures to courts," he says. "I don't understand that thinking. I think the federal NDP caucus was really quite wrong." He looked at the issue through his own experience. He had been premier in a social democratic province where there had been at least modest attempts to redistribute wealth and power. He was convinced that some of Saskatchewan's progressive social programs, including medicare, could have been struck down by a court loaded with judges drawn from Canada's conservative establishment. Saskatchewan had its own human rights code, subject to legislative override. It had been used to create affirmative action employment programs for women and native people. Blakeney feared the courts might strike down those programs if called to pass judgement on them.

Blakeney thought Broadbent had made a strategic blunder by agreeing with Trudeau right away: "I have no reason to know why Ed would do this. I don't know why he wouldn't have called a meeting of provincial NDP leaders." Howard Leeson describes the situation much more bluntly: "Blakeney had no faith in Broadbent's ability to negotiate this. It was not his forte. He didn't know the detail of constitutional negotiations. He tended to leap without looking on some things because they sounded good to him. Blakeney is a person of precision. He wanted the detail and everything on paper; he wanted to know what he was agreeing to and where it would go. He had no faith that Ed was able to carry that kind of process forward."

Broadbent has a ready defence for not postponing his support: "That's a Saskatchewan position. It's a mug's game. Then you up the ante all the time, which is what they got into. You never get enough. No, I don't think we went in too soon. If we hadn't, and I don't want to overstate it, I don't think we'd have a constitution today. They needed the extra strength at the federal level."

Most of the premiers angrily denounced Trudeau after his October announcement. Blakeney played it low key. He told the group gathered in his office that night that he intended to "mumble awhile," and publicly, that's just what he did. The leader of the federal NDP had come out immediately in favour, and any division of opinion would be embarrassing. Blakeney called a cabinet meeting the following morning. His ministers were "one hundred and two per cent" against making any deal with Trudeau. "I remember sitting around in cabinet and the ministers saying, 'The public want you to say no to anything Trudeau says, and there is no reason why we should agree to anything if we're thinking about our political future here in Saskatchewan'." Despite that hostility, Blakeney hoped he could make a deal. He thought the country needed it, and that Trudeau would be hard to stop in any event.

Cabinet decided to send Romanow to Ottawa on the weekend. He met with the federal NDP caucus on Sunday, October 5th. He warned them that Saskatchewan would not go along, at least not right away. The province intended to negotiate its own changes directly with Jean Chrétien and Michael Kirby, the senior federal advisor. Leeson, who was at the meeting, recalls, "That was a bit dismaying for Ed Broadbent. I think he had indicated to Trudeau that he thought he could deliver Blakeney on this question, that he had spoken to Blakeney and that it sounded pretty good to him. Trudeau thought that he actually would get the agreement not only of Broadbent, but of Blakeney." On the same trip east, Romanow and Leeson met with Chrétien and Kirby, and made the same points. Blakeney wanted to negotiate on his own behalf, and demanded written rather than verbal agreements. Chrétien was annoyed, almost harsh. He had thought Saskatchewan was on side, and now the province came demanding changes. Leeson says, "This caused a bit of a split which carried right through between Trudeau and Blakeney during this period. From our side, we thought that there was a package which wasn't there. We went down in good faith to try to negotiate something else, and we were met with reluctance and suspicion."

The premiers soon got into the act as well. They met in Toronto, and six of them said they were going to challenge Trudeau's unilateral action in court. Blakeney refused to join them. "I was very upset that Trudeau would proceed this way, but I was attempting to stay back a bit because I didn't want to embarrass either myself or Ed Broadbent, or disclose the split between us on this issue. Ed was all for the proposed federal action and I thought that was a very unusual and mistaken position for the federal caucus to take." While the hard-line provinces were preparing for their day in court, Saskatchewan spent October and November looking for a deal, talking to the federal government, but also to other provinces, including British Columbia and Ontario.

Blakeney spoke with Trudeau on the telephone five days after his announcement, and again at the end of October when the Prime Minister visited Regina on other business. The meeting was in Blakeney's office. "I said, 'Fair enough'," Blakeney recalls. " 'You have decided to go unilaterally, but surely you're not going to go unilaterally before making a reference to the Supreme Court.' And Trudeau said, 'Yes I am.' And I said, 'This is not right, not proper, not in the scheme of things. This is not within what is permissible.' He said, 'No, this is a political issue'."

Trudeau's action drove a wedge between the federal and the Saskatchewan NDP. It also had a minor disruptive effect within the Saskatchewan camp. Blakeney was prepared to compromise on unilateralism, as much as it offended his view of Canada. His analysis had led him to believe that it might not be possible to stop Trudeau on strictly legal grounds. He was prepared to trade off an unsavoury process for clear gains on other important issues.

"He split things into two parts," Leeson says: "the substance of the package and the process. He never agreed with the process, the unilateral action. On the other side, he thought that the substantive package had some merit if you could get some changes to the proposed charter of rights, the amending formula, and something on natural resources. He was willing to negotiate the substance of the package, and I think he thought that Trudeau was much more open to change that he really was. In addition, there were all the inside pressures in the NDP, the national leader attempting to get the Premier on side. There was a lot of pressure on Blakeney."

Romanow and Leeson were hawks on the question of Trudeau's unilateral action. "The view of Romanow and myself and others in the department," Leeson says, "was that we ought not to agree. There was a substantial split in judgement." The division was serious enough that at one point Leeson submitted his resignation, but Romanow wouldn't accept it. There were other differences, too. Romanow and Leeson liked the idea of a charter to protect the rights of individuals. They thought Blakeney's views were well considered, but not in tune with the times. Leeson also liked the idea of a referendum. It would involve individual Canadians in the constitutional decision, rather than restricting debate to the 11 first ministers. Blakeney thought a referendum would further divide the country, and he believed that Trudeau would manipulate the wording of the question and the timing of the vote.

Blakeney prevailed. He agreed that he could accept a limited charter, if legislatures had a right to override its provisions. The talks with Ottawa continued, but they didn't really get anywhere. Blakeney and Broadbent remained in contact, and Broadbent was in touch with Trudeau. A new element of strain arose when it became apparent that Broadbent's staff had news from the Liberals about the negotiations with Saskatchewan. Blakeney warned Broadbent that discussions between the two of them must not find their way to Kirby and Chrétien. "Our staff believed that if we were negotiating with another province, and if we kept the federal NDP informed, then it got to Chrétien right away," Blakeney says. "We reached the conclusion that we could not deal with the federal NDP unless we wanted to give the same information to the federal government. There was a great deal of bitterness."

A Joint Parliamentary Committee had begun to hold public hearings on the Trudeau proposal. Blakeney appeared before the committee in mid-December to present a brief. He said that Saskatchewan would withhold judgement until the committee's final resolution went back to Parliament, but without significant change, Saskatchewan would oppose Trudeau. There had been little contact with the federal negotiators since late November. Blakeney assumed they were no longer interested in talks. He thought he would wait for the Commons report, then join the opposing provinces. Early in the New Year Blakeney and Broadbent talked again on the telephone. Broadbent was trying to open the talks between Saskatchewan and Ottawa again. Blakeney was testy: "I do not know who to speak with. Chrétien is soft on detail, we have talked the principles to death. They are a pack of liars and I do not believe them." He ended, though, by saying he might talk one last time, but told Broadbent that he should take the conversation as "advance warning." Saskatchewan would likely come out against Trudeau.

Kirby and Trudeau had shifted their approach. They began to place less emphasis on winning over the remaining provinces, and more on appealing directly to the public, and to interest groups demanding additions to the constitutional package. They began talking with native leaders about including an aboriginal rights clause. Broadbent had demanded it in return for continued NDP support. The clause was actually drafted in his crowded office, with native leaders spilling off the couch and chairs and onto the window ledges. But six provinces were challenging the charter in court, and the British Parliament was unhappy about Trudeau's process. Trudeau and Kirby decided to pursue a dual strategy: first, to win over interest groups and the public; second, to convince at least one more province to support them. They hoped that would placate the British. Saskatchewan and Blakeney seemed the only possibility, but Blakeney had been so sure there would be no negotiations that he had made plans to slip away to Hawaii.

On January 14th, Chrétien called Romanow to resume negotiations. Romanow gave him a shopping list. On January 20th Marc Lalonde called to set off a new round of talks (by that time Chrétien had been hospitalized for exhaustion). On the 21st Romanow and Leeson, Kirby, and other federal officials began two days of meetings in a Toronto hotel. Lalonde flew in on January 23rd, and the meetings shifted to the Constellation Hotel near the Toronto airport. The talks centred on Saskatchewan's proposals for more concessions from Ottawa on resources—discussed, but never agreed on in October and November—and on the referendum provision. It was agreed that a province could, in extraordinary circumstances, limit production, as Saskatchewan had done with potash. It was also agreed that Ottawa would have to get the support of at least several provinces before holding a referendum on constitutional questions.

Romanow was in telephone contact with Blakeney, who said he wanted to see the proposals on paper, and also to get the sense of the negotiations personally from Romanow and Leeson. "Our recommendation to Blakeney," Romanow says, "was that we just don't buy it. I remember the long pause at the other end of the phone and Al says, 'Well, I think I want to do this, Roy.' He thought that a breakthrough would be very important."

The federal authorities decided to send Fred Gibson, one of their officials from the meetings, along to answer Blakeney's questions. Trudeau gave him a letter of agreement for Blakeney to sign. The understanding was that Blakeney would make his decision by late Monday so it could be announced to the Parliamentary committee.

Romanow and Leeson were to fly from Toronto with Air Canada on Sunday, January 25th. They arrived at the airport to be told their plane was delayed, and only later did Leeson notice on the terminal screen that the flight had been cancelled. They scrambled to book another aboard United Airlines, which sent them through Los Angeles. They arrived in Honolulu late Sunday night, and emerged from the jet red-eyed, carrying their winter overcoats and boots with them into the tropical night. They booked into a hotel called the Ilikai. Blakeney flew in on Monday morning.

The three of them spent the day in a hotel room, examining the information word-by-word, calling on Gibson when they needed him. "The thing I remember," Leeson says, "is that here you have the person who later becomes the head of the spy agency CSIS, Fred Gibson, and ourselves, and we can't go to some agency and say we want something typed up because they might say, 'Hey did you know they're here negotiating the constitution of Canada?'" They didn't finish on Monday, and worked on into Tuesday. Cabinet had met in Regina. "They communicated the political message," Romanow says, "that we shouldn't do it. They simply did not want us to sign. This had gone far enough. We didn't want to be perceived as being in bed with Trudeau." Lorne Nystrom had also called Blakeney and warned him against signing.

Blakeney had spent his days at the beach thinking about the constitution. "My reaction," he says, "was a couple of weeks late realizing what was happening here. I'm going to be committed to Trudeau, and I'm not going to be able to off-load if he keeps adding things on. I'm not in control in any way in this agenda." He was increasingly uneasy about Saskatchewan trying to negotiate bilaterally in a game where there were so many competing interests. But he thought the bitter constitutional wrangling was dangerous for the country.

While Kirby and Trudeau were negotiating with Saskatchewan, they were also meeting others. They were talking with native leaders, for instance, about entrenching aboriginal rights in the constitution. Blakeney was not opposed to that, but he was concerned that it was one more item being added on. Then Gibson announced that rights for the handicapped had been added as well. Again, Saskatchewan did not disagree, but Blakeney became even more uneasy about the apparent open-endedness of the process. Where would it end? Ottawa had also agreed to the addition of property rights to the charter of rights. They were in negotiations with the Senators. Romanow thought he had an agreement with Lalonde about the Senate: in a new constitution the Senate would not have a veto over constitutional amendments. But that had been an add-on to the rushed Toronto discussions, a verbal agreement with no accompanying text. Romanow briefed Blakeney about it when he arrived in Hawaii.

Blakeney and Trudeau were scheduled to talk on the telephone on Monday evening. Blakeney had initialled, but not signed, his draft letter of acceptance and given it to Gibson. He wanted to double check with Trudeau on the question of the Senate veto. The conversation didn't occur at the appointed time. Blakeney was told that Trudeau had been on the road from Montreal to Ottawa when his limousine got a flat tire. The Premier used the respite to probe Romanow and Leeson further on exactly what had been said in Toronto about the Senate. They were uncertain enough to contact Gibson. He had, in fact, brought some federal paper with him, with orders to show it only if asked. When Blakeney read it in detail, the news was bad. Trudeau had indeed given the Senators a veto over constitutional amendments in future, in return for their agreement not to delay passage of Trudeau's existing package. "By Tuesday morning," Romanow says, "for a number of reasons—I don't know what went on in his mind—Blakeney made the decision, just momentarily by himself. He was out on the balcony pacing, and he came back and said, 'I don't think I'll do it.' I was there watching."

The conversation between Trudeau and Blakeney on Tuesday was anti-climactic. There was no high emotion, just a flat and cautious tone: Blakeney said no. Kirby later upbraided Leeson, telling him that Trudeau was "wild" about the failed Hawaii negotiations. Trudeau thought Blakeney was a ditherer or had never been serious about a deal. The Hawaii episode soured whatever good will might have existed between them.

Blakeney admits that the "Senate was the occasion" to pull the plug: "Once you got on the Trudeau train there was no way to get off." While the Senate veto was the final straw, Blakeney disagrees with those who said it was merely an excuse for not making the deal. Stanley Knowles, among others, argued that the constitutional resolution simply maintained the status quo for the Senate, and it was not worth scuttling the charter for that. Blakeney, who wanted the Senate abolished, responds: "I think they were out to lunch. I think that if the NDP won the House of Commons and wanted to bring about major change, the Senate could undertake very significant delaying tactics. I cast my mind on what would have happened in Saskatchewan in 1962 if we had had a provincial Senate controlled by the opposition party. Anyone who believes that wouldn't happen is unusually naïve. I don't believe the concessions on the Senate were unimportant."

It's arguable whether the Senate veto was a worthy reason to scuttle an entire constitutional deal. But the charge (made by Liberals and a few New Democrats) that Blakeney would have found some other reason to demur had the Senate question not arisen does not make sense. He had already initialled the letter of acceptance; it would have been difficult to renege if Trudeau had agreed with him on the Senate. It is possible that he maintained the issue as a hedge, and was happy to have it at the end. Still, by agreeing to limit the Senate veto, Trudeau would have had him on side.

Saskatchewan's decision to oppose made for testy times within the NDP. Romanow made a quick trip east early in February to explain the decision to the federal caucus. He was met by the rumour that Trudeau had offered Blakeney everything he had asked for, but the Premier had still refused to sign. Some federal caucus members, including Ed Broadbent, felt the Senate issue was an excuse.

Relations cooled quickly. Early in March Dick Proctor, Blakeney's man in Ottawa, wrote to Broadbent's chief of staff to inform him of a change in communications procedure. Blakeney would keep Broadbent "as informed as possible on positions of the Government of Saskatchewan," but he would do so on paper, using telex or a fax machine. "There is little doubt," Proctor wrote, "[that] misunderstandings and misconceptions have occurred. It is the Premier's feeling that some of this has been the result of telephone conversations and the nuances that are drawn from those conversations." The leaders could still talk on the telephone, but anything official would move on paper.

Early in February Blakeney announced that Saskatchewan could not support Trudeau. The day before, four members of the federal NDP caucus, all of them from Saskatchewan, had publicly broken ranks with Broadbent and said they would oppose the constitutional resolution when it was voted on in the Commons. Lorne Nystrom, Simon de Jong, Stan Hovdebo, and Doug Anguish said the resolution lacked the sufficient provincial accord— essentially the Blakeney position. Two others MPs, Les Benjamin and Father Bob Ogle, supported Broadbent within the caucus, although Ogle eventually abstained when the vote came to the House.

Blakeney's clear break with the federal party necessitated a certain amount of internal housekeeping. He had considered the position of other provincial NDP leaders, and contacted them in turn, presenting each with a strategy aimed at minimizing political damage. In Manitoba, Howard Pawley would soon face an election against Sterling Lyon. Blakeney assured him that "our first priority is to get you elected," and advised that when he released his statement, Pawley should "please duck." He offered to send someone to brief Pawley's people on the detail and wisdom of Saskatchewan's position.

With his friend Grant Notley from Alberta, the telephone discussion centred around how to put enough heat on Broadbent to change his position, but not enough to threaten his leadership. With Dave Barrett in British Columbia, the task was more difficult. Barrett supported Broadbent and wished the constitutional debate would go away. Above all, he did not want to be seen on Trudeau's side when Bill Bennett was a chippy Trudeau foe. Blakeney considered Barrett a loose cannon. When he called him in February, he had already mapped out Barrett's media strategy. "The purpose of my call," Blakeney told him, "is to suggest to you, if you could see your way clear on this, to respond if asked. If not asked, not to respond at all. If asked about the difference between myself and Ed Broadbent, to say that you had not seen Blakeney's statement, that the final report of the committee wasn't down, that you would be reviewing the matter, et cetera. . . ."

Despite Blakeney's warnings, Barrett told reporters in March that he agreed with Trudeau that the premiers had become a "laughing stock" because of their inability to agree on anything. He added that they should stop their whimpering. Barrett later apologized to Blakeney through Romanow.

In March, there was a secret Sunday afternoon meeting of the NDP leaders, old and new, in a hotel in Hull. Broadbent and Blakeney argued their positions. Tommy Douglas and David Lewis were there, and took Broadbent's side. As Blakeney recalls it, Broadbent and Douglas argued that the unilateral process was flawed, but the charter of rights made it worthwhile. Blakeney said it was not acceptable to freeze the provinces out of so important a change: "The appeals of T. C. and Ed were much more to the merit of their position without acknowledging any merit of mine. David, the supreme logician that he was, said, 'Now let's take your logic and mine and see where it leads us.' But nothing was resolved. We just did not see eye to eye."

Broadbent recalls the meeting vividly. "There wasn't the reconciliation between Allan and myself that David had hoped for. And David and Tommy were on my side, on the federal side, in that dispute. Allan might have perceived the meeting as a sort of ganging up of three against one, and that is not an unreasonable perception. The meeting could well have been to have Tommy and David try to move him closer to the federal position." Blakeney left quickly and did not notice it, but after the meeting Lewis, near death from leukemia, broke down and wept on Broadbent's shoulder. "I'll always remember that," Broadbent says. "The two of us standing in a rather open square in front of the hotel parking lot, and David was a very sad man that day. It was a poignant experience."

David Lewis died in May. Blakeney, Douglas, and Broadbent had their chance to debate the issue again in July. The occasion was the NDP annual convention on the UBC campus in Vancouver. It wasn't quite a showdown, because party officials had worked out a speakers' list. The party's giants, past and present, lined up at the microphones. Broadbent, Barrett, Bob White, Tommy Douglas, and Stanley Knowles spoke in favour of the federal position. Blakeney, Romanow, Nystrom, and Notley spoke for the Saskatchewan position. At the end of the day, Broadbent's forces had won two-thirds of the convention. The debate had been a stirring tribute to democratic tradition and to the party. Arguments usually heard in only backrooms were finally voiced in public, and the air was cleared—at least somewhat.

Those were among the most difficult times ever for the New Democratic Party. Les Benjamin, MP for Regina West, says he had "given up" on the premiers after the Victoria constitutional conference in 1971. He thought Trudeau was right to act unilaterally, and he supported Broadbent. During the height of the disagreement Benjamin was asked by Broadbent, who couldn't make it, to deliver the leader's report to the Saskatchewan NDP convention. He read Broadbent's speech; when he finished, nobody applauded. Later, at a party event in the Regina Lakeview constituency, both Benjamin and his wife, Connie, were snubbed. "I remember one couple came up and said, 'That's the last time we lift a finger for you. There'll be no more signs on our lawn for you or anything else.' These were people I'd known for years. That really hurt. Three or four different people made some pretty mean remarks to Connie the same night. She came over and said, 'We have to leave.' We got our coats and left. She was crying."

Time has blunted some of the hard feelings within the party, but not all of them. Howard Leeson still says Broadbent had an "Oshawa view of the world." Broadbent says Leeson was "anti-Quebec." Blakeney and Broadbent admit that the constitutional drama placed a strain on their relationship, but each insists that things remained civil between them. The day after the 1988 federal election, in which the high hopes of the NDP had not been fulfilled, one of the first calls Broadbent received was from Blakeney.

In April, Blakeney had joined the six dissident premiers. Nova Scotia made the same decision, and so was born the "gang of eight." It was an uneasy, unlikely alliance. Blakeney was in league with a batch of Conservative premiers against a proposal that was supported by his own federal party. René Lévesque and his nimble minister, Claude Morin, were there, too. They had tried to take Quebec out of Canada; less than a year later, they were making common cause with seven predominantly anglophone provinces against a prime minister from Quebec. Blakeney knew, and so did everyone else, that this was a "defensive alliance" to stop Trudeau from acting on his own. He made it clear that, when that was achieved, the provinces must be free to deal on their own once again.

Saskatchewan approached the constitutional negotiations very much as a middle power. Blakeney had waited until the last moment to declare himself. He thought it was a principled position. He was not obstructing the process for the sake of doing so, but he would not agree to a deal until more of his conditions had been met. He did not dare to be seen as soft on Trudeau, but neither did he want to create unnecessary problems for Broadbent. It was not an easy combination to manage, and it earned him the contempt and enmity of Trudeau, of premiers like Lévesque, and even of some colleagues in the NDP.

Some premiers in the gang of eight—Lougheed and Lévesque among them—held that every province had to agree to constitutional change before it could occur. Blakeney had never believed that, and he thought that Lévesque would simply use that position to defeat the process of change. The atmosphere wasn't improved by the fact that Lévesque was preparing for an election, and Lougheed was involved in negotiations with Ottawa over oil prices.

These differing views became evident as the Supreme Court of Canada began to hear the provinces' case in April. Blakeney had a close hand in planning Saskatchewan's position, although Ken Lysyk, the Deputy Attorney General, drafted most of the arguments. Saskatchewan argued, first, that it was illegal for Ottawa to amend the constitution unilaterally; second, that unilateral action offended political convention, because federal governments had always obtained provincial consent for constitutional changes. Saskatchewan conceded that not all provinces had to agree, but that a "sufficient measure of provincial consent" was needed for change to occur. Saskatchewan did not say how many provinces would comprise "sufficient measure," and it said the court should not have to specify a number, either.

When the judgement arrived in September, it was obvious that Saskatchewan's argument had been influential. The court ruled that Trudeau's action was not illegal, but that it did offend Canadian political conventions. Following Saskatchewan's argument, the court did not specify how many provinces must agree to constitutional change. It was, in effect, telling Trudeau and the premiers to go back to the negotiating table. That set the stage for a dramatic week in November.

The government conference centre in Ottawa is a square, ponderous building of grey stone a couple of blocks east of the Houses of Parliament, and immediately across Wellington Street from the equally ponderous Château Laurier. On Monday, November 2nd, six weeks after the Supreme Court judgement, the ministers began meeting again for a last try at breaking the constitutional impasse. Blakeney and the Saskatchewan team were staying at the Château. The hotel is connected to the centre by a tunnel under Wellington Street.

On the night of the Supreme Court decision in September, Romanow had been in Ottawa. He and Roy McMurtry met informally with Chrétien at his home. The talk turned to the deal that Ottawa and the provinces would eventually have to make. Within days informal talks were breaking out all over the place, at least among those provinces which were not solidly opposed to a deal. The gang of eight met twice, but had not been able to put together an effective common front because their final goals were quite different. Romanow warned the group that now that Trudeau had been stopped, or at least slowed down, Saskatchewan was looking for a deal. Claude Morin accused him of duplicity in sitting at the table with the gang of eight while looking for a deal with Ottawa. By the time Trudeau dropped the gavel on November 2nd, no one trusted anyone.

The first ministers made opening statements on national television on Monday. Later, the sessions moved behind closed doors upstairs. Blakeney said that Saskatchewan would accept the entrenchment of basic rights in a constitution, but any other entrenched rights must be subject to an override by the legislatures. The day ended with no agreement. The Tuesday morning session concentrated on Trudeau's proposal for a referendum to break constitutional deadlocks. Most of the premiers, Blakeney included, opposed the idea. There was no public session in the afternoon, and there appeared to be no new proposals coming out of the closed sessions. Blakeney told the gang of eight that Saskatchewan would put forward a new proposal on Wednesday morning, and he had drafters work through the night.

Chrétien called Romanow early Wednesday morning. He wanted to talk. They decided to meet in federal offices at the conference centre, and they invited Roy McMurtry to join them. They sat with their feet up and talked about the bare elements of a possible agreement. Romanow scribbled on a yellow notepad. Among other things, they discussed abandoning the provinces' demand that each have a veto over constitutional change. At one time or another both Quebec and Ontario had said they could live without it, in return for other concessions. If the largest provinces could yield on the veto, the others might, too. In return, Ottawa would scale down its charter of rights, a major sticking point with several premiers. Trudeau would not accept provinces opting out of federal programs with compensation, so that option was scratched.

In the first ministers' meeting on Wednesday morning, Blakeney put forward a new proposal his staff had prepared the previous night, but the others weren't interested. The session wore on, with Trudeau and Lévesque squaring off like game-cocks. But the morning chat among Romanow, McMurtry, and Chrétien had obviously had an effect. During a late afternoon coffee break, Bill Davis and Trudeau invited Blakeney into a back room and put a proposal to him—one which discarded the single province veto, and in which there was a limited charter of rights, subject to legislative override. Blakeney thought the Davis-Trudeau proposal "an enormous breakthrough," but he played it cool. He said he would think about it. "I came out," he says, "and talked to Roy and said, 'You talk to Chrétien to see if Trudeau and Davis are just jacking around, or whether there is anything to this'."

Romanow and Chrétien had been talking in snatches throughout the day. Romanow sought him out again. "Romanow came back," Blakeney says, "and he told me 'This is for real'." Blakeney asked him to get something in writing from Chrétien, then headed off to find Lougheed. "I talked to Lougheed and said, 'I think this is for real'." They agreed that there would be a drafting session that night in Blakeney's rooms in the Château.

Romanow and Chrétien headed off in search of a place to talk. They found a pantry, and began where they had left off that morning. They decided they needed McMurtry—or rather, they needed Ontario, and McMurtry had a lot of influence with Davis—and went looking for him. In that small room the so-called "kitchen accord" was born, and found its way into political folklore. The rough elements of the deal were written hastily on Romanow's notepad.

Officials from Saskatchewan, Newfoundland, British Columbia, and Alberta gathered in Blakeney's suite early in the evening. An all-night drafting session began. Saskatchewan kept Ontario informed; at one point Romanow accompanied McMurtry to brief Davis in his room. Davis, in turn, was on the telephone to Trudeau. A pattern had developed over the long months of frustrating negotiations. Davis communicated with Trudeau, Blakeney with Lougheed and, through him, to the hard-line provinces.

The only two provinces not included in the marathon night session were Manitoba and Quebec. "We didn't get in touch with the Lyon and Lévesque people," Blakeney says, "because we didn't think they would be contributing to coming up with this compromise. Obviously we were going to try to come up with something that would put some pressure on them, but there's no point in trying to put pressure on them until you have a consensus."

Blakeney says the drafting work and the all-night negotiations succeeded more swiftly than he had expected. What emerged as a result of the night's labours was a two-page agreement which included: a constitutional amending formula (at least seven provinces with 50 per cent of the Canadian population had to agree to any constitutional changes); a charter of rights, much of which could be overruled by the legislatures; and a clause which allowed for provinces to opt out of federal programs, but not to be compensated if they did. There was a special provision for Quebec to opt out of educational or social programs with compensation. The group decided that the only provinces bound by minority language rights would be those that consented; others could opt in at a later time. Premiers who had not been at the drafting session, including Bennett, Lougheed, Davis, and Hatfield, had by the morning been informed by their officials. They agreed to the deal. Lyon, who was fighting a provincial election, had left for home the previous day. He was informed of the deal on Thursday morning, and had little choice but to agree; on the eve of an election he did not want to be seen alone with Quebec opposing the agreement.

Lévesque found out about the agreement only when he arrived for a breakfast meeting with the tattered gang of eight. While the other delegations had worked through the night, he had been asleep in a hotel room in Hull. They had excluded Quebec, and at the breakfast table he accused them of treachery. He had earlier, as a price for joining the gang of eight, agreed to give up Quebec's traditional veto on constitutional change. But he had demanded in return that Quebec must be able to opt out of federal programs, with compensation. He privately believed the opting out clause was a way to build, "little by little," an "associate state." Opting out was, for Lévesque, more important than a veto. Trudeau had been against the idea, and had referred to it derisively as "opting out of Canada." His compromise this night had been to agree that Quebec would be compensated when it opted out of social or educational programs, but not otherwise.

Chrétien's officials had been kept informed throughout the night. On the Thursday morning, Chrétien and Trudeau negotiated some slight changes. It was all over by lunch. The politicians were relieved, but probably no more so than the citizens of Canada.

As expected, Lévesque refused to sign the constitutional agreement. In the succeeding weeks he was, by turns, angry and anguished. He described Quebec's exclusion that night as "the most despicable betrayal." His lieutenant, Claude Morin, was so angry with Romanow that he still does not speak to him. Blakeney insists that Lévesque and Morin would not have signed any deal which was acceptable to Trudeau; their intent was to prevent any constitutional reform which would undercut their ultimate goals of sovereignty.

Lévesque was not the only one who felt betrayed. Most of the constitutional working drafts coming into the final conference had contained a guarantee that aboriginal rights would be protected. The Indians, Inuit, and Métis had all been accepted as having aboriginal rights in a clause written into the Constitution Act. But in the hard bargaining of the final 24 hours, that clause was allowed to slip off the table. While Blakeney had agreed to having the clause in the constitution, he did say that no one had defined the term "aboriginal rights" to his satisfaction. Most Indians in Saskatchewan had signed treaties, and Blakeney was solid in his support of the rights they conferred. He thought of Indian self-government in terms of municipal models. There was some friction over that with Sol Sanderson, Chief of the Federation of Saskatchewan Indian Nations. Sanderson spoke not of municipalities, but of sovereign Indian nations.

Even so, Blakeney's greater problem was with the Métis. They had no treaties or special status. If they could win recognition as an aboriginal people in the constitution, their future case for self-government and land would be greatly strengthened. Blakeney did not accept that, legally or historically, they had aboriginal rights. "Blakeney didn't go to bat for us," Jim Sinclair says. "He could have passed legislation that would have provided us with land, and some form of aboriginal government. He could have prepared us for the constitution, much the same as Alberta's done with its Métis people."

When native groups learned what had happened in Ottawa, they were angry. The FSIN met with Blakeney within the week. He told them that Saskatchewan had wanted to keep the aboriginal rights clause, but allowed its deletion when it became obvious that British Columbia, with many unsettled land claims, would never sign such an agreement. He promised that if the accord were re-opened for any reason, he would insist that the clause be reinserted.

He didn't have to wait long. It was Blakeney, perhaps more than any other premier, who had insisted that there be a clause allowing legislatures to make laws "notwithstanding" the entrenchment of certain rights in the constitution. He believed that elected assemblies, not the courts, must remain the final arbiters of rights. In the last, long days of constitutional negotiations, his will prevailed. Trudeau did not approve, but in the end he agreed.

Many citizens' groups had argued for a charter of rights that would be free of legislative override. Among them was the National Action Committee on the Status of Women. It was a question of principle. They favoured a charter of rights. National women's groups also pushed for a separate clause in the constitution which guaranteed equality of the sexes. An existing clause (15) stipulated that there could be no discrimination based on age, religion, ethnic origin, or sex. But women wanted a separate clause which referred solely to sexual equality. Chrétien had eventually agreed to include it. Section 28 guaranteed rights equally to both sexes.

On the day following the constitutional agreement Flora Macdonald asked in the House of Commons whether legislatures could override Section 28. Trudeau said he didn't know, but the next time the question came up, he said the provincial right to override did include Section 28. That created an immediate sense of outrage, with women's groups mobilizing quickly and with great effect. They wanted Section 28 to stand "free and clear," not subject to change by any legislature. Chrétien, Trudeau, and the premiers soon came under intense pressure to re-open the accord.

There were two questions: one of principle, the other a logical detail. Blakeney's opinion, shared by federal lawyers, was that Section 15 and Section 28 had the same effect: they both guaranteed sexual equality. If the first was to be subject to legislative override, it seemed obvious that the second should be, too. The point of principle went back to Blakeney's views about legislatures having the final word on rights. But there was an additional complication. Blakeney feared that any clause that guaranteed equality of the sexes might jeopardize his affirmative action plans for women in Saskatchewan. In strictly legal terms, it could be argued that affirmative action programs discriminate against men. He wanted a legislative override to protect those programs in case a legal challenge was mounted against them.

The women's lobby was effective. All three federal parties quickly agreed to the change. Chrétien began to call the provinces to get their agreement, but he said it would have to be unanimous. By Monday, November 16th, five provinces had agreed. The next day Chrétien called Blakeney, but the premier refused to budge. He made his point about affirmative action programs. He also raised the case of aboriginal rights. He had made a promise. Saskatchewan sent Chrétien a draft amendment which Blakeney believed would allow Section 28 to stand, and also protect affirmative action programs. Chrétien refused it.

Blakeney was receiving telexes and calls from colleagues in the NDP—Broadbent, Pauline Jewett, Alexa McDonough, and Stephen Lewis. He reluctantly agreed to give in on the sexual equality clause, but he stood firm in his position on aboriginal rights. On Wednesday, November 18th, Romanow made the Saskatchewan position official in a telex to Chrétien: Saskatchewan would "agree with reluctance" to the changes in Section 28 if the aboriginal rights clause were reinstated. Blakeney, to his dismay, watched the CBC national news report that night that Saskatchewan was still refusing to budge on the sexual equality clause.

On Thursday, he became the topic of discussion in the House of Commons. Liberal Ursula Appolloni rose to say, "It was reported that the Premier of Saskatchewan was preventing Canadian women from having full equality of rights." Trudeau got up and mockingly extended his sympathy to NDP members for the conduct of the Saskatchewan premier. The Commons passed a unanimous motion calling on Saskatchewan to support a free-standing equal rights clause. If one MP had shouted "no," the motion would not have passed.

Blakeney was livid. He called a news conference. He asked where the Liberals had received their information about his position. He tabled a copy of Romanow's telex to Chrétien. He believed that not only the Liberals, but at least one member of the NDP federal caucus had the information on Saskatchewan's position. "I was very angry with the federal NDP," Blakeney says. "I think one of them should have said no. All it took was one."

Women in Saskatchewan had been organizing for a protest at the Legislature on Saturday night. Their ranks were swelled by people attending a women's health conference in Regina that weekend, and a separate Liberal political event. Blakeney spoke to the crowd from the steps of the Legislature. He admitted that he was upset, and he admits now that he was "tired and angry." He told them about the telegram to the federal government, and said it was "totally inexcusable" that in the Commons they "allowed Saskatchewan to be portrayed as the last bastion of male chauvinism." When he was accused of trading women's rights for aboriginal rights, he made no apologies. "I said all the constitutional negotiations were trading rights," he recalls. "And then I got a little chippy with some of them. 'Why are you abandoning the Indians? You've got all this organizing power and you're using it solely for yourself. These people don't have the organizing power, but instead of saying we should have both aboriginal rights and sexual equality, you want it only for yourself'."

He also attempted to describe, in detail and historical perspective, his position on how Section 28 might affect affirmative action programs. His explanation fell flat. He may have been right, but he was not in tune with the crowd. Chrétien's people had begun to talk to the other premiers about reinserting the aboriginal rights clause. It was Blakeney's condition, and he stood firm. Bennett and Lougheed were opposed, but agreed to it on the weekend of November 21st. Lougheed insisted on a slightly altered wording. Chrétien accepted, and so did Blakeney. On Tuesday, November 24th, Chrétien announced that Section 28 would stand alone, and that Section 35, applying to aboriginal rights, would be reinstated. Most people breathed a sigh of relief. Blakeney continued to do a slow burn. "In due course it all died down," he says, "except it left a residue of bitterness with me. I don't have many in public life, just two or three, and this is one of them. I've always felt in personal terms that the Status of Women people didn't acquit themselves with dignity and fairness on that occasion." Nor has he ever quite forgiven the national media, particularly the CBC, for what he saw as their constant bias in favour of the Trudeau-Davis position, and against that of the opposing provinces.

Blakeney was glad it was over. He regretted that Quebec had been isolated, but believed he and the others had worked to get most of that province's demands into the constitution. The rest would have to be dealt with in future negotiations. He had helped to prevent Trudeau's acting unilaterally. He had been instrumental in maintaining the primacy of elected officials over appointed judges. He thought Saskatchewan had made some important gains in its jurisdiction over resources. By Christmas of 1981, all but the formalities were behind them. It was time to turn his full attention back to provincial affairs—and the election he planned to call in 1982.

# Chapter Twenty

# Defeat

The NDP had only once called an April election—when Woodrow Lloyd went down to defeat in 1964. The weather was beastly throughout much of the 1982 contest, with late snow storms and sub-zero temperatures. But April 26th was sunny and warm. Dick Proctor, a press aide who had been one of the boys on the bus during the 28-day campaign, went to Blakeney's house that Monday morning to accompany the Premier and Anne, along with some television reporters, to the polling station. Later they walked back to the house together. "As we were standing on the lawn chatting," Proctor says, "there were a couple of people who had just gone in to vote as well, neighbours who were coming by to say hello. Blakeney turned to me and said, 'See, they're very friendly.' He was telling me that he was the Premier, and he fully expected to be the Premier at the end of that evening."

The script had unfolded just as Elwood Cowley and Gordon MacMurchy had said it would back in 1978: fight Trudeau, and find a big agricultural issue. Blakeney had fought Trudeau on the constitution, although eventually they made a deal. On the farm issue, the NDP had chosen what appeared to be a sure winner. The federal Liberals wanted to change the Crow rate, the subsidized price western farmers paid the railways for shipping their grain to eastern and foreign markets. The railways also wanted to abandon thousands of kilometres of unprofitable branch lines to small town grain elevators. Emmett Hall, a retired Justice of the Supreme Court, had been named to head a Royal Commission. It played to big audiences throughout the prairies. People begged Hall to keep the rails, their towns, and their way of life. He concluded that the Crow rate and two-thirds of the rail lines should remain. The NDP had chosen that as an issue. A few days before the election call, Gordon MacMurchy had put the strategy this way to Blakeney: "It's Blakeney/MacMurchy and the farmers versus Pépin, the railways, and the Conservatives."

The polls seemed to be right; the NDP had the support of almost 50 per cent of decided voters. Bill Knight, the NDP campaign chairman, was telling reporters that those numbers would translate into an even bigger victory than 1978. The Tories responded by opening the file on their Decima Research poll, which showed them only a few percentage points behind.

Beyond the chosen issues, Knight had two other arrows in his quiver. First, there was the NDP record for economic management. The province's Heritage Fund—income from mineral resources—had assets of about $1 billion. Much of it was invested in the public potash, oil, and uranium corporations, although the majority of the fund each year was used for general revenues. The unemployment rate was three points below the national average. The budget was balanced, and the province's international credit rating was excellent.

Then there was Allan Blakeney, the man responsible for that good management. The NDP counted on Blakeney's leadership as its campaign ace, if one were needed. Eastern reporters were calling him "cool and capable." The NDP campaign slogan was "Tested and Trusted." It was the same theme the party had used in the 1960 election.

In contrast, Grant Devine, a 37-year-old agricultural economist, was practically unknown. He had run and lost in Saskatoon in 1978. The next year he won the Tory leadership when Dick Collver resigned. In 1980 he lost a byelection in Estevan—considered a safe Tory seat—and suffered the embarrassment of having to lead his party from the public gallery. The NDP liked to call him "Dr Invisible," a jibe they were to regret.

Blakeney was at the height of his powers after his win in 1978. His leadership was unchallenged. The government bore his stamp: honest and professional. Even businessmen were singing his praises. He had shone in the constitutional negotiations. He planned to lead his party to victory one more time, staying on until 1985, his 60th year. Then he would move graciously into a post-political career, possibly lecturing at a university.

Beneath the confident surface, Blakeney and at least some of the people around him had become uneasy by about 1980. The CCF-NDP tradition was one of faith in government as an instrument of the people's will. "I believe in government," Woodrow Lloyd had said, "[as] the most effective method of implementing the conscious will of people." The NDP traditionally ran a high-service administration, and Blakeney had taken his to a new level of complexity and organization.

Elsewhere, however, there were very different trends. Margaret Thatcher had been elected Prime Minister of Britain in 1979. Her government, she promised, would "stop trying to step in and make decisions for you that you should be free to make on your own." She vowed to reduce taxes and stomp on trade unions. The next year Ronald Reagan won the Presidency of the United States. His Democratic predecessor, Jimmy Carter, had talked about government's role in curing social ills. Reagan's response was, "Government is not the solution to our problem; government is the problem." In his October 1980 debate with Carter, Reagan told Americans to ask themselves one question: "Are you better off than you were four years ago?" It was an appeal to individual self-interest rather than national well-being. Reagan promised to slash taxes, de-regulate industry, and clean up the bungling bureaucracy.

Both Reagan and Thatcher had run against government, and both had won. In Canada, Joe Clark and the Conservatives defeated the Liberals in 1979. The Trudeau government had accumulated worrisome deficits. But more important, inflation, which had been at 11 and 12 per cent in 1974–75, was back in double digits by 1980. People were feeling vulnerable and insecure. They were also tired of Trudeau's arrogance, and of the constant bickering between provincial and federal governments. Then, as Trudeau replaced the short-lived Clark government, there was the prospect of more wearisome constitutional battles.

Blakeney sensed something was changing, and he put people to work analyzing the problems. But this wasn't a specific, identifiable problem, such as how to organize a potash corporation. It had to do with a subtle consciousness emerging among citizens who themselves weren't really aware of its meaning. In September 1980 cabinet had a go at analysis during a think-tank session at Saint Peter's Abbey in Muenster. Blakeney threw out a question: "Where are we going?" He told the cabinet that since 1971 their focus had been the economy and broad social programs. But was that enough? There was greater prosperity, but it didn't add up to the good life. What could the government do to give people a greater feeling of satisfaction?

Grant Mitchell took notes as the ministers began to respond. MacMurchy felt the question was how to handle wealth; there was a need for a brother's-keeper approach to avoid becoming like Alberta. Cowley said the party's left was dead; there were no original ideas coming forward, like the Land Bank; lifestyle issues posed difficulties to the party if government was too involved. Murray Koskie believed the NDP was no longer very far in front on social issues.

Romanow asked, "Do we dare to be different? Ideology does exist for us, but can we be different than Alberta on energy? On Canada? Our agricultural policies are different. Also communications. However, the politics of regionalism is swamping other ideologies."

Smishek felt that groups the party had relied on in the past for ideas—co-operatives, labour unions, farm organizations—had lost their zip. Tchorzewski believed the big crusades had been fought and won.

Cowley, responding again, said, "We don't want to turn off the cowboys. We are the governing party. We appealed to upwardly mobile people in the last election, but we still have social feeling. Farms are getting bigger.

We should resist it, but we can't stop it because we don't have the political will."

Rolfes: "We should keep in mind that we could be in trouble if there was a real alternative."

McArthur: "We need a cause or two. We talk about the social arena, but we have no plans on the table. We're tuned in as far as economic development in the resource area, but we're tuning ourselves out in the agricultural arena."

Grant Mitchell, during his tenure as Deputy Minister of the Environment, had been away from the central action. When he returned as Cabinet Secretary, he was concerned about what he found. He obviously took the Muenster discussion to heart. He later went to dinner with several powerful civil servants who comprised the government's Economic Development Group: Garry Beatty from the Crown Investments Corporation; Murray Wallace, Blakeney's Deputy Minister; and Rob Douglas from Finance. There was a perception, Mitchell said, that the government's main focus was "the development of a form of state capitalism." He wanted to know how to stimulate new social policy. At Muenster, cabinet had talked about the need to do that. If Saskatchewan was becoming a have province, could it become a have province with a difference?

After the dinner meeting, Mitchell made more notes about the discussion and sent them on to Blakeney. "They insist that the focus must be on the current thrust," he wrote. "The argument is that Saskatchewan must attempt to carve out a piece of the western economic action; otherwise it will all go to Alberta. While they recognize that some cabinet ministers are calling for development of a major social program plank before the next election, it is my view that they feel this is a necessary political gimmick, and they are not very enthusiastic about any expensive new program.

"At the end," Mitchell concluded, "I expressed concern about the prospect of continued major commitment of financial and management resources to economic development. If this must be so, can we not hang new social programs on the economic development thrust—focus on education and training, economic opportunities for disadvantaged and natives, lifestyle (recreation, culture programs)?"

Later in 1980, Blakeney had his new Deputy Minister, John Sinclair, convene other senior civil servants in a "soft-side" seminar. Again, the consensus was that the government was spending too much time on the economy and not enough on the quality of life. There was talk about "water and sewer" socialism not being enough for the 1980s, about the need for socialism with a human face. Sinclair commented on how young professional women in the civil service viewed the government: "I get the impression that we are up against a very major structural barrier, something almost akin to a class struggle. I wonder about our intellectual capacity to understand the future into which we are moving."

Sinclair provided Blakeney with a new perspective on opponents of the government's uranium policy. Most of the cabinet looked on them as immature troublemakers. It was Sinclair who pointed out that the ethic underlying the opposition related to the "conserver society."

Blakeney had civil servants prepare papers for him. One of his planners, Marvin Blauer, reported in late 1980 about societal changes he was observing: "Though difficult to define and harder still to deal with, alienation cannot be ignored. Activist governments within a democratic system depend upon an activist population."

Blakeney called on Meyer Brownstone, his colleague of the 1950s, for some advice on policy. Brownstone had been on the left of the party during the Douglas years, and had criticized the CCF for being too conservative—accepting the limited capitalist models of community involvement and democratic participation. Blakeney brought him to Regina to meet with him and with some civil servants. Brownstone reported that among the planners he found little "sense of history"—they were technocratically, but not politically, developed. He praised the affirmative action programs, and he recommended a big push on day care and communications policy.

Activists within the party frequently observed that the civil service was competent, but unsympathetic to the historical goals of the CCF-NDP. By 1980, some of the familiar faces at the centre were gone. Kinzel had retired. Bolstad had become director of the Meewasin Valley Authority in Saskatoon. There were mutterings about the "Queen's crowd" around Blakeney (referring to Queen's University in Kingston, Ontario), and how they had the Premier's ear. "Blakeney was always saying what whizzes the Finance people were," says Ed Whelan, who left government after being dropped from the cabinet in 1979. "The elected people couldn't get to him."

Blakeney's Executive Council office had become larger and more layered. By 1981 he had a staff of 22, including a Deputy Minister, a Principal Secretary, an Assistant Principal Secretary, and a Government Organization Co-ordinator. The secretariat—executive assistants, correspondence secretaries, and receptionists—had their own director in Valerie Preston. Ted Bowen, a speech writer who left the Premier's Office about then, says, "It got more and more formal, and more difficult to work there." Bill Parker, Blakeney's executive assistant for constituency matters, agrees: "After 1980 or '81 the office got a lot bigger, and there were personality conflicts. Valerie was a tough lady, and she had her struggles with [Deputy Premier] Murray Wallace, who wanted to show her who wore the pants. She would come back fuming, occasionally in tears, and would take it out on people under her."

Blakeney tried to respond to the concern that his government was growing stale. He made a significant cabinet shuffle in 1979, moving in several younger men—McArthur, Hammersmith, Reg Gross, and Murray Koskie—and dropping some others, including Whelan, Byers, and Adolph

Matsalla. In the fall of 1980, Eiling Kramer and Jack Messer both resigned their seats. Kramer had run in 1978 only because the NDP was afraid of losing the Battleford seat, so his resignation was expected. Messer's quitting at age 40 came as a surprise to everyone. He said he wanted to pursue business interests. There were rumours that he had been fired, but both he and Blakeney deny that. In December 1980, Blakeney added Dwayne Lingenfelter and Bob Long to the cabinet.

In the civil service, Blakeney called on Mitchell and Mel Derrick, the two key members of his 1971 transition team. He had Mitchell conduct a study of government organization, with an emphasis on how to decentralize services. Derrick's job was to look for ways to strengthen senior management. Blakeney had decided there was a developing morale problem. Derrick was to find ways—including better pay and sabbaticals—to keep the managers challenged and contented.

The major social programs of the 1978–82 period were affirmative action for women, the handicapped, and native people. Planning had begun earlier, but the programs didn't arrive until 1980. As the NDP was preparing for an election in 1982, affirmative action had yet to have a significant impact. Blakeney recognized that the programs, which were aimed at disadvantaged people, might not be popular with the middle class, but he was hopeful that the majority of Saskatchewan citizens were prepared to support programs that didn't immediately benefit them.

While affirmative action was an emerging preoccupation in the cities, Indian land entitlements was the controversial issue in the countryside. All levels of government agreed that the Indians had land coming to them, but the transfer was extremely slow. By 1981, after five years of negotiations, a mere 73,000 acres had changed hands. There was a backlash in farming areas where the bands wanted acreage that was held in government-owned community pastures. Reeves and municipal councillors claimed they would lose their tax base on any land that became part of an Indian reserve. The influential Saskatchewan Wildlife Federation was opposed to the process as well, ostensibly because more reserved land would mean more Indian hunting.

NDP polls indicated that people thought the government was doing too much for Indians. Caucus members brought back negative reports from rural Saskatchewan. Blakeney says the tax base problems could have been negotiated. He recognized the objections for what they were: "Many of these were just surrogates for a lack of cordiality to the idea of having land around their area owned by Indian people. And I was disappointed at that."

David Ahenakew, the former Chief of the Federation of Saskatchewan Indians, says the delays in land transfers were frustrating, but he recognized the government's problem: "The politics was heating up. We became a back room issue, and Devine and his cronies did a good job here. The

Wildlife Federation all of a sudden was up there blasting the daylights out of the NDP. The NDP's popularity was going down. We were the prime issue."

Officially, cabinet was in favour of the land transfers. The government's negotiator, Rob Milen, says that Blakeney and Bowerman were both supportive, despite the political risks. Other ministers, and their departmental bureaucracies, were not; Milen names Messer, Romanow, Herman Rolfes, Murray Koskie, and Norm Vickars. "It was continually a brawl. The government departments were always fighting everything that went forward." Ministers also resisted committing crown land in northern Saskatchewan which had hydro or mineral potential.

The first major agreement nearing completion was with the Fond du Lac band near Lake Athabasca. The deal had been negotiated in 1980, and required only ministerial signatures. Milen says that at the eleventh hour the document was referred to the Attorney General for a legal opinion. "Romanow seized it," says Milen, "and put an articling student in charge of all the negotiations." Milen says that he had coffee with Romanow, who told him he was being removed from land entitlements negotiations. Milen quit. Romanow says he has no recollection of the coffee session, or of pulling Milen off the case. He says Milen's minister, Ted Bowerman, would never have allowed such interference. Milen was without work for the next six months, and believes he was black-listed by government ministers.

David Ahenakew agrees that it was Romanow who applied the brakes on land entitlements, but is typically charitable in his assessment: "Romanow was the guy that felt the winds out there, the political feelings of the people. You can't blame Romanow because he sensed there would be a backlash." The issue of land entitlements, a matter of conscience rather than popular politics, was put into slow motion in anticipation of the 1982 election.

In economic policy, the government had set its course. The potash and uranium ventures had developed momentum, and cabinet was bloody-minded about seeing them through. During the potash takeover, the opposition criticized the government for borrowing money to buy mines which were already in place and producing. They said it was a waste of money, that no new wealth was being created. Blakeney began receiving cheques from supporters to help pay for the mines. That gave some ministers the idea that it would be a popular move to allow people to participate directly in the purchase. In 1976 cabinet had considered the idea of Potash Investment Certificates. Walter Smishek, the Finance Minister, recommended that five-year certificates be made available for purchase by Saskatchewan citizens, but both the Potash Corporation and his own department argued against the idea. They said it was an expensive way to raise money which could be borrowed more cheaply in the market. Smishek argued for it anyway. "Despite their advice," he said, "I feel, and

I know that most caucus members feel, that we should move and move quickly in providing for citizen participation in potash." Cabinet turned the idea down.

By early 1982 there was a recession in Canada, but Saskatchewan's economy was booming. While Blakeney's planners were predicting continued growth, there were some soft spots, and some troubling indicators. Potash was one of them; Blakeney was told there would be a "severe decline" in the market. That would threaten the dividends the corporation paid to the government. It had political implications, too. Plans for expansion might have to be shelved; there could even be layoffs.

But the most serious immediate problems were high interest rates and inflation. In 1981, the national rate of inflation was 12.5 per cent. In a clumsy attempt to control it, the Bank of Canada had hiked the prime interest rate to a ruinous 22.75 per cent. Rates on consumer loans were running at an all-time high of 25 per cent. Homeowners renewing their mortgages were sometimes facing payment increases of $1,000 per month. Some people simply closed their doors and walked away. Farmers who had bought land during the good years of the 1970s were facing ruin.

Blakeney didn't set interest rates. He criticized the Bank of Canada and the federal government, but he made no promises of direct provincial help. There was pressure within cabinet to do something, but Blakeney resisted. "There was general prosperity here," he says, "but by this time there was a substantial recession in Ontario. Our advisors said, and I believed, that this was going to hit us in a couple of years, perhaps less. The government of Saskatchewan would need all its resources simply to maintain the programs we had. We shouldn't be promising any lavish new spending programs because the money wasn't going to be there." In particular, he resisted a proposal to provide each Saskatchewan citizen with a small pay-out from potash revenues. He thought it would be politically popular, but financially irresponsible.

The Finance Minister, Ed Tchorzewski, tabled a budget in March 1982. It was balanced, and contained no tax increases. There was something for a lot of different groups, but no universal bonanzas. The most expensive items were a large increase in money for building nursing homes, and another for subsidized low income housing and apartment construction. Tchorzewski announced a modest $20-million program to ease mortgage rates, but only for people whose family income was less than $35,000 a year.

There was a nasty matter to attend to before the decks were cleared for an election: hospital workers in Saskatchewan, members of the Canadian Union of Public Employees, had been on strike during March. Gordon Snyder, the Labour Minister, tried to settle the dispute before an election was called. He thought the workers were blackmailing the government; they thought he was threatening them with the heavy hand of the state if they didn't settle. On March 28th, the government passed legislation sending them back to work, and banning any strikes during an election campaign. Less than twenty-four hours later Blakeney called the election.

The Conservatives had been caught off guard in the first days of the 1978 campaign. They weren't about to repeat the mistake. Devine made two expensive promises within the first week: he would remove the provincial tax from gasoline; and he promised a mortgage protection plan which was far richer than the one the NDP had announced. The Conservatives would place a ceiling of 13.25 per cent on mortgages. The government would make up the difference between that amount and the going rate, no matter what the income of the mortgage holder. Devine made a raft of other promises, including one to reduce personal income taxes by 10 per cent. His evening rallies took the form of revival meetings. The man the NDP called Dr Invisible suddenly emerged as a powerful platform speaker. He attacked the NDP for wasting the taxpayers' money on resource investments and advertisements for the "Family of Crown Corporations." The Conservatives went on the offensive on health care, too: Devine charged that the NDP had cut back health care spending. He talked about the province's young people having to leave to find work. The sons and daughters of Saskatchewan, he said, would all be invited back home after a Tory victory.

The upbeat Tory campaign was in marked contrast to the NDP's dismal first week. Blakeney announced the election at his nominating convention on a Saturday night. He had to push past a noisy union demonstration to get into the hall. While he spoke, demonstrators outside banged on a metal door behind the stage. He had to run the gauntlet of another angry union crowd at Roy Romanow's nominating convention on Sunday night. By then, the Canadian Union of Public Employees had made an unprecedented move, deciding not to support the NDP with either money or workers. The union believed that sending them back to work was a cynical ploy to appeal to right-wing voters, particularly in rural areas, and demonstrators continued to dog the campaign. On Tuesday night, Blakeney got into a confrontation with CUPE protestors in Prince Albert. Irked by the presence of a radio reporter's microphone, he shoved it out of the way. The media began to report on the Premier's temperament, and that frustrated him even more.

The NDP had few promises to announce. All of the talk from retreats, the planning sessions, and the research papers had yielded little in the way of new policy. Blakeney began to criticize the cost of Tory promises: Devine's programs on mortgages and the gasoline tax would cost $250 million in the first year, and that didn't include the promise to reduce income tax. Where would they get the money? They would either have to chop programs or run a deficit. They would dry up the Heritage Fund. He also pointed out that Devine's promise to cut the gas tax by 40 cents a gallon was hardly possible, since the tax was only 29 cents. That figure was independently verified, but facts did nothing to stop the Tories. Devine told people not to fill their tanks until after election day, then went on to promise eight per cent loans to young farmers buying land. He also promised a gradual removal of provincial sales tax. The cost of Tory promises would approach between $750 million and $1 billion in the first year of government. The price tag on NDP promises was a paltry $165 million.

In reacting to the Tories, Blakeney and the NDP fell into the same trap they had set for Ross Thatcher in 1971. Blakeney was running on his record; he was "Tried and Trusted." Devine was new and exciting. He promised tax reductions and government subsidies at every turn. "There's so much more we can be" was the official Tory campaign slogan, and Devine's favourite line.

The NDP campaign was in the grip of desperation by week three. They tried to shift the focus to health care, warning, in shades of 1978, that the Tories would ruin medicare. There were also a series of hurried new promises which had not been planned for the campaign: a universal dental care plan, free eyeglasses for senior citizens, and a straight $2,000 grant for each first-time home buyer in the province. Late in the campaign Bill Knight attempted to use the leadership trump card—isolating Blakeney on Devine as they had isolated him on Collver in 1978. Blakeney even indulged in a mild form of mud-slinging, calling Devine "Mr Incredible" and reminding people that the Tory leader had never been elected to anything.

Entirely forgotten in the campaign was the Crow rate. It was to have been the NDP's magnetic issue in the countryside. It might have worked against the Liberals, but the Tories were the provincial opposition. Devine said he would fight to keep the Crow, too. End of issue.

The NDP crowds were modest in size, and quiet. The Tories were packing them in at boisterous rallies where Devine spoke with the conviction of an evangelist. In the end, the NDP called on its fabled organization to work the doorstep and get the vote out. Roy Romanow all but neglected his own riding, and drove the province corner-to-corner, attempting to minimize the damage and stir the troops.

On Monday, April 26th, Blakeney was at home watching television as the returns began to come in. One of the first was from Saskatoon Westmount, a traditionally safe NDP seat represented by John Brockelbank. The tally showed the Conservatives ahead. Blakeney turned to his aide, Bill Gillies, and said, "Ah, they've got that one reversed." The whole evening was reversed, and before it was finished Allan Blakeney had suffered the most complete electoral defeat in Saskatchewan history. The Conservatives won 54 per cent of the vote and 55 of the 64 seats (one was contested and they later won it in a byelection, leaving the NDP with eight members). Later that night, Blakeney left the funereal atmosphere of the empty banquet hall where the NDP victory party was to have been held. With Anne and a handful of aides, he drove over to the Tory celebration at the Regina Inn. In a scene reminiscent of Ross Thatcher's wading into a jubilant NDP crowd 11 years earlier, Blakeney wedged his way into the room and congratulated the Tories on their victory.

It was a crushing blow. Blakeney retained his Elphinstone seat, but only two of his ministers—Koskie and Lingenfelter—survived. In Saskatoon, Roy Romanow lost by 13 votes to a university student. He was so crushed that he said he would not challenge the results. Everyone was incredulous, including Blakeney, Devine, and the voters.

An NDP activist in Saskatoon recalls watching the early results on television. When she saw Henry Baker and Herman Rolfes defeated, she felt almost pleased because they were among her least favourite MLAs. Minutes later it occurred to her that the whole government was going down.

Don Anderson, a former Executive Assistant of Blakeney's, had gone to work for the Retail, Wholesale, and Department Store Union. He had been upset by the government's ordering hospital workers back to work on the eve of the election, but nevertheless he campaigned for the party. He was in Moose Jaw on election evening. "I stopped in to pick up a box of beer after the polls closed and the government had changed," he says. "As I was leaving the bar this young guy came in who was a good solid member of our union, and he was just gleeful. He was just shouting: 'We got rid of those bastards.' I knew exactly what he meant. He was so happy to get rid of the NDP that it wasn't funny. And I remember my feelings at the time. I believed that the NDP deserved to be defeated, but I didn't think that the people of Saskatchewan deserved the Conservatives."

In Regina, campaign worker Sandy Cameron sat in the desolate committee rooms on election night and told a *Leader-Post* reporter: "The government stopped listening to the people and worried too much about just being good administrators." The phrase that began to spread, now that even party loyalists were free to say it, was "out of touch."

The next day a subdued and ashen Allan Blakeney met reporters. The NDP had clearly "misread the polls." He had not received the right information "either from my people or my pores." Campaign co-ordinator Bill Knight had been hailed as a genius after the 1978 victory. He and the cabinet's political committee were soon to become the objects of bitter, but usually private, criticism. Knight had confidently been predicting as many as 50 seats when the election was called. "I dropped 11 pounds in the first week of that campaign," he now says. "I knew within 24 or 36 hours of being into it we were dead meat." One analysis suggests that the poll results looked promising among decided voters, and Knight assumed that the undecided vote would break evenly. It didn't.

Blakeney now admits that others saw trouble before he did. "I remember

Roy meeting me in Saskatoon and asking me whether I thought we were going to win. I said, 'It's going to be a near thing, but I think we'll squeeze by.' And he said, 'I don't think we will'. "

Everyone had a theory about the loss. Suddenly the party was full of people who had advised against an April election, who had advised against running on the Crow rate, who had warned Blakeney that he and the cabinet had grown out of touch. "We had a council meeting before the election was called," Elwood Cowley says. "We told them basically, 'We're thinking about having an election in April. What do you think?' Cheers, roar. 'Give them hell! We'll beat the shit out of them!' About ten weeks later, I was in Prince Albert at a Council meeting, and I had these same people up there saying, 'I told you so.' I should have recorded their speeches."

Cowley says he knew by the second week of the campaign that it was lost, but he thought he was safe in Biggar. "Very friendly people were wishing me luck. What I didn't know was that they were wishing me luck in my new job." When the talk turned to scapegoats, Dick Proctor, once a sports reporter at *The Globe and Mail,* remarked that a loss of such magnitude had to have been a team effort. Blakeney later quoted the line approvingly.

By the time he reported to the convention later in the year, Blakeney had come to his own conclusions. The success of NDP resource programs in the face of a looming recession, he said, led to "a perception that our government was well off, but the people were not." He also said the NDP had done a poor job of communicating its message—that the resource policies and the crown corporations "were the means to provide society with the general wealth to help the less fortunate among us." The NDP had alienated the middle class by helping the poor, and the Tories had done a masterful job of capitalizing on the NDP's weaknesses.

The line within the party was that the problem had not been policy, or arrogance, or aloofness, but poor communications. The Tories had won by appealing to people's greed. Commentators of both the right and the left—in *Alberta Report* and *Briarpatch* magazines—were much harsher. Some of the party's own people were, too. Doug McArthur believes that the cabinet existed at an "immense distance" from the people. People were hurting from high interest rates, and the government was obsessed with competence and balanced budgets: "No one should ever make the mistake of thinking that we didn't fail the political challenge of that time. We did, badly."

Ultimately, the weight of defeat had to fall on the leader. Blakeney bottled up his feelings, as was his habit in times of crisis. Garry Aldridge, who was to remain as a caucus researcher through the next difficult years, says his boss was in the office the day after the debacle, preparing for opposition. He analyzed the defeat, but said nothing about his feelings. According to Anne Blakeney, he didn't talk about it much even to her: "Anything he felt he just absorbed silently. He said nothing to reflect on anybody else. Not many people can do that. Most of us have to complain."

There were friends who wished he would talk, who wished he would allow them to help. Zenny Burton, an acquaintance of many years, says, "He bore that election defeat all by himself. He didn't allow anybody to come close to him so that he could discuss it, and so that he could say how he felt. I think that is sad. That would have helped him. And there were people around who were prepared to talk, relate to him. He kept you at bay."

Blakeney found quickly, as he had in 1964, that a defeated politician soon leaves the spotlight. He missed being Premier. What he did not miss was being the centre of attention at the many social occasions which accompanied the job. Now at a public event he might be seen picking gingerly at the food while other guests gathered around the newly-elected Conservative politicians. It didn't seem to bother him. Bill Knight always said that, even as Premier, Blakeney could disappear into a crowd. It became much easier to do after April 1982.

Grant Devine declared Saskatchewan officially "open for business." Ross Thatcher had used the same slogan 15 years earlier. Devine's message, and apparent belief, was that a government which was friendly to enterprise would attract industry and diversity. The NDP was out; business investment would flood in. Ross Thatcher had moved quickly to give the oil industry a royalty holiday. Now Colin Thatcher, Devine's Energy Minister and Ross's son, announced a similar program. Where Ross Thatcher and Grant Devine differed, however, was on spending. Thatcher had run a tight-fisted government; Devine was profligate from the start. Buoyed by the New Right theories of Reaganomics, he believed that cutting corporate taxes would create more than enough economic activity to compensate for lost revenue. Saskatchewan people, as he had promised in the election, could have it all: lower taxes and government largesse.

The Tories kept their promises on the gasoline tax, and the home and farm mortgage programs. The result was a $227 million deficit in 1982–83, a year in which the provincial economy was growing. Devine's second year in power coincided with a downturn in the national economy, but Saskatchewan continued to prosper. The Premier accepted it as a sign of success for his policies. He declared that Saskatchewan "refused to participate in the recession," and he ran a $331 million deficit. There was drought in 1984, but again resource prices were good, and there was growth. The government ran a deficit of $379 million.

Depressed grain prices didn't hit Saskatchewan until three years into Devine's administration. CCF governments had faced farm slumps, including drought, in 1957 and 1961. The Liberal government had faced agricultural recession in 1969 and 1970. The Tories began to face them in 1985. Before the hard times hit, they had accumulated a deficit of almost $1 billion.

Devine's first mandate was characterized more by deficits than by shifts in economic policy, but many of the familiar neo-conservative signals were there. Saskatchewan labour legislation was rewritten in favour of employers. Increases in the minimum wage were stalled. The Women's Division was collapsed, and its remaining functions moved back into a government department. Affirmative action programs were reduced. Money for native political organizations was cut back. The Department of Northern Saskatchewan was dismantled. The Land Bank was dismantled. Spending on a government program of matching grants for the Third World was cut by half. A welfare reform package reduced rates for single people. Reputable studies indicated that there was hunger in Saskatchewan. As the recession hit, growing numbers of poor and unemployed people came to depend on food banks, a new symbol of the mean 1980s.

The government was not nearly so tight-fisted with other members of society. There were reductions in royalties for the oil, potash, and uranium industries. The government sold Department of Highways construction equipment to the private sector at bargain prices, then gave them the road work. It bailed out depositors after Regina's Pioneer Trust collapsed. It created a stock savings plan, allowing investors to deduct one-third of the cost of share purchases in Saskatchewan companies from their income tax. It offered Peter Pocklington $21 million in subsidized loans to build bacon processing and curing plants, and a packing plant in North Battleford.

There was plenty to criticize and oppose, but for a couple of years Blakeney and his dispirited rump didn't seem up to it. The Tories had so many members that they spilled over onto the other side of the House. They were a new crew. Not one of the 56-member caucus had ever been in government. An intense animosity had built, particularly since the 1978 election. Blakeney was now seated amid Conservatives who heckled him mercilessly. "I was offended no end," he says, "at the way the Tories approached the House. All they wanted to do was shout, and they sat a couple of people next to me, so that whenever I spoke they shouted behind me so that I really couldn't hear myself. This was Sveinson's and Maxwell's job. These were tactics I had not seen in the House, and certainly I wouldn't have dreamed of using them in 1971."

Blakeney's old Liberal opponent, Dave Steuart, dropped in once or twice to watch the debates. "Blakeney got up to speak and it was just unbelievable," he says. "They wouldn't even let the guy get a word in edgewise. They were shouting at him from every side." Steuart says that something had changed in Saskatchewan politics since the old days of the Liberal and NDP debates: "This hatred just built up. It's there. You just have to go over there."

The defeat left Blakeney without his most able members. Lingenfelter, Koskie, and Shillington had all been ministers, although none had been among Blakeney's most stalwart front benchers. Along with the others— Lawrence Yew and Freddie Thompson from the north, Norm Lusney and Allan Engel from the countryside—they formed a motley crew in the Legislature. Blakeney was discouraged: "Things just looked hopeless. And without being disloyal to my colleagues, we didn't really have a strong caucus."

Blakeney preferred a lower key approach to opposition, for both personal and tactical reasons. He believed the government's credibility would soon wear thin, and he wanted the NDP to be seen as the credible alternative. But among those who had survived the Monday Night Massacre in 1982 were Koskie, Lingenfelter, and Engel, some of the NDP's chippiest players in the House. They wanted to fight, bare knuckles, with the Tories at every turn. Blakeney's caucus, in fact, was so enthusiastic in its heckling that the leader once interrupted one of his own speeches to tell Engel to shut up.

A former Blakeney staffer describes the scene in opposition: "Blakeney's caucus was not very supportive. A few thought they should have been cabinet ministers, and still bore a grudge. They also blamed him for the loss. He knew some of them would have liked to see him go."

The party was in shock, and some people were looking for scapegoats. Bill Knight was soon gone, to become Ed Broadbent's Principal Secretary. Blakeney's leadership was never challenged, at least not openly. He says he would have preferred to quit, but felt he couldn't. All the potential leadership candidates, with the possible exception of Lingenfelter, had been defeated. He believed there was no hope for an NDP victory in 1986. He thought he should stay on to rebuild the party, then give way to a new leader after another election.

Anne Blakeney was upset. She was prepared to second guess and blame people, but her husband didn't want to talk about that. She gently nudged him about retiring. He said he couldn't until the party was ready. "That would have been enough for me not to press farther," Anne says. Her Christmas letter of 1982 provides an understated description of the year just past: "Then the provincial election in late April and voila—out on our ear. It was a great surprise and something of a shock—followed, as all the wives noticed first, by a feeling of lightness and relaxation.

"Not much change for our family however. Allan, as Leader of the Opposition, and his small staff have a great deal to accomplish. But the pressure is gone, people treat us as human beings again—a lot of it feels good."

They visited provincial parks in the spring, spent the summer in the Maritimes, and in the fall he went to China as a guest of the China-Canada Friendship Association. She took university classes in French. He was on the road throughout the province, more so in her view than he had been as Premier. In her 1983 Christmas letter she described his life as "peripatetic."

He attempted to encourage policy renewal, but the party wasn't ready for energetic policy debates. The NDP did, however, reverse itself on uranium mining, and resolved to phase out the mines as other northern jobs became available. Uranium never did become the bonanza the planners had promised. Their most conservative projection had been for an accumulated government royalty income of $950 million by 1987. The actual amount was about $200 million. The mines did increase northern employment, but less than had been anticipated. The companies had promised 50 per cent of the jobs to northerners, but the figure is closer to 25 per cent, fewer than 400 jobs. The industry admits that it has not kept its part of the bargain, and should never have agreed to specific employment targets. In 1985, the Inter-Church Uranium Committee was able to prove that Canadian uranium entering an American plant was routinely routed both to peaceful and nuclear weapons uses. Blakeney dutifully defended the party's new position to phase out mining, although never very convincingly; he hasn't changed his mind about uranium development.

Then he faced the draining process of hunting for new candidates. Many of the people he approached said no. He had finally become convinced, in defeat, that he had to be more active in recruiting women. Alexa McDonough, the NDP leader in Nova Scotia, had a blunt talk with him, and told him that Saskatchewan had a responsibility to set an example. The message finally hit home. Blakeney made the calls and paid the visits. The NDP had 5 female candidates in 1982, but 11 in 1986.

After the defeat in 1982 Blakeney seemed to sag. One reporter said he appeared to have aged 15 years in a few weeks. There appeared suddenly to be more grey in his hair, less spring in his step, and more soft weight on his short frame. Roy Romanow recalls a meeting with him at the Holiday Inn in Saskatoon shortly after the election: "People streamed by him, the odd person would say hello. But here was this powerful, thoughtful, tremendous Premier, by all measures a terrific person, and now he's just a nobody."

Blakeney was there to convince Romanow to initiate a court challenge regarding the election result in Riversdale. Romanow balked. He told Blakeney that he didn't want to go back into a House with only eight NDP members. Romanow recalls Blakeney saying, "Well, how do you think I feel about it? I have to do it, and you have to do it." Romanow did it, but the challenge failed.

What had looked hopeless in 1982 began to look more promising by 1985. The Tories' spending was out of control. They showed no apparent ability to manage. Their "open for business" campaign had fallen flat: total investment in Saskatchewan in 1986 was marginally less in real dollars than it had been in 1982. The Tories had alienated a lot of people through their patronage appointments, which had included René Archambault, Grant Devine's brother-in-law. They were brutal in their gutting of the civil service. A study conducted at the University of Saskatchewan by Hans J. Michelmann and Geoffrey S. Steeves indicated that virtually none of the deputy ministers survived, and the firings did not stop there.

When Blakeney told the party in 1982 that Devine would lead a one-term government, he didn't believe it himself. Even party loyalists thought he was "whistling past the graveyard." But by 1984 he began to believe the NDP had a chance of winning in 1986. That posed a new problem. He had planned to fight one more election, then hand the leadership over in opposition. Now, with winning a possibility, he had to decide whether he was the best person to lead the party into the election.

Blakeney does not say it, but the implication is that he assumed Romanow would be his best successor. Romanow wasn't in the House. To the annoyance of many in the party, he even delayed his decision to seek a nomination until March 1986. By then Ed Tchorzewski, who was also interested in the leadership, had won a byelection in Regina and was back in the House. "I think I know Roy well enough," Blakeney says, "to know that if I'd quit in 1985, he would have stood. But I wasn't sure of that. He was kind of discouraged with politics after '82 and it took him a long time to bounce back.

"I wasn't quite sure who the alternative was. When it began to be clear that Roy was a possibility, and that Ed Tchorzewski was a possibility, I began to give serious consideration to resigning."

He decided to stay, and he's still not sure it was the right decision. His rationale was that if he should win the election, he could make some of the tough economic decisions facing a new government, then leave the premiership to his successor. But there was another reason, according to people who know Blakeney well. He is a competitive politician. He had been defeated by Devine and was offended by the Tories. He wanted to beat them, and then leave as a winner.

He gave it a good run in October 1986. This time the Tories were ready to run their man one-on-one against Blakeney. In the Legislature a favourite, if unoriginal, Tory jibe was to refer to the NDP caucus as "Snow White and the seven dwarfs." When the campaign began, the Tory television ads showed Devine, in cowboy boots and a club jacket, hopping onto a combine. They played his youth against Blakeney's age. They also played Devine's populism against Blakeney's intellect. Devine ridiculed Blakeney as having added wrinkles, but no new ideas since 1982. Devine even claimed that Tommy Douglas, if he were alive, would be supporting Devine rather than Blakeney. Douglas wasn't alive, of course. He had died in February. It was left to his widow, Irma, to write a public letter saying she was distraught to hear that Devine "could so misrepresent the meaning of Tommy's life."

Blakeney refused to respond to personal jibes. Despite a slow start, NDP support continued to build. It would be an exaggeration to say that the party approached the election with many new policy ideas. But given the humiliating defeat in 1982, they provided a respectable showing. On election day, Blakeney polled 3,500 votes more than Devine across the province. Many of those votes were piled up in city constituencies, where the Tories were virtually wiped out. The Conservatives won just as completely in the countryside—in Saskatchewan the rural seats contain 37 per cent of the voters, but 45 per cent of the seats. Devine won 38 seats, Blakeney 25, and the Liberals 1. This time as he spoke to reporters amid the din of post-election festivities, Blakeney described the results not as a "defeat, but more of a disappointment." Four and a half years earlier it would have sounded hollow, but on this night Blakeney could paraphrase Rudyard Kipling: "I would say you have to meet triumph and disaster and treat those two imposters just the same."

# Chapter Twenty-One

# Life after Politics

After the loss in October 1986, there was no question in Blakeney's mind about his leaving. He wanted it to be sooner rather than later, and he told the party so immediately. They asked him to wait, preferring not to have a change in leadership until closer to the next election. He was co-operative, but firm: "I indicated that in no case would I stay on beyond December 31st, 1987. I would work with them on any date up to that, but after that I was gone and they could do what they liked." He'd been in the Legislature for 26 years, 16 as leader, and 11 as Premier. He had now lost two elections. The NDP had a strong caucus with a handful of people who might seek the leadership—Romanow, Tchorzewski, Lingenfelter, possibly even Louise Simard or Pat Atkinson. Blakeney wanted to get on with the rest of his life. He did not want a restive caucus waiting for him to leave. He wanted no replays of that painful night when Woodrow Lloyd resigned—wounded, and burning with indignation.

Anne Blakeney not only concurred in her husband's decision to leave; she had begun to insist. Her impatience showed in the 1986 Christmas letter. Blakeney had been campaigning throughout the province all year, she said, while she was home waiting; she "had not spent time alone like that since marriage." The children were gone, working or going to school, and her husband was on the road. They had begun to talk about the future, but much of it was in the hands of Saskatchewan voters. "I was thinking," she says, "that we never had a beginning to our marriage. We plunged into politics right at the start, and now I'm ready for a honeymoon. I'm ready to have him to myself. When is it ever going to happen? It seemed to go on about two years more than I was prepared for."

Within a month of the 1986 election, Blakeney said publicly that he would not lead the party into another. In August 1987, he announced that he would be stepping down before the year's end. During the news conference at Tommy Douglas House, Blakeney was unemotional. They had been the most "exciting, challenging and enjoyable years" of his life, he said, but it was time to go. At the NDP Provincial Council meeting in Prince Albert shortly before, the scene had been more intimate. He told the councillors that he had spent his life in politics doing what he wanted to do, and working near the limit of his capacity with people whom he liked and trusted. He came close to breaking down during his address—a shock to the councillors who had never seen him show emotion. The party planned a leadership convention in November.

He stepped down as leader on November 6th, and was saluted by all sides in the usually raucous Legislative Chamber. The members passed a unanimous motion praising him for his "leadership, statesmanship, and dedication to the public interest." In his reply, Blakeney joked that he had just taken his pulse to convince himself that he hadn't stumbled into a posthumous motion of condolence.

The people in his caucus office had planned a less formal gathering following the ceremonies in the chambers. The staff, caucus, and some party stalwarts milled about in the cramped suite of opposition offices. Small groups formed and reformed amid the buzz of conversation and the glare of television lights. A passing shot in the evening news showed Blakeney, one hand in his pocket, the other clutching a plastic glass, standing at the edge of a conversation, peeking in, as though not wanting to intrude. It was one of those occasions when television caught the mood perfectly. After 26 years in the House, Blakeney was still an inherently shy man, with little inclination to participate in that endless river of gossip and small talk which inevitably surrounds politics. Blakeney remembered some work he had to complete in his office, and left the party early.

The NDP convention in Regina that same weekend acclaimed Roy Romanow as Blakeney's successor, and Leader of the Opposition.

Willie Hodgson had worked in the federal and provincial civil service for more than 20 years. She lived in Moose Jaw and commuted daily to her job with the Public Service Commission in Regina. She later told CBC Radio that on Tuesday, May 12, 1987 she was at home with a cold. She received a telephone call from her boss. Someone was on the way out to see her. The office had been rife with rumours that there was a bloodbath coming in the civil service. Hodgson asked, heart pounding, if she was going to be fired. No, she was told, nothing like that.

She had barely hung up the telephone when her doorbell rang. A young man was at the door. He identified himself as from the consulting firm of Stevenson, Kellogg, Ernst, and Whinney. He was acting for the Government of Saskatchewan. He told her she had been fired. She was not to return to the office for her personal effects until she had made an appointment. In shock, she mumbled something about having files she would have to tidy up. He told her that under no circumstances was she to go to the office alone. He demanded that she hand over her key, then invited her to accompany him to a local hotel where counsellors were standing by.

Numbly, she followed him, only to find a room filled with provincial civil servants in the same state of shock and confusion. One of the people she recognized was Dr. Andrew Nicol, a 57-year-old man who had been principal of the Saskatchewan Technical Institute in Moose Jaw for seven years. He had received his news in a similarly abrupt manner that morning, and was led away without a chance even to clean out his desk. Hodgson, Nicol, and the others in the room were treated to a fast-paced performance by the consultants. They were told to look ahead, and not to dwell on the past (i.e., that morning). They were told that this was the first day of the rest of their lives. They were all going on to bigger and better things. The firm had imported a small army of workers to deliver the harsh news to hundreds of government workers throughout the province on the same day.

After the 1982 election Grant Devine said that Saskatchewan was so well endowed that you could mismanage it and still turn a profit. By 1986 the province had an accumulated deficit of $2 billion. The Premier did not see it as a great problem. He said during the 1986 campaign that people would prefer to have the government in debt than to be in debt themselves. The major Conservative promise was a home renovation program which cost $170 million in its first year. (The NDP had promised an expensive mortgage and home program of their own).

Throughout the campaign, Devine had talked about "building Saskatchewan," about momentum and enthusiasm. Within three months of the election, Finance Minister Gary Lane discovered that the province was facing a financial crisis. He announced late in January 1987 that the deficit for 1986–87 alone could soar to $1.2 billion or more—200 per cent higher than his budget had predicted a mere nine months earlier. The only alternative, he said, would be to chop programs and lay off government workers.

Throughout the spring of 1987, Devine and his ministers closeted themselves in meeting rooms to hack and slash both the civil service and community-based programs. The casualties were announced in a string of daily news releases. By June 1987, the Saskatchewan Government Employees' Union estimated that 2,600 jobs had been lost. The list of those summarily fired included hundreds of teachers in technical schools and community colleges, 400 dental nurses, managers at the Saskatchewan Housing Corporation, and curriculum developers in the Department of Education. Many of the other cutbacks were delivered by slashing the budgets of, or completely disbanding, third party health and social service agencies—day care centres, home care programs, women's transition houses, community mental health programs. Grants to all municipalities, school boards, and universities were reduced. Benefits from the prescription drug program became subject to a deductible.

The Conservatives discovered more than the deficit; they accepted privatization as their political salvation. Devine had promised after his victory in 1982 that there would be no general selling off of crown corporations. But following 1986 he began to import the New Right agenda of Margaret Thatcher and Ronald Reagan. Thatcher's privatization guru, Oliver Letwin, was a visitor and advisor in Saskatchewan. So was Michael Walker, the head of Vancouver's Fraser Institute, which had lent a hand to Bill Bennett in similar moves in British Columbia. The Devine government needed an ideological issue to divert attention from the sad state of the economy. Selling off crown corporations was also a way to raise money. But despite the cutbacks and the sell-offs, the accumulated deficit by early 1989 was $3.7 billion—approximately $3,700 for each person in Saskatchewan.

The government had sold part, or all, of Saskoil, Saskatchewan Minerals, the Prince Albert pulp mill, the Meadow Lake sawmill, and government coal mines. They announced plans to divide Saskatchewan Government Insurance, keeping automobile insurance, and selling the more profitable general insurance business. They put a large chunk of the Potash Corporation of Saskatchewan on the block. Finally, they separated the profitable natural gas utility from SaskPower and created a company called SaskEnergy, which they planned to sell. The Tories had the momentum. Devine reflected on the situation at a dinner held in his honour: "We've got a tiger by the tail on a downhill drive and we're going for it."

Romanow had taken over as NDP leader in November 1987. People in his own party believed that he was playing it too safe. The Conservatives were on the offensive with their privatization plans, and the NDP had done little to stop them. Between 4,000 and 7,000 people marched on the Legislature in June 1987 in a demonstration organized by a grassroots coalition. The NDP appeared weak in its response to the popular sense of outrage.

Then in April 1989, when the Conservatives introduced a bill to sell SaskEnergy, Romanow said they had "crossed the Rubicon." He led the NDP members out of the Legislature and paralyzed its operation. He and the caucus hit the road, taking their case to rallies across the province. They said they would not allow the Tories to sell a prized utility. The first general sense of Romanow's approach to economic policy began to emerge. He would paint the Tories as extremist ideologues who had imported the privatization idea from Britain; he called it "an old idea disguised as a new fad." Its results would be both reduced services and a drain of profits to out-of-province investors. Romanow appealed to the "powerful and pragmatic tradition of the mixed economy," and to "made-in-Saskatchewan" rather than imported solutions.

Shutting down the House was a gamble that paid off. It stopped the train. While Romanow and his caucus were taking the privatization issue to nightly rallies, the media began polling: only 22 per cent of those asked supported the SaskEnergy privatization. When asked for whom they would vote if an election were called the next day, 33 per cent said Conservative, and 54 per cent said NDP.

Devine backed away, and set up a commission to study the SaskEnergy sale. He returned from a summer of poor polls a chastened man; he had undergone a similar conversion prior to the 1986 election. He was going to listen to the people. He established Consensus Saskatchewan, advertised as a non-partisan group of 100 citizens who will hold hearings throughout the province to find what the people have to say about Saskatchewan's troubled situation.

The problems are considerable. The Tories overshot their announced 1989 deficit by $160 million. They are projecting another, their ninth in succession, for 1990. The accumulated deficit is $4.8 billion. Interest charges alone amount to almost $500 million a year—$57 thousand an hour. Among the budget expenditures, only health and education cost more than carrying charges on the debt. The province has had its credit rating reduced by the international lenders, which means it will pay a higher rate of interest to service the debt. The NDP now talk of reducing the accumulated deficit to zero in 15 years. Everything will have to go right for that to happen.

Blakeney has watched the privatization debate from a distance, and with some anguish. Crown corporations were always central to his vision for developing Saskatchewan. He's been close to them since his first days in the province. He believes that, because they are accountable to the cabinet and the Legislature, they are a means of democratizing the economy. They ensure that control over economic decisions remains in Saskatchewan. The alternative is control exercised from elsewhere, and a depopulated Saskatchewan. He is reluctant to become personal in his criticism of the man who has placed the crowns on the auction block. In an interview taped for CBC Radio shortly after he resigned in 1987, Blakeney was asked what he thought of Devine. He looked at the interviewer and vigorously shook his head, refusing to answer. There was complete silence in the room. When the tape recorder was turned off after the interview, he said his response would have sounded like "sour grapes." He will admit, privately, that Devine has become an effective politician, but remains a "woefully inadequate administrator."

Blakeney spent his last day in the House in March 1988, then he made a quick, clean break. From late April through June, he and Anne travelled through Egypt and Greece, then in continental Europe by train. They spent much of the later summer of 1988 disengaging themselves from both office and home. He spent his days sifting through files and sending them off to the Saskatchewan archives. She sorted through 30 years of household and family effects. They held an auction at which many of their possessions, including gifts and souvenirs he had received as Premier, were sold. They donated the proceeds to the Regina Elphinstone constituency. They were not yet sure if they should make plans to settle somewhere or, in Anne's words, to "be grasshoppers." Wherever they were, they wanted to be less encumbered by possessions. They had already sold the house at King Street and moved into a smaller Regina condominium. There hadn't been much time to plan, but now there were decisions to be made. "We envisioned moving around for some time," Anne says, "of not making any fixed plans till we had our thoughts reorganized. When you've had your nose to one grindstone for a long time, it's hard to imagine what to do next."

For the fall, he had accepted the Bora Laskin Chair in Public Law at Osgoode Hall in Toronto. The invitation came from the Dean, Jim MacPherson, who had been Director of Constitutional Law for the Attorney General's department in Saskatchewan between 1981 and 1985. He admired Blakeney, although he barely knew him then. MacPherson left to take a job with the Supreme Court of Canada, and moved to Osgoode in early 1988. Even before he had taken up his duties officially, he approached Blakeney, who had just resigned as leader. "I was looking for a politician with an intellectual bent," MacPherson says. "I wanted an eminent Canadian from outside of Ontario." Blakeney came to mind immediately, as did Pierre Marc Johnson, who had stepped down as Parti Quebecois leader. MacPherson landed both of them.

He says Blakeney fit into the academic environment immediately. "He's very smart. He knows a lot of Canadian constitutional law. He's a very good lawyer. He won the students and the faculty over with his intellect and his decency." Blakeney's friend of many years, Tommy McLeod, says he liked the university environment right away: "Happy as a pig in a puddle. He went into it with some misgivings. He's a perfectionist. His big concern was that he wouldn't be able to get this stuff across to students. But the guy is a natural teacher and now is really quite pleased with himself."

The Laskin chair is a one-year appointment. MacPherson was so impressed that he offered a permanent position. Blakeney declined, although he did go back for a second year. He enjoyed the two years at Osgoode Hall, and was professionally happy in Toronto. But neither he nor Anne liked the size of the city or its frenetic pace. What they did enjoy, after all the years in politics, was the anonymity.

The Blakeneys lived in two different Toronto houses in two years, homes let by professors on sabbatical. They travelled frequently to Ottawa to visit friends and their four children, all adults now, who have settled there. The children say their parents are in frequent contact, but are a self-contained couple. They go about their lives and make decisions without much need for family consultation. Barbara, the eldest, says that as adolescents and young adults they were itinerants, moving away from home and back frequently with books and clothes and records. Now she says it's her parents who are footloose. "I think they're like 19-year-olds now. You can't say where a 19-year-old will be in two years."

Some family patterns have persisted. Margaret, the youngest at 22, says she was never certain when her father was going to be around, so her mother was always the "chief communications centre." David, 26, says that's still the case: "If you phone them and Dad answers, the first instinct is ask for Mom. Then you talk to her, even if it's got something to do with him. He's probably busy or distracted."

Anne says that getting away from the pressure of politics has had a salutary effect on her husband. But some of the habits of a professional lifetime don't fade easily. As Premier, he always had a staff of secretaries and assistants. He has never learned to type, and still does not find computers very friendly. They were given a laptop as a gift; Anne uses it to keep up with correspondence. He now takes his own telephone messages.

He has also carried over his penchant for sorting out his problems and options, then presenting his brief. "His mindset," says Anne, "is such that he figures out what he wants to do, and when he has it all clear in his mind, it should flow right away. That doesn't always give me as much warning as I would like. Sometimes it would seem to me he could alert a person a day or two in advance. But it usually works out."

The Blakeneys aren't rich, but they're comfortable enough to travel, and to choose where they want to live. He received severance pay of approximately $60,000 when he left the Legislature, and his annual pension is around $40,000. They own their condominium jointly. He still owns the bungalow he built as part of the Lakeview housing co-operative in 1952. He has a neighbour rent it for him. They retain the cottage they purchased at Kanata Valley north of Regina. They have stubbornly resisted lawns and plumbing, and the cabin remains rustic, without telephone or an indoor toilet. The value of their two houses and the cottage—all modest buildings in a slow market—probably doesn't exceed $130,000.

He bought term deposits, RRSPs, and occasionally some shares in large companies (never companies doing business with the government), but says he did not get rich while in politics. "If you're careful, as I was, you have some savings. You don't get wealthy, but it's a pretty fair pension plan. I'm comfortable enough." Tommy McLeod says Blakeney could have made a mint as a corporate lawyer. "You just wouldn't think of Al doing that. It isn't his way of life."

The long-established habits of frugality remain. The Blakeney Oldsmobile is several years old. Their condominium, while comfortable, is only 1,400 square feet. Neither Blakeney nor Anne has used the time away from politics to cultivate a taste for fashionable clothes. Correspondence from them is apt to arrive in used brown envelopes with new white stickers pasted over the old address labels.

They like to travel, and plan to do more. A couple of weeks in the winter sun has become an annual ritual. They gained some publicity which they would happily have avoided in a 1988 Christmas trip to Cuba. While Anne remained ashore, Blakeney and Margaret boarded a boat which was to take her scuba diving and him fishing. The boat appeared suspiciously small for the large group that boarded. He thought it was going to take them across the harbour to a larger boat for the trip out to sea. To his surprise, it headed out of the harbour, and soon began to take on water. When it came time to abandon ship, there were only a few lifeboats. Most of the passengers jumped into the choppy water, trying to stay afloat until help came.

For the next two hours, those passengers who could treaded water; others tried to cling to the hull of the capsized boat, which was covered with barnacles. In the oily ocean waters, easily in sight of the Cuban coast, Blakeney alternately treaded water and clung to the boat. His earlier habit of swimming in the mornings while he was Premier may have saved him. He received deep gashes in his leg from the time he spent clutching the boat, but he was able to stay afloat, and even to help others around him. Before help came in the form of Cuban military helicopters and speed boats, however, several passengers had been lost.

Blakeney appeared on the front pages and the national television news when he returned to Canada. He was furious with the lack of care and safety taken by the Canadian and Cuban tour operators, and with their reluctance to accept any responsibility. On a voluntary basis, he took on the case of negotiating compensation for the lost effects. Part of the compensation was another, free trip to Cuba last winter. He went into the water, but always with his toes planted firmly in the sand.

They haven't decided where they will settle permanently. "My crystal ball doesn't tell me very much," Anne says. "I think that I am more tuned into enjoyment of the physical surroundings than Allan is. But those physical surroundings can be in a variety of places." While they lived two winters in Toronto, they spent their first two summers after politics in Saskatchewan. "The clear air, the quality of the sunshine, the light in the sky, the look of the fields: we thoroughly enjoyed it," she says.

He had spent the summers preparing for his law lectures, but the months were relatively relaxed. They like to go for walks along nearby Wascana Creek as it winds through their section of the city. They spend extended weekends at their cottage. After long years of having his household tools locked away, Blakeney has begun to do some of his own small repairs at the beach. He wears old work pants and a red plaid shirt when he clears brush. When he wore the red shirt for a television commercial during the 1986 election campaign, he was ridiculed by the Conservatives as an "urban cowboy." But he has since been paid the ultimate Saskatchewan compliment. Jack Kinzel, Blakeney's political colleague of many years, spends summers with his wife Betty in the little hamlet of Silton, near the Blakeneys' cottage. "A car drove up one day," Betty says, "and you could plainly see this farmer and his wife sitting in it. We didn't know who it was. When they got out, it was Al and Anne Blakeney. It's the first time he ever looked like a farmer, cap and all."

Blakeney has deliberately maintained a modest post-leadership profile. Ed Broadbent wanted him to run federally in 1988. There was a new constituency in Regina, and Blakeney would almost certainly have had the nomination. He decided he didn't want it. "I'd had 28 years in politics, and Anne and I had decided I simply didn't want to commit to another four."

Jim MacPherson, the Osgoode dean, says one of the attractions of Toronto was that Blakeney wanted to be away from Saskatchewan for awhile: "He wanted to give the new leader a free hand." Blakeney rarely speaks at home. He did talk—about potash—at a summer fund-raising dinner in Regina in 1989. When he met with reporters following the speech, he firmly avoided responding to any questions about what current NDP policy should be on potash privatization. There was a new leader and caucus, he said, who could better answer those questions.

He has also moved quietly at the federal level—too quietly for some of his colleagues who think he should have more to say, given his experience and the respect he commands. He says that he's no longer "on the firing line," and it would be presumptuous of him to advise elected members. "I never really fancied myself a political strategist, and I'm not a particularly good advisor to a party that is in opposition."

He did get involved, behind the scenes, in the federal NDP leadership race in 1989. He was part of a group of New Democrats who tried to convince Stephen Lewis to run. Later, Blakeney approached Bob Rae. He did not believe that the leader should come from the west simply because the majority of elected MPs are from there. "I think Stephen has a breadth of experience and an ability to project the aims and objectives of the party which is very outstanding. While Bob Rae is not in Stephen's class as a communicator, he is an exceedingly sound, intelligent man who would provide great leadership. The others were much lesser known quantities, and I think that's true of Audrey right now. She's an interesting and lively woman without any particular background in politics, and therefore must be unknown. Barrett—a very engaging style, but not a traditional NDP style, and I'm not sure we could build around it."

Alexa McDonough was one of the people who, along with Blakeney, spent an evening trying to convince Lewis to run. "Allan Blakeney was absolutely in his element," she says. "Everybody was deferring to his long experience and his vision of the country and the party. I remember how awe-struck some of the people in the room were with his seasoned, sage view of things. Everybody realized that here was a guy who's done it all, and his ability to share all of that was quite phenomenal." Publicly, Blakeney did not admit a leadership preference, and he will not say who he eventually supported.

He's more forthcoming with advice in areas where he considers himself most competent—in the organization and economic policies of governments once they are elected. He has already talked to both Romanow and British Columbia's Mike Harcourt about what to expect if they move into government. Garry Aldridge, Blakeney's former assistant, says, "If you asked Allan Blakeney what are the 30 things you need to do in the transition to new government, he could give you that checklist off the top of his head. But he would never give it unless asked. He's not somebody who sticks his nose into what he thinks is somebody else's business. He's very unassuming."

Blakeney may soon be called on to provide more of that advice in Saskatchewan. This fall and winter he'll be in Saskatoon, as the Law Federation of Saskatchewan Professor of Public Law. It's another short-term distinguished professorship, this time at the University of Saskatchewan. It's a logical appointment, but Blakeney would also take great pleasure at being on hand for an election and a change in government. Romanow wants to run his own show, but he's pleased that Blakeney will be nearby to offer quiet advice.

In the writing he has done since his retirement from politics, Blakeney concentrates on administration rather than what he calls "the broad sweep of ideas." He says, "I've always had an interest in administration as a technique, and not many other people seem to have it. They seem to think that administration comes like manna from heaven. What I find I am the bearer of is a great Saskatchewan tradition of public administration, a civil service which was good and which had both the Mafia and the Boat People [civil servants who left Saskatchewan in 1964 and 1982 respectively] make their mark wherever they went.

"Perhaps I should have been more of a proselytizer, but I always felt more comfortable in the other realm. I felt I was being preachy in the proselytizing role. I assumed that people knew what their moral roots were. They didn't need to be reminded, but wanted to know what they should do about it. In my speeches in later years, I have been trying to expand on broader themes."

Some people think Blakeney is too reticent in promoting his views. John Richards, the former renegade MLA in Blakeney's caucus, says that Blakeney's reticence is frustrating. "I wish he would, as an elder statesman, be more public about what he has himself contributed, on the legitimate and necessary role for good public administration and rational policy making as a part of the left. But I have the feeling that it isn't his instinct to want to do this."

One of the "broader themes" that Blakeney is speaking and writing about is the economy. He believes the NDP will forever be consigned to the margins of Canadian politics unless the party convinces people that it could manage the economy. His prescription includes deficit reduction, an industrial strategy, and a heightened commitment to environmental protection. He believes all of those policies must be pursued through the negotiation of a national "social contract," something he has been talking about since the 1960s.

He accepts that there is a global challenge to Canadian industry from both the established and the newly-emerging industrial economies. Canada will not be able to save all its industrial jobs, so it will have to create new ones, and do it in a way which supports those who work in declining industries. That can best be accomplished not by following the Tory model, which emphasizes privatization and attacks trade unions, but by pursuing a mixed economy. The major planners and players would be government, private enterprise, and labour. They would enter into a form of joint planning toward industrial goals and societal rewards. Japan has done some of that, and other countries more similar to Canada have as well: Austria, the Netherlands, West Germany.

"Clearly, our strengths are still distributional justice," he says of the NDP. "We want fair shares for all in a free society. We want a fairer tax system and we want to continue to offer a broad range of educational and health services. Those things we want. We want to review the damage of the Conservative wrecking crew.

"Having said that, it's not enough. We still have to offer some sort of blueprint for the management of the Canadian economy to produce these results. It is because of our inability to convince the Canadian people that we can keep wealth production going that they are unwilling to accept our distributional views. We must talk in terms of a European democratic socialism, about co-operation between management, government, and labour to set some broad economic goals for the government, and pursue them as some governments have done with a good deal of success. We need to talk about the social contract.

"We also want more fiscal prudence. I don't know what we can say about a Conservative government which says it's for fiscal prudence, and since 1984 has run up more debt than we did from 1867 to 1964. I think we have to confront that—why you should have balanced budgets."

Labour is accustomed to hearing talk about a tri-partite approach to the economy whenever government and business want to rationalize the imposition of wage restraints or outright controls. Blakeney's model would involve workers trading off some gains in return for an improved "social wage," including social and educational programs and, he believes, less likelihood of inflation. Critics say it's usually wages, not prices, that are controlled when workers get involved in voluntary restraint. They also say that co-operation at the level Blakeney desires would lead to a state of decision-making so highly centralized that it would hamper the local political sense of democracy and community.

Blakeney replies that neither democracy nor the economy has suffered in those countries which have pursued the social contract. But he admits that there is little support for his economic thinking within the NDP. "The trade unions in Canada are very nervous about it, and that explains the nervousness of the federal NDP on it." When he becomes frustrated with critics of the idea, he paraphrases an old Clarence Fines maxim: "Don't tell me what won't work; tell me what will."

Another of the broader themes Blakeney has begun to talk and write about is what he calls "the nature of Canada." His views, developed by years of experience at the constitutional bargaining table, are balanced and complex. He argued throughout the constitutional process for more power and control at the provincial level. Yet he has always believed the central government must remain strong enough to guarantee national independence, and to direct the economy. He opposed the Free Trade Agreement, which he says will bind the hands of the government forever. It is his concern for the role of the federal state which made him critical of the Meech Lake agreement. He feared that the accord's allowing provinces to opt out of national cost-shared programs—with compensation—would have meant that no new programs would be launched. Programs such as hospitalization and medicare always involve tax dollars from the larger provinces subsidizing programs in the smaller ones. The temptation for Ontario and Quebec to opt out of national programs with compensation, he believes, would become overwhelming: "Since those programs have done so much to weld this country together, and to define what we mean by being Canadian, we should not restrict that power."

Blakeney deliberately maintained a low profile during the frantic weeks preceding the failure of the Meech Lake Accord in June. He did not want to upstage either Romanow or Audrey McLaughlin. He is impatient, however, with those talking in "apocalyptic" terms about the demise of Canada because Meech Lake failed. He thought the Meech proposals were so flawed that they could not be supported, but says the chance to improve upon them will come again.

Tommy Douglas said in 1978 that Allan Blakeney "proved social democracy is not just an impossible dream." Blakeney never talked much about dreams. That was one of his failings as a politician. His greatest strength was not as a leader who could, by vision or rhetoric, inspire and revitalize the people's movement which had been the Saskatchewan CCF. The movement may even have waned under his tutelage, but it was certainly waning before his time, anyway. It's not easy to maintain a co-operative ethos amid the individualism of North America. Blakeney is a principled pragmatist, a decent, extremely capable man, who gave intelligent and honest government. As the NDP struggles to convince Canadians that it could govern, that it is an alternative worthy of their consideration, the value of Blakeney's contribution—as ordinary as it appears—is apparent. He once said that he would like to be remembered as someone who "ran a good shop." That was Allan Blakeney's New Deal. It's a promise he kept.

# Notes

Abbreviations Used:

AEB    Allan Emrys Blakeney
SAB    Saskatchewan Archives Board
SSP    Saskatoon *Star-Phoenix*
RLP    Regina *Leader-Post*

Allan Blakeney's papers are found at the Saskatchewan Archives Board in Regina. Their use is restricted, and requires written permission from Mr. Blakeney. There are numerous Finding Aides which act as a guide to the voluminous collection. In citing sources for this book I have used the SAB call numbers, so that each source can easily be traced to its file. Where possible I have also dated the source, since most files contain a number of documents, ordered chronologically. Anyone with permission to use the papers can easily locate the documents I have used. I have also provided the call numbers for the SAB photographs I have used, so they can be easily located as well. When I refer to Personal Papers, I am talking about those which Mr. Blakeney keeps at home, and which he lent to me.

## Jeddore
6    Walter Stewart describes the loyalists: *True Blue: The Loyalist Legend* (Toronto: Colliers, 1985), see pp. 5, 122, 239.
8    "A modestly comfortable life." SAB, R–8537. Taped interview with Judy Steed, February 18, 1982.
8    "Serene" and "steeped in security." SAB, R–8328 and R–8329. Taped interview with Jean Larmour, October 14, 1982.
11    Most Talkative student: Bridgewater High School Yearbook, 1941–42, p. 15.
11    "A lawyer and a politician": Ibid, p. 41.

## Dalhousie and Oxford
13    "Never one of the boys": Susan Swedberg-Kohli, "Blakeney: The Politician and the Man," *Sask Report*, October 1987, p. 15.
13    "I'm not one of the boys": Ibid.
13    Investing council reserves in victory loans: *Pharohs*, Dalhousie student yearbook, 1945.
13    "Left Turn Canada": Robert Bothwell, Ian Drummond, John English, *Canada since 1945: Power, politics, and provincialism* (Toronto: University of Toronto Press, 1981), pp. 65–69.
15    "Law and Canadian politics": *Pharohs* 1945.
15    "Grace and charm to the group." *Pharohs* 1947.
16    "Discussion groups and student government": AEB, Personal Papers.
16    Biscuits were not available: AEB, Personal Papers, "To Rhodes Scholars for 1947."
18    Morgan Phillips, the Labour Party secretary: AEB, Personal Papers. David Lewis letter, November 24, 1947.
18    His chances would be excellent indeed: AEB, Personal Papers. Lloyd Shaw letter, September 28, 1948.

## The Civil Service
20    "Present government of Saskatchewan": AEB, Personal Papers, Letter to George Tamaki, undated. Tamaki replied on August 12, 1949. There are several other letters to prospective employers.
21    It "wasn't Paris": Susan Swedberg-Kohli, "The Politician and The Man," *Sask Report*, October, 1987, p. 13.
22    Expanded rural and social services: information in the next few paragraphs borrows from articles by George Cadbury and Meyer Brownstone in *Essays on the Left*, Laurier LaPierre et al (Toronto: McClelland and Stewart, 1971). See also Thomas H. and Ian McLeod, *Tommy Douglas: The Road To Jerusalem*, (Edmonton: Hurtig Publishers, 1987).
23    On the afternoon of Christmas day: Allan Blakeney, "The Early Douglas Years in Saskatchewan," *Newest Review*, May 1987, p. 11.
25    "Jim Darling, Charlie Williams": SAB, Blakeney interview with Jean Larmour.
26    The "co-operative commonwealth": Meyer Brownstone, *Essays on the Left*, p. 65.
26    Should be socialists: McLeods, *Tommy Douglas*, p. 130.
29    "State of bereaved shock": RLP, March 5, 1974, p. 18.
29    "So many things were guessed at": Ibid.
29    "Had my fill of concert going": Ibid.
30    A beige straw hat: Ibid.

## Politics
31    "A much better job than I have done.": RLP, April 20, 1960, p. 1.
32    "He had persuaded Blakeney to run.": Judy Steed, *The Globe and Mail*, February 27, 1982, p. 10.
32    "As thick or as thin as you wish.": RLP, April 20, 1960.
32    Spent on its entire campaign: E. A. Tollefson, *Bitter Medicine—The Saskatoon Medicare Feud* (Saskatoon: Modern Press, 1964) p. 54.
32    A public relations man: *The Commonwealth*, July 20, 1960, p. 11. See also June 1, 1960, p. 1.
33    "Garbage of Europe": Ibid, p. 8.
34    "I think I was the key political figure": Swedberg-Kohli, *Sask Report*, October 1987, p. 14.
34    Pile-o'-Bones Creek: Wascana is a Cree word meaning "pile of bones." The bones described were the bleached carcasses of buffalo, slaughtered by the white man for sport.
36    "A right wing socialist party": Blakeney Personal Papers, Letter, undated.
36    Lloyd easily defeated the only challenger: *The Commonwealth*, November 1, 1961, p. 1.
36    A deficit of $2.4 million: Legislature of Saskatchewan, *Debates and Proceedings*, March 9, 1962, p. 14.
37    Greater equity for its citizens: Ibid.

## Medicare
38    Anne wrote a simple letter: Blakeney Personal Papers.
39    "So near to his departure": interview with Walter Smishek.
39    Needed Blakeney for Treasurer: interview with Bill Davies.
40    Included danger pay: interview with Bill Davies.
41    "Can't It Happen Here?": Robin Badgley and Samuel Wolfe, *Doctor's Strike* (Toronto: Macmillan, 1967), pp. 90–91. This book presents a good description of events preceding and during the strike.
42    "You are going to lose your doctors": Ibid.

42    "I love free swinging freedom": SSP July 7, 1962, pp. 2 and 3.
42    "God help us if it doesn't": Badgley and Wolfe, p. 65.
42    Wastebasket beside his bed: interview with Bill Davies.
43    "Down with dictators": see the film, *Bitter Medicine*, National Film Board.
43    "Freedom is being extinguished": Badgley and Wolfe, p. 67.
44    "Slightly of the ham variety": SAB-Saskatoon. AEB interview with
      E. A. Tollefson, May 26, 1966.

Opposition
46    Radical activity of the 1940s: See McLeods, *Tommy Douglas*, pp. 180–93.
46    Called an election and lost: for an account of the 1964 election see
      James A. Dosman, "The Medical Care Issue as a Factor in the Electoral
      Defeat of the Saskatchewan Government in 1964," MA thesis, University of
      Saskatchewan, 1979.
46    Unite opposition behind Thatcher: Ibid, pp. 142–43.
46    Social Credit vote . . . collapsed: Ibid, p. 148.
49    Verged on nihilism: David Smith, "Rumours of Glory," *Newest Review*,
      December, 1987, p. 14. Book review.
49    Economic stagnation and big government: a good description of the Thatcher
      years is Dale Eisler's *Rumours of Glory* (Edmonton: Hurtig Publishers, 1987).
50    For 30 per cent of the equity: Eisler, p. 169.
51    Calling Thatcher a tyrant: Eisler, p. 205.
51    The only minister Thatcher trusted: Ibid, p. 222.
53    Laid up with a bad back: Dianne Lloyd, *Woodrow: A Biography of
      Woodrow S. Lloyd* (The Woodrow Lloyd Memorial Fund, 1979), pp. 149,
      150, 156.
53    "Essential revolutions": SAB-Saskatoon, NDP Papers, A670 Box 1, 1965.
54    "His sense of responsibility and his vanity": Dianne Lloyd, pp. 162–63.
54    Publicly owned oil and potash developments: see John Richards and Larry
      Pratt, *Prairie Capitalism: Power and Influence in the New West* (Toronto:
      McClelland and Stewart, 1979), p. 252. This is an excellent book outlining
      the history of resource policies in Saskatchewan and Alberta.

The Waffle
56    "Waffle to the right": There is doubt about who said this. The McLeods say
      it may have been Ed Broadbent, but no one, including Broadbent's
      biographer, Judy Steed, seems certain. A thorough background on the Waffle
      can be found in "Pie in the Sky: A History of the Ontario Waffle," *Canadian
      Dimension*, October–November 1980. The waffle quote used here originates
      from that article, but carries no attribution. *Briarpatch* magazine carried an
      historical account of the Saskatchewan Waffle in articles during the fall and
      winter of 1989–90.
56    "A truly socialist party": author's library, from the mimeograph "For An
      Independent Socialist Canada," p. 1.
56    "Ambiguous and ambivalent": McLeods, *Tommy Douglas*, p. 279.
57    "Slightly left of centre moderate": *The Globe and Mail*, November 1, 1969,
      p. 12.
57    "A real debt": Ibid.
58    Would not have done him justice: the description of Lloyd owes to John
      Richards, "The Left of the NDP," *Western Canadian Politics: The Radical
      Tradition*, ed. Don Kerr (Edmonton: Newest Institute for Western Canadian
      Studies Inc., 1981), p. 71.
60    Profound effect on his thinking: Ibid.

60 Farmers trying to get established: *The Commonwealth*, February 18, 1970, p. 7. This edition carries a review of NDP farm policy.
62 Davies was furious: interview with Bill Davies.
62 Disagreed with the Waffle's organizing tactics: interview with Reverend Don Faris.
62 A counter-resolution that carried narrowly: *The Commonwealth*, March 18, 1970, p. 7.
63 Lloyd had begun to run out of patience: SAB, R–800.II.4.a. Dec. 3, 1969.
63 Appeared in *The Commonwealth:* March 18, 1970, p. 9.
63 "Disastrous way to run a political party": SAB, R–1143.X.2.c. March 23, 1970.
63 "Retiring land at assessed value": SAB, R–1284.V.D.7. "Draft Statement of Purpose." Records of the Saskatchewan Waffle.
64 "Caucus saw red": see Robert Walker letter to *The Commonwealth*, May 27, 1970, p. 10.
64 Told their own story: SAB, R–800, I. 226.
64 "George Taylor refused to attend": conversation with George Taylor.
65 Have not discussed publicly: there is one account of that evening: "The Meaning of Woodrow Lloyd's Resignation," *Next Year Country*, April, 1983. While useful, it does not include comments from members of caucus.
66 Caught off guard by Walker's attack: interviews with Frank Coburn, Walter Smishek, Bill Davies.
67 And had told him so: *The Commonwealth*, June 10, 1970, p. 10. Bob Walker is no longer alive. He maintained to the end that there had been no conspiracy, and was bitter about being labelled disloyal to Lloyd.
67 Within weeks of the session's ending: interview with Walter Smishek.

## Leadership
69 He mentioned Lloyd's encouragement: RLP, April 16, 1970, p. 3.
71 "Dead end reform": RLP, May 26, 1970, p. 1.
71 "I totally reject it": SSP, May 27, 1970, p. 3.
71 A motion of appreciation to him: RLP, May 27, 1970, p. 24.
72 "Superficial and too ambitious": interview with Dr. Frank Coburn.
72 "Seminar in Yorkton": see *The Commonwealth*, February 18, 1970, p. 7, and March 4, 1970.
73 "To purchase that leased land": RLP, May 26, 1970, p. 1.
73 "Suggesting nationalization of farmlands": SSP, May 27, 1970, p. 3.
73 Misinterpreted by opponents: *The Commonwealth*, June 10, 1970, p. 9.
73 Purchased at the higher "productive value.": *The Commonwealth*, May 27, 1970, p. 6.
73 Voluntary or otherwise: SSP, June 23, 1970, p. 4
73 "Deteriorated under Thatcher": RLP, June 2, 1970, p. 3.
74 "An appendage of our elected representatives": SSP, July 26, 1970, p. 3.
74 Made the left even angrier: RLP, July 4, 1970, p. 16.
75 Blakeney expected to lead: see RLP coverage of convention, July 3, 4 and 6, 1970.
75 To seek a nomination: RLP, July 6, 1970, p. 4.

## New Deal '71
77 An election on June 23rd: RLP, May 26, 1971, p. 1.
77 It was Romanow they had feared: interview with Dave Steuart.
77 "Little Allan in wonderland": Eisler, *Rumours of Glory*, p. 265.
77 "rather square": SAB, R–800, I. 188. f. "Notes on Meeting re Party Leader and Image," January 5, 1971.

78    Popular prose package called *New Deal for People*: (Regina: Service Printing Co., 1971).

79    Harsh and irritable: see Eisler, pp. 261–65, for one description of the 1971 campaign.

79    "Where the voters are": RLP, June 14, 1971.

79    The issue was agriculture: Ibid, May 26, 1971, p. 1.

80    "Capitalist economic doctrine": See *New Deal for People*, p. 1. The policies summarized here are drawn from the booklet.

82    "Magnificent election": RLP, June 24, 1971, p. 3.

82    Back in the hands of the people: Ibid.

## Premier Administrator

84    The entire ceremony took 45 minutes: RLP, June 30, 1971, p. 1.

84    Remain in cabinet throughout the Blakeney years: Ibid, p. 3, for a description of the cabinet portfolios.

85    Kramer lobbied vigorously: interviews—one not for attribution, the second with Dave Steuart.

87    Kinzel's role as writer and advisor: SAB, R–800, V. 184. a.

87    From $50 thousand to $170 thousand: SAB, R–565, IV. 1. b.

87    "Nor believe in our policies": SAB, R–800, V. 319. a.

88    Blakeney set up a small task force: SAB, R–565, IV. 6. a.

88    Hired Hubert Prefontaine: Prefontaine was later killed in a plane crash.

91    The speech passed into literature: Allan Blakeney, "The Relationship Between Provincial Ministers and their Deputy Ministers," *Canadian Public Administration*, XV, 1 (Spring 1972), pp. 42–45. See also SAB, R–565. IV. 6. a, September 17, 1971, for a Blakeney memo to cabinet on the same topic.

91    Would have occurred in any event: John Richards and Larry Pratt, *Prairie Capitalism*, pp. xii, 37–38. Richards says the waning of the NDP's populist coalition was regrettable, but also inevitable, as the task of governing grew more complex. He says it is to the party's credit that it has maintained its degree of popular participation within the alienating political environment of North America.

91    When he was late for meetings: McLeods, *Tommy Douglas*, p. 125.

92    "Words with Latin roots": SAB, R–800 V. 264. c. Memo from Wes Bolstad, "Staff Work for the Premier," May 1, p. 1978.

93    "With Tommy Douglas it took 30 seconds": conversation with Ed Whelan.

94    He would initiate the conversation: Bolstad, "Staff Work for the Premier."

95    Like Tommy Douglas, he chose to isolate himself: for Douglas's social habits while Premier, see McLeods, pp. 181–82.

## Premier Politician

99    "Healthy round of applause": SAB, Saskatoon. Don Kerr Papers. A–230, Carton One. NDP Council meeting of October 30–31, 1971.

99    One of "many inputs": "The Blakeney Government One Year After." Paper by Saskatchewan Waffle Movement, p. 7. Author's collection.

99    The early years of the CCF: see McLeods, *Tommy Douglas*, p. 126.

101    "And even my physical presence": SAB, R–800.I.148.e. May 3, 1971.

101    None of the left's 12 candidates: RLP, December 6, 1971.

102    Denouncing each other: Don Kerr Papers, "A Letter of Withdrawal from the Waffle," February 1, 1976.

102    Waiting for a box lunch: RLP, November 20, 1973.

## The Farm

104    To answer for itself: SAB, R–8537. Interview with Judy Steed, February 18, 1982.

104     When Senator David Kroll visited the Prince Albert area: I was a reporter for the Prince Albert *Daily Herald,* and accompanied Kroll's group for a day.

104     Ran their machines on used oil: my father was one of the farmers who had to resort to this indignity.

104     The provincial population shrank by 44,000: *Saskatchewan Economic Review* (Regina: Saskatchewan Bureau of Statistics, Government of Saskatchewan, 1973).

104     "Maximum number of family farms": *New Deal for People,* p. 1.

105     "Tinkering with tenure": SAB, R–800.I.222. Blakeney letter to Ove Hanson, November 26, 1970.

105     An ideological commitment to public ownership: Seymour Martin Lipsett, *Agrarian Socialism* (Berkeley: University of California Press, 1971), p. 175.

105     "Rented, not sold to smaller farmers": *Royal Commission on Agriculture and Rural Life,* (Regina: Government of Saskatchewan, 1955-57), Volume 1, Report #5, p. 155.

106     And leased back to farm families: SSP, August 17, 1972.

106     Borrowing money to buy the land: SAB, R–800.III.27.a, December 10, 1971.

107     Messer argued before cabinet: Ibid., April 12, 1972; November 22, 1972.

107     "Requisite philosophical outlook": SAB, R–800, V. 218. a, July 11 & 18, 1972.

107     As a third commissioner: Ibid, August 3, 1972.

107     He wrote from New Brunswick: SAB, R–800, I. 102. a.

107     "2100 farmers who wanted to sell": these and following figures are taken from reports of the Saskatchewan Land Bank Commission, 1973–78.

108     "At least offer a fair price": SAB, R–800, I. 102. a. Letter from Ed Harris, Chamberlain, February 9, 1974.

109     Wheat was selling at $5.00 a bushel: *Saskatchewan Economic Review,* 1983. Note: The report contains tables going back for years.

109     The Land Bank's average purchasing price almost tripled: Saskatchewan Land Bank Commission, *Annual Report,* 1978.

109     He announced a "10-year rate": SAB, I. 102. a, January 8, 1974.

109     In November rents were raised again: Ibid, November 25, 1974.

109     "Merely tenants of the government": *A New Direction: Saskatchewan Liberal Statement of Policy '75* (Regina: Saskatchewan Liberal Association, 1975) pp. 1, 2. Quote taken from *Canada, What's Left?,* Eds. John Richards and Don Kerr (Edmonton: NeWest Press, 1986), p. 27.

110     "Stayed in Ukraine": *Canada, What's Left?* p. 27.

111     "A frank political assessment": SAB, R–800, I. 102. d. See also Ibid., July 28, Aug, 3, 9, 17.

111     "It would not be met by [my] program": Ibid, August 3, 1977.

111     "An alternate land tenure system": Ibid, October 4, 1977. The responses of MacMurchy and Cowley are found in the same memo.

112     Completely out of the Land Bank: Ibid, October 4, 1977.

112     A study by Peter Woroby: SAB, R–800.V.206. Woroby's study was called: *Division of Saskatchewan into Administrative Areas.*

112     Another study by John Archer: SAB, R–800. V. 271. w. *Report of the Rural Advisory Group,* November 1976.

## The North
114     What he thought of their criticisms: RLP. June 7, 1974, p. 1. I also use descriptions of the meeting from interviews with former DNS employees.

115     Should be transferred to the province: Dianne Lloyd, *Woodrow,* p. 140.

115     The *New Deal for People* promised: See *New Deal,* p. 19.

115     Protect the potential of northern Saskatchewan: RLP, June 7, 1970, p. 1.

115    The NDP had been talking about it: See Helen Buckley, J. E. M. Kew,
       John B. Hauley, "The Indians and Métis of Northern Saskatchewan"
       (Saskatoon: Center for Community Studies, 1963). Al Johnson had prepared a
       report on a single northern agency in 1959, which was discussed by cabinet.
       Northern CCFers had made such a proposal, too. In 1960, the government
       had the Center for Community Studies begin a comprehensive study on the
       north. The center urged a single northern agency, but the Lloyd cabinet did
       not pursue it.

116    They were trained mainly as game wardens: Murray Dobbin, *The One-And-A-
       Half Men* (Vancouver: New Star Books, 1981), p. 212.

116    Eiling Kramer resisted: "See Robert S. Hauck, "The Policy-Making in the
       Department of Northern Saskatchewan, 1972–77," MA thesis, University of
       Saskatchewan, 1981, p. 20. See also the footnote for p. 20, found on p. 48.

117    "Re-occupying the Colony": *Next Year Country*, December 1972, p. 25.

117    Dangerous proponents of class struggle: SAB, R–565, VII. 163. a. File 2
       (of 5). Letter from Wilf Churchman to AEB, August 2, 1973.

118    He talked about the ruling classes: Howard Adams, "The Politics of the
       Native Movement," two-page mimeograph, undated. Author's library. See also
       Donald Purich, *The Métis* (Toronto: James Lorimer, 1988), pp. 160–63.

119    Sinclair wrote to Blakeney: SAB, R–565, VII. 163. a. Blakeney to file,
       November 10, 1971, File 1.

119    It should pick up most of the costs: Ibid., Sinclair to AEB, January 14, 1972,
       File 1.

119    A more organized approach: Ibid., Bowerman to Sinclair, February 4, 1972,
       File 1.

119    The notes backed his contention: Ibid., notes taken for the Premier by Don
       McMillan, special assistant, and Gerry Wilson, Executive Assistant. File 1.

119    Métis people wanted to be planners: Ibid., January 18, 1972.

119    The results of those consultations: Ibid, "Statement of Northern
       Administration and Legislation in Northern Saskatchewan," January 9, 1973,
       File 2.

119    Divide people along racial lines: Ibid., Bowerman to Sinclair, February 20,
       1973.

120    He said they had no claim to aboriginal rights: RLP, December 18, 1981,
       p. 4.

120    "Building another empire in the north": SAB, R–565, VII. 163, Sinclair to
       Blakeney, September 29, 1972, File 1.

120    Travelling on Métis Society money: Ibid., see Contact Airways travel voucher
       for Ray Jones, September 14, 1973.

120    The Liberals had also contributed to the Jones campaign: interview with Dave
       Steuart.

121    That the government initiate criminal proceedings: SAB, R–565, VII. 163. a.
       March 22, 1974, File 3. Howard Adams letter to Ed Tchorzewski.

121    "Appears to be unjustified": Ibid., May 31, 1974, Kujawa to Roy Romanow,
       File 3.

121    Trying to buy peace: Ibid., Adams to Blakeney, July 5, 1974, File 3.

121    The society had run up a deficit: Ibid., December 19, 1974. MacMurchy to
       cabinet, File 3.

121    The Métis would disrupt Blakeney's northern cabinet tour: Ibid., Kinzel to
       Blakeney, May 29, 1974, File 3.

121    A dissident group of Sinclair's executive: RLP. July 4, 1974, p. 1. See also
       *New Breed*, September 1974, p. 3.

122  The Regina police were called: SAB, R–565, VII. 163. a. R. N. Filson to D. Chisholm, June 26, 1974, File 3.

122  "Money to the society": Ibid., undated, File 3. See also RLP, July 4, 1974.

122  "Look like a picnic": Prince Albert *Daily Herald*, September 28, 1974.

122  A four-hour blow-out: SAB, R–565, VII. 163. a. October 21, 1974, File 3.

123  Ahenakew declined: it should be noted that after his tenure as FSI chief, Ahenakew was involved in some contract consulting work for the NDP government.

124  15 bands had about a million acres coming: *Indian Lands and Canada's Responsibility: The Saskatchewan Position*, booklet, Province of Saskatchewan, undated.

### New Deal '75

126  Increased by six times: these and following figures are drawn from the *Saskatchewan Economic Review* for years during the 1970s.

126  Gartner had delivered his New Deal report card: SAB, R–565, IV. 91. d. *New Deal for People Review*: Ibid., February 14, 1974 and May 1974. The following list of NDP achievements, and the remaining agenda, are drawn from this report.

128  For the prairie market: *Saskatchewan Business Journal*, Winter–Spring, 1972, p. 13.

128  A malting plant was built: SAB, R–565. III. 393. e.

128  A 45 per cent interest in Intercontinental Packers: Ibid., g.

128  An announced Rumanian tractor plant: SAB, R–800, V. 202. a & e. Thorson to cabinet, March 24, 1972 and May 17, 1972.

129  No success on a Daimler-Benz truck plant: Ibid., V. 23. e.

129  "Saskatchewan will have to deal differently": Ibid., V. 202. a. June 1972.

130  Blakeney devoted a cabinet meeting to "stock taking": SAB, R–565, III. 393. e.

130  CIGOL court battle: Canadian Industrial Oil and Gas was an independent company exploring in Saskatchewan. Its lawsuit was a test case on behalf of the industry. Eventually, it went to the Supreme Court.

130  Assessed on the basis of "significant benefit": SAB, R–800. V. 202. h. *Foreign Investment Policy: Government of Saskatchewan.*

130  "The less the government wishes to become involved": Ibid., V. 319. g.

130  His wish list: SAB, R–565, IV. 91. d, March 20, 1974.

131  Professional services in rural areas: Ibid.

131  A cabinet planning conference: SAB, R–800. IV. 11. a, November 5, 1974.

131  To open negotiations with Eldorado: Ibid.

131  The 1975 election platform: *New Deal '75* (Regina: New Democratic Party of Saskatchewan, 1975), 25 pages.

133  Some of the companies wrote the script: *Prairie Capitalism*, pp. 207–08.

134  "Mandate to protect our resources": SSP, May 13, 1975.

134  The perennial issue of rail line abandonment: Ibid.

134  Campaign against the Land Bank struck a nerve: Ibid., May 17, 1975. The story quotes candidate John Brockelbank.

134  Saskatchewan Investment Opportunities Corporation: Ibid., May 27, 1975.

135  "The NDP will be gone!": Ibid., June 10, 1975.

### Potash

137  Potassium chloride was first discovered: there are several good historical descriptions of the potash industry in Saskatchewan. See John Richards and Larry Pratt, *Prairie Capitalism*, pp. 187-213. A second is a lengthy speech

delivered by Allan Blakeney in Regina on July 19, 1989. It is untitled, and will be referred to simply as "Blakeney." The notes are in the author's possession. A third good source is John S. Burton and Department of Mineral Resources, "A Potash Policy for Saskatchewan," February 1974. It will be referred to as "Burton." It is located at SAB, R–565, III. 508. b.

137     "Maintaining a viable industry": Ibid., 508. a, July 21, 1971.

137     Retain the plan with no major changes: SAB, R–565. III. 510. See also Burton, p. 14.

138     Effectively dictating the province's position: Ibid., III. 508. a.

138     "Make it work even better": Burton, p. 14. See also SAB, R–565. III. 510.

138     The potash producers accused one of their number: SAB, R–565. III. 508. a. See C. J. Kelly to Bowerman, October 8, 1971, and Bowerman to all producers, October 12, 1971.

138     IMC vigorously denied it: Ibid., Nelson White of IMC to Bowerman, November 9, 1971.

139     "Sharpen our swords": Blakeney, July 19, 1989.

139     Assumed a role for public ownership: Burton, pp. 19–21.

139     "Special potash task force": SAB, R–565. III. 511, December, 1982.

139     "He was quite short": Ibid., Hubert Prefontaine to AEB, December 18, 1972.

139     Thorson ran a group of his own: SAB, R–565. III. 510. Thorson to AEB, February 18, 1972 and March 9, 1972.

139     Why the "central government" was so interested in potash: SAB, R–565. III. 510.

139     The bureaucrats from Mineral Resources: SAB, R–565. III. 508. b. See Cabinet Minutes 4460, July 5, 1973. See also R–565. V. 261. e. Thorson presentation to cabinet, December 14, 1972.

139     Burton pushed for greater public ownership: SAB, R–565. III. 508. b. Memo to AEB, June 29, 1973. Burton's position is discussed at July 5, 1973 cabinet meeting.

139     He wanted cabinet to engage in a "stock-taking": SAB, R–565. III. 313. a. September 17, 1973.

140     "Should assume public ownership of the potash industry": R–565. III. 511. a. October 11, 1973. See also Burton report of July 5, 1973 in same file.

140     "Make potash mines less profitable": SAB, R–800. XXXV. 217. Policy Paper, October 11, 1973, Gerry Gartner.

140     The government might build a mine of its own: Richard Shaffner, *New Risks in Resource Development* (C. D. Howe Research Institute, 1976), p. 15. See also SAB, R–565. V. 261. h).

140     Suggested just such a possibility: SAB, R–565, III. 510. Memo from Roy Meldrum to AEB, November 7, 1972, p. 6.

141     "Could get accurate once in awhile": SSP, May 8, 1975.

141     "Public ownership of these resources and industries": *New Deal '75*, p. 5.

141     Cancelling $200 million of planned expansion: Maureen Appel Molot and Jeanne Kirk Laux, "The Politics of Nationalization," *Canadian Journal of Political Science*, June 1979, p. 233.

142     Eleven potash companies went to court: Ibid., p. 295.

142     "Those attacks could be effectively repulsed": Blakeney, July 19, 1989.

142     A publicly owned potash industry as his legacy: *Prairie Capitalism*, p. 268.

143     How a takeover might affect markets: interview with George Cadbury.

143     Blakeney urged Don Tansley: interview with Don Tansley.

144     "Producing mines in the province": Lieutenant-Governor's statements quoted in Dennis Gruending, "Takeover: Premier Blakeney Gambles on the Future,"

*The Last Post*, February 1976, p. 4. Much of the following description of the opposition and business is taken from this article.

146 This time he was in charge: SAB, R–565. III. 510. Also author's collection, "Meetings with Potash Companies," Memo from Flo Wilke to AEB, November 17, 1975.

146 A media blitz which cost them $130,000: see Dennis Gruending, "The Reporter as TV Interviewer, Paid but Unedited: Is it P.R. or Journalism?," *Content*, May 1976, pp. 6–7.

146 Only 22 per cent were in favour: *Financial Post*, February 14, 1976, and *Financial Times*, February 2, 1976. Both cited in Molot, p. 243.

146 The government's own opinion poll: SAB, R–800. V. 316. l.

147 "Deep shit from a publicity point of view": SAB, R–800. V. 313.

147 The bureaucratic response came quickly: Ibid., "Notes on Potash Project," March 8, 1976.

147 Two half-hour television programs were produced: Ibid., *Content*.

148 The government should go with a defensive strategy: SAB, R–800. XLIX. 4. c. "Ways to Meet the 'Potash vs. People' Issue."

148 The State Department sent a memorandum: SAB, R–800. V. 316. a. See also R–565. IX. 3. See also Molot, p. 235. The American response is discussed in this article, pp. 235–42.

149 There would be an assured supply of Saskatchewan potash: Ibid., p. 240.

149 "Raising $75 million": Ibid., p. 242.

150 60 per cent of people approved of public ownership in potash: SAB, R–800. V. 316. l.

## Uranium

151 Met by Premier Lloyd: *The Commonwealth*, May 2, 1962, p. 5.

151 Those bombs relied on Canadian uranium: see Ron Finch, *Exporting Danger: A History of the Canadian Nuclear Energy Export Programme* (Montreal: Black Rose Books, 1986), pp. 17–35.

151 Center for Community Studies: "The Indians and Métis of Northern Saskatchewan," p. 42.

152 Organized a price-fixing cartel: See Peter Cook, "How Uranium Cartel Was Formed," *Financial Times of Canada*, September 20, 1976.

152 Cowley recommended in March 1974: SAB, R–800, V. 261. h. See Mineral Resources memo March 20, 1974; also Cowley memo regarding joint ventures, May 1, 1974.

153 Offer the government a 50 per cent stake: Ibid., i. See Cowley memo, January 22, 1975.

153 A two-day cabinet planning session: SAB, R–565, IV. 11. a. See Gerry Gartner's summarizing letters to various ministers, November 4, 1975.

153 Kim Thorson was instructed to approach Eldorado Nuclear Ltd.: Ibid., see Gartner to Cowley.

153 John Wiebe was an earnest, good-natured Mennonite farmer: I did not know Mr Wiebe then, but five years later he became my father-in-law.

154 Blakeney had promised a new government department: *New Deal for People*, p. 17.

154 Blakeney favoured Richard's argument: SAB, R–565, III. 167. a.

155 Only if the public pressed it: SAB, R–800, V. 261. j, September 17, 1976.

155 "They tend to believe in confrontation": SAB, R–800, V. 136. j. Byers to cabinet, September 21, 1976.

155 He recommended a Royal Commission: SAB, R–800, XXXII. 171, October 1976.

156   He wanted at least two points of view: SAB, R–800, V. 136. j. Bolstad memo to officials, October 18, 1976.
156   Blakeney wanted "solidarity" on uranium development policy: Ibid. Bolstad to cabinet Uranium Committee, October 18, 1976.
156   Bolstad warned Whelan: Ibid., November 3, 1976.
156   A joint resolution arrived: *The Commonwealth*, November 3, 1976, pp. 11–12.
156   Deliberately impeded the work: "Why Clare Powell Resigned," *The Commonwealth*, December 1, 1976, p. 16.
156   To make no "new" commitments: Ibid., p. 10.
157   His amendments won the day: Ibid.
157   It would have "wide terms of reference": Ibid., p. 9.
157   The first right of refusal on Cluff Lake shares: SAB, R–800, V. 261. i, Whelan to cabinet, December 5, 1975.
157   The agreement had been negotiated but not signed: Ibid., V. 136. j, Byers to cabinet, December 21, 1976.
157   Road construction could always begin before the announcement: Ibid., Byers to cabinet, November 19, 1976.
158   Messer wrote to cabinet: Ibid., November 22, 1976.
158   Some cabinet members think not: Ibid., Bolstad to Byers, November 24, 1976.
158   Would convince them to change their minds: Ibid., Byers to cabinet, December 6, 1976.
158   A firm rap on the knuckles: Ibid., December 8, 1976.
159   They urged abandoning the previous week's position: Ibid., December 21, 1976.
160   Had made her pro-nuclear sentiments known: see John Joseph Gunn, "The Political and Theoretical Conflict Over Saskatchewan Uranium Development"; Master's Thesis, Department of Political Science, University of Regina, 1982, p. 145, footnote #31.
160   He had approached Dr J. W. T. Spinks: Ibid., k, Byers to cabinet, January 20, 1977.
160   Spinks had been involved: J. W. T. Spinks, *Two Blades of Grass: An Autobiography*, (Saskatoon: Western Producer Prairie Books, 1980), p. 64. Spinks describes his involvement in the Manhattan Project.
160   He had a bias in favour of uranium development: Ibid.
160   They were asked to investigate the wider question: *The Cluff Lake Board of Inquiry*, Volume 1. June 1978, p. 15.
160   They chose to interpret that as a mandate: Ibid. pp. 18–19.
160   Reluctantly he agreed to a reporting date of November 1: SAB, R–800, V. 136. k, Byers to cabinet, January 27, 1976.
161   Cluff Lake was a committed project: RLP, March 18, 1977, p. 1, and March 22, 1977, p. 16.
161   Cabinet decided on Messer's advice: SAB, R–800, V. 261. j, Messer to cabinet, February 11, 1977.
161   "The government's commitment to public hearings": SAB, R–800, V. 319. q. Bolstad to AEB, February 16, 1977.
161   Bayda gave the green light: see *Cluff*, Volumes I and II, May 29, 1978.
162   A bonanza of between $1.5 and $3 billion: Ibid. Volume I, p. 453.
162   Saskatchewan's uranium players and the weapons industry: see, for example, Peter D. Jones, "Who really is AMOK?" *Prairie Messenger*, March 2, 1980. See also *Atoms for War/Atoms for Peace: The Saskatchewan Connection*, (Saskatoon: Inter-Church Uranium Committee, 1980), p. 3. Author's collection.
162   The mineral could always be obtained elsewhere: *Cluff*, Volume 2, p. 714.

163 Social impact of the Warman development: *Why People Say No to a Uranium Refinery at Warman, Saskatchewan* (Regina: Regina Group for a Non-Nuclear Society, 1980), pp. 27, 37, 46.

163 The Blakeney government had insisted: SAB, R–800, V. 373. e), December 9, 1974, Report of cabinet discussion. See also SAB, R–800, V. 453, Letter from Eldorado's President Nick Ediger to Industry Minister Kim Thorson, February 6, 1975.

163 The Dundurn military base, south of Saskatoon: Ibid., September 16, 1976.

163 The company refused: for a thorough chronology regarding Warman, see SAB, R–800.V.453, Wendy Macdonald, April 1980.

164 To drain lakes which lay above the ore body: SAB, R–800, XXXI. 73, Bob Patton to SSP, October 15, 1979. Patton's description is lengthy and provides details of the de-watering.

164 RGNNS went to court: RLP, September 5, 1979.

164 Informed the department that the action had been invalid: SAB, R–800, XXXI. 73, Daryl Bogdasavich to Grant Mitchell, October 3, 1979.

164 The province had not complied with the letter of the law: Ibid., November 13, 1979. Bowerman to Bob Patton.

164 A technical error had been made: RLP, November 7, 1979.

164 Signed quietly with the company in 1978: RLP, February 24, 1979.

164 Kramer had been lobbying for it: SAB, R–800, V. 193. g, October 17, 1977.

165 "All phases of the environmental procedures": SAB, R–800, XXX1. 75, Byers to cabinet, July 24, 1978.

165 Was only narrowly defeated: Ibid., Bill Allen to AEB regarding caucus unease over Key Lake road.

165 A high profile fight with SMDC: Ibid., XXXI. 87. Bolstad to Cowley.

165 Too close to the next election: SAB, R–800, V. 447. January 24, 1980.

166 Pursue the attack on mining with an increased vigour: SAB, R–800, V. 59. c, Messer to cabinet, February 1980.

166 They were "mistaken": this quote and associated information taken from "The Significant Minority," an unpublished paper written by Rolando Ramirez and Dennis Gruending in 1981. Author's collection.

166 Ted Bowerman invited citizens: SAB, R–800, XXXI. 86, February 20, 1981.

167 "The argument is as invalid here as there": Reverend David Petrie to AEB, December 7, 1981. Author's collection.

**The New Politics**

169 Richard Gwyn's story: *Toronto Star,* November 15, 1975, p. C. 1.

169 Paul Grescoe's article: *Canadian Magazine,* March 13, 1976.

169 Blakeney's New Deal: *Weekend Magazine,* February 3, 1979.

169 Blakeney's Mission: *Maclean's,* December 26, 1977.

169 Best premier in the country: Grescoe, p. 6.

169 "Utterly indefatigable": Zwarun, p. 25.

169 "Can match wits with Pierre Trudeau": Dizard, p. 12.

170 Costing Saskatchewan taxpayers $575 million a year: Allan E. Blakeney, Speech at Osgoode Hall, April 10, 1980, p. 17. Speeches collected in bound volume entitled *The Future of Canada.*

170 A pep talk to help improve morale: SAB, R–800, V. 319. q. Bolstad to AEB, March 31, 1977.

171 He agreed with the principle of wage and price controls: RLP, October 14, 1975, p. 1; October 15, 1975, p. 3.

171 1,000 workers jammed into the Legislative rotunda: RLP, October 14, 1976, p. 1.

171   The SFL rallied 4,000 workers: RLP, February 3, 1976, p. 1.
172   "Our relationship with labour is terrible": SAB, R–565, III. 235. a, b, August 12, 1976.
172   "We're not very far from you": Transcript of Dick Collver interview by Maggie Siggins, University of Regina Archives, p. 6.
173   Homosexuals in the NDP cabinet: *Moose Jaw Times-Herald*, March 1, 1979, p. 4.
173   A nasty lawsuit between him and the Baltzans: SSP, January 28, 1978, p. 31. See also April 11, 1978, p. 25.
173   Bad debts which Collver had: RLP, May 5, 1978, p. 1.
173   Rumours about a Swiss bank account: SSP, October 7, 1978, p. 26.
174   The best Premier in Canada: advertisement in SSP, October 11, 1978, p. 4.
174   The court released judgements: SSP, October 4, 1978, p. 1.
174   Blakeney went on a minor rampage: Ibid., October 5, 1978, p. 22.
175   "Richard Nixon of the Prairies": *Maclean's*, October 1978.
175   "Let us share socialistically": SSP, October 7, 1978, p. 31.
175   Had once been in jail in the United States: Ibid., October 14, 1978, p. 28.
175   A blind trust with former Justice Emmett Hall: SSP, October 6, 1978, p. 9.
175   Shabby treatment Collver had received: RLP, October 19, 1978, p. 3.
175   "You'd think they would learn": Ibid.
175   "Nasty comments about my mother": conversation with Wes Robbins.
176   Cowley and MacMurchy made their report: SAB, R–800, V. 127. November 7, 1978.
176   "Our farm vote was in trouble": Ibid.
177   "Deserves a medal": Ibid.

Economic and Social Policy
178   Blakeney made the right choices in concentrating on resources: John Richards and Larry Pratt, *Prairie Capitalism*, p. 317.
178   Assets of $3.5 billion: G. H. Beatty, "Accountability and Government Control of Crown Corporations," Remarks to the National Conference on Crown Corporations and Public Policy, Carleton University, Ottawa, October 16, 1980, p. 11.
179   An organization of "shadow managers": Ibid., p. 20.
179   "Provide employment to northern residents": SAB, R–800, V. 293. j. Messer to cabinet, February 11, 1977.
180   Gave Saskatchewan a glowing AA in 1979: *Saskatchewan Into the Eighties* (Regina: Government of Saskatchewan, 1980), pp. 25–30.
180   What medicare had been to the 60s: SAB-Saskatoon. Call Number A670, Box 16. File: Council Minutes 1977, May 28–29.
180   Virtual full employment during several years: statistics used here are taken from various editions of the *Saskatchewan Economic Review*.
180   Social assistance rates remained below the poverty line: Bonnie Jeffrey and Andy Shadrack, *Living Without Power* (Social Administration Research Unit, Faculty of Social Work, University of Regina, 1986), p. 59.
181   As much as the poorest 50 per cent: Gordon W. Ternowetsky, *Income Inequality in Saskatchewan 1971–81: Charting New Research Guidelines in the Relationship Between Poverty Lines, Income Adequacy and Equality* (Social Administration Research Unit, Faculty of Social Work, University of Regina, 1985), p. 8.
181   His confidential background report in 1976: "Data Sheet on Saskatchewan Natives," Planning and Research, Executive Council, 1976. This report was leaked to me and remains in my library.

182  "Social ills of the native population": SAB, R–1143, XXII. 48, September 24, 1974.
182  A thorough review of the government's relationship with native people: SAB, R–800, V. 168. l.
182  He named a cabinet committee: Ibid., V. 408 and 409.
182  Racial discrimination was the underlying problem: Ibid., R–800, V. 168. l. Svenson's study was entitled *The Dimensions of Indian and Native Urban Poverty in Saskatchewan*. (The Social Planning Secretariat, February 14, 1979). The study is included in the SAB file.
182  A four-year affirmative action program: Ibid. The blueprint for the program was a document called *Attacking Urban Native Poverty: Alternative Government Responses* (The Social Planning Secretariat), May 15, 1979.
182  Some of the documents were leaked to the CBC: See RLP, September 20, 1979, and September 22, 1979.
183  Committee on People of Indian Ancestry: SAB, R–800, V. 259.
183  "Well, it is serious": SAB, R–800, LXII. 30. b. AEB memo to cabinet, January 19, 1981.
184  Equals both in politics and the economy: Seymour Martin Lipset, *Agrarian Socialism* (Berkeley: University of California Press, 1971), p. 163.
184  "Women's dream of justice and equality": Georgina M. Taylor, "The Women Shall Help to Lead the Way: Saskatchewan CCF-NDP Women candidates in Provincial and Federal Elections, 1934–65," in *Building the Co-operative Commonwealth: Essays on the Democratic Socialist Tradition in Canada*, Ed. J. William Brennan (Regina: Canadian Plains Research Centre, University of Regina, 1984), p. 141.
185  Fewer than 300 were women: *Saskatchewan Advisory Council on the Status of Women Interim Report*, 1974–75, p. 35.
185  That number had increased to 34 per cent: Ibid., 1980–81.
185  40 per cent of married women were working: Ibid., 1974–75, p. 11.
185  "Did not meet the need": Ibid., 1975–76, p. 26.
185  "Felt strongly" about the government's lack of action: Ibid., 1979–80.
185  Half the money allocated to parental subsidies wasn't used: Bonnie Jeffrey, "Women and the NDP," *Briarpatch*, December 1973.
186  The average wage of women: Ibid.
187  Why females have not been winning competitions: SAB, R–800, XXXII. 152, AEB to Walter Smishek, May 1, 1978.
187  Serious work began on affirmative action programs: SAB, R–800, V. 168. k, Memo from John Scratch to cabinet, May 23, 1978. See also "Women's Bureau and Women's Division," in *Saskatchewan Department of Labour Annual Report*, 1980–81, p. 47.
187  Blakeney thought it too complicated for employers to use: SAB, R–800, V. 307. a. Memo September 10, 1981.

Constitution
189  Trudeau and the premiers came within a whisker: the story of Canada's constitution-making has been told well elsewhere. Two books are particularly useful for descriptive background about the constitutional process: Robert Sheppard and Michael Valpy, *The National Deal* (Toronto: Fleet Books, 1982), and Roy Romanow, John White, and Howard Leeson, *Canada Notwithstanding: The Making of the Constitution 1976–1982* (Toronto: Carswell/Metheun, 1984). I will not provide notes on general information covered in these and other sources. I will note mainly that information which has not been publicly documented previously.

190    Blakeney had been active in the debate: see "The Future of Canada:
       Speeches and Interviews by Hon. Allan Blakeney in the course of a trip to
       Ontario and Quebec, April 1980," published by the Government of
       Saskatchewan.
190    Saskatchewan needed a strong federation: Ibid., Speech to Montreal Chamber
       of Commerce, p. 13 ff.
190    Blakeney was interested in a new constitutional bargain: Ibid., Speech to
       Queen's Law Students, April 10, 1981, p. 10.
190    His best relationships were with Lougheed: Blakeney's views on other
       premiers paraphrased from interviews with the author.
192    The CCF had been calling for a Charter of Rights since the 1940s: See
       Walter Surma Tarnopolsky, Ed., *The Canadian Bill of Rights.* 2nd Ed.
       (Toronto: Macmillan of Canada, 1975), p. 11–12. CCF MPs called for a Bill of
       Rights, and Saskatchewan's provincial Bill of Rights under Douglas was the
       first in Canada.
193    Had ordered the province to pay $500 million back to the oil companies: see
       Chapter 17.
193    Cowley and MacMurchy told him to fight Trudeau: Ibid.
194    He and Broadbent talked on the telephone on September 16th: SAB, R–800,
       XXI. 9, AEB memo to file.
194    He called Saskatchewan that same afternoon: Ibid., Handwritten notes of
       telephone conversation between AEB and Broadbent, October 2, 1980.
196    "I believe deeply in that": interview with Ed Broadbent. For more detail on
       the constitutional negotiations from Broadbent's point of view, see Judy Steed,
       *Ed Broadbent: The Pursuit of Power,* Chapter Seven.
197    He intended to "mumble awhile": interview with Dick Proctor.
199    Blakeney warned Broadbent that discussions between the two of them must
       not find their way to Kirby: SAB, R–800, XXI. 9, Notes of telephone
       conversation between AEB and Broadbent, November 21, 1980.
199    Early in the New Year Blakeney and Broadbent talked again on the
       telephone: Ibid., January 12, 1981.
199    The clause was actually drafted in his crowded office: Valpy, p. 168.
201    Trudeau was "wild": SAB, R–800, XXV. 30, Leeson memo to AEB, June 26, 1981.
202    Romanow made a quick trip east: SAB, R–800, XXI. 2.
202    Anything official would move on paper: Ibid., XXI. 9. Letter from Dick
       Proctor to Norm Simon, March 11, 1981.
203    He offered to send someone to brief Pawley's people: Ibid., XXI. 10. Notes of
       telephone conversation between AEB and Pawley, February 6, 1981.
203    With his friend Grant Notley from Alberta: Ibid. Howard Leeson also
       participated in the conversation with Notley.
203    Blakeney had already mapped out what Barrett's media strategy should be:
       SAB, R–800, XXI. 10, February 13, 1981.
203    The premiers had become a laughingstock: Ibid., XXI. 20. Barrett's activity is
       described in a memo from Romanow to AEB, March 31, 1981.
204    The debate had been a stirring tribute: for descriptions of the convention
       debate see Valpy, pp. 133–34, and Steed, pp. 263–65.
204    The day after the election in 1988: interview with Ed Broadbent.
205    Earned him the enmity of Lévesque: Quebec later accused Saskatchewan of
       betraying the gang of eight by seeking a constitutional compromise in the fall
       of 1981. Background documentation indicates Saskatchewan made clear its
       desire to negotiate a constitutional settlement once Trudeau had been

stopped in his unilateral action. See for example, SAB, R–800, XXV. 28, Romanow memo to AEB June 10, 1981; also Ibid., XXVII. 2. Leeson to file October 14, 1981.

205    Saskatchewan conceded that not all provinces had to agree: for a more detailed review of Saskatchewan's position, see Romanow et al., pp. 177–85.

205    Following Saskatchewan's argument the court did not specify: Ibid.

206    The deal which Ottawa and the provinces would have to make: Valpy, p. 252.

206    Talks were breaking out: Ibid., pp. 256–59.

206    Romanow warned the group Saskatchewan was looking for a deal: see Valpy, p. 260, and Romanow et al., pp. 191–92.

208    To build an "associate state": *René Lévesque: Memoirs* (Toronto: McClelland and Stewart, 1986), pp. 325–26. Lévesque describes why he agreed to give up Quebec's traditional demand for a veto on constitutional change.

208    "The most despicable betrayal": Ibid., p. 333.

208    Claude Morin was so angry with Romanow: interview with Bob Weese.

209    National women's groups pushed for a separate clause: Penney Kome, *The Taking of 28* (Toronto: Women's Educational Press, 1983), pp. 23–25.

210    Flora Macdonald asked in the Commons: Ibid., p. 40.

210    The premiers soon came under intense pressure: see Ibid., pp. 89–95 for a description of the lobbying campaign.

210    Romanow made the Saskatchewan position official: SAB, R–800, XXVIII. 5. Telex from Romanow to Chrétien, November 18, 1981.

210    Ursula Appolloni rose to say: RLP, Friday, November 20, 1981.

211    Blakeney was livid: Ibid.

211    Blakeney spoke to the crowd: RLP Monday, November 23, 1981, p. 4. See also SAB, R–800, XXXVIII. 5.

## Defeat

213    "It's Blakeney/MacMurchy and the farmers versus Pépin: SAB, R–800, V. 106. d, MacMurchy to AEB, March 23, 1982.

214    Bill Knight was telling reporters: RLP, April 1, 1982, p. 4.

214    "Cool and capable": Judy Steed, "Cool and Capable, that's Blakeney," *The Globe and Mail*, February 27, 1982, p. 10.

214    "I believe in government": quoted in Meyer Brownstone, "The Douglas-Lloyd Governments: Innovation and Bureaucratic Adaption," *Essays on the Left*, Eds. Laurier Lapierre et al (Toronto: McClelland and Stewart, 1971), p. 65.

214    "You should be free to make on your own": *Chronicle of the 20th Century* (Mount Kicso, New York: Chronicle Publications, 1987), p. 1155.

215    "Government *is* the problem": Ibid., p. 1184.

215    Think-tank session at Saint Peter's Abbey: SAB, R–800. XXXV. 83. September 18, 1980.

215    He went to dinner with several powerful civil servants: SAB, R–800, V. 119. January 11, 1980.

216    Mitchell made more notes about the discussion: Ibid., February 14, 1980.

216    A "soft-side" seminar: Ibid., V. 410.

217    Related to the "conserver society": SAB, R–800, LXII. 10. gg. August 25, 1981.

217    "Activist governments depend upon an activist population": Ibid. V. 410. "Social Policy Determinants for the '80s," prepared by Marvin Blauer, Planning Bureau, October 1980.

217    Brownstone reported that he found little "sense of history": SAB, R–800, V. 40. November 27, 1980.

218    He had Mitchell do a study on government organization: SAB, R–800, XXXV. 89.

218   Derrick's job was to look for ways to strengthen senior management: Ibid.
218   A mere 73,000 acres had changed hands: *Saskatchewan Indian Treaty Land Entitlement Rights* (Regina: Federation of Saskatchewan Indians, May 1981, Rev. Ed.), p. 3. Author's library.
220   Citizen participation in potash: SAB, R–800, V. 168. g. August 26, 1976.
220   A "severe decline" in the potash market: Ibid., V. 316. m, December 15, 1981.
220   Tchorzewski announced a modest $20-million program to ease mortgage rates: *The Globe and Mail*, March 19, 1982, p. 5.
221   Devine made two expensive promises within the first week: *The Globe and Mail*, April 26, 1982, p. 4.
221   Reduce personal income taxes by 10 per cent: RLP, April 23, 1982, p. C. 1.
221   Demonstrators banged on a metal door: RLP, March 29, 1982, p. 3.
221   The Canadian Union of Public Employees had made an unprecedented move: Ibid.
221   Irked by the presence of a radio reporter's microphone: Ibid., April 24, 1982.
222   The tax was only 29 cents: RLP, April 15, 1982, p. 4. See also *The Globe and Mail*, April 26, 1982, p. 4.
222   The cost of Tory promises: *The Globe and Mail*, April 26, 1982, p. 4. See also *McLean's*, April 26, 1982, p. 29.
222   The Tories would ruin medicare: RLP, April 5, 1982.
222   A straight $2,000 grant: RLP, April 14, 1982.
222   Blakeney even indulged in a mild form of mud slinging: Ibid., *McLean's*, April 26, 1982.
223   "The government stopped listening to the people": Ibid.
223   The NDP "clearly misread the polls": RLP, April 28, 1982, p. 4.
224   By the time he reported to the convention: *The Commonwealth*, November 10, 1982, p. 1.
224   Commentators of both the right and left: See *Alberta Report*, May 10, 1982, p. 52, and *Canadian Dimension*, March 1983.
225   A $227 million deficit: RLP, March 30, 1990, p. 3. This article details the budget deficits in each year following 1982. Information about resource and grain prices in this and following years is gleaned from the Government of Saskatchewan's *Economic Review*.
225   "Refused to participate in the recession": Ibid., *Economic Review*, 1983, p. 1.
226   Reputable studies indicated that there was hunger in Saskatchewan: Graham Riches, *Food Banks and the Welfare Crisis* (Ottawa: Canadian Council on Social Development, 1986), pp. 5, 15, 42, 43.
226   It bailed out depositors: James Pitsula and Ken Rasmussen, *Privatizing a Province: The New Right in Saskatchewan* (Vancouver: New Star Books, 1990), pp. 266–71, 58–59.
226   $21 million in subsidized loans: RLP, December 12, 1985, pp. 1, 10.
228   A royalty income of $950 million: *The Cluff Lake Board of Inquiry*, Volume I, p. 453.
228   The actual amount was about $200 million: Matthew Hudivik, "Uranium Mining and Jobs: Setting the Record Straight," *Briarpatch*, June 1988, p. 13.
228   The figure is closer to 25 per cent: *The Globe and Mail*, September 6, 1988.
228   The industry admits it has not kept its part of the bargain: Ibid., June 20, 1988.
228   To both the peaceful and weapons' streams: *Catholic New Times*, October 27, 1985, p. 1.
229   Virtually none of the deputy ministers survived: SAB, R–1143, IX. 3. d. Hans J. Michelmann and Geoffrey S. Steeves, "Consolidation of Power in Saskatchewan: The Conservative Transformation of the Public Service," pp. 12–18.
229   "Snow White and the seven dwarfs": *Western Report*, October 13, 1986, p. 14.
229   Having added wrinkles: RLP, September 22, 1986, p. 4.

229    Tommy Douglas would be supporting Devine: Ibid.
229    "Misrepresent the meaning of Tommy's life": RLP, October 4, 1986.
230    The rural seats contained 37 per cent of the voters: *Western Report*, December 29, 1986, p. 5.
230    "And treat those two imposters just the same": Ibid., October 21, 1986, p. C. 1.

## Life after Politics
231    During the news conference at Tommy Douglas House: RLP, August 8, 1987, p. 1.
232    Praising him for his leadership: Ibid., November 6, 1987.
232    She later told CBC Radio: *Morning Edition*, CBC Radio Saskatchewan, May 19, 1987. Tape in author's library.
233    One of the people she recognized was Dr Andrew Nicol: Ibid. See also RLP, May 15, 1987.
233    Accumulated deficit of $2 billion: RLP, March 30, 1990. Story and graph detail yearly deficits since 1982.
233    A home renovation program: Ibid., March 6, 1987, p. B. 7.
233    Lane discovered that the province was facing a financial crisis: RLP, January 28, 1987, p. 1.
233    2,600 jobs had been lost: News Release, SGEU, June 16, 1987, p. 2.
234    Became subject to a deductible: "Choices: A Report and Analysis of the Saskatchewan Government's Economic and Budget Priorities." This document provides a list of jobs and services lost. It was compiled by the SGEU and the National Union of Provincial Government Employees.
234    No general selling off of crown corporations: *The Globe and Mail*, April 29, 1982, p. 5.
234    Michael Walker, the head of Vancouver's Fraser Institute: RLP, June 15, 1987, p. D. 1.
234    The accumulated deficit was $3.7 billion: Ibid., March 30, 1990, p. C. 3.
234    A way to raise new money: Paul Martin, "Reshaping Saskatchewan," *Saskatchewan Business*, September 1988, pp. 6–8.
234    "We've got a tiger by the tail": RLP, April 22, 1989, p. 5.
234    Between 4,000 and 7,000 people: Ibid., June 22, 1987. For reports of other demonstrations see *The Globe and Mail*, May 2, 1987, p. 3.
234    "An old idea disguised as a new fad": RLP, May 6, 1989, p. 7.
235    Only 22 per cent supported the SaskEnergy privatization: Ibid., p. 5.
235    Overshot their 1989 deficit by $160 million: Ibid. March 30, 1990, p. C. 3.
235    The province had had its credit rating reduced: *The Globe and Mail Report on Business*, June 2, 1990, p. 2.
235    Reducing the accumulated deficit to zero in 15 years: "Notes for Remarks," Roy Romanow, Leader's Business Dinner, Regina, March 13, 1990. Author's library.
235    In an interview taped for CBC Radio: interview done by author and aired on *Morning Edition*, November 11, 1987. Tape in author's library.
237    Received severance pay of about $60,000: RLP, June 8, 1988, p. 9.
242    "We should not restrict that power": See also Allan E. Blakeney, "The Spending Power" and "The Amending Formula," in Lorne Ingle, Ed., *Meech Lake Reconsidered* (Hull: Voyageur Publishing, 1989).
242    "Not just an impossible dream": Judy Steed, *The Globe and Mail*, February 27, 1982, p. 10.
243    "Ran a good shop": Ibid.

# Index

Aboriginal rights, 115–16, 118–20, 123–25, 199, 201, 209–10, 218–19
Abortion, 186
Adams, Howard, 118, 121
Advisory Committee on the Status of Women, 185
Affirmative action, 182–84, 187, 196, 210–11, 218, 226
Ahenakew, David, 123–24, 183, 218–19
Aldridge, Garry, 93, 224, 240
Allen, Bill, 72, 132
Amok, 152, 154, 156–57, 159, 161–62, 183
Anderson, Dr. Alan, 163
Anderson, Don, 223
Anguish, Doug, 203
Appolloni, Ursula, 210
Archambault, René, 229
Archer, Dr. John, 112–13
Argue, Senator Hazen, 46, 66
Atkinson, Pat, 231
Atkinson, Roy, 58

Baker, Henry, 31–32, 69, 223
Barnhart, Gordon, 51
Barootes, Staff, 41
Barrett, Dave, 203–4, 239
Bastedo, Lt.-Gov. Frank, 44
Bastedo, Lillian, 36
Bayda, Mr. Justice E. D, 160
Bayda Inquiry. See Cluff Lake Board of Inquiry
Beatty, Garry, 88, 118, 142, 143, 146–48, 179, 216
Beke, John, 47
Benjamin, Connie, 204
Benjamin, Les, 71, 203–4
Bennett, Bill, 190, 203, 208, 211, 234
Berezowsky, Bill, 62, 70
Beveridge, Sir William, 13, 17
Bill 2 (Essential Services Act), 50, 52, 79–80
Bill 42, 133
Bishop, Rod, 121
Black Panthers, 122
Blakeney, Allan: and aboriginal rights, 116, 119–20, 124–25, 201, 209–10; and cabinet, 84–86, 88–91, 116, 129–30, 143–44, 147, 155–58, 163, 217–18; and Molly Schwartz, 15–16, 18–19; as administrator, 2–3, 86–88, 90–94, 136, 138–39, 141–43, 146, 155, 178–80, 182, 195, 214, 217, 240; as cabinet minister, 33–37, 39–41, 44–45; as civil servant, 1, 20, 21–23, 25–27; as politician, 2–3, 96, 98–103, 173, 176; childhood, 7–8, 10–11; at Dalhousie, 11–12, 14–15; early CCF activity, 13–15, 18; early politician, 26–27, 30–31, 33; early years in Regina, 21, 23–25; family background, 5–7; family life (adult), 3, 25, 27–28, 30, 34–35, 45, 47–48, 54–55, 94–95, 227–28, 231, 237; friendships, 3, 15, 23–26, 49, 69, 95; law practice, 20, 27–28, 34, 47; legislative assembly, 52, 226, 232; medicare, 32–33, 38–39, 40, 42, 44–45; native people, 114–16, 122–25, 181–84, 209, 218–19; NDP leadership, 1, 54–55; 69–73, 75–76, 229, 231–32; opposition, 47, 52–54; 225–28; Oxford, 1, 16–20; post-politics, 4, 235, 236, 237, 238; religion, 6, 9, 25, 166–67; social policy, 180, 183–88; Waffle, 56–58, 61, 64, 67–72, 100–1; work habits, 3, 92–94

Blakeney, Anne, 3, 28–29, 34, 38, 45, 47–49, 58, 82, 84, 92, 98, 167, 182, 190–91, 213, 223, 225, 227, 231, 236–37
Blakeney, Barbara, 25, 48, 55, 95, 237
Blakeney, Bertha, 5, 7–8
Blakeney, Beryle, 7, 9, 11
Blakeney, Chambers, 6
Blakeney, David, (ancestor), 6
Blakeney, David, 45, 95, 237
Blakeney, Elizabeth, 5
Blakeney, Hugh, 25, 48, 95
Blakeney, John Cline, 5–8, 11, 14
Blakeney, John Davies, 8, 11
Blakeney, Luke, 6
Blakeney, Margaret, 49, 95, 237–38
Blakeney, Molly, 21, 23–25, 27–28. See also Blakeney, Allan and Molly Schwartz
Blakeney, Sarah, 6
Blakeney, Silas, 6
Blauer, Marvin, 217
Bolstad, Wes, 88–92, 94, 99, 111, 117–18, 131, 146–47, 156, 158, 161, 165, 170, 217
Bourassa, Robert, 189
Bowen, Ted, 93, 217
Bowerman, Ted, 53, 60, 64–65, 70, 84, 116–19, 124, 137–38, 154, 164, 166, 182–83, 219
Bridgewater, N.S., 7, 19
Bridgewater Baptist Church, 9
Bridgewater High School, 11
Broadbent, Ed, 56, 100, 194–97, 199, 202–4, 210, 227, 239
Brockelbank, J. H., 25–26, 36, 65, 74, 137
Brockelbank, John, 70, 86, 222
Brown, Caroline, 59
Brown, Larry, 171–72
Brown, Lorne, 59
Brownstone, Meyer, 23–24, 26, 50, 217
Buchanan, John, 190
Budgets, Sask.: (1962), 36; (1968), 52; (1982), 220; (1987), 233–34
Burton, James, 97
Burton, John, 71, 95, 139, 142, 146
Burton, Zenny, 225
Byers, Neil, 70, 84, 154–56, 158–60, 164, 217

Cadbury, Barbara, 25
Cadbury, George, 22–23, 25, 88, 143
Cameron, Sandy, 223
Canadian Industrial Oil and Gas (CIGOL), 170
Canadian Medical Association, 32, 42
Canadian Pacific, 137
Canadian Potash Producers' Association, 146
Canadian Union of Public Employees, 220–21
Caplan, Gerry, 56
Carter, Jimmy, 214–15
Cass–Beggs, David, 49–50
CBC, 158, 182, 210–11, 232, 235
CCF/NDP (Philosophy–History), 13, 21, 23, 25–27, 32, 35–36, 46–47, 53–54, 56–57, 59–61, 63–64, 67, 71, 73–76, 91, 100–3, 105, 113–15, 131, 145, 151, 156, 159, 163, 168, 184, 187–88, 192, 195, 198, 203–4, 214–15, 217, 223, 241–42
Center for Community Studies, 151
Central Canada Potash, 133, 138, 140, 144, 170
CF Industries, 138, 149
Chretien, Jean, 115, 191, 197, 199, 200, 206–8, 210–11

Churchman, Wilf, 117
Citizens in Defence of Medicare, 41
Civic Reform Association, 30
Clark, Joe, 195, 215
Cluff Lake, 152, 154, 156–58, 161–62
Cluff Lake Board of Inquiry, 157–61
Co-op Implements, 129
Co-operative Refinery, 130
Coburn, Frank, 57, 64, 66, 72, 101, 126
Cody, Don, 86
College of Physicians and Surgeons, 32, 39, 44
Collver, Dick, 132, 134, 150, 170, 172–73, 214
Commissariate de l'Energie Atomique, 162
Commonwealth, The, 18, 51, 63, 67, 73, 155
Community Capital Fund, 112, 127
Community clinics, 44, 45, 81
Community colleges, 127
Community schools, 184
Consensus Saskatchewan, 235
Constitution: aboriginal rights, 199, 209–11; amending formula, 189, 205, 208; charter of rights, 190, 192–95, 198–99, 201–3, 206–9; final negotiations, 206–9; legislative override, 199, 206, 208–10; NDP divisions, 194–99, 201–4; opting out, 207–8; provincial opposition, 177, 190, 193, 197–99, 202, 205–6; Quebec's position, 189–90, 193, 205–6, 208, 212; referendum, 195, 200, 206; resources, 138, 189–90, 193–96; Senate, 201–2; Supreme Court, 198, 205–6; unilateral action, 194–95, 198, 205; women's rights, 209–11
Conway, John, 62, 73
Cooper, Marjorie, 31–32, 67, 87
Cowley, Elwood, 86, 90, 99, 108, 110, 112, 136, 140, 141–44, 147, 152, 157, 160, 165, 170, 172, 176–77, 179, 213, 215, 224
Crow Rate, 176, 213, 222, 224
Crown Investments Corporation (CIC), 178–79
Currie, Bev, 60, 63, 65, 67–68, 73–75

Daimler-Benz, 129
Darling, Jim, 25
Davies, Bertha May. See Blakeney, Bertha
Davies Bill, 39–40, 42, 62, 66–68, 70
Davis, William, 4, 190, 207–8
Day care, 81, 127, 184–86
de Jong, Simon, 203
Decima Research, 214
Deficits, 215, 225–26, 233–34
Department of Northern Saskatchewan (DNS), 85, 114–20, 121, 125, 226
Derrick, Mel, 87, 117, 218
Deterrent fees, 52, 80
Devine, Grant, 4, 214, 218, 221–23, 225–26, 229, 233–35
Dewhurst, Fred, 65–66, 70
Diefenbaker, John, 172
Disberry, Mr. Justice D. C., 133, 141
Dizard, John, 169
Doell, Leonard, 163
Dombowsky, David, 141–44, 146–47, 149, 179
Douglas, Tommy, 21, 25, 31, 35–36, 38–39, 41, 43, 46, 56, 72, 74, 77, 86, 90–91, 93, 95, 115, 172, 203–4, 242
Dunsky's (advertising agency), 111, 147
Duval Corporation of Canada, 137, 149
Dyck, Bev, 164

Economic Advisory and Planning Board, 22
Ediger, Nick, 153
Eisenhauer, Jo, 10
Eldorado Nuclear Ltd., 131, 153, 163, 165
Elections Canada: (1935), 11; (1945), 13; (1979), 189, 215; (1980), 189
Elections Sask.: (1944), 13; (1964), 46–47, 49; (1967), 51, 53; (1971), 77–82, 115; (1975), 110, 126–27, 130–35, 141; (1978), 162, 170–74; (1982), 4, 213–14, 221–24; (1986), 229–30
Enders, Thomas, 148
Energy and Resource Fund, 149. *See also* Heritage Fund
Engel, Allan, 113, 227
Erb, Walter, 41, 46, 66

Family Income Plan, 180
Faris, Rev. Don, 61–62, 72, 80–81, 101–2, 132, 172
Farm Credit Corporation, 107, 112
FarmStart, 126
Federal-provincial relations, 132–35, 138, 142, 150, 169, 189–90, 194, 196
Federation of Saskatchewan Indian Nations. *See* Federation of Saskatchewan Indians
Federation of Saskatchewan Indians (FSI), 120–21, 123, 160, 183, 209
Fines, Clarence, 22, 25, 31–33, 35–36, 90
Fisher, Douglas, 147
Fraser Institute, 234
Free Trade Agreement, 242
Fullerton, Douglas, 143
Fulton, Davey, 44

Gabriel Dumont College, 184
Gartner, Gerry, 118, 126, 139
Gibson, Fred, 200–1
Gilbey, Bill, 59
Gillies, Bill, 195, 222
Gonick, Cy, 56
Gordon, Mardi, 20, 28
Gorham, Anne. *See* Blakeney, Anne
Government Finance Office (GFO), 1, 20–22, 26–27, 178
Gow, Donald, 10
Gow, Frank, 10
Grescoe, Paul, 169
Griffin, Jim, 47
Groome, Dr. Agnes, 160
Gross, Reg, 113, 217
Guaranteed Income Supplement, 180
Gudmundson, Carol, 56, 64–66, 68, 100
Gudmundson, Fred, 62, 64
Gulf Minerals, 154
Guy, Allan, 120
Gwyn, Richard, 169

Habitat conference, 154
Hall, Emmett, 175–76, 213
Hammersmith, Jerry, 183, 217
Haney, Bill, 28
Haney, Marj, 28
Harding, Bill, 155, 160
Hatfield, Richard, 208
Haughn, Margie, 10
Havey, Clint, 15, 18
Heritage Fund, 180, 214, 221
Hewitt, Alvin, 101
Hill, Fred, 41
Hindle, Byron, 111
Hjertaas, Dr. Orville, 39, 71
Hodgson, Willie, 232
Hog Marketing Commission, (Sask.), 127
Hovdebo, Stan, 203
Hudson Bay Mining and Smelting, 137
Hudson's Bay Company, 115, 117
Human rights commission (Sask.), 127

Independent Boundaries Commission, 127
*Indian Head News*, 41
Indian Land Entitlements, 124, 218–19
Industrial Development Fund, 23, 27. *See also* Saskatchewan Economic Development Corporation
Industrial development policy, 112, 128–31, 153, 178, 179, 180

Inexco, 152
Inflation, 220
Institute of Public Administration of Canada, 91
Inter-Church Uranium Committee, 228
Intercontinental Packers, 128
Interest rates, 220
International Minerals and Chemicals, 137
International Women's Year, 185
IPSCO, 23, 128, 178

Jeddore, 5
Jewett, Pauline, 210
Johnson, Al, 23, 29, 34–35, 39, 50, 181
Johnson, Pierre Marc, 236
Jones, Ray, 120

Kaeding, Edgar, 110–12
Katz, Dr. Leon, 155
Keep Our Doctors Committee (KOD), 41–43
Kenney, Kendall, 12, 14
Kerr, Don, 99
Key Lake, 152, 154, 161, 164–65, 179
Key Lake "de-watering", 164
King, Carlyle, 98
Kinzel, Betty, 239
Kinzel, Jack, 2, 79–82, 86–87, 92, 144, 147–48, 217, 239
Kirby, Michael, 197, 199–201
Kitchen accord, 207
Klenavic, John, 166
Knight, Bill, 97, 99, 103, 132, 167, 173–74, 176, 194, 214, 222–23, 225, 227
Knowles, Stanley, 25, 202, 204
Koskie, Murray, 166, 215, 217, 219, 223, 227
Kowalchuk, John, 60, 66, 70, 86
Kramer, Eiling, 65, 71, 85, 90, 116, 164, 218
Kroll, Senator David, 104
Kujawa, Serge, 121
Kuziak, Sheila, 101
Kwasnica, Myro, 60, 66, 70

Labour Court, 79
Labour Standards Act, 186
Labour unions, 35–36, 50, 59, 145, 220–23, 241–42
Lalonde, Marc, 191, 200–1
Land Bank, 63, 72–74, 78, 81, 84, 105–9, 111–13, 126–27, 133–35, 170, 215, 226
Land prices, 109
Landlord-Tenant Act, 127
Lane, Gary, 233
Lang, Otto, 52, 59, 71, 80, 145
LaPierre, Laurier, 56
Larson, Leonard, 62
Laskin, Chief Justice Bora, 170
Lawson, Bruce, 79, 142
Laxer, Jim, 59, 100
Lee, Tim, 41–43
Leeson, Howard, 191, 197–98, 200–1, 204
Letwin, Oliver, 234
Levesque, Rene, 189–90, 205, 207–8
Lewis, David, 14, 18, 58, 86, 100–1, 203–4
Lewis, Stephen, 101, 210, 239
Lingenfelter, Dwayne, 113, 218, 223, 227, 231
Lloyd, Dianne, 54
Lloyd, Roy, 88, 111, 142, 146, 162
Lloyd, Woodrow, 25, 33–36, 39, 41, 43–44, 46, 48–49, 52, 54, 56, 58–64, 66–69, 71–73, 77–78, 81, 82, 84, 86–88, 95, 98, 100, 115, 133, 151, 214
Long, Bob, 218
Lougheed, Peter, 4, 145, 169, 190, 205, 207–8, 211
Lower Inventories for Tomorrow (LIFT), 53
Lusney, Norm, 227
Lyon, Sterling, 4, 190, 203
Lysyk, Ken, 142–43, 205

McArthur, Doug, 88, 94, 106–7, 110–11, 117–18, 162, 164, 168, 183–84, 216–17, 224
McAuley, Barbara, 10–11, 16, 19
McCallum, Dr. Kenneth, 160
McCarthyism, 79

McDermott, Dennis, 56
MacDonald, Cy, 53
Macdonald, Flora, 210
McDonough, Alexa, 14, 186, 210, 228, 239
McGovern, Senator George, 108
McKay, J. Fortesque, 26
McLaughlin, Audrey, 239
McLeod, Tommy, 23–24, 236–37
MacMurchy, Gordon, 61–62, 72–75, 81, 84–85, 90, 99–101, 111, 122, 124, 144, 154, 172, 176–77, 182–83, 213, 215
McMurtry, Rev. Joan, 167
McMurtry, Roy, 206–7
McPhee, Jack, 165
McPherson, Donald K., 41
MacPherson, Jim, 236, 239
Malone, Ted, 175
Manhattan Project, 151, 160
Matsalla, Adolph, 60, 66, 70, 218
Maxwell, Colin, 226
Meakes, Frank, 66–67, 71
Medical Care Insurance Act, 39
Medical Care Insurance Commission (Sask.), 39–40, 44–45
Medicare, 32–33, 38–39, 42, 46, 52–53, 174, 180, 196, 222, 242
Meech Lake (Accord), 242
Meewasin Valley Authority, 217
Mendel, Fred, 128
Messer, Jack, 53, 60, 65–67, 69–70, 84, 88, 90–91, 106–9, 111, 126, 144, 146–147, 156–61, 163–65, 179, 218–19
Métis Society of Saskatchewan, 114, 118–22, 209
Michelmann, Hans J., 229
Milen, Rob, 124, 219
Miller, Gerry, 79
Milner, Jim, 20
Miner, David, 107
Minimum wage, 81, 180
Mitchell, Don, 71–73, 75, 85
Mitchell, Grant, 87–88, 95, 117, 154–56, 215–16, 218
Mitchell, June, 87
Monkhouse, Lowell, 173
Morin, Claude, 205–6, 208
Moroz, Don, 182
Morris Rod Weeder, 128
Morris, W. P., 137
Moxley, Ross, 107
Murray, Father Athol, 42–43

National Action Committee on the Status of Women, 209
National Farmers' Union, 58, 62, 71, 155, 160
Native Economic Development Corporation, 182
Native Employment Program, 182
Negative advertising, 174, 176
*New Deal for People*, 1, 78–80, 82, 102, 105, 115, 119, 126, 141
New Democratic Youth, 62, 75
New Right, 4, 225
Nicol, Dr. Andrew, 233
Nollet, Toby, 70, 105
Noranda Mines, 137, 138, 146
Northern Development Board, 162
Northern Municipal Council, 120
Northern Teacher Education Program, 125
Notley, Grant, 203–4
Nystrom, Lorne, 71, 201, 203–4

Ogle, Rev. Bob, 203
Oil, Chemical, and Atomic Workers, 50
Oil industry, 50, 126, 130, 132–33, 169–70, 174, 226
Ombudsman, 81, 127
Oxford, 1, 186

Parker, Bill, 96, 217
Parsons and Whittimore, 50
Pawley, Howard, 203
Peckford, Brian, 190
Pennzoil, 137, 149
Pépin, Jean Luc, 213
Pepper, Auburn, 70
Petrie, Rev. David, 167

Phillips, Morgan, 18
Pine Hill Divinity Hall, 12
Pioneer Trust, 226
Pocklington, Peter, 226
Porteous, Lt.-Gov. George, 144
Potash: prorationing of, 81, 134, 137–38, 143; takeover of, 136, 138, 139, 140–49, 219
Potash Company of America, 137
Potash Corporation of Saskatchewan, 133, 141–43, 146–49, 178–79, 219, 234
Potash industry, 50, 126, 131, 133–34, 137–38, 140–43, 146, 149, 170, 174, 219–20, 226
Potash Investment Certificates, 219
Potter, W. P., 19
Powell, Clare, 61, 72, 86, 92, 126
PPG Industries, 137
Pradnick, Ron, 173
Prebble, Peter, 154, 160, 163–65, 168
Prefontaine, Hubert, 88, 118, 139
Prescription drug program, 127, 234
Preston, Valerie, 217
Privatization, 232–35, 241
Proctor, Dick, 194–95, 202, 213, 224
Property Improvement Grant, 127
Public Sector Price and Compensation Board, 171

Quaale, Gordon, 172

Rabbit Lake, 152–53
Rae, Bob, 239
Reagan, Ronald, 214–15, 234
Reaganomics, 225
Regina Group for a Non-Nuclear Society (RGNNS), 164
*Regina Leader-Post*, 46, 161, 164, 173
Regina Manifesto, 22, 26–27, 46, 59
Resource policy, 129, 131, 134, 152, 178–80
Retail, Wholesale, and Department Store Union, 171, 223
Rhodes Scholarship, 1
Richards, John, 85, 101–2, 142, 154, 178, 240
Robbins, Wes, 71, 86, 158, 175, 186
Rolfes, Herman, 166, 186, 216, 219, 223
Romanow, Roy, 53, 60, 65, 67–70, 73, 75, 77, 84–85, 88, 89–91, 103, 121, 142–44, 146–47, 154, 160, 164, 166, 172, 180, 191, 194, 197–98, 200, 203–4, 206–7, 210–11, 215, 219, 222–23, 228–29, 231–32, 234–35, 240
Rosaasen, Ken, 111–12
Round Table (The), 14
Royal Commission on Agriculture and Rural Life, 105, 113
Royal Commission on the Status of Women, 185
Rumanian tractor assembly plant, 128
Rural municipalities, 112–13, 218

Saddlmyer, Keith, 88
Saint John's United Church, 167
Sanderson, Sol, 183, 209
Saskatchewan Economic Development Corporation (SEDCO), 128, 153–54, 163
Saskatchewan Federation of Labour, 59, 156, 171
Saskatchewan Formula. *See* Indian Land Entitlements
Saskatchewan Government Employees' Union, 233
Saskatchewan Government Insurance, 33, 47, 173, 175, 234
Saskatchewan Government Telephones, 24
Saskatchewan Human Rights Commission, 187
Saskatchewan Indian Federated College, 184
Saskatchewan Investment Opportunities Corporation, 134
Saskatchewan Minerals, 234
Saskatchewan Mining Association, 145–46

Saskatchewan Mining Development Corporation, 152, 154, 159, 161, 163, 178–79
Saskatchewan Pension Plan, 131
Saskatchewan Power Corporation, 23, 49–50, 178, 234
Saskatchewan Securities Commission, 1, 27
Saskatchewan Transportation Company, 79
Saskatchewan Wheat Pool, 128, 130
Saskatchewan Wildlife Federation, 124, 218–19
Saskatoon Agreement, 44
Saskatoon Board of Trade, 41, 146
*Saskatoon Star-Phoenix*, 41, 46, 70–71, 145
SaskEnergy, 234–35
Sask Oil, 133, 178, 234
SaskPower. *See* Saskatchewan Power Corporation
SaskTel (Saskatchewan Telecommunications), 178
Schmeichel, Dale, 163
Schwartz, Molly. *See* Blakeney, Molly
Scott, Frank, 43
Shapiro, Jack, 57, 65–66, 68–69
Shaw, Lloyd, 14, 18
Shiell, Maisie, 154
Shillington, Ned, 227
Ship Harbour, 6
Shoyama, Tommy, 23, 35, 50
Simard, Louise, 231
Sinclair, Jim, 118–24, 181, 183, 209
Sinclair, John, 216–17
Smishek, Ruth, 95
Smishek, Walter, 39, 56, 64, 66–69, 78, 84–85, 88, 95, 100, 126, 131, 154, 156, 158, 171–72, 182–84, 187, 215, 219
Smith, Ernie, 31
Snyder, Gordon, 53, 62, 64–65, 84–85, 95, 220
Social contract, 241–42
Social Credit, 27, 46
Social gospel, 25, 35
Social policy, 215–16, 218, 222
Social Policy Secretariat, 183, 187
Sopracolle, Sister Gertrude, 163
Spinks, Dr. J. W. T., 160
Stanfield, Robert, 170
Steeves, Geoffrey S., 229
Steuart, Dave, 51–52, 62, 87, 109–10, 120, 132–35, 141, 144–45, 149, 172, 226
Stevenson, Kellogg, Ernst, and Whinney, 232
Stewart, Walter, 6
Strong, Maurice, 143
Sveinson, Bill, 226
Svenson, Ken, 181–82
Swift Canadian, 137

Tamaki, George, 20, 23
Tansley, Don, 23, 39–40, 50, 143
Task Force on Agriculture, (federal), 53, 80, 104
Taylor, Alex, 88
Taylor, George, 45, 64, 71–75, 85
Taylor, Lord Stephen, 43–44
Tchorzewski, Ed, 86, 90, 99, 166, 185–86, 215, 220, 229, 231
Telford, Gertrude, 184
Thatcher, Colin, 225
Thatcher, Margaret, 214–15, 234
Thatcher, Ross, 1, 3, 33, 43, 46–47, 49–51, 54, 59–61, 66, 77, 79–80, 82, 85, 87, 89, 132–33, 137, 191, 225
*The Commonwealth. See Commonwealth, The*
Thompson, Fred, 227
Thompson, Dr. Walter, 38
Thorson, Kim, 70, 85, 138–40, 153
Thurston, Cliff, 71
Trade Union Act, 50
Trudeau, Pierre, 4, 53, 58–59, 80, 132, 135–36, 145, 169–70, 172, 189–92, 194–95, 197–99, 201–3, 206–10, 215
Turnbull, Ollie, 36
Turner, John, 130, 140
Twigg, Merran, 186–87

United Farmers of Canada, 105
Uranerz, 152, 154
Uranium: and churches, 166; opposition to, 154–65, 168, 217; and refinery at Warman, 153–54, 162, 165; weapons connection to, 151, 162, 228
Uranium development (Sask.), 151–52, 154–65, 168, 219, 228
Uranium industry, 130–31, 151, 154, 226
U.S. Borax, 50
Use-lease program, 72, 105

Vickars, Norm, 219
Viet Nam War, 56, 59–60

Waffle, 56, 58–61, 63–68, 73, 75–76, 100–2, 105, 117
Waffle Manifesto, 56–57, 61
Wage and price controls, 99, 136, 145, 170–71
Walker, Bob, 44, 65–67, 84
Walker, Michael, 234
Wallace, Len, 172
Wallace, Murray, 94, 216–17
Warman and District Concerned Citizens, 163
Warnock, John, 71
Watkins, Mel, 56, 59
Watson, Patrick, 147
Watson, Stan, 24
Weese, Bob, 190, 194
Wesson, Gib, 107, 110
Wheat prices, 104, 109, 113, 126, 127
Whelan, Ed, 31–32, 60, 70, 93, 96, 147, 155–57, 217
Whelan, Pemrose, 60
White, Bob, 204
White, Clint, 164
Whiting, Cliff, 71
Wiebe, Elizabeth, 153
Wiebe, John, 153–54
Wilke, Flo, 86, 92–93, 98
Williams, Charlie, 25, 31–32
Wilson, Budge, 15, 19, 25, 28
Wilson, George, 14
Wilson, Gerry, 86
Wolfe, Dr. Sam, 45
Women, and the NDP, 25, 48, 184–87, 216, 228
Women's Division, 186, 226
Wood, Everett, 70, 84
Worobetz, Lt.-Gov. Stephen, 84
Woroby, Peter, 112

Yew, Lawrence, 227
Yom Kippur War, 126
Young, Fred, 14, 15

Zwarun, Suzanne, 169